P9-DFU-955

CARIBBEAN

FODOR'S TRAVEL PUBLICATIONS, INC.

NEW YORK • TORONTO • LONDON • SYDNEY • AUCKLAND

WWW.FODORS.COM

Copyright © The Automobile Association 2000
Maps copyright © The Automobile Association 2000

All rights reserved under International and Pan-American Copyright conventions. Distributed by Random House, Inc., New York. No maps, illustrations, or other portions of this book may be reproduced in any form without written permission from the publishers.

Published in the United States by Fodor's Travel Publications, Inc.
Published in the United Kingdom by A.A. Publishing

Fodor's is a registered trademark of Random House, Inc.

ISBN 0-679-00474-2
Fourth Edition

Fodor's Exploring Caribbean

Author: **James Hamlyn**; Revisions: **Justin Henderson**
Series Adviser: **Ingrid Morgan**
Joint Series Editor: **Susi Bailey**
Revisions Editor: **Grapevine Publishing Services Ltd**
Cartography: **The Automobile Association**
Cover Design: **Tigist Getachew, Fabrizio La Rocca**
Front Cover Silhouette: **Catherine Karnow**

Special Sales
Fodor's Travel Publications are available at special discounts for bulk purchases for sales promotions or premiums. Special editions, including personalized covers, excerpts of existing guides, and corporate imprints, can be created in large quantities for special needs. For more information, contact your local bookseller or write to Special Markets, Fodor's Travel Publications, 201 East 50th Street, New York, NY 10022. Inquiries from Canada should be directed to your local Canadian bookseller or sent to Random House of Canada, Ltd., Marketing Department, 2775 Matheson Blvd. East, Mississauga, Ontario L4W 4P7.

Printed in Italy by Printer Trento srl
10 9 8 7 6 5 4 3 2 1

How to use this book

ORGANIZATION

The Caribbean Is,
The Caribbean Was
Discusses aspects of life and culture in the contemporary Caribbean and explores significant periods in its history.

A–Z
Breaks down the islands into regional chapters, and covers places to visit, including walks and drives. Within this section fall the Focus On articles, which consider a variety of subjects in greater detail.

Travel Facts
Contains the strictly practical information vital for a successful trip.

Accommodations and Restaurants
Lists recommended establishments throughout the Caribbean, giving a brief summary of their attractions.

ABOUT THE RATINGS
Most places described in this book have been given a separate rating. These are as follows:

 ▶▶▶   **Do not miss**

      ▶▶   **Highly recommended**

      ▶   **Worth seeing**

MAPS
Some of the maps in this book use internationally agreed symbols to denote nation states:

BS	Bahamas
C	Cuba
CO	Colombia
CR	Costa Rica
DOM	Dominican Republic
HN	Honduras
NIC	Nicaragua
RH	Haiti
YV	Venezuela

Contents

James Hamlyn's childhood was spent on the move around the world—a habit that has stuck, particularly since he discovered the Caribbean islands a decade ago. His time now is spent island-hopping, checking out the bars and restaurants, and perfecting his skills with Caribbean dances such as the merengue. He has written several guidebooks to the Caribbean as well as many articles for American and British newspapers and magazines.

My Caribbean

Carnival. A sea of satin costumes shimmers and sparkles in the tropical sun; masqueraders strut and thrust, swaying at the hip, midriffs clamped in a conga-line like a massive sequined snake. The noise is deafening—close at hand the raucous clanging of steel bands, elsewhere the thunder of amplified soca drumbeats. Carnival typifies the exuberance of the Caribbean—the color, the high spirits and the irresistible dancing rhythms. To be part of it is an amazing experience.

After the week's nonstop dancing of Carnival, you will actually need a vacation, but then that's the Caribbean's specialty. Somewhere quiet, perhaps, on a deserted beach, a place to rest and let the ringing in your ears subside with a cocktail and an uninterrupted view over the sea to the sunset. An easygoing life among charming West Indian people, in a setting of startling tropical beauty and gentle reggae music—this is the other side to the Islands.

The Caribbean islands are ideal for a little laziness, but after a while I begin to get the itch for activity. An ideal day would be spent scuba-diving or windsurfing in the morning, enjoying lunch in the elegance of an old plantation house, with the afternoon spent walking in the rain forest or exploring a colonial city. As ever, though, the day ends with dancing in the warm tropical night, to rhythms of salsa, merengue, and zouk.

Every Caribbean traveler has their favorite island; a charmed isle where they feel they belong. You may fall in love with it the moment your feet touch the sand on coming ashore, or it may grow on you gradually, within the heady mix of tropical smells, music, and rum, but you'll know it when you find it.

My favorite island? Well, it's a tough choice and I love them all. There are about 50 islands, ranging from tiny coral outcrops to large and lively industrialized nations, and they each have their own distinct charm and appeal. Read on and you'll find out more...

James Hamlyn

The Caribbean Is

Swimmers off the south coast of Barbados

With its endless beaches, swaying palm trees and a warm turquoise sea, the Caribbean does, surprisingly, live up to its idyllic image. But the landscapes extend far beyond the travel agent's clichés—from sheer volcanic mountains and lush rain forests to inhospitable deserts; and Caribbean life has been changed beyond recognition within a relatively short space of time.

Top: St. Vincent. Above: Shaw Park Gardens, Ocho Rios, Jamaica

THE ARCHIPELAGO Stretching in an arc from the bottom of Florida to the top of South America, the Caribbean archipelago is as varied as it is beautiful. Islands range in size from Cuba (4,124 square miles) to tiny Saba (3 square miles); mountains soar to over 2 miles high in the Dominican Republic, and flat sand-spits barely reach sea level. There are extensive rain forests in Puerto Rico and Dominica, and barren cactus-filled wildernesses in Haiti and Aruba. The landscape may change around each corner, as mangrove swamp gives way to pasture land and pine forests replace palm trees. Intensive agriculture and tourist development are gradually altering the Caribbean's contours and climate. Blessed with warm weather all the year round and cooled by the Trade Winds, the region is also occasionally cursed by violent rainstorms and hurricanes.

Known for its coral reefs and its beaches (every island claims the best), the Caribbean also boasts waterfalls, hot springs, and caves. Two bizarre geological attractions are Trinidad's Pitch Lake, a seemingly inexhaustible pool of hot black tar (see page 232), and Jamaica's Cockpit Country, an inhospitable area of limestone hills and hollows, still populated by descendants of runaway slaves (see page 149).

CHANGING NATURE Humans have left an indelible impression on the Caribbean landscape. Many of the islands that were once covered in virgin rain forest are now scarred by deforestation and erosion. In Haiti, the island described by Columbus as the most beautiful he had ever seen, tree-felling and over-farming have created virtual deserts in some areas, where drought and famine are constant threats.

Strangely, little of the flora and fauna that make up the typical Caribbean landscape is indigenous to the region. Sugar cane, which still flourishes on many islands, was introduced from the Mediterranean by Spanish colonists. Other crops (bananas, citrus fruits, coffee beans) and animals (cattle, dogs, horses) came from Asia and Europe.

DIFFERENT WORLDS The past has shaped the look of the Caribbean through a variety of influences. Cities, towns, and villages bear the unmistakable imprint of former colonial powers. Spanish-built Havana, with its colonnades and plazas, seems a different world from British-built Bridgetown, with its statue of Admiral Nelson in Trafalgar Square and its "tropical Anglican" cathedral.

Differing histories have also molded the countryside itself. In the formerly Spanish colonies of Cuba, Puerto Rico, and the Dominican Republic, sugar plantations stretch to the horizon as they have for 500 years. In Haiti, however, where a slave revolution expelled the French at the beginning of the 19th century, precarious smallholdings have replaced the hated plantations.

Despite the proximity of the U.S., European influence is still keenly felt. In the French *départements d'outre-mer* of Martinique and Guadeloupe you can buy baguettes, drink *pastis* and see policemen in *képis*. There is no mistaking the Dutch style of Curaçao or Aruba, where gabled pastel warehouses lining the canal and port conjure up a tropical Amsterdam. And Britain has left the paraphernalia of colonial rule in its former possessions: red mailboxes, English place names, and cricket fields.

> ❏ The Caribbean is one of the last bastions of colonialism. Martinique, Guadeloupe, St. Barts and St. Martin are technically French *régions*; Aruba, Bonaire and Curaçao remain tied to the Netherlands; Britain still maintains Montserrat, Anguilla, and the Cayman Islands as dependent territories and the B.V.I. as a crown colony. Puerto Rico is a "free and associated state" of the U.S.A., but may one day become the 51st State. ❏

11

A dramatic Caribbean sunset over the shores of Tobago

"Out of many one people" is Jamaica's national motto, and it applies just as well to the rest of the Caribbean. The region's population is a rich mixture of African, European, American, Asian and East Indian, its legacy a fusion of slavery, colonialism, and migration. This has created a unique culture, but a strict racial hierarchy still exists.

STRANGERS IN PARADISE

The original indigenous population of the Caribbean all but disappeared within half a century of European conquest. Since then, people have come, willingly or not, from every corner of the earth. This process included one of history's biggest forced migrations—the importation of some five million African people into the Caribbean's plantation economy.

ARAWAKS AND CARIBS

Little remains of the people who predated the Caribbean's "discovery" 500 years ago. However, some of their words have entered the vocabulary—barbecue, hammock, manioc, for instance—but none of the placid Arawak people survived the cultural devastation

Top: children in Montego Bay, Jamaica
Right: a flower-seller in Jamaica balances her load with care

of the conquest. Today, only a handful of Carib descendants are still found in Dominica and St. Vincent, scraping a living by selling their handicrafts to visiting tourists.

EUROPEANS

Europe conquered, colonized, and re-created the Caribbean in its own image. The first Europeans to settle in the Caribbean named cities, villages, and rivers after more familiar places at home. But with few exceptions, the physical legacy of European domination is confined to the Spanish-speaking areas of Cuba, the Dominican Republic, and Puerto Rico, which received influxes of European immigration well into the present century. Each island has its paler-skinned elite, but Europeans as such make up a tiny minority in most Caribbean societies. The exceptions to the rule are the "poor whites" of Barbados, a community

descended from indentured British laborers that has so far refused to intermix at all with any of the other Bajan communities.

AFRICANS The great majority of Caribbean people are at least in part descended from the millions of Africans who crossed the notorious "middle passage." Africa is alive in all dimensions of local life: music, language, religion, and cooking. "Jamaica Talk," for instance, the island's patois, is largely based on West African Ashanti dialect, while African speech and customs are commonplace in Haiti and around the eastern tip of Cuba.

INDIANS Around 40 percent of the population of Trinidad is East Indian in origin. The stores and restaurants of Port of Spain are filled with the sounds, sights, and scents of the Indian subcontinent, while Hindu prayer flags surround many country-side homes. In Guyana, slightly more than half the population is Indian, descended from the indentured laborers of the 19th century.

INEQUALITIES This rich diversity of race and color conceals massive inequalities, within and between individual countries. In Haiti, for instance, the one percent of lighter-skinned mulattos dominates the black majority. In most other countries, a so-called "pigmentocracy" exists, equating light skin with economic and political power. After more than 30 years of independent government, Jamaica's P.J. Patterson is the first black politician to hold the post of Prime Minister.

Even more striking is the disparity between Caribbean countries. Some, notably Haiti and the Dominican Republic, are among the world's poorest, while others, including Puerto Rico, the Bahamas and the Virgin Islands, enjoy relatively high levels of prosperity. Economic hardship has prompted many to leave the Caribbean's poorer countries to live and work in North America and Europe. Perhaps one in seven Dominicans lives in the U.S., and almost as many Puerto Ricans live on the U.S. mainland as in Puerto Rico. In the 1950s, nearly 10 percent of all Jamaicans emigrated to Britain. These exile communities provide a lifeline to the Caribbean islanders.

A Trinidad palm-weaver

13

Mangoes, soursops, papaya, yams, breadfruit, callaloo...the list of Caribbean fruit and vegetables is never-ending. Drop a seed in the soil, and you'll have a tree inside a week, say local farmers. But despite extraordinary fertility, Caribbean agriculture faces critical problems: what to do with crops that nobody wants, and what to put in their place.

14

MARKETS The market is the traditional center of Caribbean social and economic life. By bus or on foot, the marketwomen arrive before dawn to set up their displays of fresh fruit and vegetables. Whether in the town square or simply at a rural crossroads, the market and its mostly female workforce display the vibrancy of the region's tropical agriculture. Vast piles of mysterious tubers (widely known as "ground provisions") sit side by side with bunches of green bananas and plantains, the Caribbean's starchy staples. Red-hot peppers, tangy limes, and enormous avocados are some of the other offerings. Beyond the market, most people seem to have a small piece of land, if only enough to grow a few fruit trees. While there is widespread poverty in the Caribbean, few actually go hungry.

The Caribbean is still a largely agricultural region, but important changes are taking place in what crops are grown and where they go. From the earliest colonial days, the region was an exporter of agricultural commodities, most importantly sugar. In its 18th-century heyday, Saint-Domingue (now Haiti) exported more raw sugar and created more wealth than the whole of the British empire. Sugar, the fabled "white gold," made fortunes, caused wars, and brought millions of Africans across the Atlantic in slave-ships.

> ❏ In 1975 a pound of sugar fetched 76 cents on the world market; in 1982 it was worth only 5 cents. ❏

The discovery of European sugar-beet, global overproduction, and changing diets have long since undermined the Caribbean sugar industry. Only Cuba is still heavily dependent on sugar exports, while other islands have moved away into other agro-industries. Bananas are the modern-day boom crop, especially in Dominica and St. Lucia, where they represent up to 70 percent of export earnings. Bananas grow everywhere in these small volcanic islands: up steep slopes, around every house, by the roadside. They are mostly cultivated on smallholdings by individual farmers, who pack them into boxes and drive them down to the port. After a long period of special access into the British market, Caribbean bananas are now under fire from the big plantation-based producers of Latin America who grow cheaper, if not better fruit. If Latin America can outproduce and undersell the Caribbean, it will lose another essential market.

FRAGILE FRUIT Worries about the future of the banana industry reveal the vulnerability of Caribbean agriculture. Worse even than hurricanes are unstable world commodity markets, over which small producers have no control. Every crop—sugar, coffee, cocoa, tobacco—has seen its ups and downs, and an uncertain future awaits the new "exotic nontraditionals," which farmers are now trying to export to Europe and the U.S. The current generation of export crops includes ginger, mangoes, passion fruit, and cut flowers, much of it destined for supermarkets and gourmet food stores in U.S. cities.

FISHING Lobster, red snapper, and flying fish are found on menus throughout the region. But despite extensive coastlines, most islands have to import fish. The lack of a fishing industry, in part a legacy of slavery and colonialism, has also resulted from inadequate marine nutrients, storage and marketing, as well as a risk of ciguaterra (a neuro-toxin found in tropical reef fish). Consequently, the islands depend on salted and canned fish from Canada, and fresh fish flown in from the U.S. Attempts to upgrade the fishing industry have been made, but experts warn that the Caribbean sea cannot withstand intensive fishing.

Fish for sale on Aruba

15

High in the hills of Haiti, rhythmic drum-beats, animal sacrifices, and entranced dancers swirling around a crackling bonfire are all part of the island's most famous and myster-ious religion: voodoo. It is just one of many faiths in a region that claims more churches per capita than anywhere else in the world.

A Baptist worshipper on Tobago. The Caribbean islands accommodate a vast range of religious sects and denominations, imported from all corners of the globe

RELIGION From continuous radio and T.V. broadcasts to tiny ramshackle churches on every street corner, religion is part and parcel of the Caribbean. There are mosques in Trinidad, Hindu temples in Guyana, and pilgrimage sites in the Dominican Republic. With significant communities of Jews, Muslims, and Hindus, the region is influenced by most major faiths. It is also a target for U.S.-based evangelical sects.

CHRISTIANS Most Caribbean people would describe themselves as Christians. European colonizers brought differing Christian beliefs, a fact reflected in the islands' many churches. Catholicism, officially the main faith of Haiti and the Dominican Republic, is widely practiced in the eastern Caribbean and is now tolerated in Cuba. Anglicanism holds sway in the former British colonies of Jamaica and Barbados. The influence of U.S. Protestant groups is increasingly powerful throughout the Caribbean, and these sects have joined the myriad existing churches. In Barbados, for example, it is estimated that no fewer than 140 different denominations are active, one for every 2,000 Bajans.

AFRICAN RELIGIONS Christianity was the religion of the masters; the slaves had their own faiths, brought with them from Africa. Religious beliefs and practices survived the horrors of slavery, preserving the slaves' identity and memories of their homelands. Over time, these beliefs merged with Christian religion to create new forms of faith and ceremony. These have different names on different islands (*santería* in

Cuba, *pocomania* in Jamaica), but the best known is voodoo in Haiti, where religious activity is evident in all walks of life. Each tiny village has its quota of churches—Catholic, Methodist, Baptist, and hundreds more—and every church has its faithful congregation. But there are no open signs of Haiti's other religious phenomenon. As an old joke has it, Haitians are 99 percent Christian and 100 percent voodooist. Even so, voodoo remains largely invisible to foreigners, although visitors have ample opportunity to see suitably arranged versions of the authentic ceremonies (see pages 180–181).

RASTAFARIANISM Popularized in the 1970s and 1980s by reggae stars, Rastafarianism has its roots in Jamaica, and followers on many other islands. The cult expresses many people's longing for an African identity by invoking Ethiopia as the holy land and the late Emperor Haile Selassie as a god, and promotes the smoking of ganja (marijuana) as a sacrament (see page 161).

RADICALS IN RELIGION Many priests in the Caribbean have long since left the pulpit to become involved in social and political issues. The churches have traditionally been active in health and education, and since "liberation theology" spread from Latin America during the 1970s, they have become increasingly politically outspoken. In Haiti, a radical Salesian priest, Jean-Bertrand Aristide, was elected president in 1991, only to be overthrown by the army nine months later. He was restored to power in 1994 by means of U.S.-led intervention.

Caribbean politics are anything but dull. Most people love a political argument, and insults can often fly thick and fast. Elections are usually a pretext for a party, while parliamentary procedure is guaranteed to be good entertainment. The Caribbean has had—and still has—its share of unrest, but most islands enjoy healthy democracies and lively debate.

POLITICAL SYSTEMS The region's differing regimes are an integral part of its mixed cultural heritage. The British bequeathed the "Westminster model" of parliamentary democracy, and all English-speaking islands hold regular elections. The British Queen is still nominally head of state in most Commonwealth countries, represented in each by a Governor General. The Spanish islands, meanwhile, have tended to adopt a presidential system, with a greater tradition of "strong man" leadership.

PARTY GAMES Most independent Caribbean territories have a multi-party electoral system of government. Elections are fiercely contested events and can spill over into violence. On small islands, personalities are often as important as policies, especially when most electors know the candidates personally! Problems have been greatest in Jamaica, where "political tribalism" caused around 800 deaths in the 1980 election campaign. But political violence is not common, and most states are proud of their constitutional credentials.

HOT SPOTS Of all the Caribbean territories, only two are generally agreed to have undemocratic governments. Cuba has been dominated by Fidel Castro and the Communist Party since the 1959 revolution and has ever since alienated the U.S.A. by refusing to hold free elections. Once the scene of a near-nuclear confrontation between the U.S.A. and the former U.S.S.R. in 1962, Cuba has become increasingly isolated. Economically strangled by the U.S. embargo, the island suffers intermit-

tent shortages of basic goods, but has become a popular tourist destination for Europeans, Canadians, and Latin Americans, who bringing hard currency into the economy.

Haiti has had the most turbulent political history of all the Caribbean nations. Wracked by instability and dictatorship since a slave revolution won independence from France in 1804, the country was ruled by the ruthless Duvaliers until 1986. When "Baby Doc" was finally forced to flee the country, a movement for democracy evolved, culminating in the overwhelming election triumph of a radical Roman Catholic priest, Jean-Bertrand Aristide, in 1991. Aristide was soon ousted by the military, but U.N.-imposed sanctions and a U.S. military intervention led to his restoration as president. In the years since, the U.S. presence has kept a lid on Haiti's bloody factionalism. At present, a tenuous peace is in place, although who knows long it will last?

BACKYARD POLITICS The U.S. invasion of Grenada in October 1983 was an indication of how seriously the White House viewed the rise of radicalism in its "backyard," but with the end of the Cold War, the Caribbean has lost much of its geopolitical importance in the eyes of U.S. policymakers. Since then, support for left-wing movements has dwindled, and conservatives hold power on most English-speaking islands.

TRADING PLACES Current political controversy influences the region's position in the world economy. With the coming of the North American Free Trade Agreement between the

U.S.A., Canada, and Mexico, the islands fear marginalization in trade and influence. More talk of integration and co-operation has resulted, in the hope that a united front will help them weather economic storms.

Government House, St. Thomas

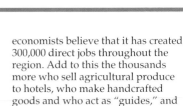

They come in the millions every year. Twelve million arrived by plane in 1992, nine million by cruise ship. Tourists are the lifeblood of the Caribbean, bringing vital dollars and jobs into the region. Although the locals may laugh at the poolside limbo lessons, they know that, for better or worse, tourism represents their economic survival.

PACKAGE HOLIDAYS With the advent of charter flights and affordable hotels, Caribbean tourism is no longer the preserve of the wealthy. In the 1950s only the rich could afford to go to the Caribbean, normally island-hopping by yacht. Now a few hundred dollars or pounds will buy an all-inclusive package deal to Antigua, Barbados, or Jamaica. All the islands are chasing the tourist jackpot; the fastest-growing vacation destination of the Caribbean is Cuba.

A modern-day "pirate ship" caters for tourists

Tourism brings an estimated $10 billion into the Caribbean economies. In the Dominican Republic, tourist earnings in 1992 exceeded all exports put together. The industry is the biggest earner in Jamaica, Barbados, and several smaller islands. Overall, economists believe that it has created 300,000 direct jobs throughout the region. Add to this the thousands more who sell agricultural produce to hotels, who make handcrafted goods and who act as "guides," and the figure may be nearer one million.

CRUISING Twice a week, the sleepy port of St. George's, Grenada, springs into frenetic action as the cruise ship arrives. As the tourists gingerly step onto *terra firma*, they are greeted by a horde of taxi-drivers, guides, vendors, and scalpers. Few of the hopeful locals will make a fortune. On average, each tourist spends a paltry $20 before returning to the safety of the cruise ship. A cruise tour may cost thousands, but little of that money reaches the islands themselves.

SPENDING Understandably, Caribbean governments and businesses prefer tourists who stay in hotels, holiday apartments and guesthouses on the islands, and spend time and money in their destinations. The multitude of restaurants, shopping malls, and souvenir stands that line the tourist resorts are proof of this single-minded pursuit of foreign currency. But foreign ownership of airlines and accommodations often means that bills are paid outside the Caribbean, reducing the hoped-for "trickle-down" effect.

More worrying still is the growing popularity of all-inclusive club vacations, where one price covers every drink or surfboard lesson. This, local restaurateurs and taxi drivers will tell you, is not a major incentive to go out and spread the wealth.

20

The Golden Lemon Hotel on St. Kitts, in the Leeward Islands

BLESSING OR CURSE? Tourism has brought welcome employment and investment to otherwise stagnant economies. For many young locals, work as a waiter or cleaner is a much better prospect than traditional farming. But tourism's impact is not all positive. Many older people complain that hustling, drugs, and petty crime have become a way of life for the young. Others feel that jealousy and resentment are inevitable consequences of the First World–Third World divide. More seriously, tourism is a shaky bet for sustainable development, as it is notoriously vulnerable to economic instability in the sender countries. Recession in North America and Europe can send Caribbean tourism revenues plummeting.

BEYOND THE BEACH Eco-tourism is the new buzzword in the local industry. Realizing that people can become bored with sand and sea, operators are now offering vacations which appeal to the adventurous and environmentally aware. You can dive among coral reefs in Belize, explore rain forests in Dominica or hike through mountains in Jamaica. Advocates of eco-tourism praise it as an intelligent use of natural resources; critics point out that in some instances it can harm the very nature that it sets out to market.

Caribbean food can be as bland or as exciting as you choose it to be. McDonalds, Kentucky Fried Chicken, and all the other familiar names are in evidence. But step outside the tourist circuit and there is food to daunt the most adventurous gastronome. Some iguana, perhaps? Or goat's offal? And don't forget the rum—the world's best.

REGIONAL FOOD Real Caribbean food reflects the many diverse influences, historical and cultural, which have shaped the region. The hearty breakfast lives on in Jamaica, but you may be offered mackerel and banana along with your bacon and eggs. In Trinidad and Guyana, the spicy *roti*, a chapati pancake often filled with curry, is an unmistakable taste of India. Meanwhile, the French territories of Martinique and Guadeloupe claim the Caribbean's most sophisticated cuisine. A classic dish is red snapper in white wine, garlic, and limes. The hamburger may have made serious inroads into regional tastes, but the imprints of Europe, Africa, and India are still very much in evidence. Supermarkets are inevitably stocked with American brands, but don't be surprised to see Camembert in Martinique, Gouda in Curaçao or Yorkshire pudding mix in Barbados.

VARIETY Most of the Caribbean islands share a few basic dishes. Rice 'n' peas (or red beans) is a staple everywhere and especially good when cooked in coconut water. Root vegetables are a cheap filler, boiled or fried, and go by literally hundreds of different names across the region. Bananas and plantains are ubiquitous, as are the common fruits such as guava, pineapple, and mango. But on top of these staples, each island has developed its own often idiosyncratic recipes. In Jamaica the national favorites are curry goat (often beef), and saltfish and ackees. The latter dish harks back to the era of slavery when salted fish was imported from Canada to feed the island's slave population. The small island of Dominica specializes in "mountain chicken," which is actually a local frog. In the Dominican Republic, *mondongo*, a tripe stew, is considered a miracle cure for a hangover.

RUM There is, of course, ample opportunity to acquire a hangover. Every island produces rum, ranging from mass-market brands to local firewater. Some of the so-called over-proof rum (140 proof) is a serious risk to health, especially when mixed into apparently innocuous cocktails. Perhaps the best way to sample the better rums is with ice and lime juice, the basis of the classic Planter's Punch cocktail. Although each island predictably claims to make the best, the better quality rums are generally those from Cuba, Haiti, Jamaica, Martinique (especially *rhums vieux*), and Barbados.

BEER The Caribbean is not a wine-producing area, but every island, however small, has its own brewery. Some international brands such as Budweiser and Guinness are widely available, but locals swear—often correctly—that their beer is better. Perhaps the best known is Jamaica's Red Stripe, but other superior brews are Barbados' Banks, Trinidad's Carib and St. Vincent's Hairoun. Less known and arguably the best is Presidente from the Dominican Republic, which often comes served in iced glasses.

HUNGER For the tourist, hunger is less of a risk than a gradually expanding waistline. Nor are many people in the main tourist islands likely to go hungry. Hardship is largely restricted to Cuba, where rationing and embargo have drastically reduced dietary intakes for the locals, and Haiti, the hemisphere's poorest nation. Equally worrying is the growing dependency of Caribbean countries on importing basic foods in order to feed their own populations. While most countries are now desperate to export their "exotic non-traditionals," they are forced to import basic ingredients such as rice, beans, and sugar for local consumption. This means that the Caribbean is now increasingly consuming what it does not produce and producing what it does not consume.

One of the Caribbean's distinctive dishes: ackees

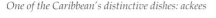

Recommended specialties

Antigua Goat water (hot goat stew) and fungi (similar to polenta).

Barbados Flying fish, dolphin (dorado or mahi mahi, not the mammal), pickled breadfruit and blood sausage.

Cuba *Moros y cristianos*—the local name for rice'n'peas.

Curaçao *Rijsttafel* ("rice table," with up to 40 different meat and vegetable dishes, originally from Indonesia).

Dominica "Mountain chicken" (a large local frog) and *agouti* (a small rodent, usually stewed or smoked).

Dominican Republic *Mondongo*, *sancocho* (a stew of made of six different meats and vegetables), *casabe* (cassava bread).

Grenada *Souse* (pig's feet stew), armadillo, iguana. Also famous for its spices, nutmeg, and mace.

Haiti *Griot* (deep-fried pork) and most French-influenced sauces.

Jamaica Saltfish and ackees, curry goat and jerk chicken, barbecued and sold from roadside stalls. Also produces Blue Mountain coffee.

Martinique and Guadaloupe *Ti-boudin* (spicy sausage), *poulet au coco* (chicken with coconut).

Puerto Rico *Pastillas* (pork, chickpeas, and raisins stuffed in dough, wrapped in plantain leaves, and steamed), the paella-like *asopao*. Puerto Rico also offers fast food, and drive-in service.

Trinidad *Roti*, *pelau* (rice and curry).

Cooling drinks are a treat and often a necessity in the Caribbean heat

The Caribbean Was

Long before Columbus "discovered" the Caribbean islands, Native Americans had started clearing the ground to build villages and plant their crops. Tribes of Arawaks and Caribs had been living on the Caribbean shores of South America since about 5000 BC, but by 1000 BC the Arawaks were fleeing their aggressive neighbors and driving out Jamaica's earliest settlers, the Ciboneys.

FIRST SETTLERS Three groups of Arawak settlers established villages on the islands: the Tainos, on Jamaica, Cuba, and Haiti; the Lucayanos, in the Bahamas; and the Borequinos, on Puerto Rico. For a few hundred years they led a peaceful life, left alone by Carib warriors. But the Caribs finally caught up and by the late 15th century, when Columbus arrived, their canoe raids and violent attacks were a constant threat.

NATIVE AMERICAN LIFE While the Arawaks learned skills such as basket-weaving and traded their crops—cassava, maize, sweet potatoes, cotton, and pepper—from island to island, the Caribs sent raiding parties to loot villages for slaves and supplies. Their expertise in making and using weapons was formidable; Caribs were fast and accurate bowmen, shooting fire- or poison-tipped arrows, and they used a variety of clubs and spears with gruesome added extras.

Nevertheless, they did develop some talents other than maiming and killing. Caribs were fine potters; each settlement had its own "trademark," often in the form of an animal, which was carved onto its pots, and, as an essentially belligerent, nomadic tribe, the Caribs excelled at canoe building.

Arawak communities were based on the family, with a *cacique* (clan chief) ruling each group of villages, helped by a committee of elders or *nitayanos*. They were also religious leaders, in touch with the ancestral and natural spirits and sometimes acting as their mouthpiece, inhaling tobacco fumes to induce a trance and

Native Americans sowing maize

conveying advice or predictions from the spirit world. *Zemis*, wooden or bone figures representing the gods of nature, were housed in special huts, set apart from the ordinary round, thatched homes of the villagers. Religious worship involved dancing, games, and tobacco-smoking; the powdered leaf was lit inside a forked tube (*tabaco*), which was wedged up the nostrils. Caves were used as burial sites by some clans (bones, canoe paddles, and *zemis* have been excavated); carvings of symbols and mask-like faces can still be seen covering cave walls and rocks on several Caribbean islands.

Fighters and killers were the respected members of Carib society. Chief warriors were elected on the basis of their performance in battle, and religious activities revolved

❑ Gold was one of the commodities traded by Arawaks, but it was prized only as an ornament. Carib warriors decorated their bodies with paint, petals, coral bracelets, and anklets, and shells or bones were worn in pierced ears, lips, and noses. Arawaks used dyed clay and grease to cover their bodies, and would bind their babies' heads to give them long, tough skulls. ❑

ceremonial; fat from the body of a brave enemy would be rubbed over Carib boys to give them courage. Even so, Carib society was undeniably brutal, and prisoners were starved and tortured before eventually being killed and served up, as a test of their endurance.

Both tribes relied to a great extent on the Caribbean's abundant marine life for much of their food, but any edible creature was regarded as fair game. Lizards, snails, and turtle eggs were all snapped up; birds were caught in nets strung between branches, and fish were hooked, speared, or even stunned by poison bark thrown into the water. Each day's catch would be added to a pepperpot, a seasoned stew left to simmer for weeks. Pepperpots (now with different ingredients) can still be sampled on Grenada (see page 52).

around appeasing a vengeful god. When European settlers arrived in the Caribbean they painted a grim picture of the Caribs as vicious cannibals who were liable to make a meal out of anyone straying onto their territory. In fact, any cannibalism which did take place is likely to have been

Symbols from a vanished world: Arawak rock carvings in Puerto Rico

After five weeks of sailing the uncharted Atlantic, Christopher Columbus and his crew were within hours of giving up their voyage of exploration when land was sighted on October 12, 1492. The sailors—who believed they had found Japan—were actually heading for the Bahamas, and were about to begin an unprecedented era of wealth, war, and oppression.

THE GREAT EXPLORER Columbus was born in Genoa in the late 1440s. He became an avid sea-voyager and a collector of maps and charts and by the 1480s, convinced that Japan and the riches of the "East Indies" could be reached by sailing west, he set about searching for the finances to back an expedition. Portugal and Britain turned him down—they had their own ideas for finding new trade routes. The Spanish monarchs, Ferdinand and Isabella, made Columbus wait five years while they drove the Moors from the country; then they agreed to his plan, eager to spread the influence of Spain and of the Catholic church, and to break the long-established Arab monopoly of trading routes to the Indies.

Columbus set out with his fleet of three ships—the *Niña*, the *Pinta* and his flagship, the *Santa Maria*—on August 3, 1492. By the time land was sighted he was having trouble preventing mutiny; the worried crew was threatening to throw Columbus overboard and head back home. After naming his first "discovery" San Salvador, the explorer persuaded some of its Arawak inhabitants— who welcomed the newcomers as protection against the Caribs—to come aboard and direct him toward Hispaniola. Here, the *Santa Maria* ran aground, leaving 40 Spaniards to build the first European fort in the Caribbean. Columbus was disappointed at the scarcity of gold and spices on the islands, but returned to

Columbus is greeted by Arawak islanders on San Salvador

Spain with a few "Indians," plants and tobacco leaves as promise of wonders yet to emerge.

THE NEW COLONIES

A second voyage followed in 1493, with a much larger fleet, bringing builders and farmers to create new settlements and priests to convert the natives. Many of the settlers were convicted criminals, pardoned on condition that they join the fleet. Before long the colonists—who had no prospect of returning home—had started to abuse the Arawaks, demanding food and taxes of gold and cotton, stealing the women and forcing the men into slavery. War broke out, and within three years, most of the 200,000 Native Americans were dead, overwhelmed by Spanish guns and

Explorer and treasure-seeker: a 16th-century Spanish portrayal of Christopher Columbus

swords or by the smallpox that the settlers had brought with them. The Europeans established a capital in Santo Domingo and a row of forts to protect their new colony.

Columbus himself returned to Spain after charting a course to Jamaica and Cuba; five years later he was back again, determined to find the mainland—which he did, after visiting Trinidad and quelling a rebellion among the Hispaniola colonists. The ambitious admiral was intensely disliked, however, and a commissioner sent by Queen Isabella to investigate complaints promptly had him arrested and shipped back to Spain. A fourth voyage also ended in disaster; after sailing along the Central American coast, Columbus's ships were wrecked off the shores of Jamaica, and the explorer and his stranded sailors had to wait for a year before a ship could be sent to rescue them.

Columbus died in 1506, having failed to supply the unlimited riches which had been promised. But a new world had been opened to Spain, with gold reserves to be mined, crops to be farmed, and souls to be saved—at the expense of many hundreds of thousands of lives.

❏ Columbus was eager to exploit the native Americans as free labor, and many were set to work mining for gold. The Spanish monarchy, however, disapproved of enslaving potential converts to Christianity, and would only sanction slavery for criminals or captured warriors. European accounts of native American atrocities and cannibalism were often invented to justify the taking of slaves. ❏

Anxious to reap the benefits of Columbus's voyages, Ferdinand and Isabella persuaded Pope Alexander VI to give them legal possession of the Americas. Under the Treaty of Tordesillas (1494), a boundary was drawn up dividing the "New World" between Spain and Portugal, and excluding the rest of Europe from claims to these territories.

LAYING DOWN THE LAW The Caribbean was to be a stepping stone for further exploration, and Spain was to have a strict monopoly over trade with the new colonies; but naturally developments did not go according to plan. In the years after

Pirates attack a Spanish ship

Columbus's last voyage, thousands of settlers arrived from Spain, eager to find gold, to own land and to be given power over a workforce of native Americans under the royal grants known as *encomiendas*. Their vicious treatment of the Arawaks

was bitterly condemned by Antonio de Montesinos, a Dominican friar, and by an ex-*encomendero*, Bartolomé de las Casas. Eventually their outspoken attacks led to two sets of laws, passed by two successive kings. In 1512 Ferdinand assented to the Laws of Burgos, dictating limited working hours and the provision of food rations for Arawak laborers; and in 1542 Charles V put an end to new grants of *encomiendas* under the New Laws. But Spain had little control over the actions of its Caribbean colonists, and by the 1520s so many native Americans had been killed off, especially by "European" diseases to which they had no immunity, that the settlers were already beginning to ship in African slaves to take their place.

CONQUISTADORES In the meantime, the search continued for richer lands, and groups of armed *conquistadores* set out to stake new claims. Juan Ponce de Léon led a party of men to conquer Puerto Rico, massacring the Borequino inhabitants and clearing the land for plantations and ranches. Diego Velázquez took three years to wipe out the Native Americans on Cuba, and by 1520 the *conquistadores* had reached Mexico and the rich prizes of the Aztec Empire. When word got out that the Spanish had struck gold on the mainland, hordes of settlers made for wider, wealthier territories. At the same time, sailors from other European countries saw an opportunity for easy money. Spanish claims to exclusive rights over the spoils of their settlements were ignored, as pirates attacked their ships and ports.

PIRATES Their cargoes were also looted by privateers, sea captains who were authorized by their governments to plunder enemy ships in time of war, and the European powers were in an almost constant state of warfare during the 17th and 18th centuries. Spain's monopoly on trade with the colonies could not be maintained. Aside from pirate attacks, the system was unwieldy and inefficient.

A buccaneer pictured in 1905

Caribbean settlers would be kept waiting for months on end, while fleets of Spanish ships loaded up with goods underwent rigorous checks at the Customs Office in Seville. Impatient with restrictions imposed by a distant state, colonists were soon doing a brisk illegal trade with ships from Britain, France, and the Netherlands, and there was little that Spain could do to stop them. Unofficial trade has continued to be part of Caribbean life ever since.

31

Looting Spanish ships was risky business, and by the early years of the 17th century the rival European powers were considering ways of earning long-term profits from Caribbean lands. While Spanish island colonies dwindled, forgotten by their home country, British and French adventurers were trying their luck at building settlements of their own.

TOBACCO Early experiments in tobacco-growing on the Guyana coast had been dismal failures; the small groups of British and French planters were soon defeated by fever and Carib attacks. In 1622 one of the Guyana colonists, Thomas Warner, decided to try the fresher climate and fertile soil of the Lesser Antilles and

take up their own plots of land. In the meantime, France was turning its attention to the Caribbean, and in 1635 Cardinal Richelieu formed a company to colonize Guadeloupe, Martinique, St. Lucia, and Grenada. For the following 10 years or so, settlers made the best living they could, fending off Carib or Spanish

Slaves being shipped from Africa were forced to dance to keep "fit"

attacks and sending home their harvests of tobacco and cotton.

set up a plantation on St. Christopher (St. Kitts). Britain, at war with Spain, was quick to see the advantages of a foothold in the "New World" and within three years the Earl of Carlisle was charged with colonizing St. Kitts, Nevis, Barbados, and Montserrat. To cultivate the land, indentured laborers were shipped from Britain, bonded to work for five years, after which they were free to

TENSION Relations between the colonies and their mother countries were uneasy: British settlers resented the imposition of rents and taxes; the French state neglected its Caribbean territories when their profits failed to live up to expectations. Colonists relied heavily on Dutch ships for their supplies and, in turn, the Dutch took every opportunity to extend their own empire, colonizing Aruba,

Curaçao, and Bonaire, which lay near Spanish mainland ports, and Saba, Sint Eustatius, and Sint Maarten, conveniently placed on their trade routes with Spain's island colonies.

SUGAR AND SLAVERY In the course of war against Spain and Portugal, the Dutch had captured several sugar plantations in Brazil, and their ships brought news of the vast profits to be made from the crop. They also seized Portugal's West African slavery centers and established a monopoly of slave provision for the labor-intensive plantations. African men, women, and children, kidnapped from their villages during midnight raids or captured and sold by rival chiefs, were shackled to each other by their necks and marched to coastal slave markets, where dealers picked the healthiest and branded them with irons. Eager for the biggest possible profit margins, captains would fill every available space on their ships, forcing the chained captives to lie shoulder to shoulder beneath the decks for their eight-week voyage. When the ships docked, the surviving slaves were auctioned off to planters, having been oiled and rubbed to cover the effects of their terrible journey.

CONFLICT In an attempt to break the Dutch hold on the slave trade, Britain attacked Dutch strongholds, triggering one of many conflicts between the colonial empires. France, Holland, Britain, and Spain were all anxious to strengthen their economies and expand their influence, and colonized islands switched hands several times, stormed by one

I would not have a Slave to till my ground
To carry me, to fan me while I sleep,
And tremble when I wake, for all the wealth
That sinews bought and sold, have ever earn'd.
We have no Slaves at home—why then abroad?
COWPER.

An 1827 condemnation of slavery

navy after another. British Lord Protector Oliver Cromwell sent a small army to Jamaica in the 1650s; in 1664 the French Minister of Finance, Jean-Baptiste Colbert, bought back Martinique, Guadeloupe, and other colonies from the private companies which had taken them over 20 years earlier. By 1678 Holland was forced to use ships registered in neutral Denmark to break through trade barriers, encouraging Danish settlement of the Virgin Islands of St. John and St. Thomas. By the end of the 17th century most of the Caribbean islands were divided between the French and British empires, which proceeded to exploit the new-found wealth of their sugar industry and the thousands of slaves who produced it.

33

During the early years of conquest and settlement, Europeans had hoped to find unlimited supplies of gold in the West Indies. In the 18th century their dreams of immense wealth were realized as the demand for "white gold" soared and the sugar islands became the Caribbean's richest exporters, supplying over 160,000 tons during the late 1760s.

Slaves working on a treadmill in Jamaica, 1830

RIGHTS OF SLAVES The rewards of this trade were restricted to a very few plantation owners—many of whom lived in Europe and left the management of their estates to agents. Even those who lived in the Caribbean tended to build their great houses at a considerable distance from the plantation fields, partly for comfort but also for security: by the 1770s slaves outnumbered whites by about 10 to one on the main sugar islands and their harsh conditions had already prompted several revolts. Strict laws were passed controlling the movements and rights of slaves: they were forbidden from gathering in large groups, from owning land, and from giving evidence in court; slaves from the same areas of Africa or with similar cultures were parted, in an attempt to dampen feelings of solidarity and close relationships. Nevertheless, African culture did survive in the traditions of story-telling (see page 61), dance and music (see pages 80–81), and spirit-worship (see pages 178–179). Many slaves risked imprisonment and whipping by running away, and over the years runaways established strong communities in inaccessible parts of the islands.

For most slaves, however, life was a constant grind for 16 to 18 hours every day, digging the fields, gathering the sugar cane, feeding it into the crushing mills or pouring boiling sugar extract into coppers. Freedom was a rare reward, granted to long-serving slaves or to the offspring of white men and slave women. Even freemen had to carry passes guaranteeing their status for seven years, and were often forbidden from owning property above a certain value.

BOOM AND DECLINE For 100 years the white minority managed to suppress slave rebellions while they kept up a steady flow of raw sugar (trade laws allowed the refining industry to operate only in the home countries). Wars continued to break out at regular intervals between the European powers, each one ending in the inevitable shuffling around of territories. By 1763, when the Seven Years War between the British and French came to an end, Britain owned five of the 10 most profitable sugar islands—Jamaica alone produced over 30,000 tons a year—and their planters had become some of the empire's most prosperous and influential men.

The rot soon set in. Plantations cost a lot of money to run, and by the late 18th century many had been overused, exhausting the soil. At the same time the French planters, who paid lower export duties, were selling cheaper sugar to more European markets, and Saint-Domingue, the French-owned part of Hispaniola, laid claim to being the Caribbean's biggest sugar producer. When the colonies in North America rebelled against "taxation without representation," sparking off the Revolutionary War, Britain forbade the Caribbean planters from trading with the mainland, cutting off a valuable source of income. The Americans turned to French and Spanish sugar islands instead, and British islands were forced to find ways to cut costs and provide their own supplies. New crops were planted, such as mangoes and breadfruit trees (brought by Captain Bligh of *Bounty* fame in 1793), and botanical gardens were opened to cultivate the plants; coffee, cotton, and spices were grown to supplement the main sugar crop. But, by the end of the 18th century, most of the sugar islands were in decline, and the West Indies were on the verge of radical, social and economic change.

A Caribbean sugar mill, 1816

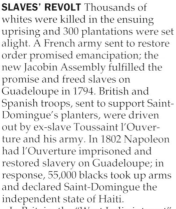

Anti-slavery movements were gathering force in late 18th-century Europe. In France the issue was brought to a head with the Revolution in 1789. The National Assembly resisted the demands of abolitionists such as the Paris-based Société des Amis des Noirs, and in Saint-Domingue the free "coloreds," angered by government failure to grant them full legal rights, armed their own slaves.

SLAVES' REVOLT Thousands of whites were killed in the ensuing uprising and 300 plantations were set alight. A French army sent to restore order promised emancipation; the new Jacobin Assembly fulfilled the promise and freed slaves on Guadeloupe in 1794. British and Spanish troops, sent to support Saint-Domingue's planters, were driven out by ex-slave Toussaint l'Ouverture and his army. In 1802 Napoleon had l'Ouverture imprisoned and restored slavery on Guadeloupe; in response, 55,000 blacks took up arms and declared Saint-Domingue the independent state of Haiti.

In Britain, the "West India interest" was losing ground with the decline of sugar profits, and slavery was abolished in 1834. Ex-slaves were obliged to serve four years of unpaid "apprenticeship," but many fled from the cane fields and set up their own plots of land; on Jamaica sugar production slumped by 50 percent. To make up the labor shortage planters took on immigrants as indentured laborers; by 1917 about 280,000 indentured workers from the Indian subcontinent had moved to Jamaica and Trinidad. On islands with little spare land, ex-slaves lacked the option of cultivating their own plots, and Barbados, Antigua, and St. Kitts continued to prosper as sugar islands for many years. Emancipation alarmed the old plantocracy, who feared the loss of political dominence. In 1865, after an episode of violent racial conflict in Morant Bay, Jamaica's assembly asked to be replaced with direct rule, and by 1898 Britain had imposed the status of Crown Colony on almost all of its Caribbean Islands.

The French finally abolished slavery on its remaining islands in 1848;

Emancipation portrayed by François Auguste Biard, 1848

Edmund Burke speaks out against slavery in the British Parliament

as on the British islands, sugar production plummeted and the planters encouraged thousands of Indian laborers to take up indentures. France pursued a policy of integrating its colonies, allowing each island to send three representatives to the National Assembly and granting the vote to all adult men in 1871.

CUBA Prosperity was late coming to the Spanish possessions, Puerto Rico and Cuba, and only when trade restrictions had been lifted in the late 18th century did Cuba's sugar industry flourish. As a result, slavery was not abolished until 1886. Resentment against Spanish rule and taxes led to

fierce civil war in the 1860s and 1870s, and again in the 1890s, by which time a separatist movement had won strong U.S. support. In 1898 U.S. warships destroyed two Spanish fleets off Cuba and under the Treaty of Paris in that year the island gained independence, while Puerto Rico was ceded to America. By 1917, when Denmark sold its Virgin Islands to the Americans, the U.S. was the Caribbean's main political and economic power, funding successful sugar, banana, and coffee industries. To defend this commerce the U.S.A. intervened in the political life of Cuba, Haiti, and the Dominican Republic (western Hispaniola) during the 20th century.

The Caribbean suffered badly during the 1930s Depression. Corrupt and repressive governments exacerbated the harsh conditions on Haiti and on Cuba, where Fidel Castro's revolutionary forces took control in 1959. On the British islands economic hardship gave rise to powerful labor movements, riots, and strikes. An attempt to form a federation of British Caribbean islands failed in the late 1950s, and in the 1960s Jamaica and Trinidad were the first to gain independence, followed by nearly all the other British islands.

The late 20th century has been a time of re-evaluation in the Caribbean. Some islands have found new roles as luxury tourist destinations; many are struggling with severe economic problems and with political instability. This fascinating region is still coming to terms with its complex historical legacy of conflict and conquest.

Dancers in traditional costume

WINDWARD TRAVEL

The quickest way to travel between the islands is on one of the island-hopping planes that run up and down the island chain at least twice a day. Alternatively you can try traveling by boat. This takes time; you may have to wait several days.

THE WINDWARD ISLANDS Crowned by sheer volcanic peaks and fringed with beautiful beaches, the islands of Grenada, St. Lucia, Dominica, and St. Vincent are among the loveliest in the Caribbean region. The advent of eco-tourism has added another, adventurous dimension to the more traditional appeal of beaches, river swimming, and yachting. With the necklace of the Grenadine Islands strung between Grenada and St. Vincent offering some of the Caribbean's best sailing, each of the Windwards has its enthusiasts, and each has a range of hotels and guest-houses to suit all tastes and budgets.

The four Windward Islands lie facing the Trade Winds head on, in a line of jagged, volcanic protrusions, some still active and liable to erupt about once every 100 years.

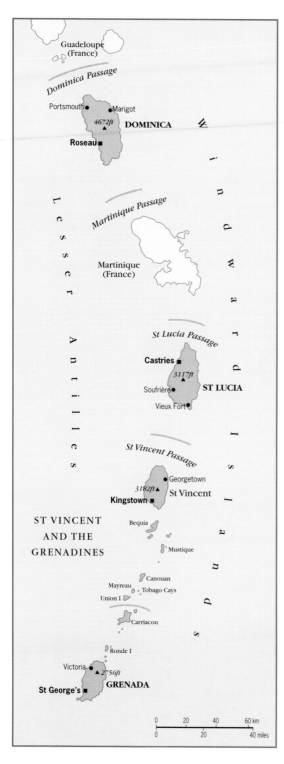

The Windward Islands

The Windward Islands

40

Calabash Hotel, L'Anse aux Epines Bay, Grenada

Regularly spaced on the tectonic fault-line between the Atlantic and Caribbean oceans, these protrusions are similar to each other in appearance, and all very small (not more than 29 miles by 16 miles), but they are nonetheless physically dramatic, with clouds hanging over the mountain peaks, and thick rain forest and bamboo covering the fertile land.

The islands no longer grow sugar, but their fertility is still the source of some wealth; fruit and vegetables are shipped as far as Trinidad and Anguilla, and the banana is an important export to Europe.

HISTORY Peaceful Arawak islanders were decimated by invading Caribs in about AD 1000; five centuries later the Caribs were defending themselves against European colonists. As late as 1748, Dominica was left to the Caribs in the Treaty of Aix-la-Chapelle. After passing between the European powers several times in the 18th century, the Windward Islands finally came into British hands, and became a Crown Colony in 1874, administered from Grenada. The islands all gained their independence from Britain in the 1970s, although they remain within the Commonwealth and still use the British judicial system.

ISLAND LIFE At one time during the to-and-fro of colonial control, all the Windwards were owned by France, and the French heritage is still strong. Names such as Beausejour Bay and Snug Corner can be seen side by side in Grenada, and French patois is spoken by the country people in Dominica, St. Lucia, and Grenada. The strongest influence, however, is African; most islanders are the descendants of African slaves, freed in 1834 and able to survive by working their own plots of land.

These are relaxed yet lively islands, both as tourist destinations—with all the sun, sea, sand, sex, dancing, and rum punches that implies—and in the local life.

The Windwards offer a remarkable breadth of tourism, from secluded mountain retreats to busy yachting marinas, and from fun-packed, all-inclusive hotels to the most sophisticated elegance. St. Lucia is the most developed island and is becoming increasingly crowded by tourists attracted to its good restaurants and hotels; Grenada, on the other hand, is developing more slowly. St. Vincent is still practically untouched, but the Grenadines offer the finest in easy island life and island-hopping by yacht (or mail-boat). Dominica, which joined in 1939, is not so developed, but offers nature tourism and scuba-diving.

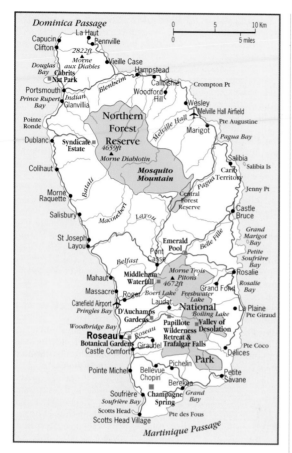

Dominica Passage

0   5   10 Km
0   5 miles

Capucin • La Haut
Clifton • Pennville
2822ft
Douglas • *Morne* • Vieille Case
Bay *aux Diables*
Cabrits • Hampstead
■ Nat Park
Portsmouth • Calibishie • Crompton Pt
Prince Rupert *Indian* Woodford •
Bay *Glanvillia* Hill • Wesley
Blenheim Melville Hall Airfield
Pointe **Northern** Melville Hall
Ronde • **Forest** Pte Augustine
Dublanc • **Reserve** Marigot
Syndicate *4659ft* *Pagua Bay*
Estate *Morne Diablotin*
Colihaut • Salibia • Salibia Is
Mosquito Carib
Mountain *Pagua* Territory
Morne • Central Jenny Pt
Raquette *Batali* Forest
Salisbury • Reserve Castle
Macoucheri *Layou* Bruce
St Joseph • Grand
Layou • Emerald *Belle Fille* Marigot
Pool *Bay*
Belfast Pont Petite
Roseau Cassé Soufrière
Bay
Mahaut • Middleham *Morne Trois* Rosalie
Waterfall ▲ *Pitons* Rosalie
Massacre • *4672ft* Grand Fond Bay
Roger Boeri Lake Freshwater
Canefield Airport Laudat Lake La Plaine
Pringles Bay D'Auchamps *Boiling Lake* Pte Giraud
Gardens **National**
Woodbridge Bay *Roseau* Papillote *Valley of*
Roseau Wilderness *Desolation*
Botanical Gardens Giraudel Retreat & Pte Coco
Castle Comfort Trafalgar Falls
Park
Pointe Michel • Bellevue Délices
Chopin Pichelin
Berekua Petite
Savane
Soufrière • Champagne *Grand*
Soufrière Bay Spring *Bay*
Scotts Head
Scotts Head Village Pte des Fous
Martinique Passage

JEAN RHYS
The novelist Jean Rhys
was born on Dominica in
1894 and lived there until
1907, when she left to
continue her education in
the U.K. After traveling to
Paris in the 1920s, Rhys
began her long writing
career, and set her most
famous work, *Wide
Sargasso Sea* (1966) in
the Caribbean. This book
describes the degenerate
and stultifying atmosphere
of colonial Caribbean life,
as seen through the eyes
of a Creole heiress, des-
tined to become
Rochester's mad wife in
Jane Eyre.

41

*Castle Bruce Bay, on the
rough Atlantic coast of
Dominica*

Dominica

Dominica claims to have a river for every day of the year
and it's probably true. A lush, green, volcanic island, it is
full of spectacular scenery and pretty coastal villages. Not
an obvious choice for beach-lovers, this is a must for naturalists and those who want to experience the simple,
small-island rural life.

At 29 miles by 16 miles, Dominica is the largest of the
Windwards—but it is also the poorest and least developed. Many islanders scrape a living on the land or by
fishing, and access to much of the country is difficult,
despite a number of new roads. For hundreds of years this
was a Carib stronghold; the descendants of those who
survived French invasion in the 18th century still live
here. Developed as a free port, Dominica made its money
from coffee, sugar, and slaves—many of whom escaped
into the jungle to live as maroons, occasionally taking up
arms against the authorities. British and French colonies
were established here in turn; positioned between the
French islands of Martinique and Guadeloupe, Dominica
had strategic value for France, and it has retained a strong
French heritage. Many of the 73,000 Dominicans are
Roman Catholics and Créole-speakers.

LIME JUICE

Dominica was at one time the biggest producer of limes in the world. One of the major buyers was Rose's, the company which supplied the British Navy with fruit juice. British sailors took a daily ration of lime in order to prevent scurvy—hence their nickname "Limeys."

MORNE TROIS PITONS NATIONAL PARK

U.N.E.S.C.O. has declared Dominica's Morne Trois Pitons National Park a World Heritage Site, thereby both celebrating and preserving its natural beauty. Guides are recommended for several of the more difficult hikes such as the Boiling Lake and the Valley of Desolation. (For information on this and the island's other magnificent parks, tel: 448-2401. There is a charge for admission.)

42

The Catholic cathedral at Roseau, completed in 1848

Dominica's capital, **Roseau▶▶**, lies in the southwest of the island; it's a small, working town of about 20,000 people, with a mixture of modern buildings and pretty stone and wooden Victorian townhouses. In the oldest part is Dawbiney Market Square, now the site of a craft market, tourist information center, and the Dominica Museum (tel: 448-8923; call for hours. *Admission charge*), which has informative descriptions of island life from colonial times to the present in pictures and exhibits, and includes volcanic geology. The new market is at the other end of the Bay Front. The Catholic cathedral, north of the old market site, was built under cover of darkness, after the government refused to support its construction. Not far from here is Fort Young, now a hotel.

The real beauty of Dominica becomes apparent on the outskirts of town. Beneath the huge white crucifix on Morne Bruce are the **Botanical Gardens▶▶**, now more like a park since the devastation from recent hurricanes, but still good for a walk to see the 150 species of plants and the endemic Dominica parrots (tel: 448-2401. *Open daily. Admission free*). The best place to see plants is directly inland in the Roseau Valley, a fantastically fertile gorge with tiny Dominican houses clinging to the slopes. At its head are the **Papillote Wilderness Retreat▶▶▶**, and three waterfalls called the **Trafalgar Falls▶▶** (see panel on page 44). The excellent D'Auchamps Gardens are halfway up the valley.

Reached along another fork in the road, the village of Laudat is an entry point to the scenic **Morne Trois Pitons National Park▶▶▶** (see panel), which takes its name from a mountain peak. The park has the best view of Dominica's forests, and walks to the Freshwater Lake (sadly the site of hydroelectric work), and the Boeri Lake. The adventurous might consider walking to the Valley of Desolation, an area of bubbling pools and mudponds, and the Boiling Lake, a crater of steaming water that can boil an egg in three minutes, and the second largest of its kind in the world.

South of the capital, the road passes a small strip of hotels in Castle Comfort, crossing lime country (see panel) to reach Soufrière, named for the nearby sulfur spring. The best sites for scuba diving are in this area. Near the pinnacles, caves, and dropoffs, a freshwater hot spring known as Champagne fizzes at scalding temperatures.

Some of the last survivors of the Carib race, which gave its name to the Caribbean, live on the east coast of Dominica. Once these proud and warlike people held sway over the Eastern Caribbean, but by the late 18th century, after a war of attrition with the expansionist Europeans, the few hundred remaining had been forced to the remotest part of Dominica and were forgotten. Only in 1903 were they officially granted their own territory.

The Caribs first appeared on the Caribbean islands around AD 1000. They came from South America (where there are still distantly related tribes) and island-hopped their way north along the chain, supplanting the peaceful Arawak tribe. Although they grew a few crops, the Caribs were mainly hunters and fishermen, who would stun parrots (for their feathers) by burning pepper beneath them, and fire arrows with amazing speed and accuracy.

Caribs were said to be cannibals, but this may well have been a lie circulated by Europeans to justify their acts of genocide. One early traveler tells of being presented with a pickled human arm, but there is little archeological evidence of systematic cannibalism.

On the beach at Castle Bruce you can watch canoes being made by traditional Carib methods (see panel). Six miles north of Castle Bruce lies the 3,700-acre Carib Tribal Reservation, which was established in 1903. (Don't expect much in the way of ancient culture and costume; the people who gave the Caribbean its name live pretty much as other West Indians.) Although there are no "pure" Caribs left, and their language has died out, their descendants still have the characteristic silky blue-black hair. In addition to canoe-building, they have maintained their woodcarving and basket-weaving skills. Carib wares are displayed and can be purchased in little thatched huts along the road. Of interest on the reservation are the Roman Catholic church, whose altar was once a canoe, and L'Escalier Tête Chien ("trail of the snake staircase"), a hardened lava flow that juts down to the ocean.

CANOES
Caribs still build their canoes in the traditional way, hollowing them out from gommier trees. In the past, a large Carib canoe could carry over 100 people. Builders would select a suitable tree and fell it, then hollow it out with tools made from conch shells. Rocks and fire were used to widen the sides, which were then built up with planks before the canoe was finally launched. A war canoe could be paddled at the same speed as a European warship in full sail.

Spaniards get a hostile reception from Caribs in 1525

Try your hand at bargaining with the ladies of the Roseau market

WILDERNESS AND WATERFALLS
At the head of the Roseau Valley, a half-hour's journey from the capital, are the Papillote Wilderness Retreat and the Trafalgar Falls (tel: 448-2401. *Admission charge*). It is possible to climb into the waterfalls, which are harnessed for hydro power as they crash onto sulfur-dyed black and orange rocks. The Papillote Wilderness Retreat (tel: 448-2287) is a 10-room hotel set in a 12-acre garden fed by a small stream from a 98-ft. waterfall. Paths wind among bamboo trees, begonias, bromeliads, and orchids, and visitors can bathe in warm springs.

The road inland from Canefield climbs into the mountains and rain forest, touching the northern limits of the National Park and giving access to **Middleham Falls▶▶** and the **Emerald Pool▶** and waterfall (pleasant but tame). From here the road descends to Castle Bruce on the coast and turns north to **Carib Territory ▶▶** (see page 43).

Back on the calmer Caribbean coast, the Layou River Gorge has good spots for swimming; beyond it, the road passes beneath Morne Diablotin (the island's highest) in the Northern Forest Reserve. Here you can arrange to walk through the rain forest to a hideout, where there is a chance you might see one of Dominica's two indigenous parrots, the Sisserou and the Jacquot.

Portsmouth, set on a huge bay in the northwest, is the island's second town and is even quieter than Roseau. Canoe trips arranged here take passengers through the Indian River mangroves; the area's malarial swamps drove British settlers to Roseau, ruining Portsmouth's chances of becoming the capital. The excellently restored **Cabrits National Park▶▶** (tel: 448-2401. *Open* daily. *Admission charge*) is an old military garrison set on the nearby promontory (cruise ships dock on the peninsula itself). Many of the barrack buildings have been repaired and there is a museum in Fort Shirley. The Park also includes a marine section, with scuba diving sites. Portsmouth's black sand beaches are passable, but Dominica's best beaches are to the east, in the hidden north coast coves; try Hampstead or Calibishie—swimmers should beware the fierce Atlantic swells.

44

Caribbean islands are best known for their picture-postcard beaches, where silken sands are lapped by gentle waves. But there are other treats for waterlovers; the mountainous interiors of many islands are laced with rivers, where cool rainwater crashes and tumbles through thick forests, and waterfalls pour into clear rockpools, making ideal spots for secluded and refreshing dips after hiking through the rain forest.

Rivers were once gathering places on the Caribbean islands. Before piped water was introduced, the population would go there to collect water and do the Monday washing, and washerwomen (*blanchisseuses* in the French Caribbean) can still occasionally be seen sudsing the clothes up at the riverside and then laying them out on the rocks to dry. Another long-standing practice was (and remains) taking a bath in the river. Although West Indians never go nude on their beaches, they do often take off their clothes in order to wash in the water.

Rivers play an important part in Caribbean folklore and legend; many islands share the legend of a beautiful girl sitting by a rockpool, combing her hair with a golden comb and perhaps granting a wish. The story goes that anyone who manages to steal her comb and take it down to the sea can keep it. The rockpools of Trinidad are said to be the home of the unpleasant Mama Dlo, the spirit of the water, who is half woman and half anaconda.

The Windward Islands are so well watered that they actually sell water to some of the drier islands; but the best islands for river bathing are the Eastern Caribbean islands from Guadeloupe down to Trinidad. There are also large rivers in the Greater Antilles. Many of the rockpools and rivers are off the beaten track and so bathers should be careful of their personal security. Rivers of slow-moving water might best be avoided—cases of bilharzia (caused by a parasitic flat-worm that enters the blood and bladder), though rare, have been known to occur.

RIVER HUNTS
On Dominica, hunting parties search the rivers by night for frogs and crabs. Hunters once used flaming torches (they are more likely to be electric flashlights nowadays) to attract the animals, which are so startled by the light that they do not even hide, can be simply picked up.

RIVERS IN RELIGION
In Haiti waterfalls have religious significance. On saints' days the Catholic and voodoo faithful gather at the riverside for ceremonies that include baptism in the waters of the cascades.

Swimmers can enjoy the pools at Dunn's River Falls in Ocho Rios, Jamaica

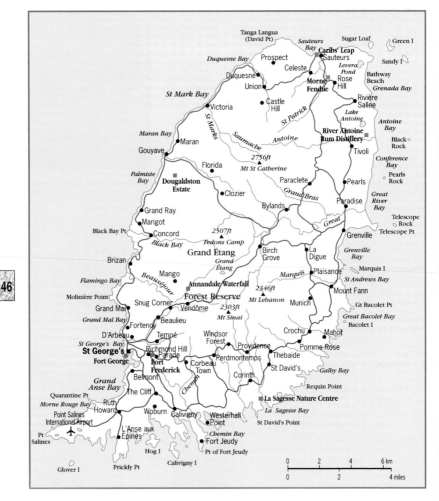

FÉDON'S CAMP

High up in Grenada's rain-forest, Fédon's Camp takes its name from French Creole planter Julien Fédon, leader of a rebellion against British authorities in 1795. Supplied by French revolutionaries in Guadeloupe, he led a brutal insurrection, and set himself up in his estate at Belvidere with 50 prisoners, all of whom were killed. The British eventually regained the island, but Fédon is thought to have escaped to Trinidad or Cuba.

Grenada

Now recovered from the political traumas of the 1980s, Grenada has relaxed into a sleepy island with the Caribbean's most picturesque port, St. George's. A warm, friendly place of small villages and mountain walks, it is ideal for either an active or a completely lazy break.

It was on Grenada that the Caribbean rum punch was perfected. In his book, *Touch the Happy Isles*, Quentin Crewe retells the story of a planter who sprinkled a mystery ingredient into his guests' glasses at a party in 1813. The addition was nutmeg and it was such a success that West Indians have used it in their recipes for rum punch ever since. The nutmeg fruit, which now appears on the Grenadian flag, was for a while one of the country's largest exports; nutmeg trees still grow all over the island. This and the many other spices grown in the hills—cinnamon, cocoa, cloves, pimento, and bay leaves—have given Grenada its title of the Caribbean's Spice Island.

Grenada is the most southerly in the chain of the Windward Islands, and is not as mountainous as the others. Of the Grenadines, its string of offshore islets surrounded by coral reefs, only two are inhabited: Carriacou and Petit Martinique. Grenada itself is developing slowly but steadily; package tourism is confined to the southwestern corner of the island, around Grand Anse and L'Anse aux Epines, where the best hotels, restaurants, and bars can be found. Elsewhere on the island you will see Grenadians living a pastoral, country life, often fishing or farming for a living.

Nowadays Grenada's atmosphere is calm and relaxed, but the island has a history of conflict and violence, aggravated by its strenghthening ties to Communist Cuba. In the recent past, the 1983 "intervention" by the U.S. and its Caribbean allies provoked strong reactions, of both outrage and approval. The troops moved in after Maurice Bishop, leader of the increasingly repressive People's Revolutionary Government, had been killed by a rival faction, along with nine of his colleagues. A return to the 1974 constitution, established when Grenada gained independence from Britain, paved the way for parliamentary elections and the island returned to a state of comparative stability. Some Grenadians still remember Maurice Bishop favorably—he had taken power in a bloodless coup, replacing the corrupt administration of Premier Eric Gairy in 1979—but only the occasional outburst of graffiti remains as a reminder of turbulent times.

ST. GEORGE'S Grenada's capital, **St. George's▶▶▶**, is a very pretty town on a natural harbor. Its Georgian stone houses and more recent concrete homes are neatly ranged in curved lines on the crumbled slopes of a long-inactive volcanic crater, their red tiled and tin roofs offset by the tropical greens of the surrounding forest. On the heights above stands a protective ring of churches and fortresses.

BEFORE THE REVOLUTION
When Eric Gairy was elected Grenada's first leader after Independence, he had already built up a large following as a member of the colonial administration, promoting the cause of the workers. However, Gairy's government grew increasingly corrupt and repressive, its policies enforced by the secret Mongoose Gang, and soon an underground anti-government movement gathered strength. The New Jewel Movement united Gairy's socialist opponents; in March 1979 it took advantage of the leader's absence from Grenada to stage a coup, and, with Cuban support, Maurice Bishop's new administration began to implement its socialist policies.

"Mango, banana and tangerine," *as sung in* Dr. No. *St. George's Market has them all*

A century ago, the cocoa estates of Grenada would ring to the sound of fiddlers, who played for the workers as they "danced" the cocoa beans. The beans were laid out on boucans, or drying trays, and the workers would shuffle through them, turning them so that they dried evenly. Spices grow throughout the Caribbean, but Grenada's mild climate and fertile soil have earned it the title of "Spice Isle."

COCOA WALKS

Cocoa trees need to be shaded from the tropical sun if they are to flourish, so planters imported the tall and bushy *bois immortelle* or *madre de cacao* trees for that purpose. Shaded by their leaves, the "cocoa walks" are cool even in the middle of the day. In January and February the *bois immortelle* flowers bright orange, and whole hillsides in Grenada, Trinidad, and Tobago are patched with flaming orange blooms.

Spice Isle produce

Nutmeg and mace The nutmeg tree (*myristica fragrans*) actually yields two spices: nutmeg and mace. This bushy tree grows to 65 feet and produces a yellow fruit like an apricot, which splits open when ripe. Its flesh, used to make preserves, protects the nut itself, which is covered with a scarlet waxy netting. This is stripped off and sold as mace, for use as a food flavoring and in cosmetics. The kernel of the nutmeg is extracted from the shell and used to flavor foods (and to treat rheumatism).

Cocoa The Aztecs used cocoa beans for barter and made their national drink, *chocolada*, with them. The cocoa tree (*theobroma*, "food of the gods") grows to about 50 feet and sprouts yellow, brown, and purple oval-shaped pods, in which the beans lie in a sweet, white, sticky pulp. These must be fermented, to strip the pulp, and then dried in the sun for several days.

Allspice "Jamaica pepper" and "pimento," as allspice is also known, is native to the Caribbean and tastes like a combination of clove, cinnamon, and nutmeg. Used mainly as a flavoring for foods, it is an essential ingredient in jerk seasoning.

Other herbs and spices Bay leaves are a well-known cooking ingredient, but they have other uses: oil taken from the leaves and twigs of the tree is used in perfumes and in bay rum (a drink and an antiseptic). Ginger was brought to the Americas from the Far East by the Spaniards. Oil of ginger is used as a pain-reliever in the Windward Islands. The sweet-smelling bark of the cinnamon tree is used in confectionery and in cooking.

48

Flags hang in the streets of St. George's in preparation for Carnival in August

The heart of town is the **Carenage►►►**, the inner harbor, where the traditional island sloops and house cruise ships tie up. Waterfront warehouses now house restaurants and bars, and water-taxis pick up passengers for the bay crossing or the return to Grand Anse.

On Young Street, the **Grenada National Museum►** (*Open* Mon–Fri 9–4:30, Sat 10–1. *Admission charge*) is set in a French stone barrack-building, and shows memorabilia including Josephine Bonaparte's childhood bathtub from Martinique, Arawak rock carvings and artifacts of the plantation era. Dominating the harbor is Fort George, also the island police headquarters, where Maurice Bishop and his supporters were killed.

Over the hill (or through the Sendall Tunnel) the other half of St. George's, the Esplanade, is on the Caribbean seafront. Once the site of the public executions, the **Market Square►►►** was not easy to reach before the tunnel was built between the town's two halves in the late 19th century. Today it also serves as the bus station for the west coast, and Saturday mornings are renowned for particular chaos, as vendors and busmen exchange shouts and jokes. Vendors hardly ever use the market buildings; they prefer to lay out their wares on tables under golfing umbrellas on the square. Near by is the Minor Spices Society, where Grenada's home-grown spices are on sale; and the **Yellow Poui Art Gallery►►** on Cross Street exhibits work by Caribbean artists.

St. George's botanical gardens, on the Lagoon, are a little run down; the Bay Gardens on Richmond Hill are a better bet, showing a range of flora from forest walkways.

GRAND ANSE Not far along the coast to the south of St. George's is **Grand Anse►►**, Grenada's best beach. There are four or five hotels on the beach itself (others are ranged behind it) and beach bars on the sand. Grand Anse is also the best area for watersports. Other good, secluded beaches, including **Morne Rouge Bay►►**, nestle in the coves toward the southwestern tip of the island.

THE BIANCA C
On the shore of the Carenage, in St. George's harbor, a statue of Christ of the Deep and a plaque commemorate those who died when a cruise ship, the *Bianca C*, caught fire in 1961. Its remains were towed out of the harbor to the southwest and sunk, and it is now the largest upright underwater wreck in the world; the stern section alone measures about 115 feet.

MAMMA'S RESTAURANT
On the road south from St. George's, excellent local meals are served at Mamma's Restaurant. Mamma herself is no longer alive, but her children continue the tradition of exotic Grenadian cuisine. About 20 dishes are offered in all, including green figs, christophene, rice in coconut milk, turtle, and even animals such as monkey, opossum, and armadillo.

The daily market is one of the liveliest and most accessible features of Caribbean life. Whether it be the overwhelming press of a large city market or a series of small stalls under a tree, the market is a vital focus of community and business. An amazing variety of goods is sold, from tropical fruit and vegetables to pots and pans, from candy and soap to human hair for braiding—all to the accompaniment of the shouts and patter of the marketeers.

THE FLOATING MARKET
Curaçao's floating market is made up of 15 or so moored boats. Vendors store their goods on board overnight and lay them out on the quayside stalls during market hours, shading them with flysheets (which are attached to the masts and rise and fall with the movement of the boats). The vendors are resupplied every few days with produce from Venezuela.

Crowds at St. George's market

CASSAVA
Cassava is a familiar item on most Caribbean vegetable stalls. Most of its 160 species contain a poisonous, cyanide-like juice that must be extracted before the vegetable can be consumed. Carib methods included grating the tuber on a sea fan coral and then squeezing the pulp in a woven bag that tightened as it was stretched. Dried cassava can be used like flour to make cassava bread and cakes (called "bammy" in Jamaica).

Caribbean markets have always been more than just a place for buying and selling. In the days before emancipation in the 19th century slaves would be allowed to make a little money by selling the fruit and vegetables they had grown. After slavery had been abolished, markets became gathering places where people would meet and swap stories. Colonial market buildings are usually made of red corrugated tin (the finest and the busiest is the Marché de Fer in Port-au-Prince in Haiti, which covers about one acre), but vendors often spread their goods out on blankets on the ground outside, rather than on the tables provided. Most stallholders are women, who sit on low boxes or benches with their skirts rolled up over their knees, shaded by two-tone golfing umbrellas. They arrive from the country in the early morning, often leaving by mid-afternoon, when the goods are sold.

Tropical vegetables are an essential feature of most Caribbean markets, and include cassava (see panel), sweet potato, which can be oval or pointed with white, purple or orange flesh; eddoe, also called dasheen, whose spherical tubers have slender stems and heart-shaped leaves; and yam, long, thin and hairy.

On Grenada's south coast, L'Anse aux Epines has a number of hotels and bars, as well as a sailing marina, and farther east, beyond the offshore island of Calivigny (where Grenadians often go for picnics), there is a charming dark sand beach with a restaurant at La Sagesse Bay. The **La Sagesse Nature Centre▶ ▶** (tel: 444-6458) is set in a 98-acre plantation, where guided trails offer interesting glimpses of varied birdlife.

A visit to the **Grand Etang National Park and Forest Reserve▶ ▶** (tel: 440-6160. *Open* daily 8:30–4) is worth the tortuous drive into the mountains. From the trails, the rainforest can be fully appreciated: ferns exploding in the upper branches of the tall trees, and the mosses and ghostly trees of the elfin forest. The Forest Centre contains a museum, and an easy walking trail circles the Grand Etang—a crater lake—which takes about 1½ hours. Longer and more strenuous trails lead to Mount Qua Qua, Concord Falls, and beyond.

From here the road descends into Grenada's most fertile valleys on the way to the Atlantic coast. In Grenville, which is not much more than a fishing village, one of Grenada's two large **nutmeg processing stations▶ ▶** is based. The **River Antoine Rum Distillery▶ ▶** shows a water-driven cane-crusher in action, and follows the long process of boiling and distilling in order to make rum; visitors can taste the extremely strong result. The cane-crusher is one of the last of its kind operating in the Caribbean region.

The road north from St. George's follows the switchbacks of the western coastline and soon reaches Molinière Point, where there is good snorkeling. At the **Dougaldston Estate▶ ▶**, just south of Gouyave, Grenadian spices are prepared for sale. The preparation of cocoa is especially interesting; in Gouyave itself there is a **nutmeg co-operative▶ ▶** (see panel. *Open* Mon–Fri 10–1, 2–4. *Admission charge*), where nutmeg and mace are prepared.

Ribbons and hair braids for the children of Grand Anse Roman Catholic School

NUTMEG PROCESSING PLANTS
It is well worth visiting either of Grenada's two main nutmeg co-operatives; one is in Gouyave, north of St. George's, and the other in Grenville on the Atlantic coast. Each factory is filled with the pungent aroma of the spice and groaning hessian sacks waiting for export. Once the mace has been stripped and graded (according to color), the nut of the nutmeg is put through a crusher and the kernel extracted from the shells. It is then put through a water test: the finest nutmegs sink and are used in food flavoring; those that float are sent to be used by the pharmaceutical industry.

The Windward Islands

The village of Sauteurs, on the northern coast, serves as a reminder of the last Carib people in Grenada, who jumped to their deaths off a cliff here (Caribs' Leap) rather than be taken prisoner by French colonists in 1651. Inland, to the southwest of Sauteurs, is the delightful **Morne Fendue►►►** (tel: 442-9330. *Open* 12:30–3), the plantation house of Betty Mascoll, where rum punch is served on the veranda and the famous lunch consists of pepperpot, a dish that can last for 60 years if replenished and boiled daily. The last pepperpot had to be abandoned during the revolution, when there was a curfew; the current pot is therefore only about a decade old. Beaches in the northern area include Bathway, where there is a protective reef against the Atlantic waves.

Carriacou and Petit Martinique Carriacou►►► is the biggest of the two inhabited islands politically attached to Grenada. Attractive, welcoming, and extremely laid-back, it measures only 5 miles by 8 miles and has 6,000 inhabitants, who earn their living by selling vegetables and livestock in Grenada, and pursuing "unofficial" trade with other islands. Boat-building is a major island tradition, and the colorful sloops constructed by hand in Windward, on the eastern coast, and Tyrrel Bay are launched with great pomp and circumstance. The festive Carriacou Regatta is held every August. Boats to Carriacou sail from the Carenage, St. George's, several times a week (they also come from Union Island farther north), and flights land at Lauriston airport. The island is graced with some magnificent beaches and its southern shore has a view stretching 25 miles to Grenada, and taking in a number of uninhabited islands and cays. Beaches to look for include Anse la Roche, Windward Beach, and Paradise Beach. Tyrrel Bay is a superb place to watch the sunset.

Petite Martinique► is situated 3 miles to the east of Carriacou, and has a resident population of around 600 independent islanders, and only one place to stay; it is basically untouched by tourism.

52

Maurice Bishop, leader of Grenada's People's Revolutionary Government in the 1980s

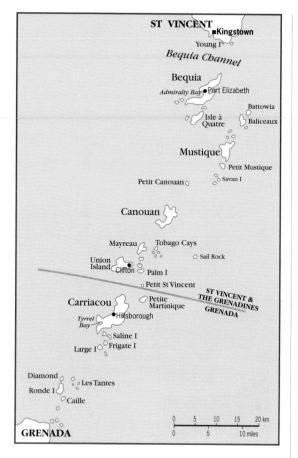

ST VINCENT ■Kingstown
Young I
Bequia Channel
Bequia
Admiralty Bay ●Port Elizabeth
Battowia
Isle à Quatre
Baliceaux
Mustique
Petit Mustique
Petit Canouan
Savan I
Canouan
Mayreau
Tobago Cays
Sail Rock
Union Island
Clifton
Palm I
Petit St Vincent
ST VINCENT & THE GRENADINES
GRENADA
Carriacou
Petite Martinique
Tyrrel Bay
Hillsborough
Saline I
Large I
Frigate I
Diamond
Les Tantes
Ronde I
Caille
GRENADA

| 0 | 5 | 10 | 15 | 20 km |
| 0 | | 5 | | 10 miles |

53

FAIR EXCHANGE
Young Island is said to have been swapped for a horse. Governor Young had brought a black charger with him to St. Vincent from Britain, and it was greatly admired by the local Carib chief, so he presented the creature to him as a gift. Some time later the two men were together on the veranda of St. Vincent's Government House, looking out toward the idyllic, forested islet just offshore. When Governor Young admired the island, the Carib chief returned the favor and made him a present of the land.

Admiralty Bay, used by the British Navy and then abandoned for lack of water, is now a favorite anchorage for yachts

The Grenadines

The Grenadines appeal to adventurous singles and couples who prefer sailing, seclusion, and sports to glitz, gambling, or designer shopping. Hotels are small, the food is simple, and the residents' hospitality provides a peaceful, laid-back atmosphere. The 32 islands and cays that make up the lush and mountainous Grenadines offer numerous unspoiled white bays and coves, and superb snorkeling, hiking, sailing, and swimming. Island-hopping by ferry is a practical alternative to flying. **Young Island▶** (tel: 458-4826) is a private resort with only about 20 cottages.

Bequia▶▶▶ lies 8½ miles south of St. Vincent. This is an island of fishermen, seafarers, boat-builders, and whalers, where tourists rub shoulders with the locals in an excellent string of bars on the waterfront in Belmont. The best places to stay include Frangipani, the Vincentian prime minister's boyhood home, and the Friendship Bay Hotel on the south coast. You can reach the excellent beaches, Princess Margaret Beach and Lower Bay, by water taxi from Port Elizabeth, or walk over to the secluded sand at Industry Bay in the east.

The graceful profiles of locally built boats are a familiar sight in the Grenadines. Brightly painted sloops still ply their trade from island to island as they have for centuries. Life in the Caribbean has always been dependent on shipping, and even now the smaller islands only really seem to come alive when crowds gather to greet the weekly boat.

Before island-hopping planes, Caribbean communities were linked by frequent boat services. Unfortunately, the use of small boats has died off on the larger islands, but part of the fun of visiting the Grenadines, the Virgin Islands, and the French islands off Guadeloupe is to hop from one island to the next by mailboat, ferry, or traditional schooner.

There is a long tradition of boat-building and sea-faring around the Caribbean islands. Caymanians and Sabans were particularly renowned as sailors and they crewed and captained vessels all over the world for the big shipping lines. Closer to home, inter-island trading was established as a necessary way of life—Anguillans would sail west to Jamaica and south to Trinidad to sell their products. Captains would fund the boat-building by traveling abroad to earn money first for the hull, then for the planking and the deck, then finally for the mast and fittings. Nowadays Grenadine sloops travel regularly to Trinidad, taking fruit and vegetables for sale and returning with goods such as potato chips and canned food. They also go as far north as Sint Maarten in the Leeward Islands, to buy supplies including export liquor and goods from Europe.

Today's master boat-builders are the Bequians and Carriacouans; although their trade is now dying, it is still possible to see hulls taking shape on the beach and being painted bright red and orange—essential for clear visibility against a turquoise sea.

Smuggling has always been part of Caribbean life. Although drugs do pass through the islands en route elsewhere, inter-island smuggling is usually confined to liquor, cigarettes, and large appliances, primarily for the avoidance of island duty. Buyers are told in advance when a boat will be putting in at a particular cove—usually in the dead of night.

54

Making sure everything is shipshape

BOAT-LAUNCHING
A boat launch is an excuse for a big party. The boat is christened and blessed by a priest with holy water (and sometimes with the blood of a goat). It is even given godparents, whose duty it is to raise it if it sinks. As the boat is launched, as many people clamber on board as possible, all dressed in their Sunday best, before returning to shore to eat and drink.

A scrubby outcrop 40 years ago, **Mustique▶▶** now has 75 of the Caribbean's most luxurious villas, 45 of which are for rent, for a small fortune (gardener, maids, cooks, and mini-moke, or donkey, thrown in). Just 1½ miles by 3 miles, Mustique has one hotel, the Cotton House (tel: 456-4777), set in a restored plantation house. Celebrities such as Mick Jagger and Princess Margaret emerge from the seclusion of their villas every Wednesday, jump-up night at Basil's beach bar on stilts (tel: 457-2713). The Caribbean seems as incidental to Mustique as it is essential to Bequia.

On **Canouan▶▶**, 800 people eke out a quiet living. This small island (3 miles by 1 mile) of gentle green peaks is rimmed with white sand. Offshore reefs protect the windward bays, and Grand Bay, on the leeward side, is a favorite yacht anchorage.

Mayreau▶▶, smaller and quieter, does not even have a jetty. Loading and unloading passengers can be a precarious business when the occasional cruise ships do put in. On the other hand, cattle are simply tossed into the sea to swim ashore. There are only 150 inhabitants and a couple of cars, but the beaches are wonderful.

Although its towering mountains make **Union Island▶** the most beautiful of the Grenadines, this is a working island; its marina and airstrip are used by a constant stream of people traveling to the quieter islands near by. Most of the 2,000 islanders are employed in the resorts or fish and trade by sea.

The five **Tobago Cays▶▶▶**, Petit Rameau, Petit Bateau, Barabal, Jamesby, and Petit Tobac, rise gently from the water, protected by a reef 1,000 yards offshore. They are uninhabited and maintained as a marine park, and offer excellent sailing and snorkeling. Close by are two tiny cays, each entirely devoted to a single luxurious hotel. **Palm Island▶▶** (tel: 458-8824) has 24 villas set on the beach or scattered among hundreds of palms. **Petit St. Vincent▶▶▶** (tel: 515/242-6951), known as PSV, specializes in low-key super-luxury, where residents communicate with room service by raising a yellow flag.

BEACHES
Beaches with bright white sand can be found throughout the Grenadines, many of them sheltered in coves formed by the irregularly shaped, mountainous islands. On the northern shore of Admiralty Bay on Bequia are the golden sands of Princess Margaret Beach and Lower Bay; Endeavour Bay is the best beach on Mustique, although the whole island is rimmed with ankle-deep, soft sand. Canouan has a number of pretty beaches and isolated coves, including Maho, Corbay, and Rameau Bay. On Mayreau the best beaches are Salt Whistle Bay and Saline Bay. One of the finest beaches in the West Indies is on Carriacou, at Anse la Roche. None of the beaches has formal facilities, but if there is a restaurant, the staff will normally let you change there.

55

Named for a governor in the 1700s, Young Island lies 200 yards off St. Vincent's southern shore

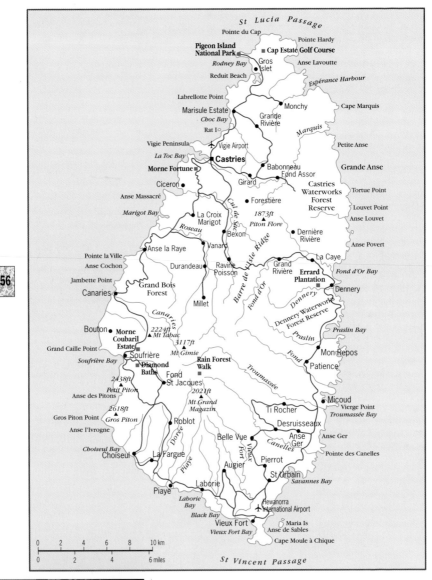

St Lucia Passage

Pointe du Cap

Pointe Hardy

Pigeon Island National Park
■ Cap Estate Golf Course

Rodney Bay
Gros Islet

Anse Lavoutte

Reduit Beach

Espérance Harbour

Labrellotte Point

Monchy

Cape Marquis

Marisule Estate
Choc Bay
Grande Rivière

Rat I○

Marquis

Vigie Peninsula
Vigie Airport

Petite Anse

La Toc Bay
Castries

Babonneau
Fond Assor

Grande Anse

Morne Fortune ■

Girard

Ciceron ●

Castries Waterworks Forest Reserve

Tortue Point

Anse Massacré

● Forestière

Louvet Point

Marigot Bay
La Croix
Marigot

1873ft
▲ Piton Flore

Anse Louvet

Roseau

Bexon

● Dernière Rivière

Anse Povert

Pointe la Ville
● Anse la Raye

Vanard

La Caye

Anse Cochon

Durandeau

Ravine Poisson

Grand Rivière

Errard Plantation

Fond d'Or Bay

Jambette Point

Fond d'Or

Dennery ●

Canaries

Grand Bois Forest

Millet

Canaries

2224ft
▲ Mt Tabac

Bouton ● **Morne Coubaril Estate**

Grand Caille Point

3117ft
▲ Mt Gimie

Praslin Bay

Soufrière

Diamond Baths

Rain Forest Walk

Mon Repos

Soufrière Bay

Fond St Jacques

Patience ●

Troumassee

2438ft
Petit Piton

2021ft
Mt Grand Magazin

Anse des Pitons

Micoud ●
Vierge Point

2618ft
Gros Piton

Ti Rocher

Troumassée Bay

Gros Piton Point

● Roblot

Desruisseaux

Anse l'Ivrogne

Belle Vue

Anse Ger

Anse Ger

Choiseul Bay
Choiseul

La Fargue

Canelles

Pierrot

Pointe des Canelles

Augier

St Urbain

Laborie

Savannes Bay

Piaye

Laborie Bay

Hewanorra International Airport

Black Bay

Vieux Fort

◌ Maria Is
Anse de Sables

Vieux Fort Bay

Cape Moule à Chique

0 2 4 6 8 10 km
0 2 4 6 miles

St Vincent Passage

56

St. Lucia

On Friday nights crowds gather at Gros Islet, a village on St. Lucia's Rodney Bay, in the north. This Caribbean jump-up transforms the settlement of wooden houses into one big street party: the thumping pulse of local soca, Martiniquan zouk, and Jamaican reggae can be heard from afar, and dancers spill onto the road, wining and grinding beneath the banks of flashing lights and the stacks of speakers, while vendors sell grilled fish and chilled beer. The heady mix of people at Gros Islet is typical of St. Lucia, where tourists and locals rub shoulders easily in the towns and on the beach. Lying between the French island of Martinique and St. Vincent to the south, this is one of the most welcoming of the Caribbean islands and has recently become a popular tourist destination, bringing in over 200,000 visitors a year. The rapid development of a tourist industry, with beach hotels and restaurants sprouting all over the island, threatens to swamp the quiet agricultural life that has characterized St. Lucia for many years, but as yet tourism is concentrated in the northwest, between the capital, Castries, and the northern tip of the island, where the best beaches are to be found. Venture into the city and beyond and there is still a beautiful island to explore, with inland rain forests and secluded coves accessible only by boat.

ISLAND LIFE St. Lucians are chatty and forthcoming, as will soon become apparent to anyone taking a walk on the streets of Castries or in the country villages. Most speak patois, a Creole language derived mainly from French, but English is the official language.

This was a British colony for one-and-a-half centuries, until Independence on December 22, 1979, but before that the island had a history of struggle and conquest. Its strategic importance sparked off several battles for its possession between the British and French until Britain finally established its possession in 1814. However the French legacy remains, in the names of many towns, the predominant religion (Catholicism) and the Creole food, which includes such delights as *soupe germou* (pumpkin soup with garlic) and *pouile dudon* (chicken cooked in coconut and sugar).

St. Lucia is the most populous (there are around 135,000 islanders) and the most developed of the Windward Islands. Besides tourism, there is some light manufacturing and an extensive agricultural sector which, until recently, depended mainly on bananas grown for export to Britain under special trade arrangements, but is now coming under threat from cheaper producers in Central America (see page 58).

PRIZE WINNERS
The island of St. Lucia can claim two Nobel Prize winners: in 1979 Sir Arthur Lewis won a Nobel Prize for Economic Sciences, and in 1992 Derek Walcott was awarded a Nobel Prize for Literature. Walcott, born in St. Lucia in 1930, was educated at the University of the West Indies and has taught in a number of American universities. He is best known for his poetry collections, including *The Fortunate Traveller* (1982), *Midsummer* (1984), and *Omeros* (1990). The last, arguably his masterwork, is an ambitious retelling of *The Odyssey* set in the islands Walcott knows so well.

Opposite: harbor view from Castries

CASTRIES St. Lucia's capital, **Castries▶▶**, was named for a French Minister of the Marine, the Maréchal de Castries, and laid out beside a natural harbor in the 1760s. It soon crept over the heights which surround the bay. Now a sprawling town of 60,000, Castries has burned down many times (most recently in 1948), and only a few colonial buildings remain. However, traditional Caribbean architecture survives on the hills around town, on Vigie Point and Morne Fortune.

The main square in the center of town has been renamed for one of St. Lucia's Nobel Prize winners, Derek Walcott. It is dominated by a huge saman tree in the center; on the south side are a number of old Creole timber-frame houses, among them the restaurant Rain, which is worth a daytime stop.

The edible banana's botanical name is Musa sapientum, *or "muse of the wise man." It is said that Southeast Asian sages would sit in the shade of banana trees, enjoy the fruit and have wise thoughts. Since the banana made its way to the Caribbean, this pastime has been readily adopted by islanders.*

"THE BANANA BOAT SONG"

Harry Belafonte's "Banana Boat Song" was originally a Jamaican working song, sung by women banana packers as they raced up and down the gangplanks, loading bunches of bananas onto the United Fruit Company ships. After working through the night, they would sing "Day-oh, day-oh" as day was dawning; the "tallyman" referred to in the song would give the workers tokens each time they came past with a load of bananas, tallying up the tokens at the end of the night and paying the women accordingly.

CLAIMS TO FAME

Bananas are highly valued by sportsmen and women, particularly tennis players and marathon runners, because they have a wide and complex range of sugars that are digested at different rates, thereby releasing energy over a longer period than other sugar foods, such as chocolate. The fruit has a rather less creditable reputation in Sri Lanka, where the story of Adam and Eve has the serpent tempting Eve not with an apple but with a banana.

Banana plants grow singly and in groves all over the Caribbean, their leaves exploding in graceful, green curves to heights of up to 20 feet. Each plant gives fruit only once before it dies, when another plant sprouts from the same root system. As they grow, they throw off drooping stems, on which the 150 or so individual bananas sprout, coming to maturity over nine months. The plants are protected from insects by blue plastic bags and some are tied with string to prevent them from falling over. Bananas grow in clusters, or "hands", of about 12; a group of 10 or so hands on a single stem is known as a "bunch." The popular yellow cavendish is the type of banana seen most in Europe and America, because it travels well, but Caribbean markets sell smaller, fatter, sweeter canary bananas (about 4 inches long) and green vegetable-bananas called plantains. Names and species vary. In the Windward Islands bananas range from big yellow *gros michels* to small "rock figs," and plantains called "green fig," "bluggo," and "buggoman."

Since the 1950s the export of bananas has improved life dramatically for many small farmers in Jamaica, the French Caribbean, and the Windward Islands. Instead of seasonal work in the cane fields, they now have a year-round income. In the Windwards, three-quarters of export earnings come from bananas. But free market agreements such as G.A.T.T. and N.A.F.T.A. have brought Caribbean bananas under threat, especially from "dollar bananas," grown more cheaply on larger Central American farms. Early in 1999, the banana dispute erupted into a major trade war.

Many West Indians prefer to carry their belongings on their heads

Diagonally opposite is the 100-year-old brick Catholic Cathedral of the Immaculate Conception (1897). A short walk away, Castries life is at its most ebullient in the market all along the waterfront in the new tin-roofed vegetable market and in the craft market.

Cruise ships dock on the north side of Castries harbor, and passengers head straight into the shopping complex at Pointe Seraphine, where the St. Lucia Tourist Board provides current information on hotels and events.

OUTSIDE CASTRIES Many of the island's hotels are set in coves north of the capital, an easy taxi or bus ride from Castries. The most popular area is **Rodney Bay▶▶**, with a marina, restaurants, hotels, and the island's liveliest beach. Reduit Beach is a long strip of white coral sand with watersports facilities, particularly busy on weekends late in May when Aqua Action takes place, a program of serious and fun watersports. Across the lagoon entrance is Gros Islet, the place to be on Friday nights.

Rodney Bay has long been a center for sailing craft and beach bars, popular with locals at weekends; before the gin-joints came Carib canoes, Spanish galleons, pirate sloops, and naval ships. Two centuries ago Admiral Rodney himself fortified **Pigeon Island▶**, across the bay

ROADSIDE REFRESHMENT
In hot weather it is essential to have a ready supply of liquid and among Windward islanders there is a tradition of selling soft drinks at the roadside. A snow cone, topped with water, sweet fruit concentrate and a straw, is a great way to keep cool. Sometimes the vendor offers a topping of condensed milk or even crushed nuts. Street snacks include locally grown peanuts, plantain chips. or coconut chips, cut from the dried copra in the center of the coconut.

59

from Reduit beach. It was designated a National Park in 1979, and its walkways pass barrack rooms and gun-pits, with a museum and restaurant at the end of the trail (tel: 452-5000. *Open 9–5. Admission charge*). There is one nine-hole golf course among the chic villas at the north of the island; and another at La Toc, south of Castries.

Different kinds of bananas and plantains are on sale in Castries market

The Windwards

The two Pitons, volcanic plugs covered by rain forest, rise dramatically from the sea in the south-west of St. Lucia

SPA FIT FOR SOLDIERS
King Louis XVI of France provided the funds to build the Diamond Baths in the 1780s after hearing of the volcanic water's healing powers, as described by the Governor, Baron de Laborie. According to reports at the time, the water was believed to cure rheumatism, among other ailments, and Louis was eager for his troops to feel the benefit. Water flows from the volcano at temperatures of about 105° Fahrenheit.

HOT WATER
The volcanic Windward Islands are active beneath the surface of the water as well as above it, and in the sea off the Pitons you will find patches of warm water let out by the Soufrière. In Dominica, for instance, the bubbles released make scuba-diving feel like swimming in champagne.

South of Castries, over Morne Fortune (pronounced "Fortunay"), there is a less feverish, less developed St. Lucia of valleys and coastal villages, where banana farmers and fishermen go about their business unaffected by tourism. Beyond Cul de Sac on the west coast is **Marigot Bay►►►**, a steep-sided inlet lined with palm trees, which served as a hideout for pirates and navies in centuries past; a couple of cafés are set on the road down to the bay, and there are bars on the beach itself. At Canaries the coast road turns inland and climbs into rainforest beneath Morne Gimie (3,117 feet), the highest peak on the island. The descent into the town of Soufrière offers magnificent views of the **Pitons►►►**, two pyramid-shaped volcanic mountains that soar from the sea to heights of 2,439 feet and 2,620 feet.

Soufrière, the first settlement on the island but rejected in favor of Castries because of its better harbor, is a town of clapboard houses with overhanging balconies. Its name comes from the nearby **Soufrière►**, the world's only drive-in volcano, a simmering cauldron of mud which can be tracked down by its foul smell. This is a solfatara—a volcanic vent that steams steadily rather than blowing cataclysmically like others in the area. Inland from Soufrière, at the **Diamond Baths►** (for a small fee) one can bathe in the naturally heated pools. Botanical gardens nearby give a good introduction to tropical flora. At the **Morne Coubaril Estate►►** you can see cocoa-making techniques, and the local product, manioc, and processing coconut. The **Central Forest Reserve►►** (tel: 452-5005) is a protected area of rain forest with walking trails, home to St. Lucia's own parrot, now near extinction.

The road from Castries down the east coast is an easier run, used to meet flights into Hewanorra international airport, near the southern tip. After passing over the rainforested Barre de l'Isle mountain range, it descends into banana plantations at Dennery before reaching the more remote villages strung out along the coast. You can visit working cocoa, coconut, and coffee plantations at the Marquis Estate at **Errard Plantation** near Jennery.

Before the age of cable T.V., whole villages would gather under a tree to enjoy an evening of storytelling. Many of the tales, often with song, centered around Anancy the Rogue and a cast of other characters—Dog, Goat, Jackass, Kisander the Cat, and Tiger—all of whom had human characteristics. Islanders still tell stories about them all over the Caribbean.

Anancy is the best-loved character in Caribbean folklore. Sometimes a man, sometimes a spider, he is a sweet-talking trickster who, as a man, is considered rather laughable because he speaks with a lisp, but who can turn into a spider and hide when the need arises. Anancy is lazy and greedy, and far happier tricking a slow neighbor out of his meal than working honestly. But he is also fully capable of outwitting his opponents—particularly Tiger, his traditional enemy. Even in his greed, Anancy wins the listener's sympathy, and is often used to deliver home truths—though storytellers may dissociate themselves from his actions by ending their tales with the words: "Jack Mantora me no choose any."

Above all, Anancy is good entertainment. When he wants a meal of crabs he dresses up as a priest and persuades them to be baptized (promptly throwing them into boiling water); having taken a bet that he cannot catch Snake, he taunts him into bragging about his length, and while measuring him against a log, ties Snake to it and captures him.

The island of Trinidad has a strong tradition of folklore, illustrated in Port of Spain's National Museum. Papa Bois, the guardian of the forest, warns animals of the hunter's presence (see panel). La Diablesse, the devil woman, appears as an old crone whose petticoats clank with chains or as an attractive girl who can drive men mad with desire, and the soucouyant is an old woman, who turns into a ball of fire at night and goes round sucking human blood.

Mama Dlo, the mother of the water, is half woman, half anaconda, and sometimes sings at the water's edge, but vanishes immediately if she is disturbed.

PAPA BOIS
Papa Bois will usually let hunters keep their kills from the forest, but if any become too greedy he will appear as a deer and lure them deep into the forest before turning back into an old man and issuing a stern warning, sometimes sentencing the offending hunter to be married to Mama Dlo.

DUENNES
Never shout the name of your child in the Trinidadian forest; it will be stolen by the Duennes. These infant tricksters, who reputedly roam among the trees, are the ghosts of children who died before they were christened, and if they hear a child's name, they will call for it and lead it away into mischief.

Top: the soucouyant
Below: Mama Dlo
Left: Papa Bois

61

The Caribbean climate is virtually ideal. Surrounded by sea, the islands enjoy an almost constantly warm temperature, even at night, and during the day the sun is tempered by the Trade Winds, cooling breezes that rise on the Atlantic. But at times, the benevolent ocean will deliver disaster in the form of a hurricane. These whirlwinds, accompanied by torrential rain, are immensely destructive. Land movement can cause chaos in the Eastern Caribbean, an area of tectonic activity where volcanoes occasionally blow and earthquakes strike.

HURRICANE SEASON
A traditional rhyme serves as a reminder of when hurricanes are most likely to strike: "June, too soon; July, stand by; September, remember; October, all over." Most hurricanes do, in fact, occur in the middle of September.

TRADE BY NAME
Although they were useful to merchant ships and used by sailors from the very first days of trans-Atlantic travel, the Trade Winds are not named for their commercial value. The term was coined in the 16th century as "tread winds"—meaning directional winds.

The calm after the storm, but a wrecked boat sits offshore after a hurricane

Trade Winds These equatorial winds flow from a high pressure area in the mid-Atlantic to low pressure regions nearer the equator. They hit the Caribbean islands from the northeast, at an angle that varies through the year because of the earth's tilting. The Trade Winds reduce humidity, while bringing plenty of rain to the more mountainous islands. Known as *Les Alizes* on the French islands, the *Passaatwinden* on Dutch land and *Brisas Aliseas* in the Spanish territories, the so-called "Christmas winds" blow most strongly in the winter months, bringing with them the balmiest temperatures.

Hurricanes Terrible damage can be inflicted by hurricanes, whose name is derived from the Carib language. They rise in the Atlantic, at the meeting point of the Trade Winds from both hemispheres (north of the equator in the summer); in a phenomenon known as the "coriolis effect," the warm, moist air rises and then condenses, releasing heat, falls and then rises again, strengthening the updraft, until eventually it begins to spiral. Immature hurricanes set off west-northwest, moving at around 12 m.p.h. and steadily building up size and power. The winds spiral inward around a vortex known as the "eye" (which is about 12 miles across), and can reach sustained speeds of up to 105 m.p.h., with bursts of around 185 m.p.h. Extending up to 500 miles across,

hurricanes are immensely powerful; their effect is measured in atom bombs per second. They are identified by a sequence of alternately male and female names.

All the Caribbean islands from Grenada northward lie in the hurricane zone, and in recent years some have been badly hit. Hurricane Gilbert swept through Jamaica and the Cayman Islands in 1988 and in 1989 Hurricane Hugo, the worst this century, laid waste to Guadeloupe, St. Croix, and Montserrat (where over 90 percent of the houses were destroyed). 1995 brought Marilyn on the heels of Luis, both causing terrible destruction in St. Maarten, Anguilla and St. Thomas in the U.S.V.I. 1998's Georges wreaked havoc in the Dominican Republic, and tore up Nevis, St. Kitts, Antigua, Puerto Rico, and Haiti.

Volcanoes The Eastern Caribbean is also an area of active volcanoes. This line of islands stretches in a curve from Saba to Grenada in the south, on the meeting point of the Atlantic and Caribbean tectonic plates. As the plates move slowly against each other, the magma (hot molton rock) contained beneath them occasionally escapes in the form of volcanic eruptions.

Volcanoes in the Eastern Caribbean all go by the name Soufrière, taken from the French word for sulfur, because of the foul smell that they give out. The most active volcanoes are on St. Vincent, Guadeloupe, and Martinique; these erupt about once every 100 years with cataclysmic lava flows and 20,000-foot plumes of smoke.

St. Lucia and Dominica have less devastating "fumarolles," where the pressure is let off constantly and much more steadily—though the heat and pressure in Dominica is enough to make a lake boil. There is also an active volcano in the Grenadines: Kick 'em Jenny is underwater at the moment, but is expected to reach the surface in the near future. Galway's Soufrière in Montserrat, normally a fumarolle, became active in 1995, showering the south of the island with ash, and erupting lava, and rendering large areas uninhabitable.

Earthquakes Another effect of living on the bridge of two tectonic plates are earthquakes, which may accompany major volcanic eruptions, and cause land slippages.

The Soufrière "drive-in" volcano, St. Lucia

63

HOME SAFE HOME
Traditional Caribbean architecture was well designed to cope with rare but severe climatic problems. Stone foundations gave a solid base during earthquakes, while a wooden upper story could wobble but survive in the windblasts of a hurricane. St. John's Cathedral in Antigua has been lined with wood to preserve it from the effects of hurricanes and earthquakes.

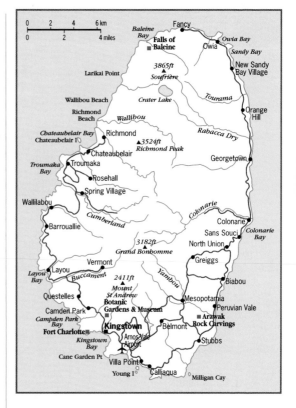

CAPTAIN BLIGH
The 18th-century mutiny on the *Bounty* has become a popular subject for films and books, but less well known is the reason for Captain Bligh's eventful voyage. He had been commissioned by the Society of West Indian Merchants to bring breadfruit plants to the West Indies from the South Pacific. Bligh's second attempt to transport the plants, in 1793 in the ship *Providence*, was more successful, and he delivered the plants to botanical gardens around the Caribbean. Trees grown from cuttings of the original plants can still be seen in the St. Vincent Botanic Gardens. The ackee tree—*Blighia sapida*—is named after the captain, who brought it to the region from West Africa.

St. Vincent

St. Vincent is a fertile and beautiful island, from its cultivated valleys to the rainforested slopes of its active volcano, the Soufrière. Linked to Grenada by the 60-mile string of the Grenadines, it is usually considered only as a starting point for yachting trips; however, its rugged east coast and fascinating Arawak settlement are well worth seeing. There is also first-rate diving and snorkeling, and hiking on trails as verdant as any in Hawaii.

The 110,000 Vincentians are mainly of African origin, the descendants of plantation slaves, but this was not always a plantation island. Like Dominica, St. Vincent was one of the last strongholds of the Carib people. Here, the local tribe, known as the Yellow Caribs, and escaped African slaves produced a race of Black Caribs, who held out against the colonists. In 1797 they were eventually defeated and their survivors were deported to Roatan, an island off Honduras. The British took over St. Vincent and

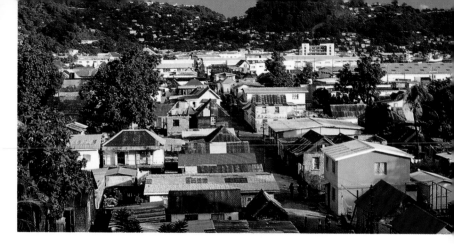

built up a trade of sugar, cotton, and arrowroot. Independence was gained in 1979, though St. Vincent remains within the British Commonwealth.

Agriculture still provides much of the island's living; exports include arrowroot starch, bananas, and coconuts. St. Vincent is relatively undeveloped, with a small area of hotels in the southeast and a few other isolated spots.

The capital of St. Vincent and the Grenadines is **Kingstown▶▶**, a few streets of Georgian townhouses with cobbled arched walkways set on a wide southwestern bay. The town is fairly quiet, except around the Grenadines pier when ships come in, and at the market on Halifax Street, the center of all island gossip. Near by are the Law Courts, where the St. Vincent Parliament sits, and the unusual gothic and romanesque Roman Catholic church, which was built in 1823.

Away from the waterfront, the ground rises through outlying suburbs to the range of hills surrounding the town. In the northwest are the 20 acres of the **St. Vincent Botanic Gardens▶▶▶** (*Open* daily 9–6), dating back to 1763. Here, species include the sealing wax palm, red hot cat tail, and roucou, used as body-paint by the Carib tribes. The St. Vincent Museum, set in the gardens, shows Amerindian relics and colonial exhibits (tel: 457-1003; *Open* Wed 9–noon, Sat 2–6. *Admission free*). On the heights to the southwest lies Fort Charlotte where, on a clear day, the view extends 65 miles south to Grenada.

Past the airport in the southeast nestles Villa Point, where restaurants and bars are set among the pretty tin-roofed villas on the waterfront, looking across a small stretch of water to Young Island. Inland are the fertile valleys where St. Vincent's market produce is grown, and at Yambou, off the road to the town of Mesopotamia, Arawak **rock carvings▶▶** date from before AD 1000.

A journey up the west coast on the Leeward Highway reveals the West Indies at its most natural: small and simple villages filled with hordes of shouting schoolchildren. There are rain forest walking trails in the **Buccament Valley▶▶**, and the hike up the Soufrière (3,865 feet) is a day's trip, best started from the Rabacca Dry River, north of Georgetown, or Richmond, north of Chateaubelair. Boats sail from Kingstown to the Falls of Baleine, a 60-foot cascade into a rockpool at the island's northern tip, past the villages of the leeward shore.

Red, rusted, and wriggly tin roofs in Kingstown, St. Vincent's capital

65

UNDER SHELTER
It rains so regularly in the Windward Islands that the old streets were built with colonnades so that the market vendors could sell their wares under cover and people would be sheltered as they walked around the town. Where other islands had wood houses (now often burned down), Kingstown has some particularly attractive stone arches and cobbles. Most modern buildings are made of concrete, and topped with tin roofs.

FORT DUVERNETTE
Young Island is the nearest of the Grenadines to St. Vincent's shore and, beyond it, perched on its 200-ft overgrown rock, is the defensive bastion that once protected the larger island's southern waters. Cannons dating from the 18th century are still at the ready, but these days only tourists are likely to invade the fort (via steps in the rockface), to enjoy the impressive views.

The Leeward Islands

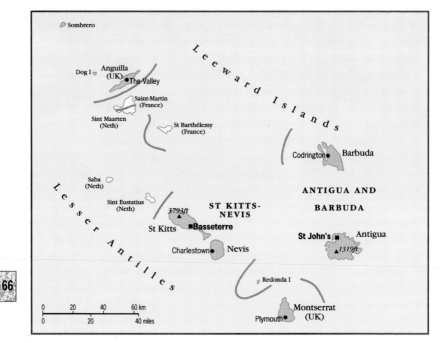

One of the Leeward islanders: a resident of Antigua

THE LEEWARD ISLANDS The English-speaking Leewards have maintained much of their small-island charm in the face of growing tourism. With a vast choice of beaches, friendly small towns, and varied local customs, they stand in refreshing contrast to the bigger tourist destinations. Antigua is the most developed vacation island; Anguilla has developed quite quickly over the past few years and St. Kitts and Nevis have followed a policy of sustainable development. Poor Montserrat, which was developing its tourism slowly, has been stopped in its tracks by the eruption of its volcano. Two centuries ago the islands were isolated outposts and fast communications were essential. Now their remoteness is a selling point, and many visitors pay a lot of money to enjoy it, particularly on Anguilla and St. Kitts.

The six Leeward Islands (they were to the lee side of ships arriving from Europe) lie in two lines. In the west, Montserrat, Nevis, and St. Kitts are the rain-forested peaks of a relatively young volcano chain (about 15 million years old). To their east are the protrusions of a much older range: Antigua, Barbuda, and, beyond the French islands of St. Barts and Saint-Martin, Anguilla, most northerly of the Lesser Antilles. Capped with coral limestone, the Lesser Antilles have some of the finest sand in the Caribbean.

HISTORY The islands are connected by a common history, having been British colonies for many years, but most have now gone their own way. The island states of Antigua and Barbuda negotiated their full independence in the early 1980s and were soon followed by St. Kitts and Nevis, but they remain in the British Commonwealth. Montserrat and Anguilla are still Crown Colonies of Britain.

British settlers first arrived at St. Kitts in 1623, but continual disputes over the island's possession raged between Britain and France right up until 1783. Using an army of slave labor, the colonizers planted sugar cane furiously and became immensely wealthy. But with the abolition of slavery in the British Empire in 1834, the Leeward Islands quickly went into decline. The freed slaves took to the land, dividing it into small individual plots, and scraped a poor living from

subsistence farming. Today you will still see subsistence farmers living on the Leeward Islands; their lifestyle is only gradually changing now after 150 years.

ISLAND LIFE The Leeward Islands' economies are precarious and, despite the success of a few small industries, all depend to some extent on tourism. This has developed steadily over the past 20 years and in places it seems to have swamped local Caribbean life and traditions, which have all but disappeared in some parts. The more developed islands, Antigua and Anguilla, tend to have better restaurants, but a stroll around Nevis, or a visit to one of its rum stores, is more likely to give a taste of local life. Each island has its special points, whether it is rum-soaked rumbustiousness during Sailing Week (usually the last week of April) on Antigua, a glimpse of the planters' leisurely way of life amid historic surroundings on St. Kitts and Nevis, the marine reserve and wildlife of Barbuda, or the deserted beaches of Anguilla. There are also good opportunities for hopping by boat and plane to other islands nearby.

The islanders are English-speakers (as they are on the nearby Dutch Windward Islands), but accents vary from island to island, as do the characteristics of their people. Distinct traces of Irish can be heard in the inflections and pronunciations of Anguillan and Montserratian islanders, which are not present in the accents of St. Kitts, Nevis, and Antigua. While there is a certain reserve and politeness on Montserrat and Nevis, the people of Anguilla and Barbuda have a reputation for a proud and independent outlook. Nevertheless, all Leeward Islanders are known for their easy-going attitude, which is well expressed in the favorite Caribbean expression "No problem."

Coconut palm silhouettes in the calm of an Antiguan sunset

REMISSIONS
The economies of the Leeward Islands have traditionally depended on "remissions" from abroad. Since the sugar industry foundered, people have either cultivated small plots of land or traveled in search of work, sending some of their earnings home to their families. Many islanders worked on the digging of the "Ditch"—the Panama Canal—and in the Dominican Republic's cane fields at the turn of the century. Later there was a rush to the oil refineries of Aruba and Curaçao, and in the 1950s and 1960s there were large influxes to Britain. Most emigration is now to the U.S.A. or Canada.

Anguilla

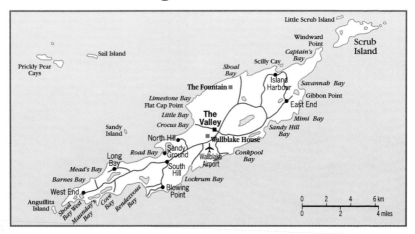

Only 20 minutes by ferry from Saint-Martin/Sint Maarten, Anguilla offers some of the Caribbean's best restaurants and beaches. There are about 30 tiny, secluded coves, snorkeling beaches, and walking strands, all with fine sand washed by a clear, turquoise sea. Anguilla has a string of luxurious hotels, though it is possible to find cheaper options: the Anguilla Tourist Office, The Valley (tel: 497-2759) can offer useful advice. There are no buses on the island,, but taxis can be picked up at the airport, from Blowing Point, or from hotels. Just 16 miles long, the island consists entirely of coral limestone. Its flat land is covered in thick scrub, steadily being cleared for building. Anguilla is a rapidly developing island, but it is still a quiet place, with little visual history and comparatively few "sights." Its chic and expensive hotels are a second home to film stars and executives who seeking a retreat from the humdrum. (Those who are wanting nightlife and shopping can always sneak over to Sint Maarten.)

It comes as a surprise to learn that this peaceful island once had a revolution (albeit bloodless). In the 1960s Anguilla became part of the Associated State of St. Kitts-

REBEL MARINE

You will soon come to know the sleek contours of boats made by Rebel Marine, an Anguillan boatyard. The gull-winged ferries that make the run from Blowing Point to Saint-Martin are made by them (as is the North Sound Express boat in the British Virgin Islands), and many others lie at anchor in Sandy Ground and around the island. The designs take traditional Anguillan lines (from a long tradition of boatbuilding) and adapt them to modern materials.

Lobsters: a specialty on the island

Nevis-Anguilla, but its inhabitants objected to St. Kitts' prominent role (see panel). Anguilla was separated from the three-island state in 1971 and regained its status as a U.K.-dependent territory. The island suffered badly in the hurricanes of 1995, but its buildings and beaches have now recovered completely.

In the middle of the island, close to the airport, is the small capital, The Valley, where the administrative offices, banks, stores, and the only hospital are all based. The other main settlements are Sandy Ground, the main port, and Island Harbour, a fishing village in the north-east, near which is the Fountain, a cave used by the indigenous Arawak Indians, where carved faces are arranged to be lit by the sun in turn. Blowing Point, on the south coast, is the ferry terminal (linked to Saint-Martin).

Beaches ring the island, and most hotels have water-sports facilities. On the north coast, near the western tip, **Barnes Bay**▶▶ is a strip of sand backed with rocks and broad-leaved sea grape trees. Heading east, **Mead's Bay**▶, a curve of deep sand, has a lovely sunset view from the Malliouhana end. Calm and protected **Road Bay**▶▶ harbors local boats and some larger ships, and has a string of restaurants and bars. Just beyond Crocus Bay is **Little Bay**▶▶▶, access to which is by boat or by climbing down the cliff, and **Limestone Bay**▶▶. **Shoal Bay**▶▶▶ has fine sand and snorkeling offshore. On the north coast lies **Captain's Bay**▶▶, a half-moon of secluded sand (ask for directions, and follow the coast-line). On the south coast, past Blowing Point, is the 2-mile **Rendezvous Bay**▶▶, a mangrove and dune-backed walking strand with a clear view of Saint-Martin and an excellent bar like a shipwrecked galleon, the *Dune*. The moorish domes of the Cap Juluca Hotel (tel: 497-6666) dominate crescent-shaped **Maunday's Bay**▶▶; beyond here, **Shoal Bay West**▶▶▶ is overlooked by the tall, white curves of the Cove Castles hotel villas (tel: 497-6801). Sandy Island and Prickly Pear Cays have fine beaches and are good for a day's sailing trip: one departs from Island Harbor for the spit of land called Scilly Cay, famed for its grilled lobster and beach party atmosphere.

THE REVOLUTION
Few small Caribbean islands have managed to sever the convenient connections made by colonial administrators, but when faced with independence from Britain in company with St. Kitts and Nevis, the Anguillans rebelled. A few shots were fired and St. Kitts policemen were expelled from the island. As tension grew, the British sent a detachment of paratroopers in 1969—an "invasion" (welcomed by the Anguillans) that was later dubbed the "Bay of Piglets." Anguilla's rebels got their way and the link with St. Kitts was cut for-ever, but a satisfactory political solution was found only in 1982, when the island was eventually granted its own constitu-tion, headed by a Council of Ministers and a House of Assembly.

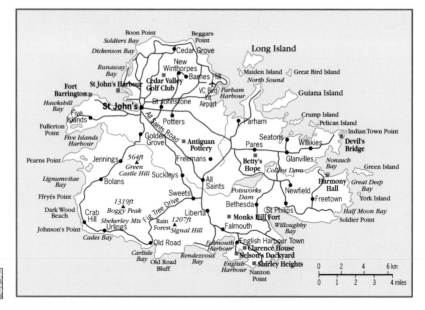

Antigua and Barbuda

The territory of Antigua and Barbuda actually consists of three islands: Antigua, the main island at 108 square miles with excellent beaches and most of the 65,000 population; Barbuda, a smaller, wooded island to the north also with excellent, undeveloped beaches; and Redonda, only a half a mile in area, an uninhabited rocky islet lying 25 miles southwest of Antigua, which has no beaches at all.

Contentment on an island cruise

Pirate ships were once feared and avoided in the Caribbean's waters; now "pirate cruises" are popular tourist attractions

ANTIGUA The largest, the most popular and the most developed of the Leewards, Antigua has a mostly dry and flat landscape. Its foremost attractions are the superb beaches, the restored historic area, Nelson's Dockyard and Falmouth Harbour, and its sailing facilities; English Harbour is a hive of sailing activity during Race Week at the end of April every year.

Antigua is made of limestone coral, covered in grassy flatlands that rise steadily to the southwest. Two centuries ago the island was blanketed with sugar cane, and ruins of the windmills in which the cane was crushed are dotted all over the island. The two main centers are the capital, St. John's, in the northwest, and English Harbour.

St. John's is a busy harbor town, particularly when a cruise ship is in dock. Founded in the early 18th century, it has attractive 19th-century buildings, with wooden gingerbread balconies. Some of the finest are in **Redcliffe Quay**▶▶—restored warehouses and townhouses now occupied by stores and cafés. Near the Tourist Information Office (Thames Street) is the Old Court House, where the **Antigua and Barbuda Museum**▶▶ (tel: 462-1469. *Open* Mon–Fri 8:30–4:30, Sat 10–2. *Admission charge*) has displays on Amerindian Antigua and the colonial past. **St. John's Cathedral**▶▶ (tel: 461-0082) is a towering building of 1848, close by the Recreation Ground where international cricket matches have been hosted here since Antigua and Barbuda became independent on November 1, 1981. **St. John's Public Market**▶, south of town, is liveliest on Saturday mornings.

Antigua's main tourist areas are to the west of the capital on the beaches of Five Islands Peninsula, and to the north on Runaway and **Dickenson Bays**▶▶. From here, the road follows the coastline north through chic, residential areas and past secluded coves to V.C. Bird International Airport (named for Vere Bird, the first Prime Minister after Independence) and the Cedar Valley Golf Club. In the eastern area of the island the coastline and sea are spectacular (but not suitable for swimming except in well-protected bays) and at Indian Town you can see the Devil's Bridge, an archway of rock carved out by the waves. The 200-year-old plantation estate of **Betty's Hope**▶, to the west, has been restored, with a visitor center, and a renovated windmill. In another windmill on the southeast coast is the **Harmony Hall**▶▶ gallery (tel: 460-4120), with works by West Indian artists.

PLANTATION ESTATE
At Betty's Hope you can see the layout of a typical Caribbean plantation estate. The windmill was placed high not only to catch the wind, but also so that the cane juice could run downhill in a sluice to the boiling house. The estate house had the best position—for the view and so that the owners could watch the activity on the estate. There is a huge cistern since, on a dry island like Antigua, water collection was vital.

73

VIV RICHARDS
Antigua's greatest hero was, for most of the 1980s, captain of perhaps the strongest West Indies cricket team ever to have played. Considered the world's finest batsman, he regularly destroyed the bowling of English, Australian, Indian, and Pakistani teams. Born in 1952, Richards played for Antigua and Leeward Islands teams soon after leaving school. He moved to Britain in 1974 to play for Somerset and in the same year played for the West Indies for the first time, becoming captain in 1984. Richards retired from international cricket in 1991.

An extraordinarily fertile and colorful marine life exists under the Caribbean waters. Corals grow like forests on the reefs and slopes, and hiding among them are weird and wonderful shellfish and crabs, while schools of tropical fish with exotic names and colors cruise by.

74

Corals, sponges, and shellfish Corals are animals that grow in salt water shallow enough to be within the range of the sunlight. Of the 75 or so species in the Caribbean Sea, about 10 account for nine-tenths of the growth. Perhaps the most familiar is the white brain coral, with a surface that resembles a human brain; other hard corals include staghorn, which grows like crusty deer antlers, elkhorn, with huge sloping branches, starlet coral, with polyps like teeth, and orange clump coral, which has a mass of tentacles. Gorgonians consist of sea fans, which face the tidal flow, sifting nutrients, and sea whips, which blow like feathers in the tide.

Sponges and anemones add their own color and variety to the marine world. Tube sponges can grow to 7 feet, in shades of pink, orange, purple and yellow, and the white cryptic sponge hides in the crevices of the reef. Anemones look like intricate flowers, with many only out at night; those which emerge during the day will often snap back into the rock if the water around them is disturbed. Shrimps (visible in daylight) often live in conjunction with anemones—the banded coral shrimp has a striking red-and-white striped body.

Night-diving reveals another, self-contained submarine society. Crabs and spiny lobsters come out for food, and starfish, some of which look like underwater plants, open up to feed in the dark. An octopus, squid, or a tiny

AQUARIUMS
Several aquariums in the Caribbean provide alternatives to viewing from glass-bottom boats for non-divers. The Guadeloupe Aquarium is between Bas du Fort and Gosier and has well-marked displays of tropical fish from the Caribbean and elsewhere. On Curaçao the Seaquarium is in the Underwater Park, east of Willemstad. A spiral-shaped aquarium operates in the Parque Lenin, south of Havana, in Cuba, but perhaps the most interesting display is at the small aquarium on the waterfront in Christiansted, St. Croix, where the underwater world is explained in fascinating detail by a guide. All aquariums charge an entry fee; prices vary, but they can be expensive.

seahorse might be spotted—though their camouflage is excellent; the sea cucumber, by contrast, is easy to make out, resembling a mobile underwater hot dog. The biggest and best known of the mollusks (shell animals), which are also best seen at night, is the conch, known as the *lambi* in the French-speaking Caribbean. Lobsters migrate in their hundreds, like a herd of galloping horses.

There are a number of species to avoid when underwater: a touch from the fire coral can give a nasty sting, as can some jellyfish. Avoid the spiny black sea urchin at all costs—its spines cause agonizing wounds if they break off in your flesh.

Fish Around a thousand species of fish live in the Caribbean, many of them on the reefs, where there is plenty of food. Schools of angel fish and butterfly fish can be seen waving in the current; the four-eye butterfly fish has an imitation pair of eyes on its tail to confuse predators. Other species are dazzlingly beautiful—such as the queen angel fish, which is a luxurious shade of velvet-like blue and gold, and the yellow and black rock beauty. Many fish have been graced with names that describe their forms and habits. Damsel fish hide and lay their eggs in the reefs, grazing on algae, and striped sergeant majors defend their eggs aggressively. Grunts are named for the noise they make when alarmed, and surgeon fish have scalpel-sharp fins in their tails.

Wrasses are scavengers that school in a harem, with one male. If the male is eaten, the biggest female simply switches sex and takes over his job. Parrotfish eat off the reef, biting the polyps and their rocky coral base, and spitting out crunched-up coral.

Predatory fish include groupers (who have been known to use scuba divers as a smokescreen in the hope of a meal—other fish are also attracted by them and come out of their crevices) as well as snappers, one of the most numerous species. They school facing into the current, all moving in time and snapping at any food that passes by. Barracuda patrol in small groups or singly, often around a chosen rock. Larger fish such as blue marlin tend to live in deep water drop-offs, where they are pursued by big-game fishing boats (see page 202).

Top: orange clown fish

EATING HABITS
The dentist or cleaner shrimp cleans the teeth of other, larger fish, thereby getting food for itself. The sponge crab takes small lumps of sponge to use as camouflage, and when it fails to find food, it takes the sponge off its back and eats it. The remora, or sucker fish, is a long, thin fish that attaches itself to a larger fish, such as a shark, and feeds off the remains of its meal.

75

CORAL CLAIMS
In 1726 the French naturalist Jean André Peyssonnel declared to the Paris Academy of Sciences that coral reefs were made up of living animals, not marine shrubs, as was generally thought. He was ridiculed and had to live out his life as a scientist in exile in Guadeloupe—and though he was proved right during his lifetime, Peyssonnel received no credit.

Above left: the beautiful angel fish is one of the prettiest in the Caribbean waters

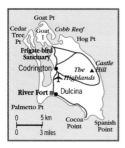

Barbuda

THE FRIGATEBIRD COLONY
The crooked wingspan and forked tail of the huge, black frigatebird is easy to recognize. Its most surprising feature is the male's gullet, a bright red balloon blown to the size of a basketball during display. Although it can be seen on Barbuda, it also flies to the other islands to feed, traveling at up to 93 miles per hour. It even attacks other birds on the wing for food, swooping in from above, grabbing the tail or leg and shaking the victim until it drops its meal. Barbuda's frigatebird sanctuary is well worth a visit; the birds soar high above it, returning to the mangroves to nest in large colonies. Located on the north end of the Codrington Lagoon, the sanctuary is only accessible by boat, and so can only be visited during daylight hours; you'll have to hire a local to take you there.

The hilly southwest of Antigua has excellent beaches, fine views from Green Castle Hill and a ring of stones thought by some to be ancient megaliths. Beneath Boggy Peak (at 1,319 feet the highest point of the island), Old Road, now a small village, was the site of Antigua's first European settlement in 1632. Nearby Fig Tree Hill is a lush valley covered with large, shiny "elephant ear" leaves and bananas, an example of vegetation more usual on the larger Windward Islands to the south.

In the southeast are the fortifications erected by British colonists when Antigua was at the height of its strategic and economic importance. Opposite Falmouth Harbour towers Monks Hill Fort, a refuge for women, children, and animals in case of attack. Beyond it are the tourist and sailing areas of English Harbour and **Nelson's Dockyard▶ ▶ ▶** (tel: 460-1053; see opposite). A short water-taxi ride across the bay brings you to **Clarence House▶ ▶**, built in 1787 for the future King William IV and now the Antiguan Governor General's official residence (open to visitors when the Governor General is not in residence). Above it are **Shirley Heights▶ ▶**, a series of Georgian barrack buildings and gun emplacements constructed in the 1780s as a defense against the French. The **Dow's Hill Interpretation Centre▶ ▶** is set among the battlements and has a multimedia show of Antiguan history, from Indian settlement through Columbus, the colonial era, to the present day.

BARBUDA Lying 30 miles to the north of Antigua, Barbuda is one of the few truly undeveloped Caribbean islands. Like Antigua, with which it was politically merged in 1860, it is all coral limestone, and has glorious beaches. Otherwise, its 60 square miles are covered in scrub, where goats, donkeys, and wild boar roam. The only town is Codrington, named for the family who owned the island and used it as a private ranch for 200 years before its incorporation into Antiguan territory. (When Antigua began negotiations for independence from Britain, it was the proud Barbudans who objected, calling for more governing powers of their own.)

Sights on Barbuda include caves in the northeast, where Indian rock carvings have survived, the **frigatebird sanctuary▶ ▶ ▶** (see panel), and River Fort, a martello tower on the south coast.

Inventive headgear on one of the streets in Codrington, Barbuda's only town

Nelson's Dockyard is as active today as it was 200 years ago, when English Harbour was the most important naval base in the area. But in place of whistles and cannon blasts, there is now a peaceful atmosphere. Preparations may occasionally be as feverish as they were during the 18th-century wars, but today's sailors are more likely to be doing battle in yacht races.

The pillars of the old Boat House and Sail Loft, where the sails were laid out for repair

77

Nelson's Dockyard is the best-preserved colonial shipyard in the Caribbean, restored over the past 40 years into one of its top sailing destinations. Covered in bougainvillea and hibiscus, the beautiful old stone warehouses contain hotels, bars, galleries, and a museum; but life still centers on the harbor, where boats line the wharves.

Set on Antigua in a deep and sinuous bay, the dockyard was first developed in 1725 as a victualing and repair station. Ships sheltered here during hurricanes and could be careened (beached on their sides) to clean their bottoms of barnacles and weeds. Eventually the dockyard became one of the most important stations in the British Caribbean, and the massive fortifications of Shirley Heights were built in order to defend it.

The dockyard's first building is the old Pitch and Tar Store (pitch from Trinidad was used to waterproof ships' hulls), now housing the Admiral's Inn, a small hotel whose restaurant/bar is *the* spot for the yachting set. Next door are the pillars of the old Boat House and Sail Loft (the building has lost its upper story), where ships' sails were laid out for repair. A museum in the Naval Officer's House, across the way, has recently been restored and has excellent hands-on exhibits, maps and model ships from the dockyard's heyday. Next door is the Old Copper and Lumber Store, where sheet metal and wood were kept, and able seamen slept in upstairs dormitories; today the old store houses a comfortable hotel. In September 1998 Hurricane Georges seriously damaged the Dockyard seawall and the old officers' quarters building. The restoration of the seawall in 1999, costing $3 million, has enabled the officers' quarters (previously converted to stores and galleries) to reopen.

NELSON
It is unlikely that Horatio Nelson would ever have consented to give his name to the dockyard. The famous British admiral served here between 1784 and 1787 while he was captain of H.M.S. *Boreas*—and he hated it, considering the dockyard itself a "vile spot." He was lonely and had the unpleasant job of putting a stop to unofficial trading between the Leeward Islanders and ships from the young American nation. At one point Nelson was confined on board for eight weeks, knowing that if he set foot ashore he would be arrested by the resentful planters. He returned to the Caribbean only once, for 24 hours in 1805, when he was searching for the French Admiral Villeneuve in the chase that culminated in the Battle of Trafalgar.

Hibiscus in bloom

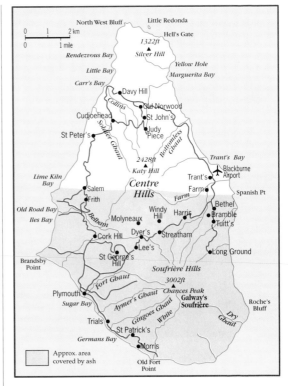

Montserrat

Montserrat has not been a viable tourist destination since 1995, when volcanic activity commenced; since then, volcanic eruptions and lava flows have transformed about two-thirds of the 39-square-mile island into an uninhabitable danger zone. However, this activity may temporarily subside and will eventually cease.

Sighted in 1493 by Christopher Columbus and named by him for the abbey in the mountains of Spain, Montserrat has long been known as the Caribbean's "Emerald Isle." With good cause: not only was this most southerly of the Leeward Islands a paradise of verdant mountains ringed by attractive beaches and tranquil bays, it was also originally settled, in the 17th century, by the descendants of Irish catholics, refugees from Protestant persecution of St. Kitts. Although Montserrat remains a British colony, the Irish gave it its nickname, and also contributed elements of Irish style: St. Patrick's Day is celebrated, and the island's stamps feature an Irish harp.

Tragically, Montserrat's emerald green has been replaced by ash gray. In the summer of 1995, after over 350 years of dormancy, Chance's Peak began erupting on the southern half of the island. A major fall of ash landed on the capital town of Plymouth, on the southwest coast, in August of that year, and the town was evacuated. By October 1995, a dome of flowing lava could be seen protruding from the crater. There was erratic volcanic

The Montserratian smile

activity until June 1997, when the dome collapsed, causing a high-speed pyroclastic flow that leveled seven villages, destroying over 200 homes and killing 19 people. This lava flow also forced the closure of the airport runway, and emitted so much ash that people were forced to wear ash masks. Two months later, a shower of red-hot rocks landed on Plymouth, which caught fire and burned. The once pretty little town is now an ash-covered ruin. Another half-dozen communities, fortunately deserted, were decimated by a lava flow in December 1997.

As well as destroying Plymouth and many other smaller towns and villages, the volcano has ruined or rendered inaccessible several of the island's main tourist attractions, including the Great Alps Waterfall and Galway's Soufrière, and it has driven the island people away. The population, once around 11,000, hovered at around 3,000 in mid-1998, although in 1999 anecdotal evidence suggested that many residents were returning from refuge in Guadelope and Antigua as the volcanic activity subsided.

At present only about one-third of Montserrat is considered safe for occupation. With Plymouth and the rest of the south uninhabitable and extremely dangerous, what remains of the population now clusters in this northerly third. At present, no one is quite certain what will happen next. A future eruption is unlikely to be so violent as to destroy the entire island, but experts warn that the current period of volcanic activity is by no means over.

Although we cannot recommend the island as a destination at this time, it is by no means inaccessible, and it might be argued that the hardy souls still living there deserve as many visitors—and dollars—as they can handle. There are no hotels open, but some privately owned villas, guest houses, and bed-and-breakfasts are taking in travelers who find disaster zones or volcanic activity to their liking. Several restaurants and bars are also open.

HELICOPTER FLIGHTS
There are daily (excepting Wednesdays) helicopter flights from Antigua departing at 7:30 AM and 4:40 PM. The flight takes about 20 minutes, and leaves Montserrat to return to Antigua about 10 minutes after landing. A ferry service also operates between the two islands. The trip takes about an hour, departing Antigua at 6:30 AM and 4 PM. Return trips are scheduled for about half an hour after arrival on Montserrat. For more information, contact Montserrat Aviation Services (tel: 491-2362/2533, fax: 491-2362); in Antigua, contact Carib World Travel (tel: 460-6101, fax: 480-2995) or Carib Aviation at V.C. Bird International Airport (tel: 462-3147). For updates on volcanic activity and listing of available accommodations, the Montserrat Tourist Board can be reached on tel: 491-2230/8730.

79

Lush vegetation typical of Montserrat

Music is played everywhere in the Caribbean: on buses, on vast personal stereos, in bars and clubs, and at Carnival, when whole islands stop work to dance in the streets. West Indians will tune almost anything to make music: wheel hubs, bamboo poles and even cheese graters, but the most famous instrument of all is the steel drum, or "pan," invented in Trinidad about 50 years ago.

Almost every Caribbean island has its own unique musical style; all of them have a strong rhythm that irresistibly inspires dancing. Particular styles of dancing vary from island to island, but the movement always centers around the hips and pelvis.

Caribbean music also incorporates a tradition of social comment. The Calypsonians of Trinidad are the most famous satirists, and many other styles have carried messages of protest: ska was a shout from the poor ghettos of Kingston in Jamaica in the 1950s, and even in Cuba, where dissent is not traditionally tolerated, "trova" songs have been known to question the integrity of party members and government officials.

Reggae and soca The British Caribbean has two main rhythms: the best known is, of course, reggae from Jamaica. This has developed full circle since Bob Marley popularized it in the 1970s, becoming dancehall in the 1980s and recently softening again to culture reggae in the mid-1990s. Soca, which originated in Trinidad, is played in the southeastern Caribbean. Soca (a contraction of "soul-calypso") consists of a fast and hard rhythm with a double beat.

Salsa and merengue Salsa comes from Puerto Rico and Cuba (other Cuban rhythms include the rumba and the cha-cha-cha). This is a bustling,

FESTIVALS
A biennial World Steel Band Festival takes place in Trinidad in November, and Pan Jazz, a mix of steel band music and jazz, is held on Tobago every March. Other music festivals include St. Croix's Jazz Festival in January, Cuba's February Jazz Festival, St. Lucia's Jazz Festival in May, Jamaica's Reggae Sunfest in July, and, in the same month, the Merengue Festival in Santo Domingo, in the Dominican Republic. The Barbados Jazz Festival takes place in January, while Easter is the opera season in Barbados.

Transforming a steel drum into a musical instrument

80

Latin rhythm; dancing partners face one another as if they were waltzing, but their legs move elastically in a subtly sensual movement. Merengue is another hip-swinging Latin rhythm, from the Dominican Republic.

Zouk and compas The French islands of Martinique and Guadeloupe have produced their own rhythm with a double beat and a very quick tempo, zouk, whose songs have French Creole lyrics. In Haiti, compas is another French-inspired, raw rhythm.

Steel pans The steel band, whose sound has come to represent the whole Caribbean, was invented in Trinidad during World War II. It started in the back streets of Port of Spain, where the discarded oil drums of Trinidad's oil industry were beaten, tuned and turned into instruments. Initially pan was regarded suspiciously by the authorities, partly because the yards where the music developed were the hangouts of ghetto gangs. But its popularity grew and soon pan replaced "tamboo bamboo" (musical bamboo poles) as the music of Carnival.

Steel pan lids are bashed out in a bowl and given a number of flat surfaces to produce different notes. There are five different ranges in the pan orchestra. Bass pan players have nine full-size drums (each one can only give three or four notes). Cello pan players have three pans which are cut down to three-quarter size, each having seven notes. Guitar pans and double second pans both come in pairs, playing notes in the middle range (the guitar pan plays chords, while the double second takes the melody). Tenor pans, or "ping pongs," are the lead instruments in the orchestra and the highest in the range. They have 30 notes, covering a two-and-a-half octave range, and are about 1 foot deep.

A steel band has as many as 120 players, and it is well worth visiting a "pan yard" to see them. Not only is the noise impressive (a symphony of pings, clangs and bongs that combine into a coherent sound) but the energetic drummers are also an entertainment in themselves.

Pan yards play all year round, but the easiest time to see them at work is during the run-up to Carnival at the beginning of the year. Steel bands with colorful names—"Desperadoes," "Renegades," and "Invaders"—have nowadays been superseded by soca as the main music of Carnival, but they still play at Jouvert, the parade which takes place on the Monday morning of Carnival week.

A musician from the Dominican Republic

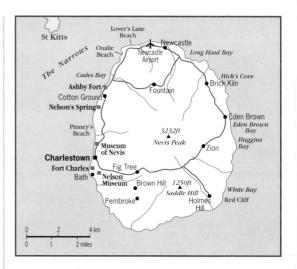

Nevis

The small volcanic island of Nevis lies between St. Kitts, across a strait called the Narrows, and Montserrat. It is almost circular—just 5½ miles by 8 miles—and rises to a central peak of 3,232 feet. A semi-permanent wreath of clouds on the summit reminded early travelers of snow and inspired the name Nuestra Señora de la Nieves—Our Lady of the Snows. Nowadays, life for the 9,000 Nevisians is pretty gentle, and the grandeur of the island's prosperous past—when it was known as the "Queen of the Caribbees"—has pretty well disappeared into the undergrowth; but the island is proud of its beautifully restored plantation houses, where many visitors stay. The atmosphere of the island has changed with the arrival of a large beach hotel—but it still has a certain regal calm, and an evening stroll along its lit walkways, while the air rings to the singing of tree frogs and flashes with fireflies, is an unforgettable experience.

Nevis is politically attached to St. Kitts (see panel) but its personality is very different. Visitors to Nevis enjoy the peace and quiet, the hammocks for snoozing, and lobster-bakes on palm-fringed beaches. The island's capital is **Charlestown▶▶**, a small collection of stone and timber-frame houses laid out irregularly on the leeward coast. Except on market days (Thursday, and Saturday morning) and when the ferry arrives from St. Kitts, the town is pretty quiet. Inland from the waterfront is Memorial Square, a triangular park overlooked by banks and stores. Nearby are the Court House and Library, and a small tourist office. At the northern end of the town is the **Museum of Nevis History▶▶** (tel: 469-0408. *Open* Mon–Fri 9–4, Sat 10–1. *Admission charge*) (see panel), set in a stone townhouse, in which the Nevis Assembly conducts its business four times a year.

North of Charlestown, **Pinney's Beach▶▶▶** is the island's best beach: a 3-mile strip of dark golden sand backed with tall palms, with magnificent views across the Narrows to St. Kitts. The island's first settlement of 80

ALEXANDER HAMILTON
Nevis's most famous son is Alexander Hamilton, who is commemorated in the museum set in his former home in Charlestown. Born in 1755, he lived here for the first five years of his life, until his mother moved to St. Croix (now one of the U.S. Virgin Islands). Impressed by the wealth of merchants on St. Thomas, he described them as "wheeling their gold through the streets in wheelbarrows." Hamilton moved to North America, where he fought in the Revolutionary War as George Washington's aide and was instrumental in establishing the American Constitution, becoming the first Secretary of the Treasury. Known as the Little Lion, because he was a short man with a fierce temper, Hamilton died in a duel in 1804. He is pictured on $10 bills.

planters, who arrived from St. Kitts in 1628, was situated here, until it was tipped into the sea by an earthquake. It is now the site of the Four Seasons Hotel, with its 18-hole golf course. The circular road passes other good beaches en route to Nevis's airport (Oualie Beach is lovely, as is Lover's Lane Beach) and the only other town, Newcastle.

To the south of Charlestown are the ruins of **Fort Charles▶**, the island's primary defense in colonial times; nearby are the old **Bath Hotel and Spring▶**, built in 1778 and now used by the Nevis police force. In its heyday as a spa hotel, the Bath welcomed thousands of aristocratic visitors, who came to take the curative waters.

The **Nelson Museum▶** (tel: 469-0408; call for hours. *Admission charge*), in the Morning Star Estate Great House, has mementoes and artifacts from the Admiral's life, including letters and pictures. At **Fig Tree Church▶**, on the road east of Charlestown, you can see a copy of the official register of Horatio Nelson's marriage to Nevisian Fanny Nisbet on March 11, 1787, during a moment off from his lonely duties around the Leeward Islands. From here you pass into the less populous eastern parts of the island, where abandoned plantations, once the focus of the island's wealth, are now only mouldering ruins.

While touring the island it is worth stopping at one of Nevis's 18th-century plantation house hotels, where lunch or dinner can be taken on the veranda. Montpelier Plantation Inn (tel: 469-3462), in the south, has cottages in its grounds; and the Hermitage Plantation (tel: 469-3477), in St. John's in the south, offers upscale accommodations and still has traces of sugar-processing equipment. The tourist office in Charlestown will supply details of other plantation houses that can be visited (Main Street; tel: 469-5521), as will the Tourist Boards (see **Travel Facts**).

Beach bar with palm-thatched parasols

83

INDEPENDENCE
The Nevisians have been posing the question of independence from St. Kitts for many years, but in 1997 the island administration pledged to go ahead with it. It must first be voted through with a two-thirds majority in the five-seat Nevis Assembly, and the Nevisians must vote "yes" in a referendum. However, it is unlikely that St. Kitts will want to let them go...

A deserted windmill stands as a reminder of colonial wealth

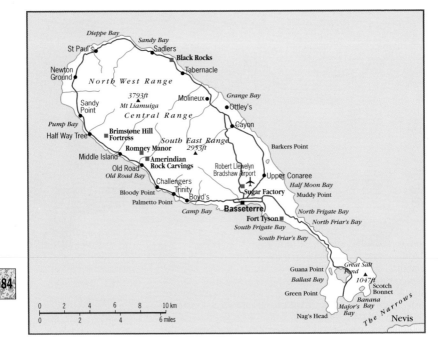

St. Kitts (St. Christopher)

Two centuries ago, most of the West Indies looked like St. Kitts, with vast tracts of bright green sugar cane swaying in the breeze, and estate houses standing aloof in colonial elegance. Many of these houses have been preserved, along with an atmosphere so English that it seems natural to play croquet and take afternoon tea. But the modern age has caught up with St. Kitts, in the form of beach tourism. The island's southeastern peninsula, which has the best golden sand beaches, has been set aside for development, and the tourist race is on—although it remains relatively low-key for the time being.

St. Kitts is larger and livelier than its sister Nevis, appealing to a more active crowd. Nevis is just a few miles to the south and the Dutch island of St. Eustatius 5 miles to the north. Measuring around 68 square miles, St. Kitts is shaped vaguely like a paddle, with forest-clad mountains and an old volcanic crater occupying its blade. In the northwest the highest peak, the 3,793-foot Mount Liamuiga, is believed to take its name from the indigenous Indian name for the island.

St. Kitts is an informal version of the island's original European name, St. Christopher, given by Columbus on his second voyage in 1493. Historically, this was the "Mother Colony" of the West Indies—the first island in the Eastern Caribbean to be settled successfully by Europeans, in 1623. British and French colonists helped each other to establish a foothold in hostile Indian and Spanish territory, before sending colonizers to other islands. Using indentured workers and slaves, they turned St. Kitts into a rich plantation island. They also

Looking toward Nevis from Timothy Hill, St. Kitts

began to fight over it, as they were to do for centuries afterwards. For proof of the bitterness of their battle, you need only visit Brimstone Hill, one of the biggest forts in the Caribbean (see page 87). An early French Governor of the island was de Poincy, whose name is remembered in the poinciana, a tree that grows all over the Caribbean islands. Together with Nevis, St. Kitts became independent in September 1983. There are 37,000 Kittitians, many working in agriculture or tourism.

Basseterre►►, the island's capital, was built on the protected Caribbean coast. Its name is one of the few remaining vestiges of the island's French heritage— unfortunately, its French buildings were all destroyed in fires. However, there are attractive British colonial timber-frame and stone buildings around the town center, some of which house cafés and restaurants. The waterfront has recently been developed on reclaimed land with stores, a marina and a new cruise ship terminal. Just behind here is the original town center, the **Circus**►►, an open traffic circle overlooked by stone buildings that have elegant upper-story balconies, with a colonial clocktower, the Berkeley Memorial at its center. Nearby is **Independence Square**►►, an open park with a fountain, poincianas and palm trees.

85

The square is surrounded by elegant townhouses, one of which contains the splendid **Spencer Cameron Gallery**►►, displaying local and expatriate Caribbean works of art, and the Catholic Cathedral of the Immaculate Conception, with its twin spires and a fine rose window. On Cayon Street is the Anglican St. George's Church, built of brown stone in traditional English parish church style. The St. Kitts Tourist Board has its office in Pelican Mall, just down from the new waterfront buildings.

Rawlins Plantation: one of a number of hotels in St. Kitts that are set in former sugar estate houses

The Black Rocks make an ideal spot for fishing

INTRIGUING TREES
The poinciana is sometimes jokingly referred to as the "tourist tree" because it turns a startlingly bright shade of red in July and August. Its pods, which look like long wooden string beans, are used by children to make music—as they make a "shack-a-shack-a-shack" noise when shaken. Another brightly flowering tree is the African tulip tree, which has red blooms all year round. It is also known as the "flame of the forest" or the "fountain tree" because its unopened buds squirt water when they are squeezed.

The main tourist area on St. Kitts is southeast of Basseterre. There are hotels, villas, a golf course, and a popular beach in **Frigate Bay▶▶**, while **Friar's Bay▶▶▶**, over the next hill, has a marvelous beach of soft golden sand, which gets busy as soon as cruise ships arrive. The new peninsular road leads past salt ponds, which used to form common ground in the days of joint English and French occupation, to the southern beaches, where there is a beach bar and superb views of the channel and of Nevis.

Northwest of the capital, the road runs past the island's light industry and emerges into sugar cane country, planted on the coastal flats beneath the central mountain range. A circular road (accompanied by a railroad to transport harvested cane) follows the coast, touching all the small Kittitian villages; it can be driven comfortably in a day. A walk into the rain forest on the mountain can be arranged by tour operators.

Old Road Bay▶ marks the site of the first British settlement and was the capital until 1727. Amerindian **rock carvings▶▶** can be seen on the Wingfield Estate, nearby. Romney Manor, a 17th-century great house set in tropical gardens, is the home of **Caribelle Batik▶▶**, a store selling silk-screened prints and clothes, where you can watch local women practicing the art of batik. At Middle Island is the **grave of Thomas Warner▶**, who led the successful settlement in 1623. From here the road soon passes under the huge defenses of **Brimstone Hill▶▶▶** (see page 87).

Around the northern tip of the island the **Black Rocks▶▶** are a curious formation of volcanic lava; from here the road leads south along the wild Atlantic coast, passing through quiet villages and returning to Basseterre via the airport and the **sugar cane factory▶▶**, which is open to visitors between January and June.

Huge forts still tower over many Caribbean settlements, monuments to an era when imperial fleets and armies were sent to defend their valuable territories. Two centuries ago the Caribbean was a hardship posting, beset by disease, and these massive bastions recall a time of violence and instability, when loud drum rolls and frantic whistle blasts would herald urgent preparations for war.

Building and maintaining a fort the size of Brimstone Hill, on St. Kitts, which could hold over 1,000 troops, involved a complex operation. Every stone had to be dragged up to the summit to create the huge structure's bastions and ramparts, inner stronghold, parade ground, barracks, cookhouses, and hospital.

Brimstone Hill (named for the satanic whiffs of sulfur from a nearby volcanic vent) took 100 years to build and was occupied by both British and French during the long 18th-century wars. In 1782 it faced its severest test when it was attacked by 8,000 French troops. The defenders, who held out for a month, were bombarded so heavily that only two rooms in the fort were left undamaged. When they eventually surrendered, the soldiers were allowed to march out with colors flying as a tribute to their bravery. A museum in Fort George, the central bastion, has exhibits explaining the history of St. Kitts and the fortress, and the store has a video presentation.

Other forts On Antigua the hills around English Harbour, an important link in the chain of British defenses, are cluttered with ramparts and barracks, described at the Dow's Hill Interpretation Centre.

Puerto Rico's two bastions overlook the approaches to San Juan, itself surrounded by walls 33 feet thick. On the point stands San Felipe del Morro, with 98-foot ramparts and a maze of tunnels; at the other end of Old San Juan is Fuerte San Cristobal, built so each of the outer bastions had to be captured before the citadel could be taken.

The most impressive Caribbean fort is Haiti's Citadelle, where 10,000 men could hold out for a year without resupply; its walls are over 100 feet high and 30 feet thick. Thousands died building it (see page 181).

CANNONS
Cannons litter the Caribbean islands, some abandoned in the forts, others put to good use, buried upright in the ground at the corners of buildings to protect them from passing truck wheels. On the British islands many cannons are printed with the cypher of King George III, a crown superimposed over the letters GR (George Rex). A small arrow can often be seen, stamped into the metal—the symbol used by naval stores.

87

A cannon at Brimstone Hill fortress covers the northern approaches from St. Eustatius

The Virgin Islands

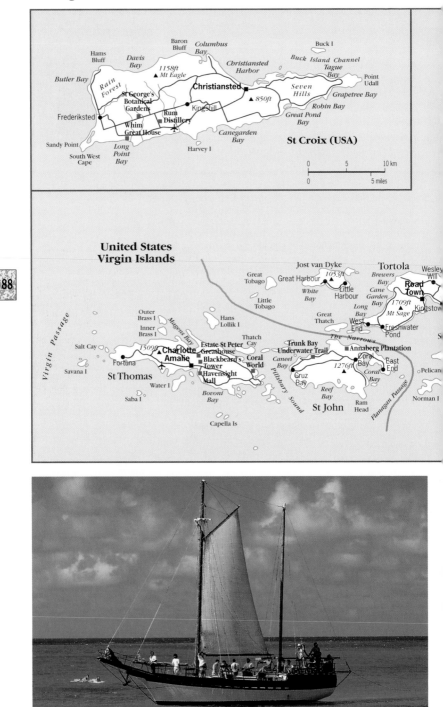

Tranquil touring among the Virgin Islands by yacht

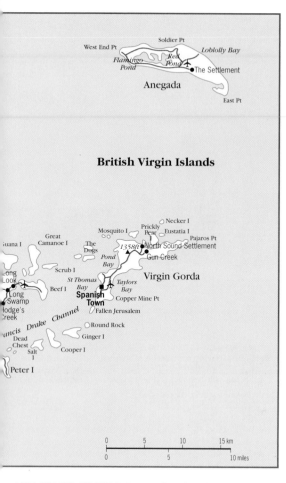

Soldier Pt

West End Pt — Loblolly Bay

Flamingo Pond — Red Pond — The Settlement

Anegada

East Pt

British Virgin Islands

Necker I

Prickly
Pear — Eustatia I

Mosquito I

Pajaros Pt

Great
Camanoe I — The Dogs — 1358ft — North Sound — Settlement

Guana I

Pond
Bay — Gun Creek

Scrub I

Long
Look — St Thomas
Bay — Virgin Gorda

Beef I — Taylors
Bay

Long
Swamp — Spanish
Town — Copper Mine Pt

Hodge's
Creek — Fallen Jerusalem

Francis — Drake Channel

Round Rock

Dead
Chest — Ginger I

Salt
I — Cooper I

Peter I

0   5   10   15 km

0   5   10 miles

THE VIRGIN ISLANDS In mood and style, the U.S. and British Virgin Islands are worlds apart. The British islands are quieter and less developed, with secluded and isolated bays and beaches, and scattered cays ideal for sailing—islanders have an old-world reserve and courtesy. The U.S. islands, St. Thomas particularly, are brash and busy and have a brisk night life. With sailing, diving, and watersports almost a way of life, these prosperous and sophisticated islands are ideal for those who don't intend to stray too far from the beach. Most visitors go to the high-rise St. Thomas or the more laid-back St. Croix, while Tortola is less crowded and largely caters to yachts.

Scattered over miles of incomparably blue sea, the Virgin Islands are, with the exception of Anegada, steep and green, the peaks of a submerged chain of volcanoes. Just under half the 90 or so islands are a British Crown Colony; the rest are "an unincorporated territory of the U.S.A." In the west are the three main United States Virgin Islands (U.S.V.I.): St. Thomas, St. John, St. Croix, and assorted cays. Sprinkled to the east, the British Virgin Islands (B.V.I.) are smaller and more numerous: the largest are Tortola and Virgin Gorda.

The Virgin Islands

A deserted sugar mill

THE DANISH IN THE CARIBBEAN

The Danes settled St. Thomas in 1665, encouraging its use as a trading base by declaring it a free port. They moved on to St. John in 1717 and St. Croix in 1733 and planted them entirely with sugar cane, bringing in slaves to work the fields. The Danes were the first to ban the slave trade, in 1792, but slavery itself continued on the islands until 1848, when the Governor went against his King's orders and declared emancipation.

In the U.S.V.I., where people work at resorts on land their forebears once owned, there is great disparity between rich and poor and some resentment toward American immigrants and tourists. In the B.V.I., people tend to own the land. There is virtually no shopping or nightlife here; on Tortola and Virgin Gorda no hotels are taller than a palm tree and most are owned by locals or expatriates. The U.S.V.I. are for visitors who want a bustling environment; the B.V.I. are for sailors and those who want to escape the crowds.

HISTORY The Virgin Islands were given their name by Columbus when he sailed among them on his second voyage of exploration. He compared the islands to the 11,000 beautiful followers of St. Ursula, who according to legend were killed by Huns on a pilgrimage to Cologne. For many years, pirates roamed their shores, waiting for ships to plunder and refitting their vessels in hidden coves. Charlotte Amalie, on St. Thomas, became a busy market place for the pirates' captured goods.

The U.S.V.I. were owned for centuries by Denmark, but not much remains of Danish influence except street and town names such as Charlotte Amalie, Christiansted, and Dronningens Gade (Charlotte Amalie's main street); the Dutch influence can be seen in the islands' many red-roofed buildings. The islands were bought by the U.S. in 1917 for $25 million.

Meanwhile the B.V.I. remained barren backwaters, planted while the going was good, but soon falling back into obscurity. At one point the British Government considered selling these islands to America as well. It never happened, but the pull to the U.S. is still strong. The B.V.I. have adopted the U.S. dollar as their currency and many islanders move to find work on St. Thomas.

ISLAND LIFE Today, the U.S.V.I. offer all the expected American comforts and conveniences (and convenience stores), with tropical setting and lilting accent. The banks are American, as are the fast food joints, the currency, the supermarkets, and the baseball. St. Thomas and St. John are geographically close, but in character they could not be farther apart. St. Thomas is overdeveloped and crowded (particularly when cruise ships put in), but offers great shopping in Charlotte Amalie, as well as good bars and restaurants. St. John, just a 20-minute ferry ride away, is quiet and undeveloped. About two-thirds of it is undisturbed jungle, protected by its National Park status. There are, nevertheless, a number of places to stay in Cruz Bay and at Coral Bay in the East End. The third island, St. Croix, and the largest of the Virgin Islands, offers a good variety of beach hotels, restaurants, and interesting town buildings in Christiansted and Frederiksted. St. Croix's first casino opened late in 1998, which should in time jazz up the nightlife.

By comparison, the pace of life on the British islands is slow and peaceful. For every 15 people who travel to the U.S.V.I. on vacation, the B.V.I. get one. Of the B.V.I.'s 150,000 or so visitors a year, three-quarters come from the U.S.—and most come to sail, without even booking into a hotel. The B.V.I. are not about discos, high-rise hotels, fast food, and casinos. They are about superb beaches, many only accessible from the sea, and excellent bars. While the U.S.V.I. have gone for numbers, the B.V.I. target bank rolls, so the islands are expensive. Tortola is the hub of B.V.I. yachting, and from here there is access by ferry to many other islands, including Virgin Gorda, with its top-rank hotels, secluded beaches, and offshore cays, or tranquil Jost van Dyke. Like the pirates of yore, you can sail among the Virgins by day and anchor in a cove for the night; but nowadays you can order dinner over the radio and have a barbecue waiting when you arrive.

A British touch on Virgin Gorda

91

Bomba's Surf Side Shack is famous for its full-moon parties

New marina developments are springing up in Tortola; this one is at Frenchman's Cay near West End

GUANA ISLAND
Guana Island is a wildlife sanctuary off the northeastern tip of Tortola. Its 847 acres are said to harbor the richest fauna seen on any island of its size in the world—from flamingos to hawks, from bats to cats, and from wild donkeys to sea turtles.

A bar sign at Frenchman's Cay, western Tortola

Tortola

A century ago, when even St. Thomas was a backwater, Tortola was written off as "forsaken." Today the island is enjoying something of a boom, which has led to growing development, as the 13,000 islanders and expatriates build on the island's towering hillsides. A dock for cruise ships has been constructed and the island is developing steadily, but there are still plenty of charming, isolated spots to be found.

Tortola is 12 miles by 3 miles and has a scrubby and meandering spine of steep mountains, rising to 1,709 feet at Mount Sage. The main settlement is Road Town, a modern, sprawling capital made up of a few streets collected around a deep bay in the southern coastline. Features include yachting marinas, a small museum, a botanical garden, bars and restaurants, and a number of stores. Tortolans live in small settlements around the coast; transportation around the island is customary taxi or rental car.

The best bays and beaches are on the island's north side. At the West End, where most of the hotels are, you will find the Pirate's Pub and the Pusser's Pub immediately after clearing customs; to the north is a perfect, isolated curve of sand called **Smuggler's Cove▶▶▶**. Heading east you come to Long Bay, a superb run of white sand, and Apple Bay, where surfers enjoy the big waves (look for Bomba's Surfside Shack, a beach bar made of driftwood). The long and lovely **Cane Garden Bay▶▶▶** has small places to stay and a string of excellent beach bars; Quito's Gazebo has live music most nights in season. From here, there is an almost impossibly steep climb to the mountain's spine, which eventually descends into Road Town.

East of Road Town, the road follows the coastline to Long Look, where there is a small town. A toll bridge leads to Beef Island, the site of Tortola's airport. There are good beaches here, including Josiah's Bay and **Long Bay▶▶** on Beef Island. The Last Resort is a lively restaurant and bar on an island in Trellis Bay, and you can also spend the day on Marina Cay, which has good watersports; there is a free ferry.

Virgin Gorda

Virgin Gorda is even quieter than Tortola, but it has some chic resorts hidden in its coves and offshore cays. Lying east of Tortola (and reached by ferry), it was patronized, like St. John in the U.S.V.I., by Laurence Rockefeller, who built the Little Dix Bay hotel here. Virgin Gorda means "the fat Virgin"—the island supposedly looks like a reclining woman. Its 8-square-mile area is divided into three mounds and covered in scrub and cactus, rising to a 1,358-foot peak in the north. The most distinctive scenery is in the south, where massive granite boulders, the Baths, form a maze of water-filled caves.

Boats from Tortola dock at the southern settlement of Spanish Town, where many of the 1,500 or so islanders live. The town is really little more than its marina, with bars and an easy-going atmosphere. Virgin Gorda's best beaches—including the Baths—are south of Spanish Town. In the southeast of the island are the ruins of an old copper mine, active during the last century.

The road to the north of the island passes isolated coves such as Savannah Bay and Pond Bay before reaching Virgin Gorda's second town, Gun Creek. This overlooks the North Sound, a stretch of water surrounded by tall peaks, cays, and small islands with fine beaches. Two splendid hotels lie at this end of the island, accessible only by boat from Gun Creek. Biras Creek (tel: 494-3555) is a place of understated wealth overlooking a calm sound, a bay (with the main beach), and wild Atlantic surf; and the Bitter End Yacht Club (tel: 494-2476) prints a newspaper showing the wide range of watersports on offer. Gathering places on the islands around the sound include a bright pink Pusser's Bar (tel: 495-7369) in Leverick Bay; an elegant restaurant, Drake's Anchorage (tel: 494-2252), on Mosquito Island; a beach bar on Prickly Pear Cay, and the tiny Saba Rock, a bar that wakes up in the evenings.

The Baths, where waves wash through tunnels and caverns made from jumbled rocks

93

THE BATHS
The Baths form a series of coves to the south of Spanish Town. Best approached by sea, the boulders are stacked in jumbled piles and backed by coconut palms. From the land you can reach them through the scrub from the Top of the Baths restaurant. Made of granite, a stone that does not normally appear in the Caribbean, they may have been carried here by glacial movement during the Ice Ages.

Watersports are an integral part of a Caribbean vacation. The warm seas and constant Trade Winds make its islands excellent places for windsurfers, scuba-divers, jet-skiers, and para-sailors. But there is nothing to beat the freedom of sailing, and the calmer stretches of sea are flecked with white as yachts of all shapes and sizes ride the ocean breezes, dolphins dipping and darting alongside their prows.

REGATTAS

The biggest annual sailing event in the Caribbean is Race Week in Antigua, which includes five days of races. A major regatta is held in the British Virgin Islands every April, and in June and July Martiniquans race the *yoles rondes*, with distinctive square sails and crews of 12 leaning out over the water on booms; in August Anguilla's race week pitches locally built boats against each other; and Carriacou, in the Grenadines, stages its own small regatta.The Caribbean Ocean Triangle Series (C.O.R.T.) sets sail in March and April, and includes the Heineken International Cup in Puerto Rico, B.V.I.'s Spring Regatta, and St. Thomas' International Rolex Cup Regatta.

A SAILOR'S ULTIMATE FANTASY

"Serious sailors will feel they've died and gone to heaven," says amiable yachtsman Colin Percy, describing the thrills he offers: seven former America's Cup yachts moored in the harbor at Philipsburg on St. Maarten, and for a price, would-be oceanic speed-sters can play Dennis Conner for a day. Percy and his crew happily organize races. Contact him at the St. Maarten 12 Metre Challenge (tel: 20045/46, fax: 26419).

With such a variety of islands lying within easy reach of one another, island-hopping by yacht is an enjoyable way of seeing the Caribbean. Yachts are readily available for four to eight people or more, and can be rented as bare-boats (no crew) or crewed (with captain and hands to order the supplies and do the sailing and cooking). All yachts have fridges, kitchenware, and bedding, most provide masks and snorkels, and some carry windsurfing and diving equipment. Day sails are available from all the islands, and most hotels have small sailboats which can be enjoyed near the shore. For a bird's-eye view, have a go at para-sailing.

The best sailing destinations are the Virgin Islands and the Grenadines. Both regions are spectacularly beautiful, with convenient sailing distances separating the islands. The Virgins have good marina facilities, but this means crowds during the high season. The Grenadines have a wilder beauty, but restaurants and bars have found their way even to many of the quieter bays.

Reliable year-round winds make windsurfing a popular Caribbean sport. The best windsurfing areas are: the Dominican Republic, particularly around Cabarete on the northern shore, where World Championships are occasionally held; Barbados's southern shore around Maxwell and Silver Sands, and Aruba. The sport is well catered for in the French Caribbean around St. François and Le Moule on Guadaloupe and in the southeast of Martinique.

Divers acknowledge the Caribbean as an ideal setting for one of the world's most exotic sports, with its vast areas of colorful coral, and its strange and beautiful tropical fish. Snorkelers, too, can enjoy access to offshore reefs from most islands; and glass-bottom boat trips provide views of underwater wonders without even the need to get wet.

Although it does not have the abundance of the Indo-Pacific area, the Caribbean can boast around 75 species of corals, which include brain corals, sea fans, and whips, hydra-headed anemones, gorgonians, and sponges. More mobile sea creatures include crabs, spiny lobsters, starfish, rays, eels, and even turtles or sharks. Diving at night reveals a completely different world, as some corals close and others open, while fish emerge to feed on them, crunching away at the polyps, or sleep tucked away in sleeping bags of mucus so that their scent cannot be picked up by predators.

DIVING SITES
The best diving sites are off the Cayman Islands, particularly Little Cayman, with sheer drops to limit-less depths, and Bonaire, where the coral-clad slopes are gentler. Saba, a steep-sided volcanic cone, has an abundance of corals and the Grenadines' waters are not as crowded.

95

As well as the natural beauties of the sea, shipwrecks are a source of endless fascination, and near some islands ships have been sunk deliberately in order to provide artificial reefs for underwater explorers. Off the shores of Anguilla, divers can swim over a 197-foot hulk sitting upright on the seabed.

Scuba diving was invented in the early 1940s and developed rapidly as a sport, popularized by divers such as Jacques Cousteau, one of its inventors. There are several suppliers in the Caribbean and diving can be easily arranged on most islands. Many hotels offer qualifying courses with the affiliated dive organizations (P.A.D.I. and N.A.U.I.); there are also non-qualifying resort courses that enable novices to dive almost immediately. (Remember to arrange personal insurance before leaving home if you intend to go diving.)

MARINE PARKS
Several islands, including the U.S. and British Virgin Islands, Saba, and Bonaim, have created marine parks around their shores in order to protect their corals and fish. Divers are forbidden from picking coral or hunting fish with spear-guns within these areas. Never buy coral jewelry on the islands—it is made from live coral, which is culled from the reef.

Smaller British Virgin Islands

Anegada▶ is not a typical Virgin Island. It stands alone, 19 miles out in the ocean, and whereas the other Virgins are tall and volcanic islands, Anegada is a 7-mile curve of coral. The island is scrubby and flat (only 30 feet at its highest point) and culminates in a submerged tail called Horseshoe Reef, a magnificent living coral expanse, which has claimed more than 300 unwary ships over the centuries. The name Anegada means "inundated"— which it occasionally is, by passing waves. Only 250 people live here, sharing the island with goats and igua-nas; their sole collection of houses is called The Settlement. The island is not much visited by tourists, but there are a couple of places to eat and stay, including a chic diving hotel, and Loblolly Bay on the north coast is the best of many beaches.

Jost van Dyke▶▶▶ is almost devoid of tourism, other than visiting yachts. It lies north of Tortola and takes its name from a Dutch pirate. Just a few hilly square miles in area, the island is reached by ferry from West End on Tortola. Great Harbour, the main port, is a port of entry to the Virgin Islands, and has a church, a police station, and a few beach bars (one of whose owners, Foxy, welcomes

Perfect peace in an ideal anchorage: Jost van Dyke

visitors with a personalized calypso). There is an excellent beach at White Bay, and yachts put in at Sandy Cay, one of a couple of sheltered cays off the island. The best time to visit Jost van Dyke is on New Year's Eve, when 2,000 or so revelers sail in for a night's drinking and dancing on the sand.

Necker Island▶▶▶ is an idyllic green speck rimmed with blinding white sand and translucent blue water. Set off the northeastern tip of Virgin Gorda, it is owned by the founder of Virgin Airlines, Richard Branson, who has built a Balinese house and rents the island to groups, families, or companies—at a high cost (tel: 800/557-4255 for details).

Sir Francis Drake Channel

Sir Francis Drake Channel is the sailing heartland of the Virgin Islands—a magnificent stretch of water off Tortola, where the white triangles of the yacht sails beat back and forth over an unbelievably blue sea. On its southern side the channel is bounded by a necklace of small, irregularly shaped islands, which run southeast in a graceful curve from Virgin Gorda to St. John in the U.S.V.I. In their isolated coves are some superb, secluded stretches of sand.

Starting in the northeast (most sailing trips sail out of Road Town South toward Peter Island, then northeast toward Gorda and Anegada), **Fallen Jerusalem** and **Round Rock** lie off Virgin Gorda. Designated a National Park, Fallen Jerusalem has rocky terrain that gives it the appearance of an ancient city in decay. **Ginger Island** is uninhabited, but the next in line, **Cooper Island▶▶**, has about 10 inhabitants—the staff of the Cooper Island Beach Club on Manchioneel Bay, which often attracts a lively crowd of "yachties" at lunch and in the evenings. Scuba-diving facilities are available, and there is a very beautiful beach.

Salt Island▶▶ takes its name from a salt pond that is still farmed. Rent, payable to the Queen of England, is set at a sack of salt a year, but apparently it has not been collected recently. This is one of the Virgin Island's most popular dive sites, with the wreck of the R.M.S. *Rhone*, which sank in the 19th century, lying offshore. Some of the wreck is shallow enough to snorkel in and you will find yourself swimming in the exhaled bubbles of divers below you. Next in line is **Peter Island▶▶**, where there is just one very chic island resort with rooms scattered along Deadman's Bay (a charming place, despite its name; tel: 495-2500). Offshore is a small outcrop called Dead Chest, where Bluebeard, a.k.a. Long John Silver, put his mutinous crew ashore with one bottle of rum. **Norman Island▶**, the last island in the chain before St. John, is also uninhabited, but is worth visiting for the eerie, waterbound caves at Treasure Point, which have excellent snorkeling, and the floating bar, the *Willie T*.

B.V.I. DIVING
The Virgin Islands have some excellent diving sites. In Sir Francis Drake Channel there are caves, pinnacles, and submerged rocks, smothered in corals and teeming with fish, some of which have become tame enough to feed. Blonde Rock, off Dead Chest, and the Dogs, off Virgin Gorda, are good examples. Anegada has many wrecks, some of them still poking above the waves where they foundered, but the most famous is that of the *Rhone*, which sank off Salt Island in 1867. This wreck was used in the filming of *The Deep* and it is possible to dive inside its bow section, which lies in 79 ft. of water. The broken pieces of its stern, including the propeller gear, are at about half this depth.

97

Sailing—the only way to travel between the many beautiful Virgin Islands

St. Croix

St. Croix (pronounced "St. Croy") is the largest of the Virgin Islands and lies alone, 31 miles to the south of the main U.S.V.I. group. This was the senior island in Danish colonial days because of its successful plantation economy, but whereas St. Thomas has been overtaken by the hustle of modern America, St. Croix has retained a quieter, historic feel, although the opening of the first of several planned casinos in 1999 may change that. Roughly twice the size of St. Thomas, it is a sparsely populated island, with varied scenery: mountains, rain forest, and beaches, and dairy and cattle-breeding farmlands.

St. Croix's main town is **Christiansted▶▶▶**, on the waterfront in the east. The Danish influence can still be seen in the town's architecture, with its terraces, patios, and arched yellow colonnades. Fort Christiansvaern was the town's old defense, and the commercial center goes up around the Old Customs House and the Scale House near the wharf, where merchants once weighed their goods. The Steeple Building contains a museum of Native American artifacts, and on King Street Government House still houses government offices. The **St. Croix Seaquarium▶▶▶** (tel: 772-1345. *Open* Wed–Sun 11–4. *Admission charge*) in the Cavarelle Arcade is worth a visit. The dry east has most of the island's hotels tucked into its coves and there are golf courses at Buccaneer Bay and Teague Bay. One of the best beaches is on Buck Island, a National Park known for its snorkeling (see **Travel Facts**).

Centerline Road heads west toward Frederiksted through agricultural land that made St. Croix wealthy during the 19th century. The **St. George Botanical Garden▶** (tel: 692-2874. *Admission charge*) is a peaceful retreat on an old plantation estate, growing Amerindian and other Cruzian plants.

Also off the main road is the Cruzian Rum Distillery, where you can view the production and buy, and beyond this is the moated **Whim Great House▶▶** (tel: 772-0598. *Open* Mon–Sat. *Admission charge*), an unusual rounded estate building restored with colonial-style antiques; in the kitchen, old utensils and sugar machinery are displayed. There are more colonnaded trading buildings in **Frederiksted▶▶** (tel: 772-2021), including restored Fort Frederik and its museum. Mahogany Road leads northward through spectacular forest.

98

For the finest sunset, a Frederiksted beach bar on the west coast is what is required

St. John

One of the most beautiful islands in the Caribbean, St. John is the smallest and least developed of the U.S.V.I. It lies just a few miles east of St. Thomas, a short ferryride across the Pillsbury Sound, but is so tranquil that it seems a world away. Two-thirds of the island are given over to a National Park, so most of its steep, volcanic hills are left to grow as natural jungle.

There are guided trails through the Park (on foot, on horseback, and even underwater through the corals of Trunk Bay), led by well-informed rangers, and there is an information center opposite Mongoose Junction just outside Cruz Bay (tel: 776 6201). On the north coast you can see the ruins of the **Annaberg Plantation▶▶**, a relic of Danish days, when the island was covered with sugar cane. Camping facilities accommodate travelers with or without tents.

Around the fringes of the National Park St. John's coastline has been developed. **Cruz Bay▶▶**, at the western tip of the island, is the main town and here you will find many good bars and restaurants, as well as the Elaine Ione Sprauve Library and Museum, which traces a slave revolt against Danish planters in 1733, soon after the island was settled; after nearly a year, the rebels were defeated by imported French troops, and many committed suicide rather than return to slavery.

The sand is crystalline and the surf gentle at Trunk Bay, on St. John's north shore

TRAVEL BETWEEN THE ISLANDS
Most of the Virgin Islands are linked by ferry: regular links connect St. Thomas (Red Hook), St. John (Cruz Bay), St. Thomas (Charlotte Amalie waterfront) and Tortola (West End and then Road Town). Sometimes the link continues to Virgin Gorda (The Valley). An irregular link also connects St. John and Tortola (West End). A hydrofoil service now connects Charlotte Amalie and Christiansted. The oft-choppy trip takes about an hour and a half each way. St. Croix is best reached by air—a novel way to make the link is by sea-plane.

Three centuries ago the Caribbean waters were infested with pirates. Bands of seaborne outlaws would lie in wait in hidden coves before taking to the high seas in their fast ships and attacking passing trade. Piracy was a dangerous lifestyle—capture usually meant death—but the rewards were great; a good haul could provide life on Easy Street for months on end.

The infamous Blackbeard

WOMEN AT SEA

Two women joined the macho world of piracy in the 18th century. Anne Bonney was the fiery daughter of an Irish lawyer, and Mary Read was brought up as a boy and served as a soldier and sailor before setting off to the Caribbean. Both women fell in with Jack Rackham and joined his pirate crew. They were all caught off the shores of Jamaica and sentenced to death; both women "pleaded their bellies" (pregnancy) and Bonney escaped execution, but Read died in prison.

Piracy started in the Caribbean soon after the word spread that the Spaniards were taking gold from the Aztecs. The stakes were high from the start—intrusion into Spanish waters was punishable by death—but adventurous interlopers like François le Clerc and Pie de Palo ("Pegleg") were willing to take the risks. British adventurers arrived in the late 16th century, including Sir John Hawkins and Francis Drake, who made their fortunes on slave-trading expeditions and later by ransacking cities on the Spanish Main.

Known variously as freebooters, buccaneers and sea rovers, pirates often started out as privateers, permitted by local governors to attack enemy shipping in times of war—but the rewards were so good that the practice was extended to include any ships that might bring in a prize, and was continued in peacetime. A single capture could bring vast riches (usually a cargo of goods—silks, arms, animals, and grog). Once these had been sold the pirates would spend their loot on alcohol and women until the money eventually ran out and they had to go in search of more.

On board ship, however, there was a strict regime. Generally pirates were accomplished sailors, who operated small, fast ships. The crew would sign "articles" stipulating their obedience to the captain and their duties: keeping their weapons clean, dispatching themselves bravely in battle, and refraining from playing cards and bringing women aboard (which carried a death penalty). Punishments included lashes of the whip and "marooning" (being left ashore on an island with water, a pistol, gunpowder, and shot). Each man had a share in any prizes captured on the venture, and injured men were compensated from the loot. There was usually a musician on board, who was expected to play six nights a week but rested on Sundays.

When faced with a pirate attack, a captain knew that he would be killed if he put up a fight. There are some particularly gruesome stories of pirates' cruelty: the Frenchman Montbars was said to cut out men's guts and make the victims dance till they died; and his compatriot l'Ollonios removed the heart of one man and fed it to another.

Gallery of rogues For a century until 1700, no ship was safe in the Caribbean, and pirates were feared and reviled. They operated from hideaways on Tortuga and, after 1691, the Bahamas. However, there is no disputing

that there were colorful characters among their ranks. Perhaps the best known Caribbean pirate was Blackbeard (Edward Teach). This huge man cultivated a diabolic image, tying ribbons in his long pigtails and beard, and putting slow-burning fuses under his hat so that he appeared to be on fire. A reward of £100 was offered for his capture and he was eventually caught after a chase at sea. Blackbeard died fighting rather than suffer the ignominies of surrendering, and his head was hung from the bowsprit of his ship.

Bartholomew Roberts is thought to have captured 400 ships in two years. He drank only tea (even when his crew was getting drunk on rum) and he always kept the Sabbath. Roberts was a dandy, going to battle in fine dress; he was killed in a skirmish with a British ship.

Stede Bonnet was a Justice of the Peace and a landowner from Barbados, who decided to buy a ship and become a pirate. Known as the "gentleman pirate," Bonnet was eventually captured. Their stories are told by Exquemeling in his *History of the Pirates*.

HENRY MORGAN
Henry Morgan was an indentured laborer who became the leader of the Port Royal buccaneers in the 1660s, directing expeditions against Spanish cities and netting 750,000 pieces of eight in an attack on Panama City, which he destroyed in the process. Having made his fortune, Morgan switched sides, becoming the Lieutenant Governor of Jamaica, a position which entailed stamping out piracy.

Treasure from the New World is loaded onto a 16th-century ship

PUTTING ON THE STYLE
As dandies and natty dressers, some pirates wore tricorn hats, coats, and cordoba boots—but looting was hot work in the Caribbean, and most wore baggy shirts and pants with no shoes. Hats included Jacobin caps and turbans, and hair was often braided and then stiffened with water and flour. Earrings were believed to improve the eyesight—and the pirate who sighted a prize gained an extra share.

St. Thomas

Cruise ships and yachts anchor side by side in St. Thomas's harbor

HURRICANES LUIS AND MARILYN
The last decade has been pretty cruel to the U.S.V.I. In 1989, Hurricane Hugo caused terrible destruction in St. Croix, then it was the turn of St. John and particularly St. Thomas, which was dealt a double blow in September 1995. First Hurricane Luis swept through, causing some destruction, and then a week later Hurricane Marilyn tore through the islands, causing maximum damage because it brought very heavy rains. The island was declared a disaster area. Many long-term residents left for good. It took over a year to rebuild because many people were uninsured (rates were so high that they could not afford them).

St. Thomas is the U.S.V.I. capital island and the most developed of all the Virgins. It is a mountainous 12 miles by 3 miles and has a population of over 50,000, so this is hardly a secluded tropical retreat; it does, however, offer excellent bars, restaurants, and clubs, many of which are concentrated around **Charlotte Amalie▶▶▶**.

Charlotte Amalie owes its birth and its still thriving life to a fine harbor, sheltered by hills and protected by islands. Pirate ships and ocean traders once brought the business here; now it arrives on cruise ships and yachts. For every visitor who disembarks, three come on cruises, primarily to shop—for gold, French perfume, Colombian emeralds and Balinese wood carvings. The town has another side, however: the arched façades of its stone trading buildings downtown and the elegant hillside mansions retain an atmosphere of centuries past.

The cooler slopes above Charlotte Amalie are dotted with grand mansions, linked by stepped alleyways and sinuous roads. **Government House▶** (1867), once the seat of the Danish council and now the Governor's official residence, stands above the town center; inside the room, murals depict Columbus's arrival on St. Croix in 1493 and the handover of the U.S.V.I. from the Danes to the U.S. Just above it is Blackbeard's Tower (where the pirate was supposed to have lived), reached by the 99 Steps (there are actually 102 of them!). Even beyond Charlotte Amalie, the hillsides are covered with houses. On the spine of the hills above the town is Drake's Seat, where the mariner supposedly watched for Spanish ships; the view is magnificent. There are botanical gardens at **Estate St. Peter Greathouse▶▶** (tel: 774-4999. *Open* daily 9–5) high above the north coast. In the east of the island beyond Red Hook, the ferry point for St. John, you will find **Coral World▶▶** (tel: 774-2955) with an underwater observation tower and aquarium, badly damaged in Hurricane Marilyn but now rebuilt and much improved.

Most of the beaches on St. Thomas are heavily developed (except Magens Bay, on the National Geographic's Top 10 Beaches list), so it is easy to find watersports.

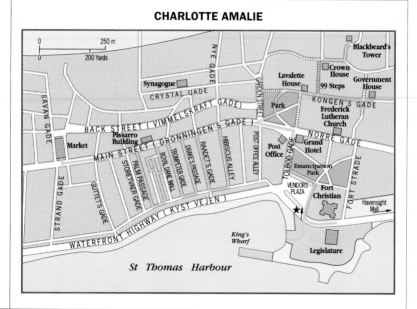

CHARLOTTE AMALIE

St Thomas Harbour

103

Walk

Charlotte Amalie

Ferries arrive at Charlotte Amalie's waterfront downtown, as will the planned seaplane service, but many visitors disembark at the yacht marina or cruise-ship dock across the harbor, and stumble straight into Havensight Mall, the first of the island's shopping centers, which was converted from a series of warehouses. Safari buses and taxis provide transportation for passengers from here into town. In town, the Paradise Point Tram (tel: 774-9809) provides visitors with a 7-minute, 700ft lift to a spectacular viewpoint overlooking the town and bay. Catch it along Long Bay Road.

Charlotte Amalie's old trading streets are laid out in a gridiron pattern with a series of narrow alleys with stores and restaurants running down to the waterfront. As you arrive, you will pass the light green **Virgin Islands Legislature Building**▶, which was built by the Danes as a police barracks in 1874 and now houses the

U.S.V.I. Senate. Across the road is the dark red and gold **Fort Christian**▶▶, which dates from the Danes' arrival in the 1660s, and now contains the Virgin Islands Museum, tracing early and colonial life on St. Thomas.

Beyond the old Grand Hotel and the neoclassical Post Office, at the head of Main Street, is the main shopping area. Here, the brick and stone buildings bear well-known names such as Ralph Lauren alongside local stores such as A. H. Riise (selling perfumes, jewelry, crystal, and watches). Wander through the small alleys and passages that wind between Main Street and the waterfront, where there are yet more stores and pleasant cafés. A plaque on Main Street, between A. H. Riise and the town's market, marks the birthplace of the Impressionist painter Camille Pissarro.

The 19th-century Virgin Islands Legislature Building, on the waterfront, has become the headquarters of the U.S.V.I. Senate

The French Antilles

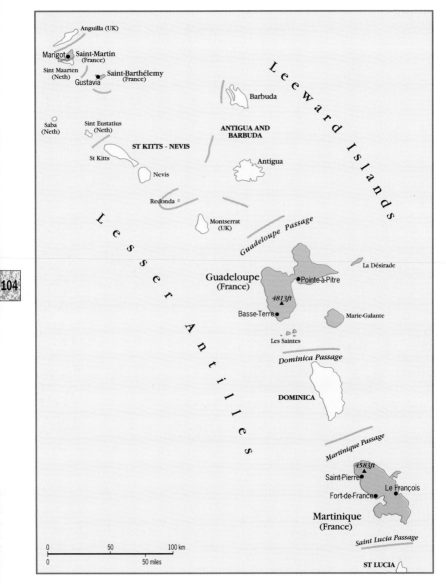

The French Antilles map:

- Anguilla (UK)
- Marigot • Saint-Martin (France)
- Sint Maarten (Neth)
- Gustavia • Saint-Barthélemy (France)
- Saba (Neth)
- Sint Eustatius (Neth)
- **ST KITTS - NEVIS**
- St Kitts
- Nevis
- Redonda
- Barbuda
- **ANTIGUA AND BARBUDA**
- Antigua
- *Leeward Islands*
- Montserrat (UK)
- *Guadeloupe Passage*
- *Lesser Antilles*
- Guadeloupe (France)
- La Désirade
- Pointe-à-Pitre
- 4813ft ▲
- Basse-Terre •
- Marie-Galante
- Les Saintes
- *Dominica Passage*
- **DOMINICA**
- *Martinique Passage*
- 4583ft ▲
- Saint-Pierre •
- Fort-de-France •
- Le François •
- **Martinique (France)**
- *Saint Lucia Passage*
- **ST LUCIA**

Scale: 0 — 50 — 100 km
0 — 50 miles

THE FRENCH ANTILLES Unmistakably French in their food, culture and general outlook, the "overseas departments" of Martinique and Guadeloupe combine tropical scenery with a sophisticated European lifestyle. Visitors can explore Guadeloupe's rainforests, Martinique's historic towns and villages, the restaurants of St. Martin, and the chic beach resorts of Saint-Barthélemy; Pointe-à-Pitre and Fort-de-France provide bustling town life, while the tiny isles of Les Saintes, La Désirade, and Marie-Galante offer white sand beaches and quiet island life. Variety and beauty are the hallmarks of the French West Indies, made up of the single island of Martinique and the six islands which comprise the *Région* of Guadeloupe. The main

island, Guadeloupe, is actually two islets of contrasting landscapes, linked by a small land bridge. The administrative *Région* of Guadeloupe is an archipelago, consisting of the islands of Les Saintes, La Désirade, Marie-Galante, and Saint-Barthélemy, as well as the half-French, half-Dutch island of Saint-Martin/Sint Maarten. As the French islands are in the northern and center sector of the Antilles, they enjoy similar climates and vegetation. Only one of the islands (Martinique) is in the region defined by the Windward group.

Lying between the Caribbean Sea and the Atlantic Ocean, the French Antilles, spread across 350 miles of sea, include two of the region's three volcanically active

French stores under the tropical sun in Guadeloupe

islands. Apart from the inner, Caribbean side of Guadeloupe and central/northern Martinique (which are covered in tropical mountain forest), the islands are green and humid, with excellent beaches and deep coves and bays. The eastern section of Guadeloupe remains part of an arc of limestone isles, and the western parts are a continuation of the volcanic link. Also in this chain, Martinique, the largest volcanic connection of the Windward islands, has three major peaks. Guadeloupe's volcano, Soufrière, is at 4,813 feet the highest peak to be found in the Eastern Caribbean.

The names given to the main islands in the Carib language—*Karukera* ("Island of Beautiful Waters") for Guadeloupe and *Madinia* or *Madinina* ("Island of Flowers") for Martinique—illustrate the mystical appeal of these islands. Even the half-island of Saint-Martin has a relatively fertile, scrub-clad, hilly terrain. The smaller islands off Guadeloupe and the northerly island of the French Antilles, Saint-Barthélemy, are arid and rocky, with sparse, drought-loving vegetation; Guadeloupe's limestone islands and the volcanic Les Saintes feature coral reefs and beautiful, sandy beaches. Karst landscape on Marie-Galante and Saint-Barthélemy (and on some parts of Guadeloupe), together with poor soil, generally restrict arable cultivation, unlike the rich, watered lands of most of Guadeloupe, Martinique, and Saint-Martin.

Although situated in and among staunchly British or Dutch islands, the French Antilles have maintained their unmistakable French air. Rather than negotiating a political break with her colonies, France has taken the view that they should be a full part of the republic, and since 1974 Guadeloupe and Martinique have had the right to elect their own representatives to the National Assembly. A small independence movement has emerged in Guadeloupe, and there are still occasional protests. In Martinique, the statue of Josephine Bonaparte, who was born on the island, was beheaded as a protest against French colonial dominance (her head was never found).

HISTORY French settlers first colonized Guadeloupe and Martinique in 1635, and African slaves were shipped in to work the new sugar plantations. By 1669, Martinique was such a successful colony that the French moved their administrative base there from St. Kitts. In the wake of the French Revolution, Guadeloupe's slaves were freed, their colonial masters were killed and their plantations wiped out. Martinique reacted differently, calling on the British to maintain the status quo. Slavery was re-introduced in

1802 and the British occupied Guadeloupe, but France confirmed her hold on the island in 1815—which was unfortunate for the slaves, for although slavery was abolished in the British colonies in the 1830s, emancipation did not come to the French territories until 1848. To fill the labor gap, the French Antilles encouraged the immigration of thousands of East Indians, who moved in as indentured laborers.

In the 1930s, Martinique became a center for the black consciousness movement known as *Négritude*, led by Aimé Césaire and Etienne Lero. Guadeloupe and Martinique were granted departmental status in 1946, giving them equal rights with every other *Département* in mainland France.

ISLAND LIFE The French Antilles have capitalized on their greatest assets: the vivacious mingling of races from many lands, and the enchanting surroundings. Tourism has brought an unprecedented influx of revenue and has transformed the lot of the islands without undermining their natural beauty or affecting the local way of life. The people of Martinique and Guadeloupe are known for their physical beauty and Gallic style. Although French is the official language and French influence permeates island life, from the food and buildings to the designer stores and the *boules* games, there is also a distinctively Caribbean side to the culture. The air pulses to zouk, a classic Caribbean beat; the countryside is laden with rain forest, sugar cane, and tropical fruit; and the people speak a unique Creole, heard everywhere—although its exclusion from official life has made it something of a poor relation.

With the mingled attributes of a robust culture, fertile soil, and abundant seas, a climate combining aridity with high rainfall, and all the requisites of the voracious tourist trade, the French Antilles seem to have arrived at a fairly happy balance of nature and development. Certainly they are among the most attractive and peaceful islands to be found in the entire Caribbean region.

CREOLE CUISINE
The French Caribbean has a strong tradition of Creole cooking, turning the techniques of French cuisine to Caribbean ingredients, including seafood and tropical fruits. Many restaurants serve classic and *nouvelle* French cuisine and some also offer the Caribbean equivalent, *nouvelle cuisine créole*. *Blaff* is a traditional manner of frying fish in spices; for *court bouillon*, fish is poached in a special liquid of lime, wine, and onion and tomatoes. *Touffe* uses a casserole and *colombo* is a sort of Caribbean curry. You may come across *z'habitants*, a local dish of crayfish. *Accras* are batter balls, usually made with fish, and *souskai* is a way of marinating fruit.

107

Hobie cats on a Saint-Martin beach

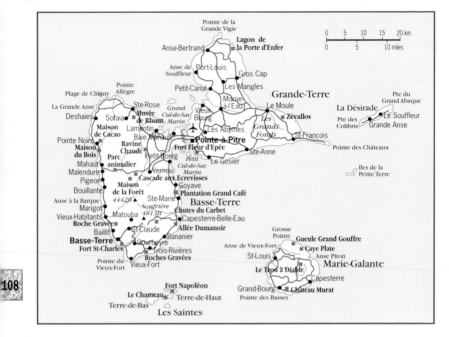

Map showing: Pointe de la Grande Vigie, Lagon de la Porte d'Enfer, Anse-Bertrand, Port-Louis, Anse de Souffleur, Gros Cap, Petit-Canal, Les Mangles, Plage de Clogny, Pointe Allègre, Grande-Terre, Pte du Grand Abaque, Ste-Rose, Grand Cul-de-Sac Marin, Vieux Bourg, Morne-à-l'Eau, Le Moule, La Désirade, La Grande Anse, Musée de Rhum, Zévallos, Le Souffleur, Deshaies, Sofaia, Pte des Colibris, Grande Anse, Maison de Cacao, Lamentin, Baie Mahault, Les Grands Fonds, St-Francois, Pointe Noire, Ravine Chaude, Les Abymes, Pointe-à-Pitre, Fort Fleur d'Epée, Pointe des Châteaux, Maison du Bois, Parc animalier, Petit-Bourg, Petit Cul-de-Sac Marin, Ste-Anne, Iles de la Petite Terre, Mahaut, Vernou, Le Gosier, Malendure, Cascade aux Ecrevisses, Pigeon, Maison de la Forêt, Goyave, Bouillante, Plantation Grand Café, Anse à la Barque, 4442ft, Ste-Marie, Basse-Terre, Marigot, Soufrière, Chutes du Carbet, Grosse Pointe, Vieux-Habitants, Matouba, 4813ft, Capesterre-Belle-Eau, Gueule Grand Gouffre, Roche Gravée, Allée Dumanoir, Anse de Vieux-Fort, Caye Plate, Baillif, St-Claude, Bananier, St-Louis, Anse Piton, Basse-Terre, Gourbeyre, Marie-Galante, Fort St-Charles, Trois-Rivières, Le Trou à Diable, Pointe du Vieux-Fort, Roches Gravées, Vieux-Fort, Capesterre, Fort Napoléon, Grand-Bourg, Château Murat, Le Chameau, Terre-de-Haut, Pointe des Basses, Terre-de-Bas, Les Saintes

Scale: 0 5 10 15 20 km / 0 5 10 miles

Guadeloupe

Guadeloupe has two distinct halves, like the wings of a butterfly. In the west is Basse-Terre, a rainforested volcanic monster which is similar in appearance to Dominica, farther south. The eastern wing, across the narrow Rivière-Salée (Salt River), is Grande-Terre, a relatively flat, coral-based outcrop from a much older range of volcanoes.

Many of Guadeloupe's hotels are located along the southern shore of Grande-Terre, which offers watersports and good waterfront restaurants and bistros. This "wing" of Guadeloupe is composed of a shattered limestone outcrop with karst hills, known as *montagnes russes*. Low plains (*fonds*) reach out to the white, sandy beaches and spectacular rocky cliffs along its coastline. The terrain on Basse-Terre is for the most part wild, with cascading

A cocoa tree growing on Guadeloupe

waterfalls and mountain streams. Its mountain range is the source of the Grande Rivière Goyaves, the island's longest river at nearly 20 miles. Inlets of black, volcanic-sanded beaches lie on the south and southeast coast of the island, but there are excellent golden sand beaches to be enjoyed in the northwest.

Guadeloupe's climate is tempered by the cooling northeast Trade Winds, generally no more than breezes—*Les Alizes*. Hurricanes occurred in 1979 and 1989, but the islands generally enjoy idyllic weather.

ISLAND LIFE About 410,000 people live in the archipelago of Guadeloupe, almost 50 percent of whom are under 20 years of age. Most are black or mulatto; some are descendants of early settlers—*Békés*—or of East Indian

indentured workers. Tourism and administration provide work for nearly half the population; agriculture and industry are the other economic mainstays.

Officially, the language in Guadeloupe is French. Créole, however, is the language of the people—once banned from educational establishments, but now a proud demonstration of individualism.

Waterfront market and ferry departure point, Place de la Victoire

POINTE-À-PITRE This large city, sprawling along the coastline in the crook of Guadeloupe's two large islands, has a population of about 100,000. Its heart is the **Place de la Victoire►►**, a large square set with royal palms, mango trees, statues of famous Guadeloupeans and lined with cafés, overlooking the busy harbor, La Darse, where ferries depart for the offshore islands. The tourist information office can be found near La Darse and behind the square, the cathedral, built mainly of metal in order to withstand the occasional fierce Caribbean hurricanes.

From here the crowded streets stretch in all directions, overlooked by tall houses with intricate balconies and shutters. On the rue Frébault, in the

Boats on Ste-Anne

GETTING AROUND GUADELOUPE

As one half of the island is flat, with plantations and beaches, and the other is mountainous (with a 75,000-acre National Park), Guadeloupe is no easy place to view on one excursion. Grande-Terre is criss-crossed with roads that do not give straight-forward access to all its attractions and should be divided into at least two journeys. Basse-Terre has few roads crossing its peaks and gorges; one circumnavigates the area, running around the coastline, but sightseeing needs at least three full excursions. The island's "neck," between Grande-Terre and Basse-Terre, takes yet another trip.

Chengy Hindu temple

main shopping district, a **covered market**▶▶ provides Caribbean mayhem and every imaginable kind of produce. The **Musée Schoelcher**▶▶ (tel: 82-08-04; call for hours. *Admission charge*), set in a stone and stucco house at 24 rue Reynier, shows memorabilia associated with the 19th-century campaigner against slavery, Victor Schoelcher; and the **Musée St-John Perse**▶ (*Open* Thu–Tue 8:30–11:30, 2:30–5:30. *Admission charge*), on rue Nozière, traces the life of the Nobel Prize-winning Guadeloupean poet, Alexis Saint-Léger. East of the town, the **Aquarium**▶▶▶ (tel: 90-92-38. *Open* daily 9–7) in Bas du Fort displays tropical fish, and the **Fort Fleur d'Epée**▶, an 18th-century defensive bastion built of coral rock, has been partly restored.

OUTSIDE POINTE-À-PITRE Tourism centers around the towns along Grande-Terre's south coast—Le Gosier, Ste.-Anne, and St.-François—where beaches and waterfront restaurants are packed. Farther east, the beaches are emptier, and at the Pointe des Châteaux there are superb strips of sand where nudism is permitted.

North of this coastal strip the country opens out and cane fields rustle in the breeze; here, the towns are quieter and isolated from the tourist clamor; in Morne-à-l'Eau, the cemetery is full of the distinctive local checkered gravestones, covered with black and white tiles. Some *Blancs Matignons* live in this area, the descendants of impoverished white settlers who have stayed here for centuries, choosing not to mix with black Guadeloupeans.

To the west of Pointe-à-Pitre, across the Rivière-Salée, the scenery suddenly changes and Basse-Terre's mountains tower ahead, their peaks wreathed with clouds. The quickest road to the capital town, also called Basse-Terre, runs south along the island's eastern shore. At the **Plantation Grand Café**▶, you can see a working banana plantation, and close by is an excellent rum distillery, the Distillerie Longueteau. Past Sainte-Marie, where Columbus is thought to have landed on his second voyage, the route runs through the **Allée du Manoir**▶▶, an avenue of 100-foot high royal palm trees. Inland, the Etang Zombi and the Grand Etang lakes, and three waterfalls known as the **Chutes du Carbet**▶▶, grace the slopes of the Soufrière. The coast road continues to the charming town of Trois-Rivières, scattered down the steep hillside; near the coast, where ferries depart for the nearby Saintes, there are Arawak carvings on the rocks, dating from around AD 1000, at the **Parc Archéologique des Roches Gravées**▶▶ (tel: 92-91-88. *Open* daily 9–5. *Admission charge*).

A trail on maps of Guadeloupe is marked "Trace des Contrabandiers" ("The Smugglers' Trail"). It follows the spine of mountains of Basse-Terre and carves its way through the magnificent rain forest. Two centuries ago, this was a long and possibly dangerous hike, but if no ship was available travelers simply had to walk. Such routes are now opening again as beautiful walking trails.

Waterfalls and luxuriant ferns in the Guadeloupe rain forest

PERPETUAL RAIN
Rain forests create their own rain. Atlantic winds are laden with water and when they hit the island slopes they are forced upward, condensing into huge white clouds above the mountain peaks. These clouds drop their loads onto the forest, and when the sun comes out it causes evaporation, putting water from the forest back into the sky, where it joins a never-ending cycle.

The Caribbean's mountainous islands are criss-crossed with paths. Most were cut by armies, but used by rebel maroons who hid out in the hills, and by runaway slaves. In the 19th century, walking traders would carry up to 110 pounds of goods for sale on trays placed on their heads. These *porteuses* were immensely fit, capable of walking up to 25 miles a day across the mountains.

Tropical rain forests grow on all the tall, well-watered islands of the Eastern Caribbean and in the Greater Antilles. At lower elevations gommiers and other hardwood trees such as mahogany tower over fern-covered floors, with canopies at about 80 feet, their trunks grappled by creeping vines. Above 3,200 feet are the montane or cloud forests, where ferns and orchids form graceful curves from the upper branches of the trees. Higher still, above 5,000 feet, are the elfin forests of stunted trees covered with mosses and lichens.

Most of the Eastern Caribbean islands have instituted National Parks. Forest trails have been laid on Dominica (for information, tel: 448-2401), Martinique (tel: 73-19-30), and Guadeloupe (tel: 80-05-79). Jamaica has excellent walking in the Blue Mountains (contact Maya Lodge, tel: 927-2097) and Puerto Rico has a number of National Parks (contact the Natural Resources Department, tel: 723-0028).

Virgin Islands National Park on St. John also has many hiking trails. Guided tours are the safest; even on small islands it is easy to get lost. Guides also usually know local flora, and the uses of plants in traditional medicine. Sneakers or light ankle-height boots are normally adequate; a sweater is needed for higher climbs, and a waterproof jacket for protection against downpours.

Maison de la Forêt, Guadeloupe

Morne-à-l'Eau cemetery

Spread over the hillside, Basse-Terre has more style than Pointe-à-Pitre, with attractive stone and wooden town buildings. The former **Fort St-Charles►►** (1650), overlooking the harbor, is a huge defensive bulwark with a small museum, renamed in 1990 and now known as Fort Delgrés, after a noted abolitionist, Louis Delgrés. Inland from Basse-Terre, on the slopes of the Soufrière volcano, is the town of Matouba, where a 200-year-old trail, Trace Victor Hugues, leads to hot baths fed by volcanic springs (an 18-mile haul, not to be undertaken lightly!). Near the Bains Jaunes hot springs the **Maison du Volcan►►** (tel: 80-45-33) has displays explaining volcanic activity. From here the road leads up to the crater itself, which still occasionally spews out dust and even lava.

Two alternative routes from Pointe-à-Pitre to Basse-Terre take in the north of the island. On the northern coastal route, among traditional cane-growing flats, a working sugar factory complete with steam-driven crusher operates at the **Domaine de Sévérin►►**, at Saint-Rose, and the story of sugar production is told at the **Musée de Rhum►►** (*Admission charge*). On the northwestern corner of the island are some of Guadeloupe's best beaches, particularly the Plage de Cluny and la Grande Anse, a 2-mile sweep of golden sand and palms. Near the 17th-century town of Pointe-Noire is the **Maison du Bois►**, which shows local building techniques and uses for different Caribbean woods. Also look for the **Maison de Cacao►►**, to view a pictorial illustration of the history of cocoa and chocolate.

La Traversée crosses through the middle of Basse-Terre, passing the **Cascade aux Ecrivisses►►** (tel: 80-24-25) and the **Maison de la Forêt►►**, which traces the development of the island's natural life. Past a small zoo, where forest animals are kept, the road descends to the sea and rejoins the coast road, turning south toward Basse-Terre. The Jacques Cousteau Marine Reserve is located on the popular black sand beach at Malendure.

Malendure has a string of beach bars; the Ile de Pigeon is an excellent site for scuba diving

La Darse, Pointe-à-Pitre

LA DÉSIRADE Virtually unspoiled by tourism, La Désirade offers a quiet getaway and white beaches. The "Desired One" was often the first island spotted by 16th-century sailors longing for land after a tedious Atlantic crossing. Their desire was usually frustrated, as ships would sail past this barren, windy island. Only 7 miles by 1 mile, La Désirade is a table mountain lying 5 miles east of Grande-Terre in the Atlantic. Its population of under 2,000 is spread along the southern shore between the town of Grande Anse and the village of Le Souffleur.

MARIE-GALANTE The beach at Petit Anse is the big draw of Marie-Galante, the largest of Guadeloupe's offshore islands. Almost circular in shape, it measures nearly 60 square miles and has a population of 8,000, about half of whom live in the main town of Grand-Bourg. Named by Columbus in 1493 for his flagship, *Santa Maria de Galante*, it was a longtime Carib stronghold but was eventually captured by Europeans and turned into a sugar island (Marie-Galante rum is still renowned). Beyond Grand-Bourg, ruined windmills are forlorn reminders of the sugar trade's peak. The Château Murat (for Chateau Tours, tel: 97-03-79. *Open* daily 9:15–5. *Admission charge*), a restored 18th-century plantation house east of Grand-Bourg, contains a museum, and farther inland Le Trou à Diable cavern can be explored (but sturdy footwear, a flashlight and caution are needed). There are also excellent walking paths around the island.

LES SAINTES The lures of Les Saintes include a nude beach, scuba diving, and a beautiful bay that's been called a mini Rio. These volcanic peaks lie to the south of Basse-Terre. Only two are inhabited: Terre-de-Bas and Terre-de-Haut. The 3,000 population of the former is descended from plantation slaves; **Terre-de-Haut▶▶**, which was never planted, centers around tourism, with hotels on the waterfront of Bourg, its only town. White fishermen—descended from French colonials—wear "salako" hats, similar to Chinese "coolie" hats, which are made in Terre-de-Haut, and sights include Fort Napoléon, with a museum, and a tower, Le Chameau (*Open* daily 9–12. *Admission charge*), on the island's highest point.

113

THE BATTLE OF THE SAINTS
The Battle of the Saints, so-called because it took place just off Les Saintes in 1782, was a turning point in the fight for European imperial supremacy over the Caribbean islands. It was also a first in naval terms; the British Admiral Rodney saw a gap between the French ships and managed to "break the line," splitting the French fleet into two parts so that the flagship could not communicate with most of its fleet. The battle ended in victory for the British, who held sway over Caribbean waters for the next two decades.

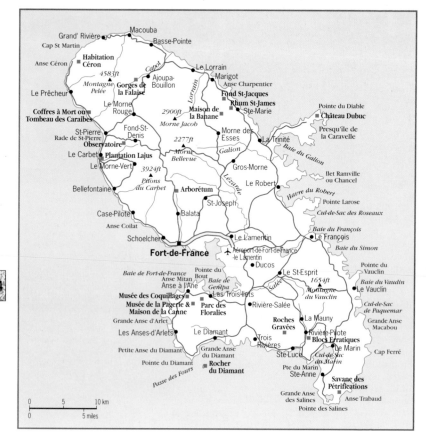

PETIT PUNCH

This popular French Caribbean drink is taken before lunch. A heap of brown sugar crystals is dashed with local white rum and stirred. A quarter of lime is squeezed in and the mix is downed in one gulp. Ice water is then swilled around to collect the last of the sugar, and downed as a chaser.

Martinique pâtisserie

Martinique

Martinique—which is far more tourist-oriented than Guadeloupe—has always been the heart of the French Caribbean. St.-Pierre, once its most important town, was known as the Paris of the Lesser Antilles, and its booming sugar trade was vitally important to the French, who were even prepared to give up their claims to territories in India and Canada in return for keeping the island in the 18th century. As its Amerindian name, *Madinina* ("Land of Flowers") implies, this is a fertile island, and since the French arrived in 1635 (they have owned it almost continuously ever since) it has been successfully farmed. Agriculture and fishing are still important and there are vast acres of bananas, pineapple, and sugar cane. Martinique lies midway down the chain of the Lesser Antilles, between the independent islands of Dominica and St. Lucia. Shaped something like a boxing glove, it measures 50 miles by 20 miles at its widest point. In the mountainous north, the highest peak, the active volcano Montagne

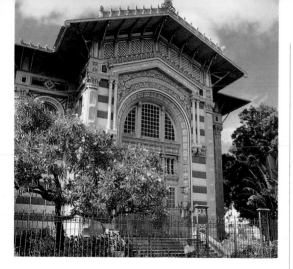

The flamboyant Schoelcher Library on La Savanne, Fort-de-France

THE HEAD CODE
There is a certain elegance and coquettish air about French Antilleans that mirrors their metropolitan counterparts. A century ago there was even a flirtatious message in the way island women wore their madras head-dresses. Tied with checkered silk material, the headdress indicated a code in the number of points protruding. One corner meant that the woman had no lover; two points meant that her heart was taken. Three points meant that officially her heart was taken, but that a man might try his luck.

Pelée, stands 4,583 feet high; rain forests cover the Pitons du Carbet, and to the south, the land descends to fertile plains and *mornes* (foothills).

The island's relatively large tourist industry is not immediately visible, as there is a strong local community. The population of 350,000 descends from a mix of French, African, East Indian, Chinese, and Arab races; French is the official language, and the French influence can be seen in everyday life, from the croissants to the Peugeot 205s. But there is also a lively Creole culture, and good Caribbean restaurants, stores, and bars.

FORT-DE-FRANCE Martinique's capital is a modern town set in a bay on the calm Caribbean shore. It has grown enormously since the eruption of Montagne Pelée devastated St.-Pierre, in 1902, and over 100,000 inhabitants now live in the center and in the suburbs that have clambered all over the surrounding hills. Overlooking the waterfront in the Baie des Flammands, the center of the town is **La Savanne▶▶**, an open park studded with 100-foot royal palm trees, where the Martiniquans take their evening walks. There is a statue (still without the head) of Josephine Bonaparte, the French empress, who was born across the bay at Trois-Ilets. You can visit Fort St. Louis, the huge fortress that protected the town from invasion in the days of the empire. The **Musée Départementale▶** (tel: 71-57-05; call for hours. *Admission charge*) has a well-presented if minimalist display of Amerindian pottery, and the most striking building is the **Bibliothèque Schoelcher▶▶** (tel: 70-26-67; call for hours. *Admission charge*), a domed structure of brightly colored metal and glass, built for the 1889 Paris Exhibition and transported here to house a library commemorating Victor Schoelcher's antislavery campaign.

Driving in Fort-de-France is not a good idea. The streets are crowded, and several are given over to markets—such as the fish market on the Rivière Madame, near the blooms and geological displays of the Parc Floral. Beyond the suburbs, the scenery turns into mountainous rain forest and sugar cane flats. Here, life is calmer and simpler: Catholic churches overlook town squares, and orange and green fishing boats are moored in the bays.

Jardin de Balata

Fans of James Bond will know that 007 was a confirmed bird-watcher. His creator, Ian Fleming, lived on the north coast of Jamaica and took the name for his famous spy from a real ornithologist, the author of The Birds of the West Indies. *The Caribbean is on migratory routes north and south and, like tourists, many birds from farther north like to winter in the Caribbean. With so many habitats (shoreline, mangrove swamp, forests) within a relatively small area, human visitors can expect to see a striking variety of different species.*

116

Top: scarlet ibis
Right: Jamaican
mountain goats

ZOOS

The Caribbean islands have a small number of zoos. In Santo Domingo, the capital of the Dominican Republic, the Parque Zoologico Nacional keeps elephants as well as tropical animals, and in Port of Spain, Trinidad, the Emperor Valley Zoo has tropical animals seen in Trinidad, including the tree porcupine, the crab-eating racoon and monkeys such as the weeping capuchin and the red howler. Animals are free to roam in the Barbados Wildlife Reserve, in the north of the island, and on Guadeloupe the Parc Zoologique et Botanique, on Road D23 in Basse-Terre, has walkways through the rainforest. There are also small zoos in Sint Maarten, and in Mayaguez, Puerto Rico.

Mangrove swamps and coastal lagoons are good places to look out for herons, ducks, and more exotic creatures such as gallinules and jacanas, whose long toes enable them to walk over lilies. Colonies of flamingoes nest on the island of Bonaire, and kingfishers can often be spotted flitting along rivers.

Pelicans are a familiar sight on many islands, flying in formation around the shoreline or diving into the sea for food. Tropicbirds occasionally soar near the coast, and the magnificent frigatebird cruises high in the air, waiting for passing meals. Gulls, terns, gannets, and boobies skim along the surface of the sea before rising and plunging to catch fish, and small crowds of oystercatchers and sandpipers walk along the beaches as they feed, dodging the breaking waves.

On open ground, the white cattle egret can be seen wherever there are grazing cows, and thrushes, finches, and larger birds, such as cuckoos and crows (called John Crows), are common. Slightly harder to spot are mockingbirds and flycatchers, which snatch up insects on the wing, and tanagers, which feed on fruit.

In contrast, some of the most familiar birds are self-assured enough to try stealing the sugar from breakfast tables: the carib grackle, which is also called a blackbird in some areas, has a V-shaped tail and displays by puffing up its feathers; and the bananaquit has distinctive yellow and black plumage.

It takes a lot of luck to see the Caribbean's more exotic birds. Shimmering hummingbirds flit around the flowers on a permanent search for nectar; the purple-throated and green-throated hummingbirds and the Antillean crested hummingbird live in most islands of the Eastern Caribbean. High in the forests there are still Caribbean parrots, though these are now an endangered species, particularly in the Eastern Caribbean, where there are parrots unique to St. Vincent, St. Lucia, and Dominica (the imperial and red-necked parrots).

The island of Trinidad is an exception in the Caribbean, both in its animal and its bird life, because it has considerable spill-over from the South American continent. Over 400 bird species make this the best island for bird-watching, but the most spectacular sight is the scarlet ibis, with its vivid red plumage and downward-curving bill. It might just be possible to see a bright blue motmot or maybe a mannikin; the male mannikin, with its white breast and black cap and wings, spends about 70 percent of its time displaying, strutting with its competitors around the female, making noises like a little firecracker and even turning somersaults.

Caribbean animals Most animals on the Caribbean islands—goats, chickens, donkeys, cattle, and even monkeys and mongeese—were imported by settlers. Indigenous survivors, most of which are endangered, include the coney, which is somewhat like a guinea pig and lives in the Jamaican John Crow mountains and in Hispaniola; the agouti, a tail-less rodent the size of a rabbit, living in the Eastern Caribbean; the American racoon; and the tatou, an armadillo that survives in Grenada. Reptiles are more widespread. Tiny geckos and lizards crawl over walls, and tree frogs peep noisily in gardens. Iguanas, which can grow to nearly 4 feet, are found on a number of islands, and the few snakes include small constrictors, and the notorious fer de lance, with eyes that glow orange at night.

Perhaps the most curious of a wide range of insects are Hercules beetles, which can measure 6 inches long and have claws protruding from their heads, and Cuban tarantulas, which can grow to the size of a man's hand.

ANIMAL SETTLERS
In the early days of European settlement, sailors would leave animals ashore and plant fruit-bearing trees on remote islands so that there would be a supply of food for anyone who might be shipwrecked. Père Labat, an early French traveler, recounts a sailors' tale that a shipwrecked crew with a pig on board should throw it into the sea and row after it, as it would know innately the direction of the nearest land.

SANDFLIES
Apart from mosquitoes, the most annoying insects that frequent beaches are sandflies. So small that they are virtually invisible, sandflies are known on some islands as "no-see-ums," and their bite causes an infuriating itch.

Iguanas live on many Caribbean islands

OUTSIDE FORT-DE-FRANCE Martinique is a large island, and although the roads are good, a leisurely circuit can take a couple of days. Buses run from the waterfront at Fort-de-France, and shared taxis follow regular routes. Car rental companies operate in Fort-de-France and the main tourist areas, and at the airport.

The closest tourist resort to Fort-de-France is Pointe du Bout and its beach, Anse Mitan, south across the bay (take a ferry from the waterfront). This is a lively area with good restaurants and cafés, though the beaches are not the best. To the south, beyond Trois-Ilets, is the **Musée de la Pagerie▶▶** (tel: 68-38-34. *Open* Tue–Sun 9–5. *Admission charge*), dedicated to Josephine Bonaparte and set in the farm where she was born. There is a golf course and a museum of sugar, the **Maison de la Canne▶▶** (tel: 68-32-04. *Open* Tue–Sun 9–5. *Admission charge*), nearby.

West along the coast, the **Musée des Coquillages▶** in Anse à l'Ane has exhibits of shells; further along, the three attractive coves at **Les Anses-d'Arlets▶▶**, isolated on the southwestern shore, are worth a detour. As the coast road winds its way to Le Diamant, it passes the solitary Diamond Rock, a few miles offshore (see panel). Working **rum distilleries▶▶** can be visited at Trois Rivières and La Mauny near Rivière-Pilote, inland from the seaside town of Sainte-Luce. Le Marin, which has a large marina, and Ste.-Anne, farther south, are the two principal tourist towns in the southeast. The area's most popular beach, the Pointe du Marin, lies between the two, but the best beaches in Martinique are at the southern tip of the island: **Grande Anse des Salines▶▶▶**, a 2-mile sweep of palm-backed sand, and nearby Anse Trabaud.

The east coast of Martinique is mainly agricultural and the sea can be rough, though there are beaches tucked into the folds of the coastline. The Caravelle Peninsula has good beaches and new hotels. At the town of Morne des Esses, locally woven baskets and mats are sold. The **Rhum St. James rum distillery▶▶** (tel: 69-30-02. *Open* Mon–Fri 9–6, Sat, Sun 9–1. *Admission free*) at Sainte-Marie and the **Maison de la Banane▶▶** inland can be visited. Near Le François, **Habitation Clément▶▶** is one of the most attractive plantation houses in the Caribbean.

St.-Pierre, once a bustling city

Balata's version of the Sacré Coeur rises out of the tropical greenery above Fort-de-France

ST-PIERRE'S SURVIVOR
At one time, St-Pierre was the most chic and stylish town in the Eastern Caribbean. It boasted a theater and a cathedral and "Pierrotins" followed Paris fashion to the letter. Although the town was almost totally destroyed by the volcanic eruption of 1902, one man was saved because he had been put in a police cell overnight after a drinking spree. The walls of the cell protected him from the heat and gases of the explosion. He later joined a circus, exhibiting himself in a reproduction of his cell.

Two spectacular roads lead north from Fort-de-France to the town of St-Pierre, one climbing into the rain-forested mountains and the other following the coast. The Route de la Trace, an old forest road cut by the Jesuits three centuries ago, climbs up through the suburb of Didier and passes through Balata, where a replica of the Sacré Coeur in Paris was built in 1923 as a World War I memorial. The road continues to the **Jardin de Balata**▶▶, where walkways lead past hundreds of tropical plants. From here, La Trace forges into the peaks of the Pitons du Carbet.

The coast road passes through fishing villages such as Case-Pilote, named for a Carib chief, and Le Carbet, where Paul Gauguin lived for two years in the 19th century; the **Musée Gauguin**▶▶ exhibits reproductions of his works. Plantation Lajus is home of Bally Rhum.

Though it was never the official capital, St.-Pierre was the business and social center of Martinique—until May 8, 1902, when the whole town was engulfed by a volcanic ash and nearly all the 26,000 residents were killed. The town is still inhabited and many of its old buildings, including the theater and some waterfront warehouses, still exist, though as ruins. The waterfront, the market and some other buildings have recently been restored. There are a couple of museums on the rue Victor Hugo—the **Musée Historique**▶, with displays about town life before 1902, and the **Musée Volcanique**▶▶ (tel: 78-15-16. *Admission charge)*, which has grim exhibits from the day of its destruction. Montagne Pelée itself looms quietly over the remains of the town. In the north of the island, you can visit the Habitation Céron, an old plantation.

St. Pierre souvenir

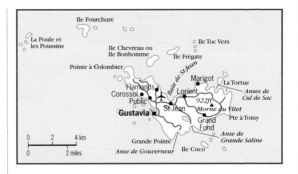

BRETON HERITAGE
St. Barts was first colonized by Bretons and Normans, and there is still a community of white Barthéleminois, whose language has retained some remnants of 17th-century Breton. Another curious hangover of their ancient heritage, still occasionally seen, is their *calèche* hats, cotton bonnets fitted with wooden slats that stick out above the face like a visor. Apart from shading the wearer from the sun, they keep away other intrusions, earning them the nickname *quichenotte*—supposedly a corruption of "kiss-me-not."

Saint-Barthélemy

Saint-Barthélemy, a tiny speck set in an aquamarine sea, has seen the full ebb and flow of Caribbean fortune. From a backwater visited occasionally by pirates it became a thriving trading post for 50 years before slipping back into obscurity. Today, the island is one of the Caribbean's most luxurious and desirable destinations.

St. Barts, as this most French of the French Caribbean islands is affectionately known, has a rarified and exclusive air. It is the favored retreat of a chic clientele of stars and the seriously rich, who zip around the island's boutiques and beaches in Suzuki jeeps and on *mobylettes* (mopeds). Tropical sophistication is taken to perfection here—at a very high price.

Although St. Barts is just under 8 square miles in size, with no hill rising above 920 feet (Morne Vitet), the scrub-covered scenery is surprisingly rough and dramatic, and six large lagoons are scattered across the landscape. The island lies 15 miles to the southeast of Saint-Martin, on the same coral geological shelf, and this gives it similarly magnificent white sand beaches. More than 20 tiny islets and islet groups lie in its waters, of which the largest is Ile Fourchue; others include the Ile Frégate twin islands, Les

Offshore islands near Saint-Barthélemy

The hair-raising landing strip at St. Barts accommodates only small planes

Balines and La Baline ("The Whales" and "The Whale"), Pain de Sucre ("Sugar Loaf"), Boulanger ("Baker") and La Poule et Les Poussins ("The Hen and Chickens").

Like Saint-Martin, St. Barts is a *commune* of Guadeloupe, 155 miles to the south, administered by a *sous-préfet* from Paris, but it has not always been French. After 100 or so years of trading with smugglers and pirates, the 1,000 French settlers learned in 1785 that the island had been leased to the Swedes in return for trading rights in the Baltic. Sweden made St. Barts a free port and for half a century the island prospered. When it was handed back to the French in 1878, its duty-free status was retained.

The capital of St. Barts is **Gustavia▶▶▶**, named for Gustav III, the Swedish King who made the 1785 exchange. It has just a few pretty streets, some with Swedish names, set on three sides of a natural harbor. In its heyday the town was defended by four fortresses, of which two, Fort Gustav and Fort Karl, can be visited. The St. Barts **museum▶▶** (tel: 27-87-27; call for hours. *Admission charge*) is set in the restored Wall House on the seaward arm of the bay. Unfortunately, much of the original town was destroyed by fire in the 1850s, but some of the old stone warehouses have been restored and now provide atmospheric settings for bars and restaurants.

St. Barts can easily be explored in a day. A drive around the steep, switchback roads takes in the occasional old church or traditional country house with plastered walls and tin roofs dotted among the modern villas. You might even hear a bit of local dialect or see an islander dressed traditionally in a long white skirt and bonnet or *calèche*. Good beaches include Anse du Gouverneur and **Anse de Grande Saline▶▶▶** on the south coast; also the Baie de St. John and Anse de Grand Cul de Sac on the north.

North of Gustavia, the road runs through Public to Corossol, an old fishing village with a shell collection at the **Inter Oceans Museum▶▶** (tel: 27-62-97. *Open* daily. *Admission charge*). The village is also the best place to find St. Barts weaving, made from the latanier palm, which grows all over the island.

To the northeast of the capital, the Plaine de la Tourmente is the site of the island's airstrip and of a graveyard. St. Jean, to the east, is one of the centers of the tourist industry, with boutiques and restaurants. At Lorient, farther east, local fishermen work as they have for centuries; beyond this point, the country opens out, though there are hotels tucked away in the bays. When the winds are up, the windsurfing is excellent in the east.

121

The Club la Banane— a tourist's-eye view of St. Barts

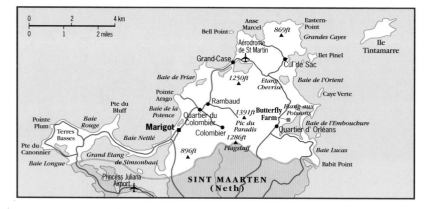

THE PARTITION
A fanciful story describes the partitioning of Saint-Martin/Sint Maarten between the French and the Dutch. Two men, one from each side, stood back to back and set off around the coastline until they met up again; the line between the departure and meeting points was to be the border. The French ended up with the larger share of the island—so the Frenchman presumably walked faster—but there are tales that the Dutchman was delayed by snoozing after too much French wine, or by a pretty French girl who happened to be passing.

Saint-Martin

The border that divides the island of Saint-Martin between France and Holland (see also pages 140–142) is barely noticeable. The countryside is much the same on both sides. Only an obelisk and a bilingual sign mark the fact that this is the smallest island in the world to be divided between two sovereign states. France, which owns the northern half of the island, looking toward Anguilla, marginally got the better of the division (see panel), with 21 of the total 37 square miles.

This is a beautiful island with tall, green and yellow concave slopes (the tallest is Pic du Paradis, at 1,391 feet), and a tortuous coastline indented with coves and superb white sand beaches. The main landmass is pierced with lagoons and salt ponds, and one "wing" is almost entirely occupied by a vast lake—one of the largest natural lakes in the Antilles, divided between the Dutch and French; the French part is attended by two low islands, Ilet Pinel ("Penal Island") and Caye Verte, to which there are daily ferry trips.

Saint-Martin is a *commune* of Guadeloupe, and has a distinctly French air—policemen wear *képis*, and French restaurants, bistros, and clothing stores line the main resorts. But the atmosphere of the island is basically international and modern, having boomed, like the Dutch side, from a lazy backwater 20 years ago to a large tourist destination. The population has exploded to 11,000 to cope with the influx of tourists; this is not the best Caribbean island for getting away from the crowds.

Marigot▶▶ is the capital on the French side, a small nexus of streets set between the Baie de Marigot and the Simpson Bay Lagoon. The few old townhouses with wrought-iron balconies and the waterfront warehouses have been restored and now buzz with shoppers and drinkers taking time out from the beach. On the Boulevard de France, overlooking the bay, is the **market square**▶▶, and the tourist office. Heading west out of town you will come to the **Musée de Saint Martin**▶▶ (tel: 87-57-21. *Open* Mon–Sat 9–1, 3–7) which traces the indigenous and colonial history of the island. The ruined Fort St. Louis, the town's defense in the days of imperial wars, still has a magnificent view over Anguilla

BIENVENUE EN PARTIE FRANÇAISE
———
WELCOME TO THE FRENCH SIDE

and the town's approaches, and overlooking the lagoon on the other side of town, the **Port la Royale**▶▶ marina is lined with cafés and restaurants.

Beyond here, some of the island's best beaches can be found in Baie Rouge and Baie Longue at the western tip of the island. The road south out of Marigot leads past the obelisk marking the border and to the main airport.

North of Marigot is a more natural Saint-Martin, although the hills are dotted everywhere with modern villas. There is a lookout near the summit of the Pic du Paradis that gives marvelous views of the nearby islands.

Beyond the local settlement of Colombier and an excellent, often uncrowded beach at Friar's Bay is the appealing town of **Grand-Case**, set along the sandy waterfront. Known as the gastronomic capital of the island, it has a row of excellent restaurants and bars set above the sea.

Past the airstrip to the east the countryside becomes surprisingly sparse, although most bays are now developed with hotels. Orléans is a 17th-century settlement, once the capital but now no more than a few villas and stores. Of the east coast beaches, the best for windsurfing are Baie de l'Embouchure and **Baie de l'Orient**, partly a nudist beach.

Marigot harbor...

...and café society

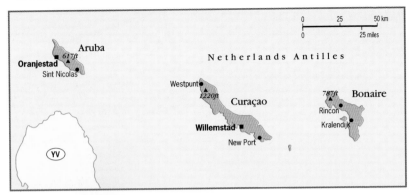

Aruba's white sand beaches

Boca Tabla, on Curaçao's northern shore

THE NETHERLANDS ANTILLES The six Dutch islands of the Caribbean carry the imprint of their colonial history; on Curaçao, even canals and gabled warehouses can be seen. The dry island of Aruba has superb beaches and Bonaire has some of the region's best preserved reefs. Aruba, Bonaire, Curaçao, and especially Sint Maarten all have developed tourist infrastructures, while the tiny outcrops of Saba and Sint Eustatius see far fewer visitors. The islands lie in two groups, separated by 500 miles of sea: the volcanic Dutch Windwards, Sint Maarten, Saba, and Sint Eustatius, nicknamed Statia (the S.S.S. islands), near the northern end of the Lesser Antilles; and the Dutch Leewards, Bonaire and Curaçao, off the coast of Venezuela. Aruba was politically part of this group until it separated from the Netherlands Antilles in 1986, but many still refer to these as the A.B.C. islands. The two groups represent some of the more beautiful—and most inhospitable—of the West Indies islands.

A Dutch heritage spanning 350 years has formed much of the character of each island. Red-bricked, pastel-painted, and gabled houses recall the heyday of the Dutch Empire, contrasting with the modern buildings erected since the oil boom of the 20th century, all set incongruously among golden beaches, coconut palms, and limpid

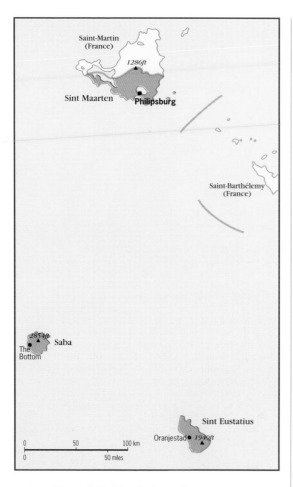

Saint-Martin
(France)

1286ft

Sint Maarten   Philipsburg

Saint-Barthélemy
(France)

285ft   Saba
The
Bottom

Sint Eustatius

Oranjestad 1979ft

0   50   100 km

0   50 miles

waters. The A.B.C. Islands have their own language, Papiamento, a curious-sounding mix of Spanish and Dutch, seeded with Portuguese, English, and African.

HISTORY The Dutch West India Company first spotted the strategic and economic significance of the Lesser Antilles in the 1620s; Sint Maarten was a neat stepping stone to Dutch colonies in Brazil, and Aruba, Bonaire, and Curaçao (colonized on a small scale by the Spanish in 1511) provided salt for the profitable herring industry at home. As trade increased—Curaçao became a center for the slave trade—so did the interest of rival empires, and during the 18th century the islands were seized by one European power after another. In 1816 the Dutch regained their hold, but the era of booming trade was over, and the islands fell into decline until the arrival of the oil companies, Royal Dutch Shell and Exxon, in the early 20th century. Refineries were set up on Aruba and Curaçao, bringing in workers from neighboring islands and new prosperity. In the 1980s the oil industry, faced with falling profits, reduced its Antilles operations, and islanders were thrown back resources from the tourist trade.

The Netherlands Antilles

A yacht-borne picnic excursion passes Saba at sunset

126

PATH TO INDEPENDENCE?

The Dutch islands were in step with the rest of the Caribbean in their growing desire for political self-government in the early part of the 20th century. Labor union movements in the oilfields increased the political awareness of the islands and a *Staten*, or Parliament, was formed in 1936. During World War II, while Holland was occupied by the Germans, the Dutch islands were left to fend for themselves and gained experience of self-government. There was not the headlong rush for independence after the war that was seen among the British islands, but autonomy was granted in 1954. Holland has stated that it will allow the islands to become fully independent when their economies are reliably stable, but many islanders prefer to remain with the Kingdom of the Netherlands for the foreseeable future.

Red roofs in The Bottom, the capital of Saba

127

Today the Netherlands Antilles are divided into three territories: Curaçao (the administrative capital), Bonaire, and the three Windward islands, Sint Maarten, Sint Eustatius and Saba. Each has its own representative body (the Island Council), elected every four years, which selects commissioners. Together they form the Executive Council for each island or island group. The Queen of the Netherlands appoints the Lieutenant-General and the island Governor, who serves a term of six years and appoints Antillian ministers. Aruba was deemed a state apart (*Status Aparte*) from the other administrations in 1986, and is now an autonomous part of the Netherlands, preparing for full independence in the near future.

"African" carvings at a craft stall in Aruba

128

Aruba

From the air, Aruba seems small and flat, with a ribbon of blinding white sand running down its western side. In fact, although the island is only 19 miles by 6 miles, its hills rise to over 490 feet, and the combined stretch of Palm Beach and Eagle Beach is one of the Caribbean's finest strips of sand. The island's distinctive beauty lies in its countryside—an almost extraterrestrial landscape full of rocky deserts, cactus jungles, and secluded coves. With its low humidity and average temperature of 82 degrees Fahrenheit, Aruba has the climate of paradise; any rain falls mostly during November. The 78,000 Arubians have a wide range of origins, including Spanish, Portuguese, East Indian, and the Caribbean, as well as Dutch. The official language is Dutch, and English is widely spoken, but most Arubians speak Papiamento, a dialect drawing from Spanish, French, Portuguese, Dutch, African, and English (see panel). Colonization came relatively late to Aruba, which was virtually ignored by

Oranjestad: a modern interpretation of traditional Dutch-Caribbean style and colors

European powers until the 20th century, and its people have retained a strong sense of independence.

The capital, **Oranjestad▶▶**, lies on the protected southwestern shore of the island; the town and its outlying suburbs are the center of Aruban life. Named for the Dutch Royal House of Orange, this is Aruba's main port; some of the older buildings around the main street, Nassaustraat, date from the oil boom earlier this century, but most are modern imitations with traditional flourishes, containing the banks and shopping malls of the modern town. A line of fishing boats forms the quayside Schooner Market, selling produce from Venezuela.

Fort Zoutman (1796) is the island's oldest building, and contains the **Museo Arubano▶** (tel: 26099), tracing Aruba's history, and the **Museo Archeologico▶** (tel: 28979), depicting indigenous life. **The Museo Numismatico▶▶** (tel: 28813), on Irausquin Plein, has a collection of 30,000 bills and coins, and there are 700 species of shell on display at the **De Man shell collection▶▶**, at 18 Morgenster Street (by appointment, tel: 24246).

To the west of Oranjestad, the coastal road runs past the cruise ship dock to Aruba's magnificent beaches: **Eagle Beach▶▶▶** ("low rise strip") and **Palm Beach▶▶▶** ("high rise strip"). There is no shortage of watersports or bars here—nor is there any lack of crowds, especially in June, when Aruba hosts the HiWinds International Windsurfing Regatta.

East of the town, the road passes through suburbs into the scrub. Sprinkled among the new houses are traditional buildings, with talismanic symbols painted on the clay walls, and roofs made of cactus wood and grass.

Aruba's highest hill is Jamanota (617 feet), but its most distinctive is the **Hooiberg▶**, standing over 540 feet high, with stairs to ease the climb. To its north are the huge, gray, and rounded **diorite boulders▶▶** at Casibari and Ayo, and on the north coast, east of Oranjestad, are the ruins of the Bushiribana gold mines, whose discovery in 1825 led to a brief gold rush (a smelting site at Balashi produced over 2 million pounds of gold).

Also in this area are the ruins of a 16th-century fortress, and at **Andicouri▶▶**, the sea has carved the spectacular Natural Bridge from the coral rock. San Nicolas is the island's second town and the site of the old oil refinery.

Aruba's Dutch legacy is still apparent...

...while tourism is taking over on its inviting beaches

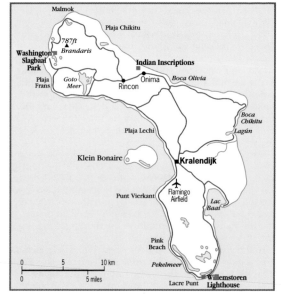

Malmok

Plaja Chikitu

787ft
Brandaris

Washington
Slagbaai
Park

Indian Inscriptions

Plaja
Frans

*Goto
Meer*

Onima

Boca Olivia

Rincon

*Boca
Chikitu*

Lagún

Plaja Lechi

Klein Bonaire

■**Kralendijk**

Punt Vierkant

Flamingo
Airfield

*Lac
Baai*

Pink
Beach

Pekelmeer

0   5   10 km

0   5 miles

Lacre Punt

**Willemstoren
Lighthouse**

*Above and far right: salt
stacks awaiting shipping
glare in the tropical sun
of Bonaire*

130

Bonaire

Bonaire is a stark desert island, perfect for the rugged
individualist who is turned off by the over-commercial-
ized high life of the other Antillean islands. A mecca for
divers, the island offers one of the most unspoiled reef
systems in the world. The water is so clear that you can
lean over the dock and look the fish straight in the eye.
This is not the island for connoisseurs of fine cuisine, nor
for shopping addicts, but what lies off its shores is guaranteed to keep divers enthralled. Most visitors to the
island come for the scuba diving. The **Bonaire Marine
Park**▶ ▶ ▶—a model of ecological conservation—almost
surrounds Bonaire itself as well as Klein Bonaire from the
high-water tidemark to a depth of nearly 200 feet. The
corals and fish are some of the finest and least disturbed
in the Caribbean, and they make Bonaire well worth visiting for a relaxing vacation with a sporting focus.

Shaped somewhat like a foot, Bonaire is a crooked 23½
miles long. In the bight of the protected coast is the foot-
ball-shaped Klein Bonaire, about to be kicked toward
Curaçao. Like its neighbors, Bonaire is dry and
windswept, covered in scrubby vegetation and dotted
with tall cacti. From the salt flats in the south, the land
rises to the 787-foot Mount Brandaris in the northwest.
Much of the coastline is limestone coral shelf, but there
are breaks in the wall where the sand collects to form
decent beaches. Two colonies of flamingoes nest on the
island and can be seen feeding in the lagoons during the
day. A circuit of the island can be completed in a day; cars
can be rented from hotels or rental companies.

Industries on Bonaire include oil bunkering (storing oil
fuel for ships), salt harvesting, and radio transmitting
stations, but tourism (mainly diving) is the most important economic sector and it has changed the island

THE SALT INDUSTRY
As you drive south on
Bonaire you will come to
the vast white stacks of
Bonaire's salt, beneath
which several cranes bus-
tle about. Salt production
has recently been revived
for industrial purposes;
sea water is let into shallow "pans" and the sun
and the wind then do their
work, evaporating the
water. The resulting brine
is channeled into other
pans to increase the evaporation effect and
eventually a bed of white
crystals appears. These
are harvested and cleaned
before being stacked by a
crane on rails in mounds
ready for shipping.

radically in the last 15 years. From a lazy backwater (which the island had remained from the moment the Dutch arrived in 1636) it has suddenly geared up for large numbers of visitors, but a certain funky sleepiness has survived. Bonaireans speak Papiamento, although Dutch is the official language and English is widely understood.

The capital, **Kralendijk▶▶**, lies in the protected bight of the western shore, on the coral (*kralen*) wall (*dijk*). A few traditional Bonaire houses, painted gold with white stucco, stand among the mostly modern buildings; bars and restaurants line the waterfront, and hotels are spread along the shores on either side of the town.

Fort Oranje, the town's old defense, now contains the island museum, displaying indigenous native American and colonial Bonairean artifacts. The whole town comes to life for Carnival and for parades and festivals during late June.

Beyond the hotel strip, going north, the road passes the oil storage depot and continues to the Goto Meer, one of the flamingoes' favored nesting spots. The island's north-western tip is made up of the 13,489-acre **Washington Slagbaai Park▶▶**, where marked roads give views of Bonaire's semi-arid flora, as well as possible glimpses of the iguana and some of the estimated 130 species of birdlife (including pelicans, bananaquits, and sandpipers). Visits can be made by car and by bicycle. Another road heads back to Kralendijk via Rincon, the island's second town, and Indian inscriptions at **Onima▶**.

A circular road runs around the southern toe of the island beyond the airport to **Pink Beach▶▶**, named for the striking color of its sand, and then to the vast white stacks of harvested salt at the **salt works▶▶** (see panel opposite). Another flamingo colony nests here. Colored obelisks stand on the coast, built as shipping guides on an otherwise indistinguishable coastline. Two groups of small huts huddled on the shore were once two-man dormitories for slaves who worked the salt pans in 1850. Lac Baai has two good beaches; nudism is permitted on one.

NATURE AND WILDLIFE
The divi-divi tree, which grows in the Dutch Leewards, has a gnarled but basically vertical trunk about 6 ft. high, but its branches are forced to grow at 90 degrees to the trunk by the strong Caribbean wind. The A.B.C. islands are mainly dry and covered with cactus and scrub. Birds include the orange and black troupial, Curaçao's national bird, and the oriole, which lays its eggs in a hanging nest 3 ft. high.

Kralendijk waterfront at dusk

131

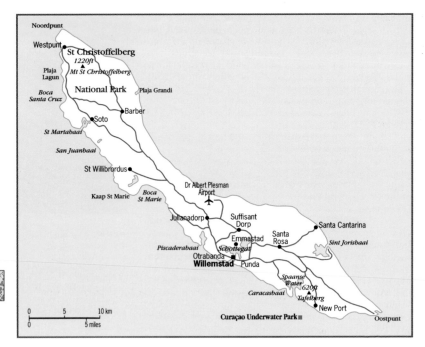

Noordpunt
Westpunt
St Christoffelberg
1220ft
Plaja Lagun
Mt St Christoffelberg
Boca Santa Cruz
National Park
Plaja Grandi
Barber
Soto
St Martabaai
San Juanbaai
St Willibrordus
Kaap St Marie
Boca St Marie
Dr Albert Plesman Airport
Julianadorp
Suffisant Dorp
Santa Cantarina
Emmastad
Santa Rosa
Sint Jorisbaai
Piscaderabaai
Schottegat
Otrabanda
Willemstad Punda
Spaanse Water
Caracasbaai
620ft
Tafelberg
New Port
Curaçao Underwater Park ■
Oostpunt

0 — 5 — 10 km
0 — 5 miles

Curaçao

In Willemstad, Curaçao's capital, handsome rows of pastel-colored townhouses look as though they were transplanted from Holland. The island's Dutch architecture makes a cheerful contrast to a terrain dotted with stark cacti. Curaçao has neither great beaches nor enchanting scenery. But watersports attract enthusiasts from all over the world, the shopping is first-rate, and some of the best reef diving is here. The sun smiles down on Curaçao, but thanks to the gentle trade winds it never gets too hot. The largest of the Netherlands Antilles, the island lies between Aruba and Bonaire, 34 miles from the coast of Venezuela. Curaçao is a long and thin island, measuring 37 miles by 9 miles, created from lava emissions encrusted with coral limestone.

HISTORY Curaçao is the traditional heart of the Dutch Caribbean, and has been the administrative capital since the Dutch arrived in 1634. Dubbed the "Land of Giants" by explorer Amerigo Vespucci, who felt dwarfed by the indigenous Caiquetios tribe, Curaçao was left alone by early colonizers, though many of its inhabitants were taken as slaves to the Hispaniola gold mines. By the early 17th century, there was a handful of Spanish settlers, but these were chased out by Dutch invaders. Slave-trading was the island's prime source of wealth, and emancipation signaled its decline. In 1915 a new source of prosperity was introduced with the building of an oil refinery, and the population soared as workers moved in. During the 1960s and 1980s the oil industry was dealt two blows: "automation," which reduced the number of

DUTCH CUISINE
Food in the Dutch Leewards is very different from dishes elsewhere in the Caribbean. A number of restaurants specialize in local cuisine, made even more exotic by its Papiamento names. Dishes include *sopi* (soup) and *stoba* (stews), made with *galina* (chicken), *bestia* (lamb), *carco* (conch) and *kreeft* (lobster) or even *juwana* (iguana). Side dishes include *snijboonchi* (stringbeans), *giambo* (cactus fruit), *funchi* (maize meal) or *toetoe* (cornmeal mixed with beans and bacon, topped with Edam cheese). *Keshi yena* is spicy chicken, covered with Dutch cheese.

employees, and the effects of rising prices. Eventually the business was wound down and there are now plans to expand the tourist industry. Duty-free shopping already attracts regular cruise ships, but there are only a few mid-range hotels on the southern shore, mainly around Willemstad, the capital. Curaçao's beaches are not the Caribbean's best, tending to be picturesque, craggy coves, but the island has some excellent restaurants.

ISLAND LIFE With 160,000 inhabitants, Curaçao is the most populous of the Netherlands Antilles, and its life as a trading port has given it an extremely varied mix of people. Though Dutch is the official language, Curaçaoans generally speak Papiamento as a first tongue; most also speak English and Spanish. Of all the Dutch Caribbean islands, Curaçao shows the strongest Dutch influence, in its buildings, its food, and its faces.

WILLEMSTAD Lying on the protected southern shore, Willemstad has developed around the Schottegat, a huge natural harbor, which attracted the first Dutch colonizers. The oldest part of the town is **Punda▶ ▶** ("the Point"), of which the main quay, the **Handelskade▶ ▶** is one of the most striking sights in the Caribbean; its buildings (such as the 1708 Penha House) combine the curly gables of Amsterdam with the bright colors of the West Indies. Like the streets behind it, the Handelskade still works as a trading area, now serving cruise-ship passengers rather than merchants. At right angles to it is the **Floating Market▶ ▶ ▶**, a line of wooden boats docked at the quayside, where you can buy fruits and vegetables shipped in from Venezuela and displayed on slab tables shaded by awnings attached to the masts, which rise and fall with the rocking of the boats.

The **Mikve Israel Synagogue▶ ▶** (tel: 461-1067), located on Columbusstraat, dates from 1732; the Jewish Historical Museum, in its courtyard, displays among other artifacts a 250-year-old ceremonial bath, and other ritual and Torah objects are still in use in services today. **Fort Amsterdam▶**, the town's original defense, was built in 1634. It is now the residence of the Governor of the Netherlands Antilles and the seat of their Parliament.

The Penha building: Dutch-influenced architecture on the Handelskade waterfront

133

Willemstad's main quay, Handelskade

134

A museum in the **Fort Church▶** (tel: 461-1139; call for hours) displays maps and religious artifacts dating back to 1635. Four other 17th-century forts surround the port, two of which are now restaurants. There is a tourist information booth under the arches of the Waterfort, and the **Plaza Biejo▶▶** is an excellent stop for lunch; customers sit at long tables, watching the pots boil before them with such popular Curaçao dishes as *stoba* (stew) and *toetoe* (see panel on page 132). Otrabanda, on the other side of

Above and above right: shading under the sails at the floating market at Willemstad

the main harbor channel, is reached by the **Konigin Emmabrug▶▶▶**, a pedestrian pontoon bridge formed by about 15 barges that move constantly on the waves, making for a bouncy walk across. Occasionally the bridge opens to let ocean-going tankers through; small passenger ferries operate at these times. In Otrabanda there are more excellent examples of the distinctive Dutch Creole architecture: colonial houses, with their orange tiles and curly gables, many painted with Curaçao gold. **The Curaçao Museum▶▶** (tel: 762-3873; call for hours), in an old townhouse once used as the naval hospital, exhibits among other interesting items part of the first airplane to fly here from the Netherlands. South of Brion Plein is the Coney Island Amusement Park; northwest of here, the Beth Haim Cemetery has some of the oldest European tombs in the Americas. The **Numismatic Museum▶▶** (tel: 46-8610; call for hours. *Admission free*) in the Central Bank building has early coins and banknotes from Dutch Antillean history and displays on minting and printing processes.

OUTSIDE WILLEMSTAD The suburbs of Willemstad creep around the Schottegat harbor, where container ports and dockyards line the shore. The autonomy monument, on the eastern side, is a 1954 sculpture of six birds, commemorating the year when the six Netherlands Antilles were granted self-rule. Farther along is the **Curaçao Liqueur Distillery**▶▶ (*Open* Mon–Fri), in the Landhuis Chobolobo, where Curaçao liqueur is produced from the peel of small, green oranges. Nearby, the Amstel Brewery can be visited on Tuesdays and Thursdays. The oil refinery on the northwest shore was once the largest in the world. The best view of its tangled pipes and chimneys is from the hills around Fort Nassau, behind Punda. Near the sports stadium is the restored 18th-century **Landhuis Brievengat**▶▶ (*Open* daily 10–5. *Admission charge*), a cochineal plantation house. Close to the airport are the **Hato Caves**▶, with Indian petroglyph drawings, as well as stalactites and stalagmites.

East of Willemstad is the **Curaçao Seaquarium**▶▶ (tel: 461-6666. *Open* daily 10–10. *Admission charge*), with re-created reefs and tropical fish. Glass-bottom boat trips and scuba diving are available in the nearby Curaçao Underwater Park, a restricted marine area, where divers can swim with rays and feed sharks through a mesh.

Westward is the bush countryside, where isolated plantation houses (*landhuisen*) stand among scrub and cacti. Near the island's western tip is **Christoffel National Park**▶▶, on the slopes of Saint Christoffelberg (1,220 feet), with marked driving and walking trails and a natural history museum (tel: 864-0363). Curaçao's best beaches are toward the western end, on the south shore.

135

Fishing in Spaanse Water, eastern Curaçao

FLAT POINT AND THE ROAD

Flat Point is, in fact, on a gentle slope, but it is the only area of Saba large enough to have an airstrip (1,300 ft. long). The Road is a feat of engineering which it was said would be impossible to build. Between Windwardside and The Bottom there is a plaque to Joseph Lambertus Hassell, who followed a correspondence course in engineering and then designed and built The Road, starting at Fort Bay and heading up to The Bottom and on to Windwardside and eventually via 19 hairpin bends down to Flat Point. The Road is still in good condition, after nearly 50 years.

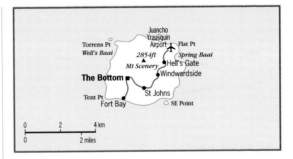

Saba

Not long ago, Saba almost passed a law decreeing that all the roofs on the island be painted red. Draconian, perhaps—but red roofs have long been a tradition on Saba. They go well with the white cottage walls, the picket fences and the striking greens of this fertile island.

Another draconian aspect of Saba is its geography. It is small, extremely rugged, and difficult to reach. Mount Scenery, the waterborne peak of an extinct volcano, soars to 2,854 feet, on an island only 3 miles by 2 miles. The 1,200 hardy Sabians have their island neatly tamed; they must, in order to survive here.

Dutch colonists from Sint Eustatius were the first Europeans to settle on the island, in 1640. Twenty-five years later, Saba was taken by a British privateer, and all non-English speakers were shipped away. In the 19th century the island was returned to Dutch possession, and Saba survived on the money sent home by its menfolk, who earned a reputation as skilled sailors, and on the lace-making and threadwork of the women. The oil boom on Aruba and Curaçao provided work for islanders in the 20th century, but after its collapse the island turned to its small tourist industry. There are a few places to stay, which are more like friendly mountain guesthouses than Caribbean beach hotels. Saba has no natural beaches, but then visitors to the island mainly come for the excellent scuba diving.

The island's four settlements are all linked by a sinuous artery, respectfully known as The Road (see panel). Its capital is a village by the name of **The Bottom▶ ▶**, thought to derive from the Dutch *Botte* (bowl), though ironically it's located 820 feet above sea level. Most of the houses do, indeed, lie at the bottom of a bowl, but new buildings are steadily creeping up the towering, forested peaks that surround it. The Governor's Residence, in the village, is an attractive balconied Caribbean house. A number of bars are run from timber-frame houses, such as Cranston's Antique Inn, where you can join the Sabans for an afternoon drink.

One of Saba's pretty white cottages

On the sheltered coast beneath The Bottom are Saba's two harbors: Ladder Bay and Fort Bay. The first is reached by steps; in the days before The Road, Sabans had to carry all their supplies up here on their shoulders. Fort Bay has been the principal port since 1972, when the jetties were built here. It is also the departure point for scuba diving operations. From here there is nowhere to go but back up to the village, from which The Road leads to St. John's, a small collection of houses built on an expanse of relatively flat ground.

Magnificent views of the coast open out 1,200 feet below as The Road reaches **Windwardside**▶▶, Saba's other principal village. The tourist office can be found here, as well as banks and hotels. Windwardside is even neater and prettier than The Bottom, its white houses set behind stone walls, with gardens of bougainvillea and hibiscus. The **Saba Museum**▶ (*Open* Mon–Fri 10–12, 1–4. *Admission charge*), set in a private home, shows Amerindian artifacts and 19th-century exhibits. Older village women still knit the renowned Saba lace, which can be bought at the Island Craft Shop, and brew "Saba Spice," a potent concoction of rum and various herbs and spices.

Beyond Windwardside is the village of Hell's Gate, and from here, The Road descends tortuously to the optimistically named Flat Point, site of the island's airstrip (see panel opposite).

Like many of the old trails used by the islanders before The Road was constructed, the steep path to the top of Mount Scenery has carefully laid steps (they start just outside Windwardside) leading through the rainforest and elfin forest; on a clear day the views from this laborious climb are superb.

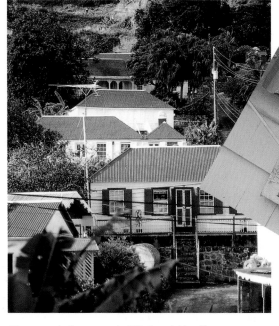

Houses stacked top-to-toe in Windwardside village

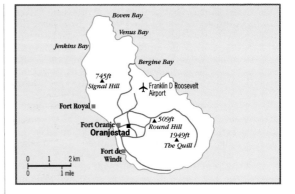

Map labels:
Boven Bay
Venus Bay
Jenkins Bay
Bergine Bay
745ft
Signal Hill
Franklin D Roosevelt Airport
Fort Royal
509ft
Round Hill
Fort Oranje
Oranjestad
1949ft
The Quill
Fort de Windt
0   1   2 km
0   1 mile

THE FIRST SALUTE
Sint Eustatius was the first place in the world to recognize the U.S. When, in November 1776, a ship flying an unfamiliar flag arrived in harbor, the island gave the customary salute, according it an official welcome. The *Andrew Dorea* was flying the flag of the rebel American colonists and this was the first recognition of their sovereignty. The British were so angry that they persuaded the Dutch to recall the Governor responsible for the incident, de Graaff. (For the Sint Eustatius Historical Museum, tel: 82288. *Open* Mon–Fri 9–5, Sat, Sun 9–noon. *Admission charge.*)

Sint Eustatius

Two hundred years ago, Sint Eustatius was one of the richest and most important islands in the West Indies. As many as a hundred ships would put in to this busy trading port at a time. But the mile of warehouses that once ran along the Lower Town's shore has gone, and only a few walls remain from the island's era as the "Golden Rock."

Almost all of the 18th-century's booming business was breaking the trade laws, as goods which should have been sold to the colonies' governing countries were smuggled to Statia (as the island is usually known) for quick and direct payment. A brisk arms trade developed during the Revolutionary War, and as colonial powers battled over their possessions, the island changed hands over 20 times.

A Statian resident contemplates island philosophy

Statia's golden age came to an end after the British, led by Admiral Rodney, took over the island and sold off all its goods (see panel opposite).

Today Statia is a quiet backwater with only 2,100 inhabitants, mainly of African descent and English-speaking, although the official language is Dutch. The island is undeveloped—there are only a few hotel rooms and no white sand Caribbean strands—though with the help of the E.C. Statia has renovated its historical buildings. Lying 30 miles south of Sint Maarten (the main access to Statia), between the volcanic peaks of Saba and St. Kitts, the island is just 12 square miles in size. In the south rises a perfectly formed extinct volcanic cone called the Quill; the volcanic sand makes all Statia's beaches dark.

The capital and only town, Oranjestad, sits on a cliff 525 feet above the island's sheltered Caribbean coast. Its **Upper Town▶▶** has cobbled streets and a few old stone houses with wooden wraparound balconies among the newer buildings, and from its clifftop courtyard of cobbles, date palms, and cannon, **Fort Oranje▶** enjoys a superb view of the bay. The **Sint Eustatius Historical Museum▶▶** is set in de Graaff House, named for the Governor who was responsible for the First Salute (see panel opposite). There are rooms devoted to Arawak and Carib Indian culture, the colonial years, and more recent island history. Some of the Upper Town's historical buildings are no more than shells, but it is worth climbing the tower of the Dutch Reform Church for its fine view. The ruined Honen Dalim synagogue, on Synagoogpad, is one of the oldest in the western hemisphere.

Lower Town▶▶ is where the trading warehouses once stood; as trade expanded, a dyke was built to reclaim more land from the sea. An ancient stone walkway descends from Fort Oranje to the small line of restored buildings recreated with the original bricks. Statia has a growing reputation for scuba diving, and boats depart from here, heading out to the reefs offshore. Occasionally divers find blue beads, which were used as a currency on the island two centuries ago.

Beyond the town, Statia's countryside is relatively open, although modern homes are steadily filling the available space. An older Statia is still just visible in the fences of spiky agave and cactus plants and the inevitable goats. It is an easy walk to the lip of **the Quill's crater▶▶**, where lush rainforest grows down in the bowl (it can be a very slippery climb). In the south of the island there is a good view of St. Kitts from the tiny Fort de Windt; in the north, an area of uninhabited hills is the site of Statia's only major industry, an oil bunkerage and a refinery that produces 250 barrels a day.

139

ADMIRAL RODNEY'S REVENGE
A few years after the First Salute the British had their revenge when Admiral Rodney captured the harbor and kept the flags flying as though the island were open for trade, impounding 150 ships that unwittingly came into harbor. Rodney carried off the merchandise and destroyed the retaining walls. His suspicions were aroused by a sudden rise in the number of deaths on the island: Rodney had several coffins dug up, to find that merchants were hiding their gold in them.

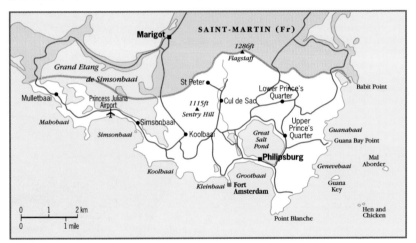

SAINT-MARTIN (Fr)

Marigot

1286ft
Flagstaff

Grand Etang
de Simsonbaai

St Peter

Lower Prince's
Quarter

Babit Point

Mulletbaai

Princess Juliana
Airport

1115ft
Sentry Hill

Cul de Sac

Mahobaai

Simsonbaai

Simsonbaai

Koolbaai

Great
Salt
Pond

Upper
Prince's
Quarter

Guanabaai

Guana Bay Point

Philipsburg

Mal
Aborder

Koolbaai

Genevebaai

Grootbaai

Kleinbaai

Fort
Amsterdam

Guana
Key

0   1   2 km
0   1 mile

Point Blanche

Hen and
Chicken

SHOPPING SPREES
Amid the vast cruise ships
that dock at Sint
Maarten's capital are
smaller, wooden craft,
whose captains also come
to enjoy some of the
Caribbean's best
shopping. Sint Maarten is
where many West Indians
go at Christmas, for wine,
electrical goods, tobacco,
and alcohol. Local yachts
make the run from as far
down as the Grenadines,
where many were built.

Philipsburg's beach

Sint Maarten

Seen from a distance, Sint Maarten appears serene and
tranquil, with land rising from the sea in graceful curves
to form steep mountain peaks. But this peaceful air belies
the hectic activity of Sint Maarten, one of the busiest and
most developed islands in the Caribbean.

Despite being just 37 square miles in area, the island is
divided between two countries (the smallest island in the
world to fly two flags). Since it was first settled in 1648, it
has been shared between the Dutch and the French (see
pages 122–123 for the French territory, Saint-Martin) and
give or take the odd invasion, relations have been pretty
amicable. There is even a peak called Mount Concordia as
a tribute to their goodwill. The island stands on the same
landmass as Anguilla and St. Barts, an ancient volcanic
bank, inactive and coral-encrusted, and has superb white
sand beaches. Dutch Sint Maarten occupies 16 square
miles in the southern part of the island.

Given its size, Sint Maarten's tourist industry is huge,
and this has changed the island dramatically over the last
20 years. There has been extensive building, and rebuild-
ing after Hurricane Luis in 1995, and the population has
increased. Though Dutch is the official language, a whole
range of spoken languages can be heard here, from
Haitian Kreyol to Papiamento to English.

The island is crammed to the hilt
with hotels, restaurants, bars, clubs,
casinos, and heavy traffic, fre-
quently jammed up. The airport at
Juliana is a hive of activity, with
flights arriving from the main
Caribbean islands as well as from
European and U.S. cities. Sint
Maarten is also popular as a cruise
ship stopover, and its status as a
duty-free port brings in about half a
million tourists a year, as well as
locals, to take advantage of the best
shopping in the Caribbean.

One of the most attractive features of Caribbean architecture is "gingerbread" design, which embellishes houses with an elaborate latticework of wood carved into squiggles, sweeps, and twirls. The term is supposedly derived from 16th-century German pastry-makers, who were known for their ornately decorated gingerbread creations.

The flamboyance of gingerbread appealed to plantation owners and estate managers, who had grand houses built to show off their wealth, with elaborate verandas overlooking their estates. Public buildings were also given the gingerbread treatment, the most fanciful of which are in Haiti. Saba, one of the Dutch Windward Islands, has several well-maintained gingerbread houses with green or red window frames, surrounded by pretty tropical blooms, concentrated in a small area (Windwardside and The Bottom). Gingerbread's popularity spread, and the style was taken up in the U.S. during the prosperous 1860s and 1870s, after the Civil War. Good examples can be seen in the beach resort of Cape May, New Jersey.

Traditionally, Caribbean houses were constructed in wood, as there was no need for the warmth provided by stone and brick. Wood was cheaper and buildings could even be dismantled and taken away (in Barbados, farmers' homes were known as "chattel" houses because they could be moved with other goods and chattels). These houses, their walls made from strips of clapboard and their roofs tiled with wooden shingles, are steadily disappearing as the islands develop, but you will see examples of them if you drive through the country.

Curaçao, Bonaire and Aruba's houses are made with brick and plaster—wood was scarce and at risk from fire, so its use in building was banned. The walls are painted in gold, light brown, purple, and deep green, and the effect is completed with orange "dakpannen," clay roof tiles, and white borders. The story goes that Admiral Kikkert, a Governor of Curaçao, suffered from headaches brought on by the reflection of the sun in Willemstad's whitewashed buildings, so he ordered that they be painted any color other than white.

Old San Juan's city hall, Puerto Rico

COUNTRY SHACKS
Traditional Caribbean country shacks were made with "wattle and daub," a latticework of springy twigs covered in mud and dried in the sun. The roof was topped with thatch, providing a cool indoor environment. More recently, concrete has become popular as a hurricane-resistant building material.

A restored colonial house in French Saint-Martin

A West Indian market in the mural—tourists shopping in real life at Philipsburg

PETER STUYVESANT
Peter Stuyvesant was an early Governor of Curaçao (in 1638) and later of all the Dutch possessions in the Americas, which he governed from Nieuw Amsterdam (New York). An autocratic leader, he lost his right leg in a fight for Sint Maarten in 1644 and wore a silver ornamented false leg as a replacement. Stuyvesant was forced to surrender the North American possessions to the British in 1664, but later returned to live in the Great Bouwery in Manhattan until his death in 1672.

The capital and main town on the Dutch side of Sint Maarten is **Philipsburg▶**, set on a narrow spit of land between Great Bay and the Great Salt Pond (the source of the salt which originally attracted the Dutch West India Company to the island). It has just four streets and a sprinkling of traditional houses among an otherwise modern town that has sprouted since the tourist boom. The town faces south, towards Saba and Sint Eustatius, the other two Dutch Windward Islands.

Visitors who stream off the cruise ships arrive at de Ruyterplein, a small square which is the setting for the pretty Old Courthouse Building and a tourist information office. Leading through it is Front Street, Philipsburg's mile-long shopping arcade, where the best of the duty-free bargains can be found—European fashion, jewelry, crystal, and porcelain—as well as plenty of cafés and bars. In an arcade at the head of Front Street, the **Sint Maarten Museum▶** (tel: 24927) has exhibits of pre-Columbian and colonial island life. Its displays highlight the contrasting lifestyles with items such as Native American pottery and Delft dinner services. Behind the West Indian Tavern are the ruins of a 300-year-old synagogue, the first on the island. The town's founder, John Philips, is buried in an 18th-century cemetery to the west of Philipsburg.

Philipsburg's outlying areas completely encircle the lagoon, and determined shoppers will find yet more arcades around its shores, but generally this is where the islanders live. A **zoo▶** (tel: 32030; call for hours) on the Madame Estate keeps animals from South America and the Caribbean area. Farther afield, Sint Maarten's eastern side is relatively untouched and secluded.

The main route out of Philipsburg is often clogged with traffic; in Koolbaai (Cole Bay), a left turn leads alongside the Simpson Bay Lagoon to the busiest tourist area. Simsonbaai (Simpson Bay) itself has a good beach, and beyond the airport are Mandsaoi (Mano Bay) and Mulletbaai (Mullet Bay), with watersports, stores, and a golf course. The road to Marigot crosses the border, which is marked only with an obelisk and a sign saying *Bienvenue à la Partie Française.*

Almost every brochure for a Caribbean vacation includes a picture of a waiter with a tray of sweet and exotic tropical fruit. Not all will be in season at any one time, but a visit to the market is always worthwhile for the displays of this fertile region's appetizing produce.

143

The pineapple, used by Native Americans for food and wine-making, grows on a stem in the center of a low bush of about 30 stiff, spiky, cactus-like leaves, and takes about 15 months to mature. Black pineapples are slightly smaller and sweeter.

Pawpaw, or papaya, grows on a tall and slender tree of very light wood. The fruit, which matures to yellow and orange, can grow to 18 inches in length. Papaya is said to be good for high blood pressure, and the seeds are used as a remedy for constipation.

The fruit of the soursop, which is not sour at all, is irregularly shaped, sometimes oval, with small, black hooks protruding from its aromatic, light green skin. Inside, black seeds sit in a white, pulpy flesh that tastes like a combination of mango and pineapple. Its seeds make it difficult to eat fresh—so it is probably best tasted in ice-cream.

Related to the soursop, the sweetsop looks like a fleshy green pine cone. It is known locally as the sugar apple or custard apple; its seeds are contained in a sweet, creamy pulp, rather like custard.

Guava fruit is really an outsize berry, which turns from green to yellow when ripening. Inside, its seeds sit in a

white or pink pulp. Guava has a bittersweet taste and provides five times as much Vitamin C as orange juice.

Mango trees, although not native to the Caribbean, grow throughout the region; their yellow and red fruits have some of the sweetest-tasting flesh of all. Other exotic fruits include the Otaheite apple, shaped like a pear with a red skin and a crisp white pulp, or the carambola, yellow-skinned with crunchy white flesh, which is shaped like a five-pointed star when cut cross-section.

TENDER FRUIT
Papain, from the papaya, is used as a meat tenderizer; West Indians simply wrap their meat in pawpaw leaf and leave it to stand. Pineapple is also a meat tenderizer, with pretty powerful effects: stranded soldiers on a South Sea island during World War II found that their teeth fell out if they ate too much of the fruit.

Young breadfruit, usually eaten baked or roasted

HYBRID FRUIT
Jamaica has created two hybrids of other citruses. The ortanique is part orange, part tangerine; the size of the former but with a skin that peels like the latter. The lumpy ugli fruit is a cross between a grapefruit, an orange, and a tangerine.

144

Great Courland Bay, one of a number of deep, palm-fringed coves cut into Tobago's northern shore

OTHER CARIBBEAN STATES The larger, independent nation states of the Caribbean, separated by physical and cultural obstacles (and often suspicious of each other, if not openly hostile), are marked by their diversity. Jamaica's lushness and extensive rainforests are a reminder of what Haiti, 100 miles east, must have been before generations of impoverished peasants cleared the hillsides in search of charcoal. Jamaica has all the attributes of the travel agency clichés—beaches, rivers, mountains—but it also has social and economic problems, as any visitor to downtown Kingston will see. Cuba is cracking and crumbling behind its wall of isolation. The colonial splendor of old Havana is gradually collapsing

Other Caribbean states

from neglect; yet this was once the most inviting tropical resort in the world. Haiti and the Dominican Republic share an island, but their border is more often closed than open. For all the Dominican Republic's colonial treasures and natural beauty, thousands of poor islanders risk their lives each year to cross the Mona Passage to Puerto Rico, where rural and U.S.-influenced lifestyles exist side by side. The oil-producing nation of Trinidad and Tobago, famous for its Carnival and calypso, faces an uncertain future after years of wealth; while Barbados is perhaps the most developed of all the islands. No two islands are similar. If you want to know more than a little piece of the Caribbean, explore some of these fascinating states.

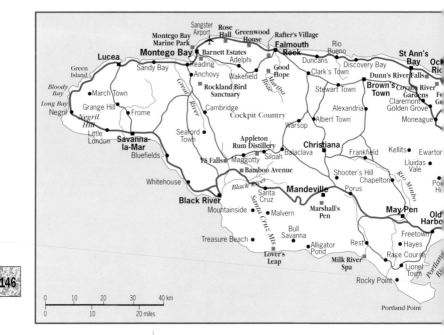

Jamaica

The third-largest island in the Caribbean (after Cuba and Hispaniola), the English-speaking nation of Jamaica enjoys a self-sufficiency based on tourism, agriculture, and mining. Its attractions include jungle mountaintops, clear waterfalls, and unforgettable beaches, yet the country's greatest resource may very well be the Jamaicans themselves. Although 95 percent of the population trace their bloodlines to Africa, their national origins lie elsewhere: in Europe, the Middle East, India, China, South America, and many of the other islands in the Caribbean. The music, art, and cuisine of Jamaica are vibrant, with a spirit easy to sense but as hard to describe as the rhythms of reggae or a flourish of the streetwise patois.

HISTORY Jamaica was born of strife, as a colonial outpost, first of 16th-century Spanish settlers (who destroyed the Arawak inhabitants) and then of the British, who cut their plantations in the hills. Pirates brawled on the coastline, and the flourishing plantations, worked by slaves, were attacked by runaway maroons (see panel). Uprisings

*Jahbah's health food
center in Negril*

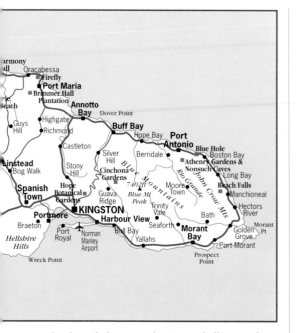

MAROONS

The maroons were a community of runaways who lived high in the inaccessible Jamaican interior, in the John Crow Mountains in the northeast and the Cockpit Country in the northwest. Their name comes from the Spanish word *cimarrón* ("wild"); the earliest maroons were slaves left behind by the Spaniards when they fled from the British in 1655. Maroons were highly successful guerrilas and were never conquered; eventually the colonial authorities were reduced to negotiating with them, agreeing to guarantee their freedom and a considerable measure of self-government (which they still have today), in return for certain conditions, which included returning runaway slaves.

among the slaves led to several serious rebellions and terrible bloodshed, and even after their emancipation in the 19th century the hardship and violence continued. Demonstrations marked the run-up to full enfranchisement in 1944, and preceded complete independence from the U.K. in 1962.

Over the past 30 years the island has built one of the biggest tourist industries in the Caribbean, providing easy access from Europe and the U.S. and a full range of accommodation: beachfront luxury, all-inclusives (offering entertainment and accommodation), guesthouses on the cliffs in Negril, villas, and mountain retreats. The resort towns of Montego Bay, and Negril have good restaurants and lively bars and nightclubs.

ISLAND LIFE Jamaica is a cultural leader in the Caribbean; its boisterous culture of reggae and rastafari is known throughout the world and attracts visitors who are looking for a little more than the traditional Caribbean image of sun, sea, and sand. Economically, though, the 2.5 million islanders have not had an easy ride recently; rising prices for imports and a fall in earnings from the main export, bauxite, led to austerity measures in the 1980s and there is still considerable unemployment and inflation. From time to time there are outbursts—troubles tend to come to a head during the fiercely contested elections, when traditional political rivalries are at their height, particularly in Kingston.

There is no reason why this should affect visitors to the island, most of whom will be on the north coast anyway. Besides, the majority of Jamaicans are welcoming and friendly. Jamaica remains primarily a place of peace and beauty, with all the character and vibrancy that has come to characterize the Caribbean.

JAMAICAN JERK

Jerking is a special way of cooking meat that was started by the maroons in their hideaways. Originally it was wild hog, shot in the hills, that was cooked slowly in a barbecue sunk into the ground, but now you can buy jerked chicken, sausages and fish. These days there are "Jerk Centers" all over the island, but the traditional home of jerk pork, a very hot and spicy dish, is Boston Bay, near Port Antonio, where you can choose your meal, as it is cooked at a number of roadside shacks.

A safari cruise on the Black River into the mangroves of the Great Morass

SWIMS

On the road between Black River and Bamboo Avenue you will see vendors holding plastic bags of pink "swims"—local shrimps cooked in pepper sauce. Swims are tasty, but the pepper sauce, made from Scotch bonnet peppers, is very hot. The peppers get their name from their shape, said to look like a Scottish highlander's turban.

COFFEE FACTORIES

Blue Mountain coffee is renowned as some of the best in the world. At the Mavis Bank and Silver Hill coffee factories, berries are pulped and fermented to reveal the beans, which are then dried and husked before being bagged for export (much of the crop goes to Japan). Take a formal tour at Mavis Bank, or an informal one elsewhere.

▶▶ Black River

Southwest Jamaica, around Black River, is a little-known corner of the island, where a quiet, rural lifestyle still exists, relatively untouched by the development and tourism of the north coast. The fishing town of **Black River▶** is somewhat run down, although there is still some charm in its old wooden buildings, set up when logwood exports (the source of indigo before synthetic dyes were developed) brought prosperity a century ago. On the **Black River Safari▶▶** (tel: 965-2513), you can cruise along the river itself into Jamaica's largest swamp, where mangroves form a tunnel around you, and you may glimpse herons, egrets, and even crocodiles.

There are a few isolated, usually deserted bays scattered along this coastline. From Crane Beach, just outside the town, the scrubby savannah land extends to the southeast, where lone cows graze attended by white cattle egrets. It eventually reaches **Treasure Beach▶▶**, a lost and lazy settlement set on a superb strip of sand. There is a wonderfully relaxed atmosphere, providing a perfect antidote to the more commercial resorts in the north. Another good beach can be found at Bluefields, to the northwest of Black River.

Inland, north of Black River, the main road skirts the swamp and then leads to **Bamboo Avenue▶▶**, a fine sight which is worth a quick detour. For just over 3 miles the huge bamboo plants form an arch over the road, hanging in graceful bushy curves. Just north of here are the **Y.S. Falls▶▶**, a series of waterfalls and ponds where you can swim. These can sometimes be crowded with tourists, but the falls themselves are stunning.

▶▶▶ Blue Mountains

The heavily forested **Blue Mountains** tower above Kingston, but the pace of life in the small mountain communities there is much slower than the capital. **Ivor Lodge▶▶**, a traditional wooden guesthouse in Jack's Hill (a steep and winding climb, but accessible) offers a magnificent view over the city, ideal for lunch or an early

evening cocktail (tel: 977-0033). You can walk the Blue Mountains, including the 7,400-foot Blue Mountain peak, with guides arranged at the less formal **Maya Lodge►►**, close by (tel: 927-2097). Another great place to head for is higher up: Strawberry Hill, in Irish Town, is an elegant hotel with traditional architecture (tel: 944-8400). You reach it from Papine; at this point the road passes into gorges and steep-sided valleys where fruit and vegetables are grown.

At Castleton, on the road to Annotto Bay on the north coast, botanical gardens dating from 1862 are laid out beside a river; here, guides will show you exotic flora, birds, butterflies, and the ingenious trapdoor spider. There are gardens at Cinchona (reached from Clydesdale), where quinine was once extracted from cinchona trees; other places worth visiting include the World's End Rum Distillery at Guava Ridge, and the coffee factories at Mavis Bank, nearby, and at Silver Hill (see panel, opposite). The Pine Grove Hotel is a good stop for refreshment.

► Cockpit Country

The Cockpit Country lies in the northwest of Jamaica, to the south of Falmouth. This has always been one of the most inaccessible and remote areas of the island, and for years it provided a hideout for the guerilla-style runaway maroons. Its romance lies in its appearance—shaggy, pointed mountains of karst limestone—and in its names. During the maroons era, it was known as the Land of the Look Behind, and had districts such as "Quick Step" and "Me No Sen, You No Come," which were so dangerous that British soldiers would ride back to back on their horses. Even today the Cockpit Country is rarely visited by outsiders, and the few roads that run around it are rough and little used.

The **Appleton Rum Distillery►►** (tel: 963-9215. *Open* Mon–Fri 9–4. *Admission charge*) is a working sugar cane factory and rum distillery that is well worth a visit during the cane-cutting season from January to July. Tours show the newly cut cane being carted around and rolled through crushers to release the juice, which is boiled at high temperatures before being crystallized into sugar using massive centrifuges. There is a restaurant and bar at the distillery.

MANATEES
The endangered manatee is a large marine mammal that occasionally appears on the shores around Milk River and in the river estuary. Also known as the sea cow, it can grow to 13 ft. in length and can weigh up to 310 lb. With its small, rounded tail, front flippers, and tiny, under-developed eyes, the manatee is believed to have been the source of many sailors' tales of mermaids on distant rocks.

149

TREE OF LIFE
The national flower of Jamaica is the delicate, light blue bloom of the *Lignum vitae* tree. Its name means "wood of life," and it is valued for many things; the wood, which was extremely hard, is used to make axle shafts, bowling balls, and even to replace metal ball-bearings, and the resin is used in the treatment of breathing disorders.

A dance troupe in traditional costume in Kingston

▶▶ Kingston

Kingston, the capital of Jamaica, sits on the southern shore of the island, between a huge natural harbor and the Blue Mountains. It is a far cry from the north coast resort towns; Kingston is very much a Jamaican city, whose character is unaffected, in the main, by tourism. Downtown it is a melee of traffic, people, and streetside trade: noisy buses, neatly dressed schoolchildren, stray goats, and vendors touting their wares. There are not many formal "sights" here, nor much left of architectural interest, but with a population of well over half a million, Kingston is a good place to catch some genuine Jamaican life. Unfortunately, this includes a criminal element, as in most busy cities, so be careful when walking around. Avoid garrison towns and ghetto areas like Trenchtown.

The heart of downtown Kingston pulses around the **Parade▶▶**, a bus terminal and market area, where vendors sell every conceivable consumer item from the sidewalks and "busmen"—the good-humored bus ticket collectors—do their utmost to persuade passengers onto their buses, watched over by the stately Ward Theatre and Kingston Parish Church. The **National Gallery of Jamaica▶▶** (tel: 922-1563. *Open* Mon–Fri 11–4:30. *Admission charge*) offers a formal view of the island's art, and then you might visit **National Heroes Park▶▶**, with statues of the leading lights of Jamaican history and Independence (see panel).

Most visitors to the capital stay uptown in New Kingston, a business and residential area with a more relaxed tempo and good restaurants and bars. **Devon House▶▶▶** is a historic oasis in the modern town and it is worth spending time in its atmospheric grounds. The main house was constructed in 1881 in neoclassical style adapted to the tropics, and is open to visitors. Its courtyards contain stores and restaurants (tel: 929-7029. *Open* Mon–Sat 10–5. *Admission charge*). Farther along Hope Road, you pass Kings House, the Governor General's residence, and the **Tuff Gong Studio▶▶** (tel: 927-9152; call for hours. *Admission charge*), where there is a museum to the memory of Bob Marley with his gold and platinum albums on the walls. The **Hope Botanical Gardens▶▶** has an orchid house and a small zoo.

THE NATIONAL HEROES
The Jamaican national heroes, whose statues stand in Heroes Park, are Paul Bogle, a preacher, and George William Gordon, who were both blamed and executed for a rebellion in Morant Bay in 1865; Marcus Garvey, the activist and founder of the Universal Negro Improvement Association, which was so influential among black people in the early part of this century; and Independence leaders Alexander Bustamante and Norman Manley. Nanny, a female maroon leader, has recently joined the ranks of the national heroes.

SPANISH TOWN
Kingston did not become Jamaica's capital until 1872. Before that the capital was Spanish Town, where you can still see the grand old Georgian colonial administrative buildings and courthouse in the main square. In the cathedral there are tablets in the floors and walls dating back to the late 17th century. It is worth the half-day's trip from Kingston by bus or taxi to see these reminders of the past.

Devon House, New Kingston, built by George Stiebel, Jamaica's first black millionaire

Rich and debauched Port Royal earned the names "Gilded Hades" and "the wickedest city in Christendom" in the 17th century, when pirates would sail into town laden with loot and binge until their next escapade. In 1692 the revelry came to an abrupt halt. At about noon on June 7, a massive earthquake struck and the city disappeared under the waves, killing 2,000 people.

Port Royal lies on the tip of the Palisadoes Peninsula, at the mouth of Kingston Harbour. It was fortified by the British in 1655, and became a gathering place for English buccaneers. Soon, this was the Caribbean's richest town; merchants shipped their wares here for onward sale, and buccaneers, hounded from their base on Tortuga, off Haiti, brought their own loot. Taverns (one for every 10 inhabitants) were crowded with prostitutes and men were killed at the drop of a hat. When the earthquake struck, the townspeople thought it was Judgment Day. Whole streets slipped into the bay and ships were flung into the town's remains on a tidal wave. Of 3,000 houses, only 200 were left standing—but the spirit of Port Royal wasn't immediately extinguished; as the dust settled, some of the survivors simply carried on drinking.

After the earthquake, Port Royal was rebuilt, only to be devastated by a fire in 1703. Its remaining residents then moved to Kingston, leaving their town to the navy.

Port Royal today Nowadays Port Royal is a quiet village, reached by ferry from the Kingston waterfront and known for its fried fish and bammy (a flat Jamaican cake made with cassava). Fort Charles, a lumbering stone fortress whose embrasures are still lined with cannons, survived the earthquake, although it sank a few feet (tel: 922-0620). Inside, in quarters where the British Admiral Nelson stayed in 1779, the Maritime Museum, has models of ships and maritime memorabilia (tel: 924-8782). The nearby Giddy House is a Victorian armory that ended up at its weird angle and received its name in 1907, after another earthquake.

LUCKY BREAK
In the graveyard of St. Peter's Church (1725), the story of Lewis Galdy is written on his tombstone: he was "swallowed up in the Great Earthquake," but was disgorged into the sea a few minutes later as another shockwave passed, and kept swimming until he was eventually rescued by a boat. Next to him are buried the remains of three children found underneath a collapsed wall by marine archeologists and who were reburied in 1992.

151

Cannons at the ready at Fort Charles

Jamaica is musically the loudest and the most productive of all Caribbean islands. Folk culture and religious traditions have given birth to a wealth of dance rhythms, and music has a strong element of protest, developed by singers ranging from the "rude boys" of the 1960s to the dancehall singers of today. But this does not restrict the scope of musical life; tune the radio to Irie F.M. for certain proof that Jamaicans can put just about any song to reggae and make it sound good.

MARCHING BANDS
In the British Caribbean there is still a tradition of marching bands, very much in the British military fashion. Musicians dress in suitably formal and colorful tunics, but when marching, rather than keeping to a formal, disciplined style, they swagger and swing their instruments around.

Until 50 years ago, the popular dance rhythm in Jamaica was mento. With its slow, melodic sound and strong lyrics, this was similar to the old calypsos of Trinidad—and, like them, mento had a satirical edge. Ska dance music emerged in the late 1950s, at a time of political upheaval, as Jamaica moved toward independence, and was initially frowned on by the establishment; it introduced "rude boys" and usually delivered a socially conscious message.

Rocksteady, a slower version of the ska rhythm, incorporating a heavier bass riff and stronger vocals, put in a brief appearance in the mid-1960s, but it was soon

Maxi Priest and Shabba Ranks; Shaggy, top

TOASTING
Toasting developed in clubs, as D.J.s sang their quickfire lyrics over popular tunes when introducing records. This rapid, off-the-cuff patter is difficult for the uninitiated to understand, requiring a lightning mind and a good deal of skill. It is hugely popular with club-goers.

superseded by reggae. This immensely popular music combined elements of ska and rocksteady, and its "chaka-chaka" rhythm was given international appeal by bands such as Bob Marley and the Wailers, and Third World.

Reggae has had lasting success, spawning new bands in many other countries, but in Jamaica the music scene has moved on. In the 1980s it adapted rap music to produce "dancehall," a hard and repetitive rhythm overlaid with a heavy rapping voice. The strutting rude boys came to the fore again, headed by D.J.s such as Shaggy and Yellowman, the king of "slack" (vulgar songs). Other singers have begun to sing softer, more melodic songs and culture reggae.

▶▶ Mandeville

The central town of Mandeville is 2,000 feet above sea level, and enjoys a cooler climate than the coast. In imperial days beaches were considered unhealthy and the British colonials would come here for their summer retreat from Kingston. Nowadays the town is the center of a rural (and recently industrialized) area—a far cry from the beach-hustling and resorts of the north coast. There are just a few places to stay, and they have a relaxed and stately (if faded) air.

Mandeville itself was built along the lines of an English country town, with a parish church and a Georgian courthouse facing each other across the grassy common, or green. The colonials would have taken their constitutional walks here, but the green now serves as the bus terminal, and is a focus of chaotic Jamaican life.

On the hills around Mandeville is some of Jamaica's most fertile land; the roadsides are lined with stalls selling all the fruits and vegetables in season: mangoes, oranges, bananas, peanuts, and cashews. Just south of town is **Marshall's Pen▶▶** (by appointment, tel: 962-2260. *Admission charge*), a classic Jamaican mansion surrounded by gardens on what was once a coffee plantation. Built in the late 18th century, the wooden house is furnished in period style. It is possible to arrange bird-watching trips on the estate. On the coast to the south of Marshall's Pen is Lover's Leap, where there is a spectacular lookout. There are also superb views from Spur Tree Hill, southwest of Mandeville.

The region around Mandeville is Jamaica's bauxite mining country. Used to make aluminum, bauxite is a major export, and open cast mines form orange scars across the landscape before being returfed and returned to grazing land. At Shooter's Hill, to the northeast, you can arrange a tour of the Pickapeppa sauce factory (manufacturing a popular spicy sauce); ask when they are likely to be boiling up—this is the best time to visit (tel: 962-2928. *Open Mon–Fri. Admission free*). Milk River, on the south coast, is an old spa town, popular before beach vacations.

Stately Mandeville, once a colonial retreat

JAMAICAN BIRDS
Of the 250 or so birds that spend time in Jamaica (the island is on a migratory route), there are 25 native species. These include the Jamaican owl, with its eartufts and guttural whirring call; the Jamaican woodpecker, black and white except for its red head, the yellow-bellied cuckoo, which can be seen in the Mandeville area; and the Jamaican becard, which suspends its nest from a tree, entering through a hole in the bottom.

CASHEWS
The cashew nut, cultivated in the Mandeville area, grows in a shell at the end of the cashew apple on an evergreen tree. Inside the shell is an oil that can blister human skin and is poisonous if burnt; it must be dried in the sun and roasted to remove the oil before an inner shell can be broken off to reveal the nut. This laborious process is the reason why cashews are so expensive.

Other Caribbean states

154

BEACHES

Many hotels are set on beaches and most of these have watersports facilities. In Montego Bay itself Doctor's Cave Beach is the most popular choice, and tends to get very busy. There is an entry fee, but facilities include changing rooms and bars. Other strips of sand are accessible at Walter Fletcher Beach and Cornwall Beach.

THE WHITE WITCH OF ROSE HALL

The most famous mistress of Rose Hall was Annie Palmer, who lived there around 1820. Her story has no doubt been embellished over the years, but she is said to have murdered three husbands, and had many lovers, including some of her terrified slaves, maintaining her power over them through witchcraft and sometimes killing them when she lost interest. Finally she herself was murdered by one of her lovers who realized he was losing favor with her.

►► Montego Bay

Montego Bay, in the northwest, is the best known of Jamaica's resorts. Mo Bay, as it is known, is a lively town; there are plenty of bars along Gloucester Avenue and some good restaurants, both international and local, set in the old stone buildings and down on the waterfront. The hotels include some of the Caribbean's snazziest, such as the Tryall Hotel and Round Hill: these are not in the town itself, but scattered in coves along the coast to the east and west. There are many package hotels around Montego Bay, but independent travelers will also be able to find cheaper accommodation, particularly on Sunset Boulevard and Queen's Drive, and in the suburbs. Activities in the area include river rafting trips and visits to a number of great houses, which can be arranged by tour operators (see **Travel Facts**).

The heart of Montego Bay itself is **Sam Sharpe Square►►**, where vendors hawk their colored T-shirts, peanuts, and sky-juice (plastic bags of ice crystals with a dash of fruit concentrate) to passers-by. In the corner of the square is the Cage, a jail for errant slaves from the days before emancipation, and a statue of Sharpe himself, a slave leader who was executed after his sitdown strike turned into a full-blown uprising in 1831. Toward the sea from here you will find the **Craft Market►**, with souvenirs, wooden carvings, and straw hats on sale for tourists. North along Gloucester Avenue is **Doctor's Cave Beach►►**, the most popular beach in the town, and another fine Jamaican institution: the **Pork Pit►►**, where you can buy jerked chicken and pork. Tours can be made of the **Montego Bay Marine Park►** (tel: 979-2281. *Open* informal daylight hours. *Admission charge*) in glass-bottomed boats, arranged on the main beaches.

As you leave town heading east along the north coast you pass the Half Moon Club hotel and its golf course and come eventually to **Rose Hall►►►** (tel: 953-2323. *Open* daily 9–6. *Admission charge*), Jamaica's best-known great house. Set in stately gardens overlooking the coast, Rose Hall was built in the 1770s in imitation of British mansions of the period. The grand interior is furnished with antiques, but the guides concentrate on telling you about the house's former mistress, Annie Palmer (see panel). The less pretentious **Greenwood Great House►►** (tel:

Doctor's Cave Beach, Montego Bay; Jamaica's first and best-known public beach

JAMAICAN DOCTOR BIRD
The doctor bird, or the red-billed streamertail, is the Jamaican national bird and one of the prettiest hummingbirds. As its name suggests, it has a red bill; the male's chest is a shimmering fluorescent shade of green. In flight it displays a pair of back tail feathers about three times as long as its body.

SEAFORD TOWN
Seaford Town, south of Montego Bay, looks like a normal Jamaican town but has an unusual history. Lord Seaford granted the land to German settlers who came here to farm it in 1835, and their blond descendants can still be seen. A similar experiment involved importing Indian laborers to Little London on the south coast, near Savanna-la-Mar; they, too, were absorbed into the local community and culture.

155

965-1077. *Open* daily 9–6. *Admission charge*) stands on a hill about 5 miles beyond Rose Hall. Built the same period, it was owned by the family of the poet Elizabeth Barrett Browning. But perhaps the most attractive plantation house is **Good Hope▶▶** (tel: 954-3289), which has a wonderful view over the fertile Jamaican lands. It is a hotel, but can be visited for the day.

Beyond the town of Falmouth is the Martha Brae river; rafting trips start upstream at Rafter's Village (tel: 952-0889; cost of raft tour includes cocktail). At Rock, a phosphorescent lagoon glitters at night when disturbed.

Heading west from Montego Bay, the road skirts the bay itself and heads for the area of Reading, passing hillsides dotted with expensive villas. Beneath them is Catherine Hall, where the Bob Marley Performing Centre hosts the annual reggae gathering, Reggae Sunfest. The Barnett Estate is a working plantation with a wonderful stone and wood estate house that dates from the mid-1700s (tel: 952-2382. *Open* Mon–Fri 9–4. *Admission charge*). From here the coast road leads to Negril, passing on its way the mouth of the Great River, where you can take a river rafting trip (by torchlight at night), and the hotels at Round Hill and Tryall, with its golf course.

Turn south at Reading and climb immediately into the hills. Near Anchovy is the delightful **Rockland Bird Sanctuary▶** (tel: 952-2009. *Open* 2–5. *Admission charge*), best visited from 3:30 PM on. Set among fields of banana and citrus, **Belvedere Plantation▶▶** (tel: 952-6006. *Open* Mon–Sat. *Admission charge*) has re-created a village from the last century, displaying various trades, and a fascinating herb garden. There is also a garden walkway along the river with labeled plants. **Croydon in the Mountains▶▶** is worth visiting for a view of a working plantation where they grow coffee, pineapple, cocoa, and bananas.

Bob Marley shot to international fame in the 1970s, popularizing reggae and rastafari across the world. Although he had the toughest Jamaican roots, Marley was awarded Jamaica's highest public honor, the Order of Merit, and his legacy remains in hundreds of songs, which are still played all over Jamaica.

TUFF GONG
The Tuff Gong Studio was bought by Marley as his home and recording studio in 1976. Set on Hope Road in New Kingston, an uptown area of Kingston, it is a far cry from the shanties of Trenchtown. Tours of the studio show the gold records awarded for Marley's top-selling discs and video recordings of Marley performing his songs.

Robert Nesta Marley was born on February 6, 1945. Deserted by Norval Marley, her white Jamaican husband, Marley's mother, Cedella, raised Nesta in Nine Miles village, in the parish of St. Ann's, on Jamaica's north coast. When he was a youth they moved to the poorest shanty area of Kingston, and he worked as a welder.

Determined to succeed as a musician, Marley formed "The Wailing Wailers" in the early 1960s with Bunny Wailer and Peter Tosh. Together, they typified the "rude boy" image and found popular success with over 30 ska songs; but, having made little money, the band split up and Marley had to turn to welding again to make a living.

The 1970s finally brought financial success and the new Wailers were signed by Island Records. By this time Marley had become a rastafarian and the band began

MARLEY MAUSOLEUM
Bob Marley's mausoleum, in his home village of Nine Miles, is a site of pilgrimage to many fans and can be toured. Prepare for a mild onslaught of high-pressure selling, but it is interesting to see the small house and the tomb itself, which is decorated with memorabilia important to the great singer.

playing reggae. The album *Catch a Fire* hit the international charts and was followed by *Natty Dread*, *Exodus* (the best-selling album of all), *Kaya*, and *Uprising*.

By now a world-famous celebrity, Marley emigrated from Jamaica after an attempt on his life, but returned in 1978 to stage the One Love Peace Concert, in which he persuaded Prime Minister Edward Seaga and opposition leader Michael Manley to make a gesture of unity against the gangland wars which were then plaguing the island.

Bob Marley died of cancer at the early age of 36 on May 11, 1981. His body was laid to rest in a mausoleum at Nine Miles in St. Ann's (see panel).

▶▶▶ Negril

The town of Negril lies at the far western tip of Jamaica and, more than any other place on the island, typifies the Jamaican image of a hedonist's hideaway on an idyllic beach. Sunset-watching has been a hallowed pastime here since the 1960s, when the village was adopted as a home by hippies. Since then Negril has been discovered by tourists; there are large hotels on the beach and people are bussed in daily to watch the sunset from Rick's Café. But the old laid-back life still exists, and it is still possible to escape the crowds. There is not much to see in Negril—but then that is hardly the point of the town. You can expect to be hustled there—but then who could resent a vendor who arrives by canoe bearing a briefcase, or who greets you by massaging your leg with aloe?

Negril divides neatly into two halves: the beach and the cliffs. If there is a town center it is at the rotary, from where the road runs inland toward Savanna-la-Mar. To the north, the road reaches Montego Bay, alongside **Long Bay▶▶▶**, one of Jamaica's best beaches—5 miles of superb sand with hotels and beach bars (try Cosmo's at the top end) scattered along it. Beyond Hedonism II, on the point, is **Bloody Bay▶▶**, which takes its name from the days when whalers used to clean their catch here. Behind the beach is the Great Morass, a mangrove swamp that can be visited by boat to see wading birds.

South of the rotary, the coastal road of Negril's West End winds its way along the clifftops, where there are small hideaway hotels, guesthouses and bars (try the L.T.U. bar or Kaiser's and the more "jet-setty" Xtabi and Rock House). The cliffs are not very high—although they might seem so to people about to jump off into the sea, a tradition in some bars. Negril has a number of outdoor music parks where you can sometimes hear big Jamaican bands. At the southern end of Negril is the 100-foot **lighthouse▶** (*Open* daily 9–6. *Admission free*), which has good views of the surrounding area.

CALICO JACK
The infamous pirate Jack "Calico" Rackham (named for his penchant for calico underwear) was captured in Negril in 1720 and executed. With him were two women pirates, Mary Read, and Anne Bonney, who was pregnant and escaped execution, and said of him: "If he had fought like a man he would not be dying like a dog."

157

A sunset cruise off Rick's Café on the cliffs of Negril

Other Caribbean states

ACKEE AND SALTFISH

Ackee and saltfish was once a hardship food, but has now achieved the status of national dish. Ackee is the fruit of a tree that originates in Africa. Its red pods must ripen and open naturally before the lobes of yellow flesh can be taken out and boiled (otherwise it is poisonous). When cooked, ackee looks and even tastes rather like scrambled egg. Saltfish (salted cod) was the cheapest high-protein food available in the 18th century, imported to feed slaves. It has since become expensive, but this has not lessened its popularity.

COLUMBUS IN TROUBLE

After exploring the coast of Central America on his fourth voyage, Columbus was stranded with his crew when his ships sank in St. Ann's Bay in 1502. The island's inhabitants, the Arawaks, agreed to feed the explorers, but after an altercation withdrew their aid. Columbus managed to change their minds again by calling on God to take away the moon, knowing that a total eclipse of the moon was due. Eventually, as there was no sign of rescue (a ship from the Santo Domingo settlement sailed away leaving the unpopular Columbus behind), two members of the crew took a canoe and braved the seas between Jamaica and Hispaniola to fetch a ship and collect the stranded sailors.

▶▶ Ocho Rios

Halfway along the north coast, Ocho Rios is Jamaica's second biggest resort town. As in Montego Bay, the resorts are scattered for several miles on either side of the town, which itself stretches along the seafront and has become a much-frequented vacation spot for Kingstonians. Ochie, as it is affectionately known, is well provided with beaches, watersports, and entertainment; there are expensive resorts and some cheaper hotels, and a clutch of lively bars can be found on James Avenue, near the center of town. The main beach is the Ocho Rios bay public beach directly beneath the twin skyscrapers on the seafront; to the west of Ocho Rios there is a good strip of sand at Mammee Bay. Many excursions can be made into the surrounding countryside, making this a popular cruise ship destination.

The town centers around the clocktower, where cars and buses, market vendors, and the occasional goat vie with one another for supremacy. There is nothing much to see in Ocho Rios itself, but Jamaica's best-known tourist attraction, **Dunn's River Falls▶▶** (tel: 974-2857. *Admission charge*), lies to the west of town. The falls are a remarkable sight, as the river cascades over limestone outcrops, dropping steadily nearly 660 feet. Most people start at the bottom and climb through the lips and falls, pausing occasionally to swim in the pools (bathing suits are essential and sneakers are recommended). The falls are popular with tour buses and tend to be crowded with tourists; souvenirs are sold at the end of the climb.

Farther along the coast road to the west of Dunn's River Falls are a number of small towns and occasional hotels in an isolated bay. **St. Ann's Bay▶** is the birthplace of black activist Marcus Garvey. There is not much to detain you here, but spare a moment to think of

Tourists climb up Dunn's River Falls, Ocho Rios

Christopher Columbus, who was forced to spend over a year here waiting for rescue when his ships sank (see panel). Close by is the site of Jamaica's first Spanish settlement, Seville Nueva, restored as an archeological park.

The road south from Ocho Rios climbs immediately into the hills. **Coyaba River Gardens▶▶** are festooned with flowering bushes and trees set among streams and ponds. The **Shaw Park Botanical Gardens▶▶** (tel: 974-4568. *Open* daily 8:30–5. *Admission charge*) also make an interesting tour of tropical plants and lily ponds. The main road to Kingston then passes into **Fern Gully▶▶**, a deep cleft in the hills. The route runs past impressive scenery: huge ferns and trees clamber up the walls and hang over the road, blocking out the light and keeping the gully cool.

Heading east from Ocho Rios along the coast, you cross the White River, offering daytime rafting trips and torchlit night excursions with dinner included; these can be arranged at hotels. **Prospect Plantation▶** (tel: 974-2058. *Admission charge*) is a working plantation where native fruit and vegetables, including soursop, cocoa, tamarind, and ackee (see panel), are grown, and trees (bearing plaques) were planted by celebrated visitors including Winston Churchill and Charlie Chaplin. It can be toured either by tractor-drawn carriage or on horseback. **Harmony Hall▶▶** (*Open* 10–6. *Admission free*) is an art gallery set in a restored house, exhibiting works by Caribbean artists. At **Irie Beach▶▶**—not actually a beach, but a gulley inland where a river cascades over small falls into rockpools—you can swim and sit in the sun.

About 15 miles farther on—past Goldeneye, the house of James Bond's creator, Ian Fleming (which can be rented as a villa)—is **Firefly▶▶▶** (tel: 997-7201. *Open* 8:30–5. *Admission charge*), where Noel Coward lived until his death in 1973. The house itself is simple, the few furnishings and musical scores still as Coward left them, but the most spectacular feature is its view, extending for miles along the north coast as far as the Blue Mountains. Inland from Port Maria is **Brimmer Hall Plantation▶▶**, a working estate growing a range of fruit and vegetables.

Relaxation at the northeast resort of Ocho Rios

MARCUS GARVEY
Marcus Mosiah Garvey was a black activist during the early 20th century. His aim was to help Africans and their descendants improve their situation in a white-dominated, colonial world. Through his Universal Negro Improvement Association he built up a massive following in the Caribbean and the U.S., keeping in touch with the organization's branches throughout the world by means of its newspaper, *Negro World*. Garvey died in relative obscurity in Britain, but in 1964, his bones were brought back to Jamaica, where he was proclaimed the first Jamaican national hero.

Other Caribbean states

BEACHES

Set against the backdrop of the John Crow Mountains, the beaches around Port Antonio tend to be steep-sided coves, but there are pleasant strips of golden sand in the area. Be careful of currents—the sea can become rough when onshore winds are blowing. There are good beaches at Winifred and at Boston Bay, and Frenchman's Cove is often deserted. Although not a beach, the Blue Hole is a favorite spot: a stunningly blue sea pool with edges fringed by palm trees (*Admission charge*).

Street scene, Port Antonio: red roofs and telegraph poles

BANANAS GALORE

The banana trade made Port Antonio rich at the turn of the century, reaching its heyday in the 1920s. The fruit was brought down the Rio Grande on bamboo rafts, to be shipped out to the U.S. When Errol Flynn bought Navy Island in Port Antonio harbor in the late 1940s he popularized the use of these rafts for pleasure; it has since become a staple of a Jamaican vacation.

▶▶▶ Port Antonio

The northeast is a little-known corner of Jamaica, but one of the most rewarding. Although there are hotels here, the area is distinctly less commercial than the big resort towns on the north coast. Small rural communities are dotted along the steep slopes of the John Crow Mountains, which tumble down to the coast. The scenery is fertile and unspoiled; nature quickly reclaims any human invasion, with fences becoming hedges and telephone wires covered with vegetation in no time.

Port Antonio itself is a charming town with an easy, relaxed pace, set between mountains and a magnificent double harbor. The few streets of clapboard houses have become a bit run down since the decline of the town's prosperity, which flowed from the banana industry early this century, and then from its brief reign as Jamaica's most exclusive resort in the 1950s, when the likes of Errol Flynn and Bette Davis were frequent visitors.

There is a fine panorama of the town from the Bonnie View Hotel. Beneath it, behind the harbor, is the oldest part of town, with stone buildings such as the courthouse and parish church; beyond is the Point, with beautiful old wooden town houses. Just off the Point is Navy Island, once owned by Errol Flynn; his former residence is now a hotel. Not far southeast of town are Athenry Gardens, with walkways and labeled plants, and Nonsuch Caves, illuminated caverns festooned with stalactites.

East of the town, beyond the Blue Hole (see panel), is **Boston Bay▶▶▶**, the home of jerk, which is freshly cooked at roadside stalls. The **Sam Street African Art Museum▶▶**, inland of Long Bay, has fine exhibits; 6 miles farther south are **Reach Falls▶▶▶**, some of the island's prettiest and normally free of tourist buses.

Inland from Port Antonio, Berridale marks the start of the river-rafting trip on the **Rio Grande** (tel: 993-2778. *Open* 8:30–4:30. *Admission charge*) (two per raft; transportation is provided from the Rafter's Rest, on the river mouth). You descend gradually through magnificent, fertile scenery punted by a raftsman with a bamboo pole. The road then climbs farther into the John Crow Mountains and leads to **Moore Town▶**, an old maroon settlement; visits can be arranged by the Port Antonio tourist office (City Centre Plaza, tel: 993-3051). Walking tours in the hills above Port Antonio are offered by Valley Hikes (tel: 993-2543).

The word "rasta" tends to conjure up a picture of musicians dressed in red, gold, and green, and sporting hydra-heads of dense dreadlocks. But the picture is a misleading one. In Jamaica, most of the rastafarians live quiet, religious, often reclusive lives and rarely set foot in tourist-dominated towns.

Rasta beliefs first emerged during the 1930s in the poor ghettos of west Kingston as the religious crystalization of anti-colonial, black consciousness movements. Although it has often been sensationalized and misunderstood, rastafari is still a Judeo-Christian-inspired faith, and many believers carry bibles and go to services.

Rastas have no central church, but there is a system of recognized beliefs common to all followers. According to the rastafarian interpretation of the Bible, Ras (prince) Tafari is a divine incarnation, believed to have taken earthly form as the Emperor Haile Selassie of Ethiopia. To rastas, Africans are God's chosen people, and some look ahead to eventual black supremacy. Ethiopia is believed to be Zion, or heaven on earth—a belief linked with the "back to Africa" movement. Other countries, particularly Jamaica (to which blacks were forcibly brought to atone for their ancestors' sins) and white nations, are regarded as Babylon, or hell on earth.

True believers lead simple, austere lives, rejecting the trappings of modern Western life. They eat "ital" (from "vital" or natural), mostly vegetarian foods, and usually prefer herbal remedies to Western medical treatment. Most rastas wear their hair uncut and uncombed, in long, thick "dreadlocks," and most regard smoking marijuana, or "ganja" (illegal in Jamaica) as a sacred activity.

Rasta beliefs have been obscured as the following has become internationally known; many of the famous Jamaican reggae stars adopted the faith, and to the West it became associated with messages of militancy and ganja-smoking. Unfortunately, the trappings of the movement have been hijacked in the Caribbean by small-time opportunists and hustlers, who don rastas' clothing and are known as "wolves" or "dreads."

LION OF ZION
Haile Selassie was known as the "Lion of Judah"; as a proud, African animal, the lion is often used in rasta art. The lion's mane is taken to symbolize a full head of dreadlocks, and followers will consciously emulate the lion's slow, proud bearing.

161

Rasta craft market in Montego Bay

GANJA
Marijuana was introduced into the Caribbean by agricultural workers from India, who arrived as indentured laborers (on contracts to work the canefields) after the abolition of slavery in the 19th century. Smoked in a "chalice," and believed by rastas to bring wisdom, the leaf has several names, including ganja, cully weed, holy herb, and wisdom weed.

Sunrise at Cayman Brac

The Cayman Islands

Thousands of visitors fly down to the Cayman Islands for reliable sun and sand and the finest diving seas close to the mainland U.S., and the islands are well geared up to receive them. The Caymans' successful tourist industry is supplemented by the offshore finance sector; the islands' status as a tax haven and the presence of numerous millionaires has given the 32,000 Caymanians the highest average per capita income in the Caribbean—although many islanders have menial, low-income jobs.

The Cayman Islands are formed by limestone caps of submerged mountain peaks, rising 25,200 feet from the valley floor. These three British-dependent islands have distinctly different atmospheres. They lie to the northwest of Jamaica, separated into two groups. Grand Cayman, the senior island and site of the capital, George Town, is 20 miles by 7½ miles and is busy, commercial, and flat. It is also by far the most developed island of the three. About 85 miles to its northeast are the twin cays of Cayman Brac (with a population of about 1,500), and Little Cayman (which has only about 70 people), offering some of the region's best fishing.

The development of a tourist industry has only just begun here. All three islands are generally dry and scrubby, with areas of swamp, and lie very low in the water, but for all their unattractiveness above the waterline, they have some of the most impressive underwater sites and marine life in the Caribbean.

There are a number of scuba operations on the islands, diving mainly off the walls—vertical underwater drops clustered with coral—in the north and west of Grand Cayman. If you are not a diver, you can see the corals from the Atlantis Submarine (tel: 949-7700), which offers reef trips some 120 feet down near George Town.

Tourism has mainly taken hold on Grand Cayman along Seven Mile Beach, where bars and restaurants stand shoulder to shoulder among the many hotels, and from where there is an excellent view of the sunset most days. You can dine extremely well here, in chic restaurants, but there are also fast food chains and rib joints.

From Mondays to Saturdays, bars and clubs provide plenty of nightlife, and there are shows in the hotels and a couple of places to dance. Cayman Brac and Little Cayman are, on the other hand, very peaceful and quiet, and their inhabitants, like those of Grand Cayman, are generally known as some of the most easy-going people in the Caribbean.

A Cayman Islands totem pole

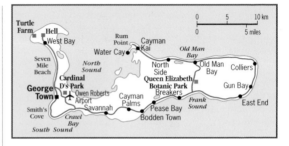

BEACHES

Seven Mile Beach is an archetypal Caribbean beach with perfect golden sand that shelves gently away to the west. The water is calm on this protected side of the island, and there are magnificent sunsets. All kinds of watersports are available here, from water-skiing to parasailing; the only problem is that it is sometimes pretty crowded. Caymanians tend to go to Smith's Cove, an inlet between the coral rocks to the south of George Town. Other beaches that are worth exploring include Cayman Kai and Water Cay, on the north coast.

GRAND CAYMAN This is the largest and most developed of the Caymans, and it is here that you will find the capital and the only real town, George Town, a small collection of wooden and concrete buildings on the waterfront in the protected southwest of the island. Its quiet streets come alive with the arrival of cruise ships and during the annual festivities, the Batabano carnival (April) and Pirates' Week (late October), when choreographed hordes of swash-bucklers carouse there. The **Cayman Islands National Museum▶▶** (tel: 949-8368. *Open Mon–Fri 9–5, Sat 10–2*) set in a traditional Caymanian building, is run by the National Trust and has excellent displays illustrating the islands' history and natural life. It includes an interesting section on the old seafaring traditions with artifacts found both on land and in the sea.

Life for most visitors to Grand Cayman is centered on Seven Mile Beach, which is heavily built up with hotels and condominiums along its (strange, given its name) 5½ mile length. Here you will find the liveliest bars and restaurants. In their prosperity, the Cayman Islands have been swamped with satellite dishes, big cars, and other trappings of North American culture, but as the tourist development thins out to the north and farther afield in the east, you will occasionally see the neat, wooden buildings of the old-time Caribbean: the white clapboard houses with their pink or blue shutters and shingle tiled roofs, set in carefully tended gardens blooming with hibiscus and bougainvillea.

Swimming with stingrays off the Cayman Islands

In West Bay, north of Seven Mile Beach, **Hell▶** is a pitted and scorched terrain of worn coral limestone (postcards mailed here will have the postmark Hell). At the **Turtle Farm▶** (*Open 9:30–5. Admission charge*) you can learn how turtles lay their eggs by crawling up onto the sand and burying them in a hole dug with their back flippers, but this is a sad place, where the animals are cooped up quite severely. About 5 percent of the turtles bred every year are released into the wild however, but turtle products may not be taken into the U.S.A. The route to the east of George Town passes Owen Roberts airport on its way to the eastern end of the island. **Cardinal D's Park▶** is a small zoo with Caribbean and other animals. Beyond here the island is undeveloped except for a few houses and isolated hotels The award-winning **Queen Elizabeth Botanic Park ▶ ▶** (tel: 947-9462. *Open* daylight hours) has a path through the Cayman forest. with signs showing the different plants.

Local straw craft in the making, Cayman Brac

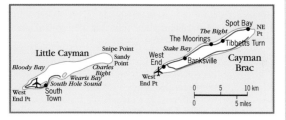

LITTLE CAYMAN AND CAYMAN BRAC The other two Cayman Islands, both thin and each about 12 miles long, lie tip to tail some 85 miles to the northeast of Grand Cayman. The channel in between them may not look dangerous but it is, in fact, a treacherously deep stretch of water. It is possible to arrange day trips by airplane to both Cayman Brac and Little Cayman. Cayman Brac takes its name from the "brac" or cliff at its eastern end, the highest point in the Caymans (a princely 148 feet). There are just 1,500 Brackers and they have a reputation for their friendly hospitality. Cayman Brac has a **museum▶** (tel: 948-2622. *Admission free*) (in Stake Bay) and a few stores, but generally it is as sleepy today as it has been for the last 100 years. Apart from the people and the opportunity to do nothing in warm surroundings, the best reason for going to Cayman Brac is the coral, where superb dive sites and snorkeling grounds can be explored around the western tip of the island. There are only five hotels on Little Cayman, offering diving and fishing facilities (around Bloody Bay, the reef wall drops off at a depth of 20 feet). The island is home to hundreds of birds, including magnificent frigatebirds, whose males puff up their red throat sacs to massive proportions in display.

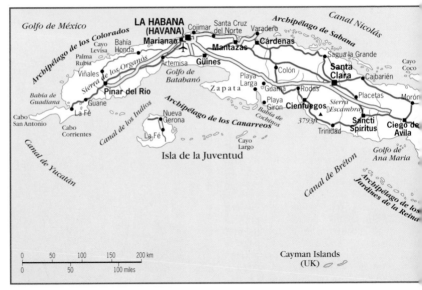

Golfo de México

LA HABANA (HAVANA)
Cojimar Santa Cruz del Norte Varadero Archipélago de Sabana Canal Nicolás
Marianao Cárdenas
Mantazas Sagua la Grande Cayo Coco
Archipélago de los Colorados Cayo Bahía Levisa Honda Palma Rubia Viñales Sierra de los Organos Artemisa Güines Colón Santa Clara Caibarién
Golfo de Batabanó Playa Larga Rodas Placetas Morón
Babía de Guadiana Pinar del Rio Zapata Guama Cienfuegos Sierra Escambray
Guane La Fé Archipélago de los Canarreos Playa Girón Bahía de Cochinos 3793ft Sancti Spiritus Ciego de Avila
Cabo San Antonio Cabo Corrientes Nueva Gerona Trinidad
Canal de los Indios La Fé Cayo Largo Golfo de Ana Maria
Isla de la Juventud Canal de Brèton Archipélago de los Jardines de la Reina
Canal de Yucatán

0   50   100   150   200 km
0   50   100 miles

Cayman Islands (UK)

166

Cuba

An extraordinary, enigmatic country, Cuba is strikingly different from other Caribbean islands—a place of revolution, violence, and hardship; but also a beautiful land where ancient and modern exist side by side.

Havana (La Habana), Cuba's capital, is less than 100 miles from Florida's Key West, but its proximity belies the political gulf between the two countries. Before the 1959 Revolution, 90 percent of visitors to Cuba were from the U.S. Today, U.S. citizens are forbidden to spend their dollars in Cuba; only excursions for scientific or research purposes are permitted, although many U.S. tourists now travel there from countries such as Canada, Jamaica, and Mexico. U.S. citizens wishing to travel in Cuba should contact the Dept. of Treasury, Washington, D.C. 20220 (tel: 202/376-0410).

Cuba lies at the gaping mouth of the Gulf of Mexico and is the largest of the Caribbean islands, a snake-like 777 miles long, though never much more than 75 miles wide. Much of the fertile, agricultural land is covered in sugar cane. There are three mountain ranges: in the west, the karst formations of the Sierra de los Organos, whose red earth is covered with tobacco plants; the Sierra de Escambray, halfway along the island; and the Sierra Maestra, in the island's eastern province, which includes Pico Turquino (6,580 feet),

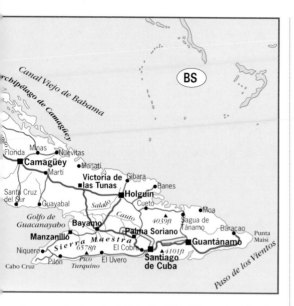

CUBAN COCKTAILS
Two of Cuba's best-known cocktails were favorites of Ernest Hemingway and he was supposed to have had a saying: "My mojito in the Bodeguita, my daiquiri in the Floridita" (the Bodeguita del Medio and El Floridita are long-established Havana restaurants). A mojito is made with rum, sugar, fresh mint leaves and Angostura Bitters (from Trinidad). It is then shaken with ice and strained into a glass. A daiquiri is also based on rum, which is blended with cane sugar and fresh fruit, so that it comes out as an ice-cold, crystalline sludge. A Cuba Libre, named soon after the Revolution, consists of rum on ice with the juice of a lime, topped with cola (a version of which the Cubans still produce).

where revolutionaries hid in the 1950s. The entire island is ringed with around 4,000 miles of sandy beaches, coral cays, islands, and large, secluded bays.

Even without American visitors, Cuba lays great emphasis on tourism. It has to, in order to bring in much-needed hard currency—especially now that financial support from the former U.S.S.R. has dried up. Europeans and Canadians flock here for inexpensive vacations; Havana and Santiago de Cuba, the second city, are now linked by air to many European capitals, including London.

HISTORY Cuba was Columbus's second landfall in 1492, and for the next four centuries Spanish adventurers arrived here expecting to make their fortunes. They decimated the indigenous population, replacing them with African slaves, who worked the prosperous sugar plantations. Over the years the slaves mingled with Spanish colonists to form today's mixed Cuban race. During the 16th and 17th centuries, "New World" treasure flooded into Spain via Havana, which quickly became the richest city in the Caribbean.

Spanish colonization gave way briefly to British rule; then the U.S. took control of the island until, in 1902, Independence was declared. In the early 1940s, Americans began to exploit Cuba and its cheap labor. The island played host to thousands of visitors from the U.S., and a wide variety of entertainments and diversions became available, ranging from privately organized gaming casinos to explicit shows. Havana's streets were the setting for extortion, illicit alcohol distribution, trade in narcotics, and prostitution. The state, under the dictatorship of Fulgencio Batista, exploited tourism at the expense of the Cuban population and the country.

Embittered Cubans, led by Dr. Fidel Castro, rose up against the Batista regime but were incarcerated on the Isla de Pinos (renamed the Isla de la Juventud after the Revolution) in 1953. On their release, Castro and the

Main square, Trinidad, Cuba

REVOLUTIONARY ART

There are no billboard advertisements in Cuba, but revolutionary posters are an art in themselves —brightly colored and featuring famous Cuban faces or working scenes. Some rail against the "Yankee Imperialists" of the United States; others show Fidel and other state heroes, such as José Martí, the poet and journalist who was killed soon after taking arms against the Spanish in 1895, and the Argentinian Che Guevara, encouraging the Cubans to fulfill their social duties.

revolutionaries undertook military training in Mexico, joined by the Argentinian doctor, Che Guevara. In 1956 they sailed to Cuba on the *Granma* and hid in the Sierra Maestra, with a band of guerillas which at one stage numbered only 12. Their following grew, as soldiers deserted Batista to join the rebels. Batista fled Cuba on January 1, 1959, and the revolutionaries took control. Castro defeated a U.S.-sponsored invasion at the Bay of Pigs in 1961, and in 1965 he made the Communist Party of Cuba the island's sole legal political party.

STAYING IN CUBA Accommodations can vary dramatically. The most popular and largest of Cuba's beach resorts is Varadero beach, in Matanzas Province, east of Havana, but there are quieter resorts around the coast, such as the Hotel Colony on Isla de la Juventud, an offshore island in the southwest. Most hotels are mid-range resorts, but luxury resorts such as the Paradiso in Varadero have risen on many beaches. Many resort hotels are joint investment ventures between Cuba and Argentina, Brazil, Canada, Germany, Spain, and France, and meet high standards. Cuba's own hotels and casual accommodations, however, leave a lot to be desired, as Cubans are restricted by a lack of facilities and supplies.

ISLAND SIGHTS AND ENTERTAINMENT The world-famous Varadero beach, Havana's East Beaches, Santa Lucia beach, and Guardalavaca and Daiquiri beaches are just some of Cuba's many seaside resorts. On the offshore cays, such as Cayo Sabinal and Cayo Coco, facilities are provided for reef snorkeling and diving trips. The most

PLAYA GIRON
PRIMERA DERROTA
DEL IMPERIALISMO
EN AMERICA
LATINA

AFTER THE REVOLUTION

For the average Cuban, life improved after the Revolution. Medical care and education became available to all and starvation became a thing of the past. At the same time, Castro established a one-party constitution, and political dissenters were simply locked up. Castro, usually known as Fidel, was a popular figurehead and to some extent he still is, though most of his population cannot now remember what life was like before the Revolution.

popular cay is Cayo Largo, off Cuba's southern shores, a coral island resort whose air links from Varadero make it an easy day's excursion. Beyond the beaches, Cuba offers some of the Caribbean's most historic areas. The Old Town of Havana is 2 square miles of cobbles, colonnades, and Spanish colonial palaces, some dating back to the early 16th century. In the south of the island is the "living museum" of 16th-century Trinidad, which recently joined Old Havana as a U.N.E.S.C.O. World Heritage site.

Although gambling is now forbidden in Cuba, it still has a lively entertainment scene, including renowned shows such as Havana's 50-year-old Tropicana and a rival nightclub on the outskirts of Santiago de Cuba city.

A good central highway and a 150-year-old railroad run down the spine of the country, and there are over 18,000 miles of roads. Facilities for car rental and chauffeur-driven cars are good, but expensive; cars available include V.W.s, Scania, Nissans, and Mercedes Benz. Cubans still drive 1950s American cars—when gas is available—and ox-carts, horses, and bicycles are common alternatives.

The cars driven by Cubans are a curious leftover from pre-Revolution days, when the island was almost an offshore state of the U.S. Dating from the 1950s—the last time Cubans were allowed to buy, or could afford, privately owned cars—these magnificent, fin-tailed beasts are adorned with a great expanse of chrome on their bumpers and fittings, and are cared for lovingly.

Domestic flights link most large towns and the Varadero beach resort, which is also joined by a highway, to Matanzas in the south. Flights within Cuba are not expensive and are generally easily booked. Independent travel is possible except in restricted areas, though it can be difficult to find meals outside resorts and accommodations can be basic. However, new lodges and camp sites, Cubatur's helpful guides, and use of tourist buses and trains have made independent touring a realistic option.

ISLAND LIFE The Cuban currency, the peso, is rarely seen by tourists, as the U.S. dollar is the most readily accepted currency. Cuban Tourism Bond Notes, or coupons, are also circulated in resort areas, as well as specially minted coins. Dollar-only stores stock everything from bikinis to toothpaste. Seeing the best of the scarce resources reserved for tourists has understandably caused resentment among Cubans, for whom life is very hard, although Cubans with dollars are now permitted to shop in them, too. Hustlers are appearing in larger numbers, and visitors should be particularly careful with their belongings in Havana and Varadero. Rationing has now reached a point where many people simply do not get enough food. Electricity is restricted and fuel for private vehicles is hard to find. Even the much-vaunted services of health care and education are under threat through lack of resources. Real progress is unlikely while the U.S. embargo continues, and, for its part, the Cuban Communist Party has shown little inclination to change. Since the embargo has loosened a little, however, things have improved slightly.

For all their difficulties, the 11 million Cubans are a lively nation, whose Latin Caribbean character shines through in their rhythmic music. It is well worth attending an evening at a *casa de la trova*, where professional musicians play in competition with one another; and in July each year the Cubans drop everything for *Carnaval*, a weekend of dancing through the streets.

169

TROVA
The trova is a special Cuban ballad which, like many Caribbean songs, has an element of social comment. Trovas are as likely to celebrate a national hero or take a swing at corruption in the Communist Party as they are to sing of love. The name "trova" is derived from the Provençal *trobar* (to compose)—as is the word troubadour, used to describe the medieval romantic poets of Languedoc.

A Cuban country house

Wrought-iron balconies, vantage points for viewing the streets in Old Havana, above; the baroque 18th-century cathedral, right

THROUGH THE KEYHOLE
It is always worth taking a look inside the buildings, both public and private, in Havana, if you can see or find your way through the front door. There may be glimpses of superb inner courtyards, with arched colonnades on each story, constructed so that the sunlight and heat did not penetrate into the rooms. Others have elaborately decorated stairways or beautiful, fan-shaped stained-glass windows.

▶▶ Havana (La Habana)

The modern city of Havana, on the north coast of Cuba near the western end of the island, has radiated outward from the earliest colony, which was settled on the western shore of Havana harbor in 1514, and is now made up of four distinct districts: Old Havana, Central Havana, Vedado, and Miramar.

Even in its dilapidated state, there is a charmed feel about **Old Havana▶▶▶**. Its tight alleys and cobbled squares, colonnades, and colonial palaces built in coral rock are strikingly beautiful compared to the present-day city's high-rise hotels. Old Havana's finest square is the Plaza de la Catedral; the 18th-century baroque cathedral sits on its northern side, flanked by the Museum of Colonial Art, the El Patio restaurant and the Postal Museum. Grass-roots capitalism has emerged in various guises in Havana, including the appearance of a colorful and interesting arts and crafts market just off the Plaza de la Catedral.

Hemingway's favorite Bodeguita del Medio restaurant is near by, as is the grand Plaza des Armas, which was originally the parade ground, with its imposing Palace of the Captain Generals. Also on the Plaza are the City Museum, the Flota House bar, a statue of Manuel Cespedes (who was a 19th-century Independence leader), and the classical-style El Templete portico, built to celebrate the first mass on Cuban soil. Just off the square, the Castillo de la Fuerza is Cuba's oldest fortress (1544), whose roof is topped by the city's symbol, the tiny golden statue of La Giraldilla. Numerous cannons, which were recently excavated near the ancient city walls, now surround the fortress.

To the west, Old Havana is bounded by the Paseo de Martí, an avenue giving easy access to the Memorial Museum, the National Museum (containing many old masterpieces), the ornate Garcia Lorca Theater, and the Capitol (a copy of Washington, D.C.'s). Overlooking Old Havana, across the port entrance, is the 16th-century fortress of El Morro, now a museum and restaurant.

Heading north through the open Parque Central, you emerge into the 19th-century Prado, a broad boulevard with a raised promenade where Habaneros sit and pass the time of day. Close by is the old Presidential Palace, an eclectic building of columns and balustrades, which now houses the Revolutionary Museum. This displays photographs, guerilla maps, and stirring revolutionary memorabilia. Outside, military hardware on show includes tanks, planes, and Castro's invasion boat.

Along the seafront, the 2-mile Malecon, a promenade where young Habaneros gather on summer evenings (and where *Carnaval* is staged), leads west to the modern districts of Havana, including Vedado. At the head of La Rampa, a bustling business street, stands the Havana Libre Hotel, built in the 1950s as the Hilton. The Bar Turquino, on the top floor, has a magnificent view of the city. South of here are the stately buildings of the City University and finally the open Plaza de la Revolucion, where a statue of national hero José Martí stands beside a huge concrete column constructed in the shape of a communist star. Political rallies are held here, and often draw up to as many as 500,000 people.

To the west of the square is the Cementerio Cristobal Colon (the Columbus Cemetery), with an impressive collection of magnificent mausoleums with exquisite stone carving—definitely not to be missed! Elsewhere, there is a wealth of galleries, museums, and palaces. A visit to the Casa de las Americas gallery, which exhibits contemporary Latin American art and craft, and has regular recitals and theatrical events, is particularly worthwhile—and Havana's excellent ice cream should be tasted at La Coppelita park on La Rampa.

HEMINGWAY'S ISLAND

Ernest Hemingway lived in Cuba during the 1940s and 1950s and he set two of his novels on the island: *Islands in the Stream* and *The Old Man and the Sea*, whose story supposedly takes place in the village of Cojimar. Two restaurants in Old Havana were particular favorites of his: the riotous Bodeguita del Medio on Calle Empredado, and the more formal and stately Floridita on Calle Obispo, where you can try some of the best lobster in the Caribbean. Hemingway lived in the suburb of San Francisco, in a hillside house called La Vigia, now open to the public. He was a keen deep-sea fisherman—a marina west of Havana bears his name.

171

THE BAY OF PIGS

The Bay of Pigs (Bahia de Cochinos) was catapulted into the headlines in April 1961 when on 1,400 Cuban exiles staged an invasion of the island, partially backed by the U.S., in order to oust Castro and his revolutionaries. It was a military fiasco and most of the exiles were rounded up within a couple of days. In Cuban revolutionary lore it was written up as the first great defeat of imperialism on Latin American soil. Castro declared Cuba communist a couple of days later.

An old West Indian legend tells of large Cuban women rolling the world's finest cigars on their thighs. Whether or not this was true, the reality nowadays is rather less picturesque, although it is still intriguing to watch Cuban cigars being rolled by hand, cut with large metal blades and pressed in antique wooden vices.

Tobacco, a bright green plant with long, oval leaves, grows on many Caribbean islands for use in cigarettes—but only Cuba and the Dominican Republic have cigar industries. The finest Cuban tobacco, reserved for its cigars, grows in the northwestern province of Pinar del Rio, where the earth is thick and deep red, and the leaves grow with a minimum of starches and sugars. Dotted around the neat tobacco fields are drying houses, with wooden walls and palm-thatch or aluminum roofs, where the leaves are cured for up to three months after picking.

Once dried, the leaves are sorted according to age—older leaves have a stronger flavor but younger leaves are more elastic and better for rolling—and are bundled off to the factories. While one factory worker sits at the head of the room, reading aloud from a newspaper, the others sit at long tables, placing "binder" leaves in their hands, laying tobacco filler (the offcuts of the last rolls) on top and then making the first, skillful roll. Each cigar is then pressed in a vise to give it the correct shape. One half of the strong, evenly colored "wrapper" leaf is then rolled around it, and finally the cigar is trimmed. After the manufacturer's bands have been slipped on, the cigars are packed in boxes, between leaves of aromatic cedar wood, for export.

Some of the most famous cigar manufacturers are based in Cuba, including Monte Cristo, Partagas, Romeo y Julietta, H. Upmann, and Davidoff. Within Cuba, cigars are remarkably cheap and factory tours can be arranged through Intur or Cubatur. Due to sanctions against the Communist regime, Cuban cigars are illegal in the U.S.

EARLY SMOKERS
Columbus was the first European to see Indians smoking tobacco, which is indigenous to the Americas. Twisted leaves would be wrapped in dried palm leaves or maize husk and smoked by Mayan Indians during religious ceremonies. The Mayans believed tobacco to be medicinal, and the word "cigar" is derived from their own term for smoking, *sik'ar*. Tobacco quickly gained popularity in Europe, where, in the 17th century, smoking was a sign of great wealth.

CIGAR TYPES
The traditional Cuban cigar is a corona, which measures about 6 in. and has straight sides, with one rounded and one cut end. The corona chica has the same shape, but is about 4 in. in length. Ideales are slender and torpedo-shaped, tapered at the lighting end, as are the smaller bouquets. Panatellas are thin and cut open at both ends; a cheroot is even thinner.

OUTSIDE HAVANA West of Havana is Pinar del Rio Province, the home of the finest Cuban tobacco. It takes a good day's drive to see the neatly ranged fields of bright green tobacco plants and thatched drying houses. There is a museum of tobacco in Pinar del Rio itself, as well as a number of cigar factories that are said to sell the best cigars in Cuba. Around Viñales the landscape is punctuated with strange karst "haystack" hills, known in Cuba as *mogotes*. Pinar del Rio contains an attractive selection of neoclassical houses, and a rum factory renowned for its wild guava-flavored rum, Guayabita de Pinar. Also worth seeing is the cathedral of San Rosendo, and the **Museo de Ciencias Naturales Sandalio de Noda▶** (*Open* Mon–Sat 8–2), which houses a collection of geological and natural history exhibits.

UNEASY LEASE
Guantanamo, a remote, easterly province, is a curious anomaly, in that there is a U.S. naval base there, on Cuban sovereign land. It was arranged on a lease in 1902, but since the Revolution the Cubans have refused to accept the nominal annual payment of $5,000.

Cienfuegos traffic

173

North of Pinar, the charming small town of **Vinales▶** is located amid the *mogotes* of the Sierra de los Organos, in an area that has been declared a national monument. Just over a mile west of town, a mural painted by Lovigildo Gonzalez, a disciple of the great Diego Rivera, can be seen; 3–4 miles north, look for the Cueva del Indio, a lovely Indian cave that can be toured on foot or in a boat. Catch a boat at Palma Rubia to get to Cayo Levisa, part of the Archipelago de los Colorados, offering a long, sandy beach with good snorkeling and scuba-diving around a reef that parallels the beach.

Hemingway aficionados might want to visit **Cojimar▶**, the village where he set his tale *The Old Man and the Sea*. Hemingway himself fished from Cojimar, and his International Fishing Tourney originated there, although it now takes place at the Hemingway Marina near Havana.

To the east of Havana is Cuba's best resort town, **Varadero▶**, where hotels and restaurants stand on the Peninsula de Hicacos' 12 miles of powder-like sand. Windsurfing and parasailing can be arranged here, and there are lively evening bars, including the Cueva del Pirata, a discotheque set in a cave. There are also museums about Cuban history and the indigenous Tainos.

The museums' themes can be further explored at the **Cueva de Ambrosio▶▶** (*Open* Tue–Sun 10–noon, 2–4. *Admission charge*), a cave containing dozens of Indian drawings discovered in 1961. Look for the cave between the Marina Chapelin and the Marina Gaviota toward the north end of the peninsula. Varadero has its share of hustlers and prostitutes, who tend to congregate toward

MONCADA GARRISON
The Moncada Garrison in Santiago, is honored in revolutionary lore as the place where Castro made his first strike against the Batista regime. On July 26, 1953, 130 young rebels assembled to the east of the city, and although some were unarmed, launched an attack. Militarily, it was a dismal failure; most were rounded up as they tried to escape, and many were killed. The survivors received long prison sentences. Moncada is recalled on the black and red party flag in the insignia "M-26-7," and July 26 has been made a national holiday.

BOTANIC GARDENS
About 10 miles east of Cienfuegos is the Jardin Botanico de Cienfuegos (*Open* daily 8–6. *Admission charge*), part of an old sugar plantation. The gardens are devoted to medicinal plants, fruit trees, orchids, bamboos, and a great collection of palm trees. It was founded by plantation owner Edwin F. Atkins in 1901.

the south end of the resort area. The international hotels can be found farther north, and the very north end of the peninsula has been designated park area and is to be left undeveloped. In general, Varadero offers a fine beach vacation, but it is totally isolated and has more in common with a typical Caribbean beach resort than with the rest of Cuba.

On the south coast beneath Varadero is the swampy Zapata Peninsula, site of the infamous Bay of Pigs invasion in 1961, and now of the Bay of Pigs Museum and a number of tourist resorts. Farther west, through the sugar flats, is the pretty town of **Cienfuegos►**, one of Cuba's major ports, where interesting buildings include the 1870 neo-Gothic Catedral Purisima Concepcion, the **Thomas Terry Theater►** (*Open* daily 9–6. *Admission free*) on the Parque Martí, decorated with an exquisite painted ceiling of muses and Cuban writers , and the Moorish-influenced Valle Palace, a decorative art museum on Punta Gorda. On the west side of Parque Martí, visit the Palacio de Ferrer, now the **Casa de Cultura Benjamin Duarte►►** (*Open* daily 9–6. *Admission charge*), a ca1894 building, and climb the tower for wonderful views.

The southern slopes of the Sierra de Escambray tumble into the sea around the town of **Trinidad►►►**. Founded in 1514 by Diego Velázquez, Trinidad was a successful shipping town in the early 19th century and has been restored to its former grandeur. The cobbled central square, Plaza Martí, one of five main squares, has beautiful colonial Spanish buildings painted yellow and complemented with bougainvillea blooms, as well as two museums: the **Museo de Architectura Colonial** (tel: 3208. *Admission charge*) and the **Museo Romantico** (tel: 4363. *Admission charge*). Next door to the Museo Romantico is

An interior in Trinidad's Museo Romantico

Trinidad's premier cathedral, the **Iglesia Parroquial de la Santisima Trinidad**►►► (*Open* daily 11:30–1, 7:30–8, mass daily 9–10 PM, tourists not allowed), built between 1817 and 1892. The largest church in Cuba, it is famed for its acoustics. Other city museums include the **Museo de Arqueologica Guamuhaya**► (tel: 3420), overviewing pre-Columbian to post-conquest times, and the **Museo de Lucha Contra Bandidos**► (tel: 4121), on the revolutionary campaign in the Escambray Mtns. The Casa de la Cultura (*Open* daily 7 AM–11 PM) on Calle Zerquera has a gallery and store; the Casa de la Trova (*Open* Mon–Sat 10 PM till the early hours) offers open-air concerts on Calle Marquez, with singing on Sunday afternoons.

The fishing village of La Boca lies just 5 miles from Trinidad; you'll pass through en route to the beach at Playa Ancon, which features lovely turquoise water, good diving 300 yards offshore and a couple of resort hotels. To the east, the ruined Torre de Iznaga is an old watchtower built to oversee slaves in the sugar cane fields.

Cuba's second town, **Santiago de Cuba**►►, commands a stunning position on a vast south-coast harbor, near the east end of the island. In the shadow of the great Sierra Maestra mountains, this city's cathedral is the oldest on the island (1514). Conquistadors Hernando Cortez and Diego Velázquez lived in the 1520 mansion on Cespedes Park, in Santiago's center. In all, the city has 14 museums, of which notable examples are the Bacardi Museum, a reminder of the rum family's origins (they moved to the Bahamas after the Revolution, and eventually to Puerto Rico), and the Museum of Carnival.

Casa de Cultura in Cienfuegos

175

Santiago has a more ethnically mixed population, having been the first Cuban city to receive slaves; French colonists fleeing Haiti's insurrection in the 18th century also arrived at Santiago, as did many migrating Jamaicans. Much of the city is organized around Cespedes Park, most prominently the recently renovated Hotel Casa Grande on the east side, and the cathedral **Santa Iglesia Basilica Metropolitana**► on the south side (*Open* daily 8 AM–12 PM). Northeast of the center lies the Plaza de la Revolucion, dedicated to the 19th-century Cuban revolutionary General Antonio Maceo. The park is dominated by a bronze statue of the general on horseback surrounded by iron machetes, as well as a galvanized steel monument to the revolution.

Santiago's architecture is eclectic, offering everything from neoclassical to Art Deco. The pastel-hued buildings are in better shape than those in most Cuban towns. The Cementerio Sant Ifigenia, northwest of town, contains Jose Marti's mausoleum; inside, a statue of Marti—surrounded by six statues of women meant to represent 19th-century Cuba's six provinces—has been positioned to receive a shaft of sun all morning.

If you have a car, take the coastal road along the Sierra Maestra, checking out the deserted, black sand beaches. High points include **El Uvero**►, about 40 miles west of Santiago, with a small museum commemorating an early battle in the revolution; and **Pico Turquino**► (reached via a turn-off 13 miles west of El Uvero), the highest peak in the Sierra Maestra at almost 6000 feet. The road continues to Pilon; in the 1950s, Castro's revolution began in this area, and there are numerous sites devoted to those days.

EL COBRE

About 6 miles west of Santiago lies El Sanctuario de Nuestra Senora de la Caridad del Cobre, or "El Cobre," the shrine to Cuba's patron saint, built above a copper mine. There's a legend attached, but more compelling is the idyllic setting in the Sierra Maestra. To get there will cost around $10 by hired car from Santiago.

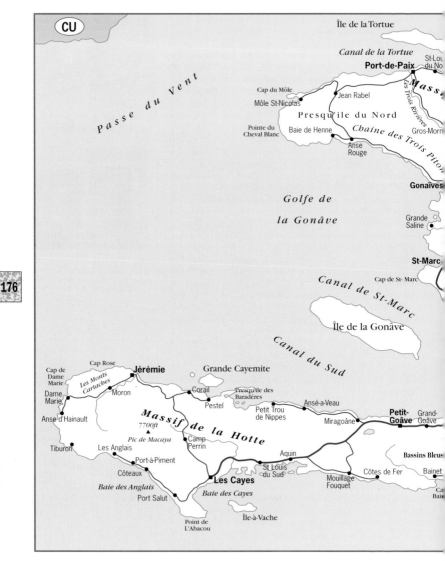

Haiti

Only 30 years ago, Haiti's excellent beaches, sophisticated hotels, and proximity to the U.S. made it one of the area's top vacation destinations. Since then, however, the political situation has become tense, with outbreaks of violence. Instability is the norm, and Haiti cannot be recommended as a tourist destination at present. When things calm down again, by all means go. Few countries contain such striking contrasts of devastating poverty and luxurious lifestyles, hardship and hope. Travel there is a bombardment of the senses: the primitivist art, adorning buildings, walls, and vehicles; the cramped, brightly painted buses and trucks, called *tap taps* (after the noise

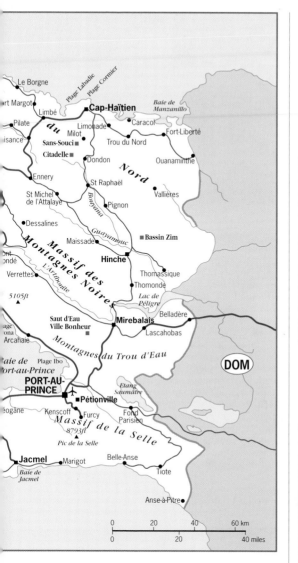

Le Borgne
rt Margot
Pilate
isance
Limbé
Cap-Haïtien
Baie de
Manzanillo
Limonade
Milot
Caracol
Fort-Liberté
Sans-Souci ■
Citadelle ■
Trou du Nord
Dondon
Ouanaminthe
Ennery
St Raphaël
Vallières
St Michel
de l'Attalaye
Pignon
Dessalines
Maissade
Bassin Zim ■
ont
ondé
Verrettes
Hinche
Thomassique
Thomonde
5105ft ▲
Lac de
Péligre
Saut d'Eau
Ville Bonheur ■
Belladère
Mirebalais
Lascahobas
age
ona
Arcahaie
Montagnes du Trou d'Eau
DOM
aie de
ort-au-Prince
Plage Ibo
PORT-AU-
PRINCE
Étang
Saumâtre
Pétionville ■
eogâne
Kenscoff
Furcy
Fond
Parisien
Massif de la Selle
8793ft ▲
Pic de la Selle
Jacmel
Marigot
Belle-Anse
Baie de
Jacmel
Tiote
Anse-à-Pitre

0   20   40   60 km
0   20   40 miles

177

*Crowds in the streets of
Port-au-Prince*

made by the original trucks), with their carved wood and
religious maxims displayed along the sides, and scenes
from the Bible on the hoods; the strange world of voodoo;
and the ceaseless hubbub of the markets. Love it or hate it,
there is nowhere in the world like Haiti.

This is not an easy island for travelers. White visitors are
particularly targeted with constant demands for money,
from people who are genuinely in dire need. Haiti's currency is the gourde (five gourdes make a *dollar haïtien*),
named for the large, hard-shelled fruit of the calabash tree
and introduced by the country's despotic leader, Henry
Christophe, in the early 19th century.

Most flights from Europe and the U.S. go to Miami for
connections to the main airport at the capital, Port-au-
Prince. Haiti's capital lies in the southwest, in the deep

Other Caribbean states

A multicolored tap tap

TOUSSAINT
Toussaint l'Ouverture is
the principal hero of
Haitian independence. A
former slave, he joined
the rebels in 1791 as a
doctor, but soon became
one of their military leaders because of his skills
on the battlefield. After
defeating French, British,
and Spanish armies, he
took over the whole of
Hispaniola. His success
provoked Napoleon
Bonaparte, who sent an
army to reclaim the
colony. Its commander,
Leclerc, lured Toussaint
into talks and took him
captive. Toussaint was
shipped to Europe and left
by Napoleon to starve and
freeze to death in prison.
As he was deported, he is
reputed to have said: "In
overthrowing me, they
have cut down in St.
Domingue the trunk of the
tree of black liberty. It will
shoot up again through
the roots, for they are
numerous and deep."
A couple of years later,
the population rebelled
and France lost the
colony forever.

*Religious and
nationalist graffiti,
Port-au-Prince*

bight of the Golfe de la Gonâve. It is a buzzing city of over
one million inhabitants, many of whom live in the shanty
towns that cluster around the main town. There are good
places to stay in Pétionville, the prosperous suburb above
the capital, well priced now in their faded grandeur, not
forgetting the beach hotels on the Côte des Arcadins
about an hour north of Port-au-Prince. There is also a
clutch of good restaurants.

Haiti occupies the western third (10,715 square miles) of
the island of Hispaniola, which it shares with the
Dominican Republic. "Haiti," the original Amerindian
name for the island, meaning "mountainous land," is an
accurate description. Shaped like a crab's claw closing
round the Golfe de la Gonâve, it is about 90 miles from
north to south and has two long mountainous ranges that
stretch west like pincers toward Cuba and Jamaica. The
highest peak is the Pic de la Selle (8,795 feet), in the southeast. The country is generally fertile and there is a variety
of scenery: good palm-backed beaches (the closest to Port-
au-Prince are Ibo beach and Kyona; Cormier and Labadie
are found outside Cap-Haïtien); cactus-covered plains,
and huge, rainforested mountains. However, in a country
of around 6 million mainly rural inhabitants, deforestation and soil erosion have now become a serious problem.

HISTORY Haiti has a history of turmoil. The first 40
European settlers, left there in 1492 by Columbus, all died
within a year. In 1697 the French were handed control of
western Hispaniola (then called
Saint Domingue) by the
Spanish, and made it an
immensely wealthy colony,
exporting sugar, coffee, and
indigo. At the end of the 18th
century, after years of torture
and starvation at the hands of
their colonial masters, the
African slaves finally rebelled,
led by Toussaint l'Ouverture.
In 1804 Haiti declared itself
independent—the world's first
black republic. Its political life
since then has been troubled:

civil war between the mulatto south and the black north was followed by a succession of tyrannical leaders and U.S. invasion in 1915. The Americans left in 1934, and in 1957 François Duvalier, "Papa Doc," became the ruthless dictator, maintaining his grip on power through the notorious secret police, the *tontons macoute*. His son, Jean Claude ("Baby Doc") continued the reign of terror and corruption until, in the mid-1980s, a movement of revolt known as Operation Deschoukay drove him out of the country. Haiti has continued to suffer political instability with a series of coups d'états and failed elections. Democratically elected President Jean-Bertrand Aristide was ousted in 1991, but then returned to power with the help of an American peacekeeping force in 1994.

ISLAND LIFE Ordinary islanders, most of whom work on the land, have suffered the consequences of corrupt and repressive government, and Haiti is now the poorest country in the western hemisphere. The majority of its population is descended from Africans; many of the small and powerful "mulatto élite" emigrated during recent troubles. French is the official language, and its influence can be heard in the everyday spoken language, Kreyol.

Haiti has an amazingly vibrant artistic and religious life. Its primitive-style art, with primary colors and almost cartoon-like forms, has been copied all over the Caribbean. Many of the traditional themes of Haitian life are portrayed, including agricultural, biblical, and voodoo scenes. Voodoo itself is a mix of Catholic and African beliefs, often sensationalized as "black magic," and running deep in the Haitian psyche. Haiti has its own dance rhythm—compas—which fills the streets during Carnival, from January 6 to Mardi Gras, before Lent. This is the best time to witness the extraordinary spirit of the Haitians, which survives despite years of insecurity and hardship. When stability returns to Haiti, it will hopefully resume its deserved place among the most interesting Caribbean destinations.

THE BLACK JACOBINS
One of the far-reaching effects of the French Revolution was to bring to a head the tensions of Haitian society in the late 18th century. Political rights, granted in theory to the mulatto population by the French National Assembly, were denied within the colony, and violence erupted. In 1791 the black population, who had suffered appallingly as slaves to the white colonists, themselves rebelled, and the country was split between the southern mulattos and the northern blacks (where Toussaint l'Ouverture rose to prominence). The story of Toussaint l'Ouverture and the Haitian revolution is told in C.L.R. James's powerful book, *The Black Jacobins*. Published in 1938, this was an influential work at a time when British West Indians were re-assessing their history and turning their minds toward Independence.

179

Fishing off the north coast town of Cap-Haïtien

Voodoo calls up sinister images: candle-lit cere-monies of dancing, chanting, and mesmeric drum rhythms; initiates in trances flailing around, intoning predictions, eating hot coals, or making animal sacrifices. There is an ele-ment of truth in these images, but voodoo should not be written off as "black magic." Widely misunderstood outside Haiti, voodoo has a deeply rooted role in everyday island life.

DUPPIES

Duppies, also known as jumbies, are the wander-ing souls of the dead. People who die unhappy or without a proper wake are said to become rest-less spirits, returning to haunt those who knew them in life. Belief in dup-pies is widespread, and even educated people who otherwise disregard obeah will acknowledge their existence.

180

Haiti is not the only island where voodoo is practiced. Other forms of the religion exist elsewhere: santería, across the border in Santo Domingo and in Cuba; poco-mania, in Jamaica, and shango, in Trinidad. In these parts of the Caribbean, however, the beliefs are gradually dying out, while in Haiti voodoo continues to touch every-one's life, and was particularly prevalent in the days of Papa Doc, who made himself a high priest of voodoo.

Like a number of the Caribbean systems of belief, voodoo has mixed African and European origins. All have a common theme in their appeals to spirits to intervene in life on earth. Spirits, or lwas, are summoned, in drum-ming and dance, to "mount" a follower, who then falls into a trance, taking on the spirit's characteristics, danc-ing and speaking in tongues or making predictions. The

A voodoo ceremony, by Gérard Valcin

ZOMBIES

There is evidence in Haiti of people turned into zom-bies ("undead" souls) while still alive. A poison is believed to reduce their metabolic rate so that they appear dead.
After burial, they are supposedly exhumed, revived and then used as slaves.

worship of spirits was originally brought by slaves from Africa and merged with Caribbean beliefs and Catholic saints. In Haitian voodoo the snake god Damballa, who makes his followers dance in a writhing motion, is equiva-lent to St. Patrick, often pictured with snakes at his feet; Ogun, the god of war, whose followers appear to be bran-dishing swords, is associated with St. James, and Erzulie is equated with the Virgin Mary. Like the angels of the Christian pantheon, lwas can be benevolent or vengeful. They come to advise, but they must also be appeased. If times are hard it is because the lwa is displeased. *Rada* lwas, such as Erzulie, are known for their wisdom and benevolence; *petro* lwas, like Tijan Petro, for their power.

Voodoo ceremonies are conducted according to a calendar, which includes important Catholic events; for example, devotees celebrate the appearance of the Virgin Mary at the Ville Bonheur waterfall near Mirebalais on July 16 each year. Here devotees, particularly those with problems of love, come to wash themselves in *Saut d'eau* (waterfall) in order to receive the blessing of Erzulie and the Virgin Mary. The usual setting for a ceremony is a village temple with a mud floor, a *hounfort*, and the ceremony proceeds under the direction of a *houngan* (priest) or a *mambo* (priestess). After recitations from the Catholic liturgy, the drums strike up with the special rhythms of the lwa to be invoked. An initiate then traces on the ground the lwa's *véver*, a complex pattern of lines laid out with cornmeal. Eventually a dancer is mounted by an lwa and exhibits his or her characteristics, either making predictions to the community, giving advice or making demands. The lwa will be presented with its favorite food or drink and eventually there may be an animal sacrifice. Followers who have been mounted apparently remember nothing after the event.

It is almost impossible for visitors to Haiti to attend a genuine voodoo ceremony, but occasional shows are held with commentaries; contact Le Péristyle de Mariani, on the outskirts of Port-au-Prince.

Obeah Another feature shared by all the Caribbean beliefs is the use of obeah, or magic, known as *myal* in the British Caribbean and *wango* in Haiti. Obeah men (*bocors* in Haiti) act as advisers and intervene in human affairs through the use of incantations and spells. These may be used to heal a sick person, to ensnare a lover or to settle a score; they may also rid a person of a vengeful duppy (ghost). Spells are set with herbal concoctions and other ingredients, such as blood, sweat, eggshells, and broken bottles. Obeah was outlawed in Jamaica as early as 1760, but it is still practiced widely, though secretly, in rural areas all over the Caribbean region.

THE DRUMS OF VOODOO
The driving force behind every voodoo ceremony is the drumming, which engenders a trance and summons a particular lwa. There are three drums of different sizes, each one carved of mahogany; and each lwa has its own particular drum rhythms.

OTHER RELIGIONS
Besides the revivalist sects of pocomania and Revival Zion, Jamaica has many spirit-based religions. Kumina is a religion with less European influence than most— probably because it arrived relatively recently, brought by free Africans who came willingly to Jamaica after emancipation in 1838. Kumina appeals to its own zombies, the spirits of ancestors, as well as to the gods of the Congo, its followers' original homeland. Convince is a faith that appeals to the African *bongo* gods and to the spirits of the maroon leaders (see panel, page 147), as does Kromanti. There are similar sects in Trinidad (the Shouters) and in St. Lucia (the Kele).

A ritual mask, which is worn by men taken over by female spirits

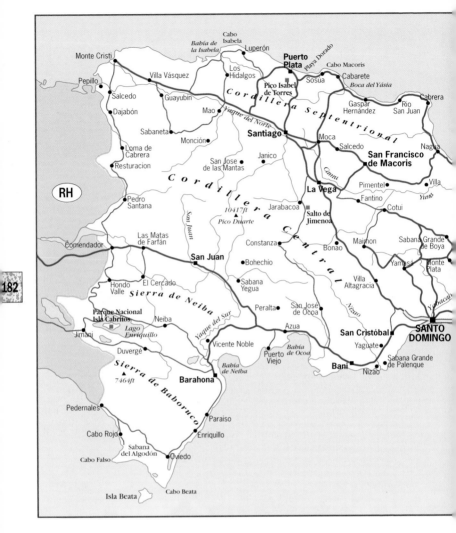

RH

182

The Dominican Republic

The country Columbus called "the fairest land under heaven" is home to the oldest European settlement in the Western Hemisphere, but the Dominican Republic has two modern faces. Its glorious beaches, fascinating colonial heritage, and mountain-top "resorts" contrast sharply with the grinding poverty of many of its islanders. With its 3,300-mile shoreline, the Dominican Republic has one of the largest tourist industries in the Caribbean. Most of its hotels are mid-range beach-front resorts, scattered in complexes along the northern and eastern shores, but other options include the luxury Casa de Campo—where polo ponies can be rented—or a hotel in Santo Domingo's historic colonial city. The island also has quiet, isolated resort towns, such as Cabarete and Las Terrenas, where you can relax in guesthouses under the

QUISQUEYA

Quisqueya was the name used by the indigenous Taino for their island when Columbus arrived in 1492. It is still used as a poetic name for Hispaniola, but principally survives as the name of a locally brewed beer. (Presidente is a lighter and slightly more bitter but tastier local beer.)

SANTERIA

Just as the Haitians have voodoo (see page 179) and the British Islands have obeah, so the Latin islands observe santeria, which is a mix of African animist beliefs and Catholic doctrine. There are the same drum-driven ceremonies, animal sacrifices and possessions, as well as witchcraft practitioners, who use local plants and other small objects to make their concoctions.

palm trees, or windsurf till you drop. The Dominican Republic is one of the cheaper and better value package tour destinations in the Caribbean, and it can be easily reached from the U.S. and Canada, both by scheduled and charter flights. Cruise ships from the U.S. stop at Puerto

Carvings set up for sale at a Dominican Republic market stall

"Mexican night" at the Playa Dorado restaurant

Plata. There are charter flights from Europe, although if you are travelling independently you may have to go via Miami or via Spain. Despite the million or so annual visitors to the island, the tourist industry is surprisingly

unobtrusive once you have left the fringe of hotels running along the coast. In contrast to many of the islands in the Caribbean, which are visibly affected by the industry, the Dominican Republic is large enough to allow independent travel and to maintain a lively local Latin culture. In September 1998 Hurricane Georges hammered the southeastern half of the country, and many hotels throughout the Republic were closed for periods from a week to several months. Most were open by Christmas, and the Dominican Republic Tourist Board reports that every hotel in the island was back in business by Easter 1999.

One of the best places in the Caribbean to immerse yourself in history is the colonial city in Santo Domingo, the oldest city in the Americas, which enjoyed its heyday in the 16th century when conquistadors came here to plan their voyages to the American mainland. Nowadays you can relax in the bars and restaurants with no fear of being arm-twisted into an invasion force. This is a Latin American island, full of surprises. Merengue music is heard everywhere; if you get on a bus, you might find the passengers singing along. Islanders gather on the plazas in the late evening to take in the cooler air; and they love to dance, so the clubs are always popular meeting places.

LA ISABELLA

Santo Domingo was not the first of the "New World" towns. La Isabella, named after the Spanish queen, was settled by one thousand willing adventurers in 1493 on the explorer's second voyage. The site is near Luperon on the north coast, but there are only archeological remains now. The colonists moved to Santo Domingo's present site in 1498 because La Isabella, set among malarial swamps, was unhealthy, and riches beckoned after gold was found nearer Hispaniola's southern shore.

The Dominican Republic forms the eastern two-thirds of the island of Hispaniola—a contraction of *La Isla Española*, as Columbus called it when he landed in 1492 (Haiti forms the western third of the island, ceded to French rule by the Spaniards in 1697). At 18,765 square miles, it is the second largest country in the Caribbean after Cuba; geographically, it is the most extreme. Topping the massive Cordillera Central, Pico Duarte (10,420 feet) is the tallest mountain in the West Indies, and in the southwest, Lago Enriquillo is a lake set in the lowest point of land, 114 feet below sea level. It encircles arid, thorny islands that serve as a protected sanctuary to exotic birds and reptiles, such as the flamingo, the iguana, and the indigenous caimen (a kind of crocodile).

In the north there are rampantly fertile mountains with crashing rivers; in the south, on the Barahona peninsula, there is desert. The greater part of the country has seemingly endless stretches of bright green hillsides and cane fields, spiked with magnificent royal palm trees.

ISLAND LIFE The 7 million or so Dominicans are of mixed African and European blood, with a strong Amerindian influence, dating from the early days of colonial settlement and recognizable in many Dominicans' distinctive straight, dark hair. This is a desperately poor nation; its poverty is particularly evident in the countryside and on the outskirts of the main towns, where many people live in makeshift shanty flats. The limited public services break down regularly (big hotels have their own power plants). Since there is no social safety net, life can be

DOMINICAN DISHES
Comida Criolla, or Creole food, as local dishes are known, includes a wide range of meats: beef, farmed by *campesinos* (cowboys) in the southeast, pork, goat (*chivo*), and chicken. These are served in rather heavy but tasty dishes such as stew, *sancocho*, which is made with a variety of meats, and *mondongo*, made with tripe. Seafood and fish are popular, as are many tropical vegetables, including plantains and cassava.

185

Fruit-sellers lay out their wares on the roadside in a Dominican Republic market

Windsurfers at the luxury resort of Casa de Campo

FRESH FRUIT MILK SHAKES

Dominicans use their fruit to the best advantage in freshly prepared drinks. *Jugo* is plain squeezed fruit juice served with ice, but the best drinks are *bastidas*, squeezed fruits whisked up with milk and ice. Flavors include *pina* (pineapple), *china* (orange), *lechola* (pawpaw), and *guanabana* (soursop).

MERENGUE

The national rhythm of the Dominican Republic is the merengue, a strongly Latin and impossibly quick beat. You will hear it played by local string bands and in the clubs, where dancers exercise their elastic legs, racing across the dance floor in a close embrace. There is a merengue festival in Santo Domingo each year, in the third week of July, when bands and dancers fill the streets.

extremely hard for the islanders, some of whom endeavour to escape to the U.S. The journey is a notoriously dangerous one, however, which many undertake in inadequate, leaking boats.

The Dominican Republic throws the contrasts of Caribbean tourism into the sharpest relief. With so many prosperous tourists passing through, opportunists have inevitably come to regard them as walking dispensers of dollars, and outside the tourist complexes you will probably be hassled for money. There is considerable prostitution—"sex tourism" has now become an established trade in some places—and unsurprisingly there is an increasing incidence of A.I.D.S., so the risks to all parties are abundantly clear.

The Dominican Republic has a troubled political tradition, which has hit ordinary Dominicans hard. Throughout the 19th century, control of the island lurched from one ruling power to another, as Spanish, Haitians, Americans, and Dominican independence fighters battled for supremacy. Independence finally came in 1844, but the country soon fell into the hands of despots, and slid into bankruptcy.

The U.S. sent troops to administer the country between 1916 and 1924, to a mixed reception from islanders, who longed for stability but resented military rule. In 1930 General Rafael Leonidas Trujillo, the Dominican army's commander, established a ruthless dictatorship, ruling the country for the next 30 years as his personal estate, organizing the "disappearance" of thousands of opponents and rifling through the treasury.

Trujillo was assassinated in 1961, and there followed a series of coups, civil war, and military intervention by the U.S. Elections were held in 1966 and won by Balaguer, who is now a blind octogenarian. Dr. Leonel Fernandez, current president of the Dominican Republic, came to office in 1996.

▶▶▶ Altos de Chavón

Altos de Chavón is near the eastern town of La Romana, attached to the Dominican Republic's premier resort, the huge and luxurious Casa de Campo. The "Heights of Chavón," standing high above the Chavón river, are a pretty replica of a medieval Spanish hilltop town. The village has a slightly unreal feel, for the 30 or so coral-rock houses are so obviously imitations. But many parts of the village are festooned with colorful bougainvillea blooms, making this a pleasant and satisfying place to spend an afternoon or evening. It is partly an artists' colony, so shopping here for crafts and art in the galleries and workshops is a treat. Hurricane Georges hit hard here: Casa de Campo was closed for repairs for almost three months.

As well as the museum of Native American history, there are good restaurants and bars. The attractive church of St. Stanislaus can be visited and there is an amphitheater where concerts are staged. Singers have included Julio Iglesias and Frank Sinatra, who sang for the inaugural concert. There are also fabulous views of the Chavón river valley, particularly when it is lit up at night. Buses connect Altos de Chavón with Casa de Campo.

▶▶ Cordillera Central

The Cordillera Central is the Dominican Republic's highest and most strikingly beautiful mountain range, which runs through the center of the country from the northwest down toward the capital. It contains the highest mountain in the Caribbean, the Pico Duarte (10,420 feet). Reaching the summit takes three days. Start at the town of La Ciénaga. Make sure to take a guide and all the food you need for the trip. Although the lower mountains are covered in beautiful royal palm trees, the pine-clad heights are tall enough to have frost; the steep and fertile valleys (where distinctly un-Caribbean fruits such as strawberries and apples prosper) are cut by cold waters from the mountains above. The towns of Constanza and Jarabacoa are cool hillside retreats, popular with visitors from the capital, who regard them as an ideal escape from the hotter zones down below. Look for the waterfalls of Aguas Blancas 12 miles from Constanza, and the 100-foot Jimenoa Falls near Jarabacoa.

NEW COMMUNITIES
As well as the community of German and Austrian Jewish refugees who were granted sanctuary in Sosúa on the north coast in the 1930s (see page 188), Trujillo invited a community of Japanese farmers in the 1950s, offering them land in return for passing on their farming skills. Some of their descendants still live and work around Constanza.

187

Tourist accommodations and tropical greenery: the north coast resort of Sosuà

BEACHES

There are fine beaches on the Amber Coast. The resorts are clustered around protected bays, where palm-backed sand shelves gently into the sea, and these are the best places to go for watersports. Sosua is the busiest, and therefore gets very crowded, but farther on there are long strips of deserted sand, battered by the Atlantic waves and winds. Cabarete is renowned for windsurfing, and also has a fine beach.

AMBER

Amber is the national gem of the Dominican Republic, which has some of the world's largest amber reserves, and a large mining area in the Cordillera Septentrional. Strictly speaking amber is not a stone, but the sap from trees that has solidified over millions of years. The youngest is the lightest in color and can be almost translucent; it is graded by color, through rich yellow to red. The most valuable are pieces with prehistoric insects or leaves preserved within them. Be wary of pieces offered to you on the streets; these may be plastic.

Restaurant in Puerto Plata

►► Puerto Plata and the Amber Coast

The Amber Coast, on the north shore, has the greatest concentration of Dominican tourism. Here, several hotel complexes cater to package tourists who fly into the international airport near Puerto Plata, but the seaside villages of Sosua and Cabarete, with excellent beaches, have bars and guesthouses that are ideal for independent travelers. Puerto Plata itself has a strong Dominican life. Attractive old Creole houses still stand in the town, and the squares, with shady trees and benches, come alive in the late afternoons with old gents and salesmen selling lottery tickets. There are just a couple of hotels on the rocky seafront, but the town has a number of good restaurants and bars (see pages 269-283). The **Amber Museum**►► (tel: 586-2848. *Open* daily 9–6. *Admission charge*), in a grand town house with classical balustrades and columns, has exhibits explaining the origin and mining process of the gem. A cable car takes passengers 2,625 feet to the top of Mount Isabel de Torres, just south of the town; its running times are unpredictable, but hotels will usually arrange seats for visitors. A statue of Christ dominates the magnificent view of the coast and the Cordillera Septentrional.

Playa Dorado is a purpose-built resort, a collection of hotels to the east of the town. It is set on a superb beach, where there are watersports and a good beach bar, but this is private and reserved for hotel guests. The resort town of **Sosúa**►► is split into two parts, set on either side of the lively Sosúa beach: Los Charramícos is the westerly, more Dominican half; El Batey has a stronger European influence, a legacy of the wave of Austrian and German Jewish refugees who came here fleeing the Holocaust (restaurants here still serve Austrian and German food). Here you will also find some of the best restaurants and small hotels.

One of the best resorts on the island, **Cabarete**►►► is a lazy seaside town with palm-thatch garden bars and beachside restaurants, patronized by windsurfers; windsurfing World Championships are occasionally held here. Beyond Cabarete, the beaches continue, on and off, for miles along the coast.

The Dominican Republic's landscape is graced by thousands of royal palm trees, soaring up to 165 feet from the ground and exploding into bushy palm fronds. Dominicans who travel away from home will often say that they miss the royal palm most of all.

Around 2,600 species of palm trees and shrubs grow in the tropics and subtropics, varying in height from 6 inches to 200 feet. Palms do not have branches, but their fronds, which can be as long as 30 feet, emerge in sequence at the top of each stem, pointing vertically at first and gradually leaning to the side as younger fronds push them aside.

The coconut palm As well as being the quintessential Caribbean palm, the coconut is the most useful and versatile. Almost all of its parts can be used: the fronds in thatch and the trunk in building; in the past, the husk of the coconut was used to weave ropes and mats; coconut flesh is eaten, and copra (dried coconut flesh) can be used to make oil for washing or burning. Coconut milk, a popular drink, has even been used as an intravenous fluid. In all the Caribbean islands, you will find vendors

THE PALMCHAT
Native to Hispaniola, the palmchat is the national bird of the Dominican Republic. It has a greenish-brown coat and a white breast with dark streaking, and lives and feeds in flocks. Its communal nest has separate compartments for up to 30 pairs, and is built on the trunk of the royal palm.

189

who will slice the top off a coconut (usually with a machete) and let you drink the liquid inside.

The royal palm This most stately and magnificent of palms grows throughout the Caribbean, and is Cuba's national tree. It can stand up to 165 feet high, with a smooth trunk as much as 3 feet thick and a bushy crown of fronds. The heart of the royal palm is used in salads, and its fruit is used for animal feed.

Other palms The cabbage palm is similar in appearance to the royal palm, although it grows only to about 130 feet. Known as the *palma cana* in Spanish, the latania palm, with fan-like fronds, is used for weaving, particularly in St. Barts. The ornamental golden palm is a bright green bush that appears in many Caribbean gardens, and the fishtail palm bears fruit that can be distilled into alcohol.

Picture-postcard views— palms and perfect water in the Dominican Republic

PALM AVENUES
Royal palms and cabbage palms are often planted to form beautiful avenues. Some of the best are the Allée Dumanoir, on Basse-Terre in Guadeloupe, and the driveway that leads to Codrington College in Barbados (see page 220).

Dawn at Las Terrenas, Samaná peninsula

BEACHES
On the northern side of the Samaná peninsula strips of golden sand stretch either side of Las Terrenas, and hotels rent out watersports equipment. On Samaná Bay itself you can arrange to visit Cayo Levantado, an offshore island, or make your way up to Las Galeras, a small beach resort in the northeast.

▶▶▶ Samaná

Isolated in the northeast, the lush Samaná peninsula is in the isolated northeast, but it is worth making the effort to get there to spend some time in the town of Las Terrenas, the island's best resort. Set on the northern shore of the peninsula across a ridge of mountains, Las Terrenas has golden sand swept by low-hanging palms. There is an easy-going feel to the place, with its string of thatched restaurants, candle-lit at night, and its few excellent hotels and guesthouses. At the Tropic Banana you can spend the afternoon listening to a Dominican string band (guitar, soul-comb and cheese-grater, and sit-on beat-box).

Set on the huge Samaná Bay (named Golfo de las Flechas, or Gulf of Arrows, by Columbus for the local Carib Indians showered him with arrows), the town of Samaná itself is not very attractive, although it has a few guesthouses and a collection of good restaurants on the waterfront. You can arrange to see the **whales▶▶▶** that collect offshore early in the year (from January to March), try your hand at deep-sea fishing, and visit the offshore island of Cayo Levantado, where there is a good beach and some facilities, and the **Los Haïtises National Park▶▶** (tel: 685-1315), where among the limestone caves and mangroves you can see terns, jacanas, and ibises. At Las Galeras, in the northeast, there is a good beach with a couple of quiet hotels.

▶ Santiago

You may only mean to pass through Santiago, the country's second city, but it makes a good traveler's stop. It is a working city set on the cliffs above the Yaque river in the Cibao Valley, one of the country's most fertile regions. Hustlers are not as active here as they are in the tourist resorts. The **Museo del Tabaco▶▶** relates the story of cigars and tobacco, which is grown in the area, and in the **Museo del Arte Folklorico▶▶** you can see exhibits of local arts and crafts and also the carnival masks worn at religious festivals.

LARIMAR
The Dominican Republic has a unique variety of turquoise, known locally as Larimar. This hard, light-blue stone, sold as jewelry throughout the country, is mined in the Bahoruco mountains on the southwestern Barahona peninsula.

Sugar was such a valuable commodity during the 17th and 18th centuries that it became known as "white gold." Empires were built on the sugar trade; whole islands were planted with sugar cane, and navies were sent to capture and defend them. Meanwhile, the planters grew rich and their African slaves lived and labored in miserable subjection.

Sugar cane (*Saccharum officinarum*) is an overgrown grass. It grows to about 12 feet, can be a green or deep purple color, and takes 18 months to mature, blooming with a tall, white, wispy ear. Cane fields are sometimes burned to rid the canes of their corn-like leaves, creating enormous columns of smoke that are visible for miles.

Cane-cutting is grueling work. In colonial times, teams of cutters would work in lines, led by singers and drummers and swinging their machetes in time to the music. Once the cane was cut, other gangs carted it off to the mill. The cane-cutting season lasted for about six months, ending in July; the annual Barbados carnival, Cropover, and the zafra in Cuba, are survivors of the end-of-season celebrations.

River Antoine Rum Distillery's sugar mill, Grenada

191

Technology has advanced from mule-driven mills to wind-driven equipment and finally steam-driven crushing machinery, but sugar production has remained basically unchanged for 350 years. Canes are cut to length and passed repeatedly through metal rollers, so that the juice runs away and the pulp, or bagasse, emerges dry. Bagasse burns well and is used to fire the engines that drive the rollers. The cane juice is clarified in the boiling house in huge copper boiling pans (which are also heated with bagasse). As it cools, the sugar crystalizes into granules. Nowadays the sugar is passed through a centrifuge, separating the crystals from the molasses, which is itself used as animal feed and for distilling rum.

In the mid-19th century, the development of sugar beet as an alternative to cane sugar began to threaten the West Indian trade, and now only a few islands cultivate sugar crops in any quantity. The biggest industries are in Cuba and the Dominican Republic, each producing about 7 million tons, and Jamaica, producing about 2½ million tons every year.

SUGAR LOAF

Sugar loaf mountains can be found all over the English-speaking world. They take their name from their steep-sided shape, which resembles the "loaf" of early sugar manufacture. Wet processed sugar would be placed in a mold like an inverted pyramid and allowed to drain, so that the brown molasses would seep to the bottom and white sugar crystals would be left at the top. When the mold was broken, a pyramid-shaped "loaf" of sugar was revealed.

Other Caribbean states

FRANCIS DRAKE

Francis Drake was something of a scourge around Santo Domingo. He first came to the Caribbean in 1565, on a voyage with Sir John Hawkins selling African slaves to the Spaniards, and later returned to pursue the more profitable action of attacking and ransoming their settlements. Drake captured Santo Domingo in 1586, setting up his headquarters in the cathedral and ransacking it for any loot he could lay his hands on; his name has been adopted by one of the city's best bars, which can become rowdy late in the evening. After gaining fame in Britain for his defeat of the Spanish Armada in 1588, Drake eventually died of dysentery off Porto Bello in Panama, in 1595.

COLUMBUS'S LIGHTHOUSE

The Faro a Colon has been dogged by bad luck since its construction was first suggested a century ago. It was eventually built to designs submitted to a competition in 1929 by a British architect, J. Gleave. The project was adopted by Trujillo in the 1930s and then abandoned because it was so expensive. In 1987 the lighthouse became the personal project of President Balaguer, who spent vast amounts of his poor country's reserves building it. It is the butt of many sarcastic jokes among Dominicans; when the lighthouse is lit, it drains electricity from the rest of the city. More imposing than attractive, it contains six museums and (it is said) the explorer's remains (*Open* Tue–Sun 10–5. *Admission charge*).

▶▶▶ Santo Domingo

Santo Domingo, the island's capital and largest city, is the oldest surviving European settlement in the Americas. Its heart is the colonial city, on the bank of the Ozama river on the island's southern shore, but La Capital, as it is known, has expanded enormously over the centuries and now has around 2 million inhabitants. It has all the problems of fast-growing cities in poor countries: congestion, inadequate electricity and water supplies, and grinding poverty. But there is also a compelling Latin vibrancy here—best seen on the **Avenida del Puerto▶▶▶**, as crowds gather for their evening promenade.

Hidden by its ancient walls above the Avenida del Puerto, the **colonial city of Santo Domingo▶▶▶** is a calm enclave, with coral-rock alleyways and shady courtyards. Its most impressive building is the **Alcazar de Colon▶▶▶**, Columbus Palace, just inside the city walls. Built in 1514 for Columbus's son Diego as his viceregal palace, the solid stone house is fronted by a double row of arches; its interior has been restored and furnished with tapestries, earthen water-pitchers and leather-bound chests. Ranged before it are the viceroy's administrative buildings, the **Atarazana▶▶**. These once contained the colonial armory and customs houses; they now house the Museum of Marine Archaeology, stores, a gallery, the Fonda restaurant, and a couple of bars, including Drake's Pub (see panel). The city's oldest surviving building is the Casa del Cordon (1503), now a bank, across the street from the post office; look for the Franciscan order's cord motif, which is carved above the door.

From the Alcazar the city walls lead to **Calle de las Damas▶▶**, named for colonial ladies who would promenade here. Set in the former colonial offices, the **Museo de las Casas Reales▶▶** (tel: 682-4802. *Open* Tue–Sat 9–4:45, Sun 10–1. *Admission charge*) has exhibits from early Spanish colonial times, including suits of armor and wall maps. The imposing **Panteon Nacional▶** (*Open* Mon–Sat 10–5), guards an eternal flame commemorating the Dominican national heroes, Duarte, Sanchez, and Mella, who formed the underground independence movement

BOCA CHICA
Boca Chica is a lively
tourist town about 20
miles east of Santo
Domingo. Popular with
Dominicans, it gets busy
at weekends; there are a
number of small
guesthouses and apart-
ments here, and many
restaurants and bars near
the beachfront.

EL CONUCO
This lively Santo Domingo
restaurant on Calle
Casimiro de Moya, deco-
rated with palm thatch
and gravel, is based on
the theme of *conuco* (the
country). Ancient farming
tools are hung on the
walls among old wives'
sayings carved on wood.
Meals are local country
fare—mainly tripe and
stews, but there are less
daunting options (such as
Creole-flavored chicken
and plantains in batter),
and the waiters, dressed
up as *campesinos* (cow-
boys), in boots, jeans, and
bandanas, have been
known to dart off in the
middle of taking an order
and start dancing.

193

La Trinitaria during the Haitian occupation in the 1830s,
and eventually won independence for the Republic in
1844. Further along the street are the cool, quiet palace
courtyard of the **Casa de Bastidas▶▶** and the **Fortaleza
Ozama▶**, a fortress whose cannons have now been set in
peaceful gardens.

The Plaza de Toledo alley leads into the Parque Colon,
Columbus Square, where a statue of the explorer overlooks benches and trees. On the southern side of the
square is the **Catedral Santa Maria de Menor, Primada de
America▶▶**, the oldest cathedral in the Americas.
Completed in 1523, the cathedral, with its pointed battlements, was said to be the burial place of Columbus until
his remains were moved to the Faro a Colon in honor of
the quincentennial celebrations in 1992—although there
are rival claims from Cuba and Spain. The cathedral is
guarded but you can usually go in to visit, where you will
see a bishop's throne made of mahogany.

From the Parque Colon, El Conde, one of the city's busi-
est shopping streets, leads up to the **Parque
Independencia▶▶**, the chaotic hub of the modern city.
All distances in the country are measured from here.
Behind the old city gates are the imposing memorial and
sunken mausoleum dedicated to Duarte, Mella, and
Sanchez. Leading off the square, the Avenida Mella is
another shopping street, where you will find the Mercado
Modelo, the lively market. To the south is the
Malecon▶▶, the palm-lined seafront boulevard where
Dominicans like to take the evening air.

Inland, the **Plaza de Cultura▶** (tel: 687-3623; call for
hours. *Admission charge*) houses the National Theater and
Modern Art Gallery and three museums. Despite its
rather dull appearance, it is worth visiting the Museum of
the Dominican Man, where exhibits trace the history of
Caribbean Indians and their customs. Visually more
impressive is the **Palacio Nacional▶**, a baroque palace
built by the dictator Trujillo on Calle Dr. Delgado.

On the city's northwestern outskirts, the **Jardin Botanico
Nacional▶▶** (tel: 687-6211; call for hours. *Admission
charge*) has an orchid house and an aquatic plant house of
flowering lilies. In the eastern suburbs, the **Faro a
Colon▶▶** is a 100-foot lighthouse built in the shape of a
cross as a monument to Columbus (see panel opposite).

Alcazar de Colon

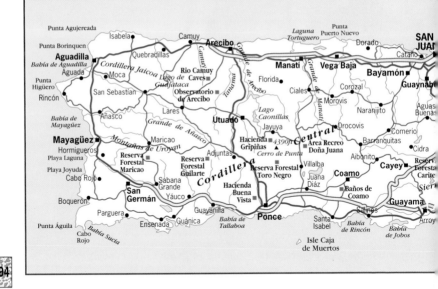

Punta Agujereada
Isabela
Camuy
Arecibo
Laguna Tortuguero
Punta Puerto Nuevo
Dorado
SAN JUAN

Punta Borinquen
Quebradillas
Cataño
Aguadilla
Bahía de Aguadilla
Aguada
Manatí
Vega Baja
Bayamón
Punta Higüero
Moca
Río Camuy
Cordillera Jaicoa
Lago de Caves
Guajataca
Florida
Ciales
Corozal
Guaynabo
Rincón
San Sebastián
Observatorio de Arecibo
Morovis
Naranjito
Aguas Buenas
Bahía de Mayagüez
Añasco
Lares
Grande de Añasco
Utuado
Lago Caonillas
Jayuya
Orocovis
Comerío
Mayagüez
Hormigueros
Maricao
Montañas de Uroyan
Hacienda Gripiñas
4390ft
Central
Area Recreo Doña Juana
Barranquitas
Cidra
Playa Laguna
Reserva Forestal Maricao
Cerro de Punta
Aibonito
Reserva Forestal Carite
Playa Joyuda
Reserva Forestal Guilarte
Adjuntas
Reserva Forestal Toro Negro
Villalba
Cayey
Cordillera
Cabo Rojo
Sábana Grande
Coamo
Sierra
San Germán
Yáuco
Hacienda Buena Vista
Juana Díaz
Baños de Coamo
Guayama
Boquerón
Parguera
Guayanilla
Bahía de Tallaboa
Ponce
Salinas
Arroyo
Punta Águila
Bahía Sucia
Ensenada
Guánica
Santa Isabel
Bahía de Rincón
Bahía de Jobos
Cabo Rojo
Isle Caja de Muertos

194

Puerto Rico

With good communications and plenty of hotels, you'll find Puerto Rico easy and attractive to explore. San Juan can claim to be the best preserved Spanish colonial city in the Caribbean and has a lively cultural and artistic life; the southwest offers the best beaches and quieter accommodation. As a semi-autonomous commonwealth territory of the U.S., Puerto Rico is well known by American travelers. It is easy to reach—flights from Miami, New York, and several other U.S. cities land at San Juan's Luis Muñoz Marin airport, as do frequent U.K. flights, and most European airlines connect at New York. It also has a large, well-organized tourist industry; the beaches around San Juan are as developed as those in Miami, and Old San Juan, seven beautifully restored blocks of 18th-century colonial buildings, has become one of the Caribbean's foremost cruise ship destinations. But there is far more to Puerto Rico than the tourist circuit. As well as a vibrant culture, the island offers endless exploration in its rain forests, caves,

Billboards are everywhere on the streets of Puerto Rico

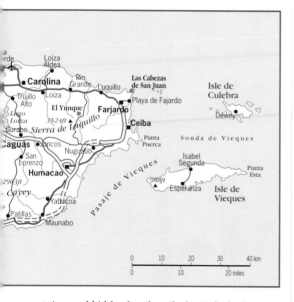

PUERTO RICAN EATING
San Juan offers food from all over the world, but it is worth tasting the local dishes. Many are based on rice, including *arroz con pollo* (spiced chicken and rice) and *asopao*, like a paella. Seafood is often spiced with traditional flavorings: *sofrito* (onion, garlic, and pepper) and *adobo* (lemon, garlic, salt, and spices). Side dishes include *mofongo* (spiced and battered plantain) and *yuca frita* (spiced cassava with cloves and parsley).

mountains, and hidden beaches, the best of which are on the southwest coast, and the two sleepy offshore islands of Vieques and Culebra. The entire island can be circumnavigated on an expressway that touches the coast at several resorts and passes through secondary towns such as Arecibo, Aguadilla, Mayagüez, and Ponce, each of which has an airport. A highway crosses the eastern part of the island from San Juan to Ponce on the south coast, and many secondary roads run into the interior.

The most easterly of the Greater Antilles, Puerto Rico lies 994 miles southeast of Miami, and is almost rectangular in shape—110 miles in length and about 37 miles from north to south. A range of mountains run through the center

TREE FROGS

The call of the coqui, a favorite Puerto Rican variety of tree frog, is almost synonymous with the tropical night. About 1½ inches long and with overlarge eyes, tree frogs can be heard in every Caribbean island (each species has a slightly different call), and they are particularly noisy at night and just after it has rained.

of the island from east to west and marks a distinct division of climate: on the north side there is rainforest, and the rain in the northwest has created amazing karst cave systems (see page 200); in the south, the land is mainly dry and cactus-covered.

HISTORY Although it was visited by Columbus during his second voyage to the Americas in 1493, Puerto Rico was not settled by Europeans until 1508, when an expedition from Santo Domingo was led by Juan Ponce de Léon, who became the island's first Governor. Having first exploited and then defeated the native Tainos Indians, Ponce de Léon died in Cuba on a search for the Fountain of Youth. His bones were brought to San Juan, and eventually laid in San Juan Cathedral.

For the next 300 years, Puerto Rico's settlers suffered constant invasion—from Caribs, pirates and raiding European armies. After decades of neglect by its mother country, the colony was revived by a Spanish envoy in the 18th century, and trade from its sugar exports began to pick up. A new constitution was granted in 1812 and an independence movement started to emerge, to be ruthlessly put down by a succession of Spanish military governors. An uprising in 1868 which led to the first declaration of a republic was soon put down by the

196

A fire engine and filigree ironwork in the restored Ponce fire station

THE U.S. CONNECTION

Puerto Ricans have formed large communities on the American mainland, particularly in New York, where they are known as Nuyoricans. The island has special Treasury laws, according to which the islanders do not pay Federal taxes, and therefore are not represented in Congress.

Spanish, but in 1897 autonomy was finally granted. Before the new government could fulfill its role, the U.S., at war with Spain, invaded the island, and seven months later Puerto Rico was ceded to the Americans. U.S. citizenship was granted to islanders in 1917, but senior government appointments remained in American hands. Initially there was a movement toward independence—a 1937 rally ended in 19 deaths after police shot at the protestors. In 1952 the island became a Commonwealth of the U.S., and recent political debate has revolved around the question of whether Puerto Rico should become the 51st State of the Union. One of the obvious benefits of the American connection is Puerto Rico's prosperity, in comparison with nearby islands.

Puerto Rico

The 17th-century Cathedral of Our Lady of Guadeloupe on the main square in Ponce

THE *GUAYABERA*
Recently, American fashions have come to Puerto Rico in a big way, but the traditional dress for men on the island is the *guayabera*. Shaped rather like a jacket or an extended shirt, this is worn as the outer garment over an undershirt or T-shirt. Most are made of cotton and are worn during the day, but there is a more formal version for evening wear, made with pineapple fiber. The *guayabera* is usually embellished with patterned embroidery, running in stripes down the chest.

Puerto Rico took a big wallop from Hurricane Georges in September 1998, but the U.S. connection turned the disaster into an economic boom, with $3.5 billion in aid pouring in to repair the 50,000 houses destroyed or severely damaged. The tourist industry was largely unaffected, and all hotel damage was quickly repaired.

ISLAND LIFE American and Latin American culture live side by side in Puerto Rico, and often meet in an incongruous mix. Both English and Spanish are widely used—Spanish is the official language of Parliament; high-rise, air-conditioned office buildings tower over traditional Caribbean markets; cable T.V., fast food and American cars are all a way of life, but so are roadside stalls and, away from the larger towns, a simple, rural existence. Like most West Indians, the 3 million Puerto Ricans constitute a racial mix and include Africans, Spaniards, Italians and Lebanese. They are strongly Catholic, and their most important festivals, the *fiestas patronales* (Saints' Days celebrations) combine a devout faith with the compulsion to dance—particularly to the salsa, a racing beat led by brass and African drums. Held by each individual town, the *fiestas* have costume balls, parades, picnics, and fairs; perhaps the most exuberant of them all is the Festival of the Innocents, in which, on December 28, the whole town of Hatillo on the north coast becomes a costumed brawl. Music festivals are held throughout the year featuring different styles of island music, such as the *danza*, the *plena*, and the *seis*.

Puerto Rico has a strong culinary tradition. Many dishes are based on rice, but plantains are also used as a staple in *mofongo* and *piñon* (see panel, page 195). Daytime snacks can often be bought at the roadside fruit stalls—try *alcapurria* and *bacalao* (crab and cod-fish batter balls) or *empañadas* and *picadillos* (meat- or cheese-filled sandwiches).

The most popular island pastimes are baseball and cock-fighting (see page 209).

Festival of the Innocents at Hatillo, on the north coast near Arecibo

Hacienda Gripiñas—colonial-style accommodations on an old coffee plantation high in the Cordillera Central

ARECIBO OBSERVATORY

The Arecibo Observatory is an impressive sight: a bright white dish, 1,300 ft. across, neatly cupped in a karst sinkhole. It listens to waves across the spectrum and bounces them back to the massive recording gear that hangs 650 ft. above the dish itself (there is a two-story building up there, too). The information is then relayed to the offices before being sent to Cornell University for analysis (tel: 878-2612. *Open* Wed–Fri noon–4, Sat, Sun, and holidays 9–4. *Admission charge*).

▶▶▶ Cordillera Central

The Cordillera Central, the major mountain range in Puerto Rico's interior, runs parallel to the coast, splayed east and west on either side of the island's highest peak, Cerro de Punta. Running through them is the **ruta panoramica**▶▶▶, a scenic road stretching over 120 miles from coast to coast, taking in forest reserves and waterfalls. It's a long trip (two or three days), particularly if you stop off to explore, but there are charming mountain hotels en route and good roadside cafés, and the journey reveals a little-known side of Puerto Rico.

The *ruta panoramica* sets off from Maunabo, in the southeast of the island, beyond the tourist resort of Palmas del Mar. From here it rises into the Cayey mountains and the **Carite Forest Reserve**▶, a cool environment with rain forest and dwarf forest inhabited by 50 species of bird, and then Cayey itself, where it crosses the main San Juan to Ponce road. It then continues to Aibonito and Barranquitas, two modern towns in steep-sided valleys. Close by is the **San Cristobal Canyon**▶▶, an impressive cleft over 650 feet deep, where there is a 100-feet waterfall. To the south, Coamo is an old colonial town, founded in 1579; the medicinal springs to its south were used by the indigenous Indians and later by Ponce de Léon. In the 19th century, they became fashionable as baths; restored as a modern *parador* (a government-run inn-cum-hotel), they still retain a period dining room.

Ascending steadily, with magnificent views, the route continues to Doña Juana Recreational Center, where there are 200-foot falls, and on to the Toro Negro Forest Reserve, a magnificent area of undeveloped forest where there are trails to the island's highest point, Cerro de Punta (4,390 foot). Just a few miles from here as the crow flies is one of the island's most charming retreats, the **Hacienda Gripiñas**▶▶▶ (tel: 828-1717). This *parador*, set in the wooden estate house of a former coffee plantation, overlooks the valley, and represents the best of old colonial Puerto Rico.

Although the *ruta panoramica* itself continues westward, it is worth making a detour to the north at the town of Utuado. Beyond another

attractive *parador*, lost in greenery on the shores of Lago Caonillas, the **Caguana Indian Ceremonial Park**▶▶ (tel: 894-7325. *Open* Wed–Sun 9–4:30. *Admission free*) is set in a valley surrounded by massive peaks. It has a small museum and about 10 *bateyes*—sports and ceremonial grounds used by the indigenous Amerindians. Surrounded by carved stones, they are believed to date from the 9th century but may be even older.

Just to the north of the park, in karst country (see page 200), is the largest radio telescope in the world, the **Arecibo Observatory**▶▶ (see panel). This 20-acre dish, owned by Cornell University, fills a whole valley and made the first discovery of quasars. Not far off is the **Rio Camuy Cave Park**▶▶ (tel: 898-3100. *Open* Wed–Sun 8–3:45. *Admission charge*), a cave system where an introductory lecture is followed by a trolleybus ride and walks through the caves. Thousands of years of dripping rainwater have created impressive stalactites and stalagmites in caverns 165 feet high. The hillside town of Lares, situated on the southern boundary of karst country, was the setting for a rebellion against Spanish authorities in 1868, revered in Puerto Rican history as the *Gito de Lares* (the Cry of Lares).

Rejoining the *ruta panoramica* itself at Adjuntas, you climb into higher hills, with superb views. The road passes through the Guilarte Forest Reserve (where there are walking trails) and near the Maricao Forest Reserve, with a fish farm and a viewing tower overlooking the entire west coast. Nearby there is another charming parador, the Hacienda Juanita. From here, the route descends to sea level, arriving at the coast at Mayagüez, the island's third largest town. The **Mayagüez Zoo**▶▶ exhibits animals in open compounds, and a wide range of tropical plants are on view in the University of Puerto Rico's Tropical Agricultural Research Station.

Tourist bus logo

199

Sun and cloud alternate all day in the lush Cordillera Central forest

The Caribbean archipelago runs southeast from the Tropic of Cancer, near the tip of Florida, down to the coast of South America, and has an impressive variety of terrain. The islands lie on the join of the Atlantic and Caribbean tectonic plates, where massive ructions have produced a string of volcanoes in the Eastern Caribbean. At the same time, the warm tropical sea has given rise to coral reefs, which have gradually clustered the islands with limestone deposits as they age and die.

CAVE VISITS

All coral-based islands have caves, carved out by rain over the millennia. The best organized cave tours include the Rio Camuy park (tel: 898-3100) in Puerto Rico and Harrison's Cave (tel: 438-6640) in Barbados. Both tours have introductory explanations and a trip on a trolleybus to view the stalactites and stalagmites. The Cueva del Indio in the Viñales region of Cuba are also worth visiting, as is Anguilla's Fountain Cave, thought to have been an Arawak religious site.

NAMES AND USES

In the British Caribbean old limestone shelves (dead coral reefs) on the seafront are known as "ironshore" and in the Spanish Caribbean as "black teeth." Many early Caribbean buildings were constructed with the bright, pitted coral rock, quarried on the islands.

Over the millennia corals have created whole islands. When a hard coral dies it leaves a limestone skeleton, on which the next generation of corals can fix itself. Eventually a reef is formed and, as the level of the sea rises and falls, the growing reef can be left exposed as land. Wave action breaks down the dead reefs, carving natural bridges, blowholes and coastal caves, as well as creating bright, white sand. The islands which form a line from Anguilla through Antigua to Grande-Terre in Guadeloupe are all coral limestone, as are the Caymans, encrusted around a string of old volcanoes that died off 100 million years ago.

In the Greater Antilles, age-old coral lime-stone has been pushed up into the mountains by seis-mic activity. There it has been eroded into areas of cone and tower karst mountains, named for a region of shaggy-topped limestone outcrops in the former Yugoslavia. Karst peaks are distinctive, steep-sided mountains between 330 feet and 660 feet tall (they once had roofs suspended between them, but these were undermined by heavy rain and collapsed long ago). From above they look like shaggy egg cartons; beneath them, the rocky earth is laced with sinkholes, caverns, and underground rivers. In Jamaica karst mountains are known as "cockpits" (steep-banked pits for cock fights). Karst peaks can also be seen around Viñales in Cuba (where they are called *mogotes*), in the Dominican Republic's Los Haïtises National Park, and in the northwest of Puerto Rico.

▶▶▶ Ponce and surrounds

Isolated from San Juan by the central mountain range, Ponce has a radically different feel from the island's capital; the area is hotter and has less rain, so its pace of life is more leisurely. The 200,000 Ponceños are renowned for their independence, and for their pride in a heritage dating from the 17th century, when Ponce de Léon's great-grandson founded the city.

Ponce's tree-lined central plaza and a number of streets surrounding it have recently been restored. Most striking is the striped red-and-black **Parque de Bombas**▶▶ (fire station), erected a century ago. Built to a Spanish-influenced Puerto Rican design, the Cathedral of Our Lady of Guadeloupe dates from 1670, and the Casa Armstrong Poventud, a turn-of-the-century townhouse, has been well restored with period furniture and now houses a tourist information office. The **Ponce Museum of Art**▶▶ (tel: 840-7363; call for hours), on the Avenida de las Americas, has an excellent collection of European and Latin American art.

One of the best views of the city is from El Vigia, the enormous cross on the hill, where an earlier version was designed to guide ships to land. **Castillo Seraites**▶▶, also on the hill, is the extravagant former family home of the distillers of local rum Don Q. Weekend ferries leave the Playa de Ponce for the small and popular offshore island Caja de Muertos (named for the coffin it resembles), which has excellent beaches and coral reefs.

The **Tibes Indian Ceremonial Center**▶▶ (tel: 840-2255. *Open* daily 9–noon, 1–4, except Wednesdays) is set in forested parkland behind the town. On an Amerindian village site, discovered in the 1970s, thatched houses and *bateyes* have been re-created, and a museum displays bones, weapons, and ceremonial figures found in the area. On Route 10, in the hills above the town, is the **Hacienda Buena Vista**▶▶ (tel: 722-5882. *Open* weekends by appointment), a restored late 19th-century coffee estate, which is worth a visit. There is a small museum and original machinery, driven by water. You will also see the bags and painted stencils that were used to export the product a century ago.

Red and black stripes on the Parque de Bombas

In his book The Old Man and the Sea, *Ernest Hemingway tells of a poor fisherman in Cuba and his fight to hook an enormous blue marlin. In another of his novels,* Islands in the Stream, *a boy and a marlin are engaged in a desperate struggle. Big-game fishing suited Hemingway's macho image, and he was one of the sport's most passionate practitioners, relishing the rich sealife of the Caribbean waters.*

BIG AND BEAUTIFUL
One of the most beautiful fish in these waters is the sailfish, a sleek fish with a silver belly, a blue back, and a large, bright blue dorsal fin that looks like a sail. It can grow to about 10 ft. in length and weigh 200 lb. Other, smaller fish include wahoo, a streamlined gray-blue fish with a crescent tail, which grows to nearly 7 ft. and can weigh up to 120 lb. and, about the same size, the tarpon, which is slim and has silvery scales. The dorado (so-called because of its golden color) or mahi-mahi has red fins and grows to about 3 ft. in length.

Barracuda

202

Big-game fishing was made possible by the invention of the motorized boat at the end of the 19th century, and fishermen soon gathered along the coasts of the Gulf Stream (Cuba, the Florida Keys, and Bimini in the Bahamas), where the biggest fish live. Today it is possible to fish off most of the Caribbean islands, and the sport is particularly popular off Cuba, Jamaica, the Dominican Republic, and the Cayman Islands.

Deep-sea fishing boats have tall upper decks, or tuna towers, from which their pilots can look out, and trail a number of lines from different rods. This is a strenuous, physical sport, and once a fish has been hooked, the fisherman will strap himself into a "fighting chair." Some species are immensely strong, weighing over 1,000 lb, and the fight can last for several hours: line is paid out in order to prevent it from snapping, allowing the fish to dive and move around. The unfortunate catch is then slowly hauled in; most fish are killed in the process (though catch-and-release fishing is increasingly popular).

The Caribbean's principal big game fish are the blue and the white marlin. Both have spears extending from their noses and long dorsal fins. The blue marlin can grow up to 1,500 lb. Other fish include tuna: yellowfin, albacore, and skipjack (the most important commercial fish, which is trawled extensively and processed in Puerto Rico) and the blue-fin tuna, which can grow to 14 feet and weigh 1,700 lb.

▶▶ San Germán and the Southwest

Puerto Ricans take their vacations in the southwest of the island. Here, the country is hotter and there are good beaches in the area; consequently, a number of small local tourist towns have collected along the coast, and come alive in the summer.

The main road from Ponce to Mayagüez cuts inland and passes close to the town of **San Germán▶▶▶**, the second on the island to be founded by the Spaniards (in 1573). It remained prominent until the 19th century, despite constant threats from pirates, and now has a university and attractive old townhouses. The **Porta Coeli Church▶▶** (1606) has been restored and now contains a museum of religious art. Contemporary art can be seen at the museum in Bahr House on Acosta Street.

A golden sunset over the hotter southwest coast of Puerto Rico, where locals go to relax

On the coast directly south of San Germán is the town of **Parguera▶▶**, which has a more hedonistic, seaside feel. Local seafood restaurants, cabins on stilts, and small villas overlook the mangroves on the coast, and the beach (not one of the best) is some way out of town. A more worthwhile local attraction is the nearby phosphorescent lake (see panel, page 210).

Perhaps the best town in the area is **Boquerón▶▶**, a small seafront resort on the southwest coast. Backed with huge palm trees, its beach is one of the island's best and gets very lively at weekends. Watersports equipment is for rent and there are several cafés. Other, more isolated beaches can be enjoyed on the island's southwestern tip near the lighthouse and the old lagoons where the islanders used to harvest salt. There is also a small forest reserve here with mangroves.

To the north along the coastline are more resort towns, with *paradores* and restaurants lining the seafront at Playa Joyuda and Playa Laguna. This west-facing coast is excellent for sunset-watching, and offshore there are a number of small islands which are rarely visited, including Desecheo and Mona, a deserted nature reserve with soaring cliffs, which can only be reached by taking a charter plane or fishing boat.

PUERTO RICAN PARADORES
The *paradores* of Puerto Rico are hotels dotted around the island, judged to be of a certain standard and style by the Tourist Board (from whom a list can be requested). They are usually small, and while they are neither fancy nor chic, they often have great local character and are generally in superb settings. Puerto Ricans themselves use *paradores*, so you are highly likely to meet islanders there. The *mesons gastronomicos* are restaurants chosen according to similar criterion specializing in local cuisine.

*Sidewalk cafés in
Old San Juan*

*The battlements of the
Castillo de San Felipe
del Morro*

▶▶▶ San Juan (Old City)

Approached from the sea, Old San Juan looks like a massive fortress. The city is enclosed by over 6 miles of walls, 50 feet high and 20 feet thick, and a ring of sentry boxes, or *garitas*. Its formidable appearance was a necessity during the turbulent days when there was continual threat of invasion; both Francis Drake and Jack Hawkins led attacks on the city in the 16th century.

Parts of San Juan date from its foundation in 1520, but most of the colonial city has been restored to its 18th-century style. The streets are laid with blue cobblestones shipped from Spain as ballast, and the wrought-iron streetlamps, balconies, and shuttered windows all add to the rather self-conscious sense of history. Admittedly this is a tourist showpiece, and it can be overrun by visitors from the cruise ships; but Old San Juan is also a city with genuine character and life.

A walk around the city can take in its main features (see **Walk**), but there is also a wealth of museums and galleries to explore, including the Pablo Casals Museum on Calle San Sebastian, where the cellist's instruments are on display; the Museo del Arte de Puerto Rico, on Calle Cristo, which houses a collection of fine arts; and the Casa del Libro, on the same street, with displays about printing and binding and a library of antiquarian books. The fortresses of San Felipe del Morro and San Cristóbal also have visitor centers. For a rest from sightseeing, try La Mallorquina restaurant, on Calle San Justo, or La Bombonera, a noisy café on Calle San Francisco; or sample a daiquiri at La Violata, on Calle Fortaleza. Late in the evening Calle de San Sebastian comes alive with promenaders taking the air.

OLD SAN JUAN

Bahía de
San Juan

Walk

Old San Juan

Start at La Casita, a colonial building near the cruise ship port on the inner harbor. Walk uphill, following the city wall to Calle San José. The Plaza de Armas is the city's main square, site of the Alcaldía (City Hall). Calle Fortaleza leads to **La Fortaleza**►► (hourly tours; tel: 721-7000, ext. 2211), used as the Governor's Mansion since its construction in 1520 and renovated in 1846.

At the foot of Calle del Cristo, lined with stores and restaurants, is the tiny **Capilla del Santo Cristo**►, a chapel marking the spot where a horseman plunged over the walls during a race around the city. Heading north, you reach the Catedral de San Juan, built

in 1540 and altered in the 19th century; Ponce de Léon's bones are entombed there. A stepped alley leads downhill to one of the city gates, and beyond the walls, parkland leads to the vast **Castillo de San Felipe del Morro**►►►, San Juan's main defense. Started in 1540, it took over 240 years to complete; its walls rise 138 feet, and it has six levels of tunnels and dungeons (tel: 729-6960 for the Park Service).

The route back to town brings you to the **Casa Blanca**►►. Built in 1521, this was the ancestral home of the Ponce de Léon family, and now contains a museum of colonial life. On the nearby **Plaza de San José**►► is the Ponce de Léon family chapel. From the **Convento Dominicano**►, with its charming inner courtyard and the Plaza del Quinto Centenario, follow the cobbled streets to the city's other defense, **Fuerte San Cristóbal**►►, a 17th-century labyrinth of tunnels: a museum explains its design. Take Calle Fortaleza to return to the dock.

One of the most seductive aspects of the Caribbean landscape is its luxuriant greenery. Some islands are so fertile that you could plant a pencil and expect it to take root. Hundreds of plants grow here, including flowering trees, tropical fruit trees, curious crops and creepers, and the infinite variety of flowers that adorns West Indian gardens.

BOTANICAL GARDENS
The Caribbean has many excellent botanical gardens: Hope Gardens, Kingston and Castleton in the Blue Mountains in Jamaica; the Jardin Botanico Nacional in Santo Domingo, capital of the Dominican Republic; the Rio Piedras Gardens in the south of San Juan, Puerto Rico; the Jardin de Balata in Martinique; the botanical garden of St. Vincent; the Flower Forest and Andromeda Gardens on Barbados; the Queen Elizabeth Botanic Park on Grand Cayman; and the Emperor Valley Gardens off the Savannah in Port of Spain, and the J.R. O'Neal Botanic Gardens in Road Town, Tortala, B.V.I.

The evergreen croton

Beaches and swamps Palm trees on the seashore, overhanging the sandy beaches, are a travel brochure cliché nowadays, but they are not the only coastal trees by far— manchioneel (see panel opposite), sea grape (with bunches of edible, bitter grapes), and sea almond trees (bearing inedible fruit) all grow near the sea, and around the swamps and coastal lagoons are the mangroves, hardy trees that have adapted to salt water and muddy ground, where they drop a tangle of buttress and aerial roots in order to support themselves. Flowering lilies can often be seen on fresh inland water.

Dry land The drier Caribbean islands, which include low-lying lands such as the Caymans, the Dutch Leewards, and the outer chain of the former British Leewards, are generally covered in green scrub, which turns to yellow as it is bleached by the sun. On Aruba and Curaçao, where this scrubland is known as *cunucu*, the cactus-like aloe vera produces oil that is used extensively in cosmetics, and the century plant throws out a 30-foot flowering stem about once every 10 years. In this poor soil the divi-divi tree grows stunted, with branches that bend over in the winds, looking like a head of windblown hair. Numerous cacti cover the arid land, and are used to make fences in many settlements.

Grasses and flowers On the more fertile islands, grassland known as savannah is grazed by cattle, and gardens situated close to sea level grow an enormous variety of flowers. The best known are bougainvillea, which bloom in spiny fingers of purple, pink, and orange, and hibiscus, with around 200 different delicate and brightly colored blooms, each of which lasts only one day. Other species to look out for include white flowering frangipani, many different-colored ixora, allamanda, and plumbago, which has purple blooms; and the more exotic garden flowers include heliconia (known as "lobster claw" because of its strange shape), red hot cat tail, a fluffy, dangling bright red bloom, and the bird of paradise (*strelitzia*), with a bird-like form. The ubiquitous anthurium, with its plastic-looking leaf and furry stigma, is used to adorn dinner tables in houses all over the Caribbean.

Flowering trees The Caribbean's many dazzling flowering trees include the yellow and pink pouis, African tulip trees, and the immortelle, which is planted to give shade to cocoa beans and makes whole valleys flame in January. The flamboyant, or poinciana, blooms red in June and July, and the ackee produces red pods, whose yellow flesh can be eaten. Other food-bearing trees include the breadfruit and the spiky breadnut; fruit trees are a valuable source of income for many islands (see page 143). The calabash fruit cannot be eaten, but its hard shell was used as a container in years gone by; and the cannon ball tree, despite its delicate flowers, grows fruit like lumps of wood. *Lignum vitae*, or the tree of life, has wood so hard and heavy that it sinks in water; mahogany tree pods release sycamore-like whirling seeds. Beware of the sharp spines on the trunk of the sandbox, so-called because its pods were used to hold sand for ink blotters. The Traveler's Tree (see panel) is so called because rain collects in the cupped spaces

THE TRAVELER'S TREE
The Traveler's Tree, also known as the compass tree because it grows pointing east and west, is sometimes (and incorrectly) called a palm tree. Its leaves grow like a fan, splaying sideways as each new leaf is superseded by another in the middle. Occasionally, a spiky, inedible fruit pokes out and reveals its strange, blue, wax-like material.

Roadside flora in Dominica

between the leaves, giving travelers a ready supply of drinking water.

Higher up the slopes of the larger islands, the vegetation changes and the forests begin. Countless varieties of ferns swirl into an impenetrable, tangled mass; vines clamber up the trunks and drop their lianas into the soil; and "air-plants," orchids and bromeliads thrive on the upper branches and telephone wires. At the highest altitudes, you will find small and stunted "dwarf forest."

FORBIDDEN FRUIT
The manchineel is a bushy evergreen whose small apples are extremely poisonous; one of Columbus's sailors tried his luck, and the fruit quickly became known as the "apple of death."

Skyscraper hotels tower above the beach at Isla Verde, San Juan

SAN JUAN SNACKS
Like other Caribbean islanders, the Puerto Ricans adore roadside snacks and there is a grand variety of tasty fillers at *kioskos* in San Juan and around the countryside. *Chicharron* is popular, although perhaps an acquired taste—spiced fried pork rind. *Bacalao* is frittered codfish, and *alca-purrias* are also fritters, either meat or local fish, fried and served on a banana leaf. *Empañadas* are strangely flattened sandwiches, and *picadillas* meat patties.

▶ San Juan (New City)

Beyond the historic walls of colonial San Juan there is a real working city with a population of over one million, and urban development has sprawled along the coast and around the lagoons. Hotels and apartment houses crowd the coastline, while farther inland there is a mixture of swank commercial buildings and poor shanties that highlight the contrasts of Puerto Rican life.

To the east of Columbus Square, which marks the edge of the colonial city, is **El Capitolio▶▶**, the seat of the Puerto Rican Senate and House of Representatives. Built in the 1920s, its style imitates that of the White House in Washington; in the rotunda, visitors can see a copy of the Puerto Rican constitution, which was originally drawn up in 1954.

Farther along the coast is **Condado▶▶**, one of the town's main tourist strips. Huge hotels, interspersed with stores and conference centers, stand right on the seafront, and behind them are streets full of restaurants and bars. This line of tall buildings extends along the coast solidly for the six or so miles to **Isla Verde▶▶**, the other main tourist area, which is crammed with luxury hotels, an interesting variety of restaurants, and bars overlooking a large, popular beach.

Inland are the working areas of the capital. Hato Rey, known for its street of glass-fronted skyscrapers, is the commercial heart of San Juan, which is one of the biggest financial markets in the Caribbean. A more traditional Caribbean market operates in Rio Piedras, with tropical fruits and vegetables on sale. To the south, the **Botanical Gardens▶** provide a green and welcome retreat from the hustle of the city and its endless traffic. A ferry ride across the bay from Old San Juan takes you to Catano, where the **Bacardi Rum Distillery and Museum▶▶** provides tours for visitors (tel: 788-1500. *Open* Mon–Sat).

As tourists have flooded into their resorts and towns, many Caribbean islands have gained reputations for their gambling centers. But beyond the roulette tables, there is a popular tradition of West Indian gambling and bar games, from domino contests to local wrestling matches or even cock fights.

Caribbean casinos have a predictable lineup of games: *vingt et un*, roulette, craps, and slot machines. If casino gambling is an important factor in your vacation choice, the following islands should be on your list: Antigua; Aruba (which has about 10 glitzy gaming rooms with cabaret shows); Bonaire (one small casino at the Flamingo Beach Hotel); the Dominican Republic (casinos in all the main resorts); Guadeloupe and Martinique (two each); Puerto Rico (a host of casinos in Condado and Isla Verde and at hotels around the island); St. Kitts (at the Jack Tar Village), St. Croix, with its first casino now open and others to come, and the Dutch side of Sint Maarten, where there are nine casinos. Opening hours vary, but many continue as long as the gamblers do.

GAMBLING TRAVELERS
Cuba was one of the biggest gambling islands, attracting thousands of U.S. visitors to its gaming houses, until 1959, when casinos and all other trappings of capitalism were outlawed by the young Cuban revolutionaries. Since then Puerto Rico (and the Bahamas, which are also close to the States) have taken over as the favorite gambling destinations for American visitors.

Cock-fighting On the French- and Spanish-speaking Caribbean islands, cock-fighting is a major spectator sport. It is a brutal event—the cocks are occasionally killed—staged in a cockpit with steeply banked seats. Cocks are prepared for weeks in advance for a fight, with special diets and grooming. On the day of the fight owners bring their birds into the ring, showing them off to the crowd and brandishing them at one another as the bets are placed. As the fight begins, two cocks lunge at each other, pecking and slashing with their claws, while the audience erupts into screams and shouts of encouragement. Raising fighting cocks was a traditional Caribbean way of becoming rich in times past. In the French Caribbean, a variation on the bloodsport theme is occasionally introduced, when mongeese and snakes are pitted against one another in a contest to the death.

Fighting cocks are a traditional way of life in Puerto Rico

DOMINOES
Played in just about every bar throughout the Caribbean, dominoes are even enjoyed by Fidel Castro, the President of Cuba. The pieces are usually laid on the playing board with a grand flourish and a loud slap; in Barbados they are referred to as "cards," and are even "shuffled" in preparation for the game.

Casa del Frances, Vieques, built as a plantation house

LUMINOUS LAKE
The phosphorescent lake at Mosquito Bay, Vieques, has an eerie beauty. At night it glows where paddles cut the water; fish leave streaks as they dart away, and in a storm the whole surface is set alight. The cause is bioluminescence; tiny creatures emitting light when agitated.

Puerto Rican license plate

▶▶ Vieques and Culebra

If you look east from Fajardo, on Puerto Rico's east coast, you will see that the sea is sprinkled with islands and cays as far as the horizon, culminating in the Virgin Islands. About 6 miles from the mainland, Vieques is the largest of the Puerto Rican islands; not far beyond it is Culebra, surrounded by a collection of little satellites. These islands are dry and low, with rolling hills and some of the best beaches in Puerto Rico. The wildlife is different from that on the mainland—you might see red-billed tropicbirds and turtles, which lay their eggs on the beach—and Culebra is partly given over to a wildlife refuge.

Vieques An hour's ferry ride from the mainland brings you to Vieques' northern shore and its main town, Isabel Segunda, where many of the island's 8,000 inhabitants live. The central square is quiet and pleasant and there is a tourist information office there. A restored 19th-century **fort▶** stands on the hill above the town. In **Esperanza▶▶**, on the southern coast, bars and restaurants are strung along the shorefront, a stone's throw from the island's best beaches. Look for the **Casa del Frances▶▶**, a stylish old plantation house. Much of the island belongs to the U.S. Navy and is used for naval exercises (to the resentment of many islanders), but at other times visitors are allowed on to the area's beaches—including Red Beach and Blue Beach. During World War II, Vieques was the fall-back base for the British Navy should Britain fall in the German invasion.

Culebra This tranquil island sits among a small crowd of tiny coral outcrops 25 miles east of the mainland. Only 2,000 islanders live on Culebra, many in the only town of Dewey, better known as Pueblo, where there is a small information office. Culebra was used as a gunnery range by the U.S. Navy for many years, but after a campaign by the islanders the government eventually withdrew in 1975. The snorkeling off Culebra is wonderful.

▶▶▶ El Yunque Rain Forest

The most accessible area of Puerto Rico from the capital is the northeast, with its rich variety of mountains, mangroves, and beaches. Perhaps the most popular tour is to El Yunque, an area of rain forest which because of its position in the far northeast of the island enjoys the best of the water-laden Atlantic winds (bringing about 120 billion gallons of rain every year).

El Yunque is approached by Route 3 from town or by following the coast road out of Isla Verde and then heading into the mountains, rampant with tropical foliage, on Route 191. In this 27,000-acre National Park, 240 species of tree grow in three different varieties of forest (rain forest, montane forest, and stunted dwarf forest, near the 3,000-foot peaks). Trails have been cut into the forest, with explanatory signboards, waterfalls, and look-out platforms. There is a visitor's center on Route 191, where information is provided about the plants and animals—such as the coquí tree frog, whose dual note echoes through the greenery—and about the 60 or so species of bird, including the endangered Puerto Rican parrot. As this is rain forest, there are frequent tropical showers, so it is advisable to take a water-proof coat.

On the far northeastern tip of the island there is another nature reserve at **Las Cabezas de San Juan▶▶**, where boardwalks lead through the mangroves past the shore and swamp birdlife. A visitor's center is housed in the old Faro (lighthouse), from which there are superb views toward the Virgin Islands. The route back to town on the north coast road passes Luquillo, site of one of the island's most popular public beaches and a string of excellent roadside snack outlets, before reaching Loíza, a poor area known for its costumed *fiesta patronal* (Santiago) on July 25. At Piñones, just before the road comes into Isla Verde, is another area of protected mangrove swamps that is the habitat of birds such as snowy egrets, pelicans, and herons. It also provides a home for a rich diversity of wildlife besides.

MANGROVE BIRDLIFE
Mangrove swamps harbor lots of crustaceans, providing food for herons, terns, sandpipers, and stilts. The easiest to visit from San Juan are Piñones (from Boca de Cangrejos marina) and Las Cabezas de San Juan. Guanica, in the southwest, is designated a World Biosphere site by U.N.E.S.C.O.

Bar at Esperanza

Other Caribbean states

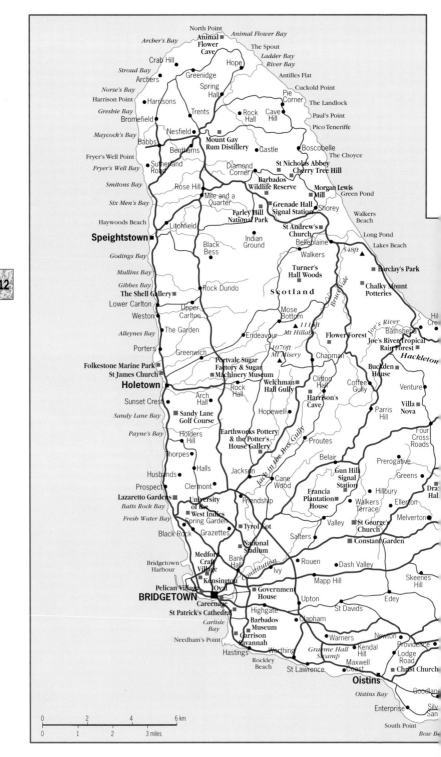

212

Barbados

Probably the most British of the Caribbean islands, Barbados has a gentle, undulating interior, ringed by safe and attractive beaches. It is relatively prosperous, relaxed, and welcoming, and has absorbed the tourist industry gradually, without allowing it to overwhelm the life and character of the island. Popular attractions include its famous rum, its lively south coast nightlife, and its passion for cricket. Away from the low-key sophistication and luxury hotels of the west coast, Barbados's (and one of the Caribbean's) premier tourist areas, are the high-rise hotels, guesthouses, and condos of the south. In contrast, the east coast is quiet and mostly undeveloped. Because the island has so many hotels and is easily

213

SETTLING BY FORCE

Three centuries ago, to be "Barbadosed" was to be sent forcibly to the West Indies. Settlers were needed on the islands and the courts deported common thieves, and prisoners of war there. They were set to work alongside indentured laborers, who sold their labor for five or seven years in return for their passage to the islands, on the understanding that they would be given land to plant at the end of their term. In the late 17th century, African slaves provided a large-scale labor force for the sugar plantations.

Nelson's statue stands in Bridgetown's Trafalgar Square

reached on regular flights from Europe and the U.S.A., good package deals are available to Barbados through tour operators and travel agents.

Barbados is one of the best Caribbean islands for an active beach vacation. By day, watersports are easy to arrange, and there are plenty of beach bars to retire to. Divers come to enjoy the marine life of the coral reefs, and several companies offer equipment rental and scuba-diving instruction. Snorkeling is an easier alternative, and nondivers have access to underwater views from the dry comfort of the **Atlantis Submarine**▶▶ (tel: /436-8929 for reservations). Barbados has more exploring potential than other islands. The interior, although nowhere near as dramatic or lush as Jamaica or St. Lucia, has pleasant scenery, with mahogany woods, cattle and black-bellied sheep grazing on rough meadows, traditional wooden chattel houses, and forests of sugar cane. There are also magnificent plantation houses—some open to the public, some still the homes of "high white" families of the old plantocracy, some the hub of working plantations, and one or two available for rent to visitors. By night there is a wide choice of nightclubs and many good restaurants, serving local as well as international food. Although not cheap, several of them include magnificent coastal settings in the price.

Shaped like a pear set at a slightly tipsy angle, Barbados is made entirely of coral limestone. It measures 21 miles by 14 miles and lies in the Atlantic Ocean, 100 miles east of the Windward Island of St. Vincent. From the western beaches, gently lapped by the Caribbean Sea, the land rises steadily through the cane fields and cultivated land of the central plains, culminating in the 985-foot

LITTLE ENGLAND
In colonial days, the leading Barbadians were proud of their association with Britain, and of being the only British Caribbean island never to be conquered by another power. They called their island, which was a highly successful colony, Little England, and having been nicknamed "Bims" by their slaves, styled themselves as inhabitants of "Bimshire," as though Barbados were a county of Britain.

King's Beach, on the west coast

Bajans "liming" (in discussion) on a fishing boat at Bridgetown

LITTLE BRISTOL
In the 17th century, during the early days of colonization, Bristol was the major port on the west coast of England, and many settlers on Barbados came originally from the West Country (Southwest England). Speightstown's West Country residents earned it the nickname Little Bristol, and their accent can still be heard in the drawled Bajan vowels.

escarpment of Hackleton's Cliff in the east. North of here is the hilly Scotland district, where the island reaches its highest point, Mount Hillaby, at 1,115 feet. Powerful Atlantic waves (nicknamed "white horses") crash constantly against the dramatic eastern shoreline, carving out bizarre rock formations (and steadily eroding the coast).

ISLAND LIFE The island's population of 265,000 is one of the densest in the world, a fact that is clearly visible in the urban sprawl radiating from Bridgetown along the western and, increasingly, the southern coasts. Solitude may be hard to find on Barbados, but the island is made special by its people. Bajans, mostly of African descent, are some of the friendliest West Indians; whether at the weekly Sunday **National Trust walk▶▶** (see side-bar) or in a local rum shop for a game of dominoes, the Bajans will give you an amiable welcome and are always ready to fill you in on all the latest island gossip.

The Barbados economy has mostly recovered from a recession in the early 1990s, and the island is busy and businesslike, with extensive building in island infrastructure. Bajans treat tourism as an important industry, and they are gracious to visitors, making this an excellent island for a first-time visit to the Caribbean.

Much is made of Barbados's Englishness, the result of a long-standing colonial connection with Britain. For a time the island was even known as Little England (see panel opposite). While it is true that Barbados has visibly kept more British traits than other islands, in their traditions and manners, the North American influence can also clearly be seen today. Since Independence in 1966, the people have started to take pride in their Afro-Caribbean heritage, and more recently have developed their indigenous Bajan culture.

RUM AND EXERCISE
The Sunday walk with the Barbados National Trust (a preservation body), and the Bajan rum store are both equally hallowed institutions. On the former, a guide leads walkers through a chosen area of historic interest (perhaps a section of old railroad, or an abandoned fort) for a couple of hours on Sunday mornings (tel: 426 2421; a small fee is charged). In the rum stores, customers may offer informal instruction in such essential pursuits as dominoes and talking politics.

Other Caribbean states

THE CAREENAGE

The Careenage takes its name from the system of tilting the hull of a ship. (A number of harbors in the Windward Islands and the nearby French islands share the same name.) A weight was attached to the ship's mast in shallow water and the ship would be tilted so that her hull and bottom were exposed, so they could be scrubbed free of barnacles and weeds.

The Careenage,
Bridgetown

▶▶ Bridgetown

The capital of Barbados lies on a broad, protected bay in the southwestern corner of the island. Old colonial buildings and modern offices stand side by side in the center of Bridgetown, but over the years the city, which has around 100,000 inhabitants, has spread steadily north and southeast along the coasts.

Bridgetown is the center of island life, where the offices of government and big business stand above lively West Indian street markets. Its traditional heart is the Careenage, a sea inlet where, in the days of seaborne travel, lighters would bring ashore passengers from the ocean-going ships. There is not much nautical activity any more (passengers now arriving by sea will usually dock at the deep-water harbor), but yachts and fishing boats still use the inlet, and bars such as the Waterfront Café cater to the landlubbers.

NELSON

Lord Nelson, "Preserver of the West Indies," arrived in pursuit of the French Admiral Villeneuve during the Napoleonic Wars and removed the threat of French invasion. Without a column to stand on, the statue in Bridgetown is a lot smaller than that in London, but it has the distinction of being 30 years older. As a legacy of the colonial era Nelson is a somewhat contentious figure, and some islanders would prefer a statue of a Bajan gracing Trafalgar Square—"Put up a Bajan man," sang the Mighty Gabby, famous calypso star and consciousness-raiser.

On the north side of the Careenage is Trafalgar Square. Smaller than its namesake in London, this square also has a statue of the Admiral Horatio Nelson (see panel). Near him stand the two distinctive colonial public buildings, built from local coral rock in the 1870s. Crenellated and with pointed arches, they have red tin roofs and green louvered windows, which keep out the sun but allow ventilation when there is a breeze. The House of Assembly, the seat of the Barbados Parliament, which was founded in 1639, is open to visitors. British monarchs from James I to Victoria are commemorated in stained-glass windows in the Parliament chamber.

At the center of Trafalgar Square is a small fountain, its bowls supported on the tails of brightly painted dolphins, which was erected in 1865 to mark the arrival of piped water—an important event in a hot town. From the square leads an important commercial street: Broad Street, where Bridgetown's major stores are housed in old colonial buildings; north of here is Swan Street, a typically Caribbean (weekday) street market where vendors stand by their colorful stalls selling anything from oranges to fluorescent shoe laces or mirror shades.

Selling fruit in the capital

BAJAN DISHES
Whatever it has taken from the British in other respects, Barbados owes little to them in the way of food. Bajan fare depends more on local ingredients, including fish and local vegetables such as yam, plantain, and sweet potato, cooked according to Amerindian and African techniques. Pepperpot is a strong tasting Amerindian stew made with meat and vegetables and served with traditional Caribbean rice and peas, cooked in coconut milk or with pumpkin fritters. Local fish and chicken are usually curried and served in Creole sauces of pepper, tomato, and onion.

St. Michael's Cathedral, a few blocks east of Trafalgar Square, was built in 1789 and provides a haven from the town's hubbub. The restored Synagogue, originally built in the 17th century, is off Magazine Lane near the law courts; in the yard is a gravestone dedicated to Benjamin Messiah, who was renowned as a circumciser, apparently performing with "Great Applause and Dexterity."

Cheapside Market, at the northwest end of Lower Broad Street, is set in a traditional tin market building and sells mainly local food and vegetables, and in the Rasta Mall goods for sale include rastafarian herbal concoctions and leather pendants from Africa. Near by, Pelican Village sells more formal arts and crafts.

In the northeastern area of the city, you will find **Tyrol Cot**▶▶ (tel: 429-0474. *Open* Mon–Fri 9–5. *Admission charge*), the elegant home of the Bajan political family, the Adams, which has provided two island prime ministers. There are artisan workshops in the grounds, set in traditional Bajan "chattel houses".

A couple of miles to the south of the Careenage is the Garrison Savannah, the military district of the colonial era. The old Georgian barrack buildings are still visible, some restored, others in decay, but the 300-acre Savannah itself is now used mainly for sports events, including horse-racing and local cricket matches. The **Barbados Museum**▶▶ (tel: 427-020. *Open* Mon–Sat 9–5. Sun 2–6. *Admission charge*), at the corner of the Savannah, is situated in the island's former prison. The museum displays aspects of life in Barbados in Amerindian and colonial times, including the old mobile chattel houses of the former slaves and the ill-fated Barbados Railway (see panel). Rooms here have been fitted using period furniture and a gallery of maps and prints is set in the old cells.

THE BARBADOS RAILWAY
During the 19th century the British built railroads throughout their empire, and despite its small size, even Barbados had one built in the 1880s. The line ran east from Bridgetown through the central sugar cane lands before descending to the Atlantic coast at Bathsheba and continuing to Belleplaine. It was used by workers coming into town in the week and was usually packed for church outings at the weekends. Having suffered financial problems from the start, it finally folded in 1937.

Sandy Lane Hotel, on the west coast

▶▶▶ Caribbean (West) Coast

The beach that stretches up the west coast of Barbados is one of the finest in the Caribbean. Its golden sand is washed by the calm Caribbean Sea, and behind the coconut palms and casuarina trees are superb hotels such as the Sandy Lane and the Coral Reef Club, long-renowned and now renovated havens of luxury which have given Barbados its name for tropical refinement. Interspersed among them are restaurants and cheaper hotels, and two golf courses: one at Sandy Lane and the other north of Speightstown at the Heywoods Hotel.

The roads north out of Bridgetown lead to the Spring Garden Highway, which comes alive each year on the first Monday in August with colorful dancing parades during the festival of **Cropover▶▶▶**. North of the town center is the Kensington Oval, the Barbados cricket stadium—the Bajans' fervor for the game makes attending a cricket match a rousing experience. On the coast nearby are the **Mountgay Visitor Centre▶▶** (tel: 42-9066. *Open* Mon–Fri 9–4, Sat 10–1) and the **Malibu Visitor Centre▶▶**, where tours include a look at the vats and the distilling process, and a taste of the rum. The history of the sugar-refining process is traced at the **Portvale Sugar Factory▶** (near Holetown), on view between February and May.

Holetown was the site of the first European settlement on Barbados in 1627, colonized after it was claimed for the British by Captain John Powell in 1625. The small but stately St. James Parish Church is notable for its English style of architecture, but Holetown today mainly consists of open spaces and an excellent string of restaurants and bars. The **Folkestone Marine Park▶** has a small marine museum and a snorkeling trail through the offshore corals, and inland lies **Harrison's Cave▶▶**, with a network of illuminated underground caverns.

Back on the coast, **Speightstown▶**, 7½ miles north of the capital, seems a sleepy town but has some good bars; beyond it, the countryside opens out to reveal cane fields, small settlements and deserted beaches. At the island's northern tip, you can visit Animal Flower Cave, named for the sea anemones or "animal flowers" that live there.

WEST COAST BEACHES
Calm and west-facing, the Caribbean coast is an almost continuous strip of beautiful sands, ideal for early morning walks or for sunset-watching. Though the beaches are never really crowded, you cannot expect to be alone here, because there are so many hotels set along the coast. There are few divisions between the beaches, and in some places you can wade through the shallows to the next beach. All beaches are public and provide a right of way, and hotels have watersports facilities—non-residents can usually negotiate their use. Paynes Bay, with its easy access and choice of watersports deals, is a good option.

Sports are unifying features of an area made diverse by its geography. Within the former British Caribbean islands, cricket is something of a religion: islanders will drop everything to listen to the commentary of an international match in which the West Indies team is playing. In the Spanish Caribbean the most popular sport is baseball, and life comes to a halt if an important game is being played.

Cricket The West Indies have had a world-class cricket team for years—a remarkable achievement for an area with so small a pool of players to choose from. Players for the team are drawn from all the British Caribbean islands, but the main centers are the islands where there are international-class (Test Match) grounds (Jamaica, Antigua, Barbados, Trinidad, and Guyana). Barbados has an impressive record, having won the inter-island competition (the Red Stripe Tournament) more often than any other team.

Cricket is played on the beaches and in back streets, with a tennis ball and sticks for stumps; tourists are often asked to join in. Success at cricket is a route to fame and wealth, so it is fiercely contested: the best attain national hero status. Famous names include Viv Richards (Antigua), Clive Lloyd (Guyana), Gary Sobers, (Barbados), and now Brian Lara (Trinidad).

OTHER SPORTS
By means of cable TV, the Caribbean is steadily being influenced by sports from America. Basketball is very popular, as is football, although the latter is restricted to the small screen, and is not played on the islands. The major participant sport in the French Caribbean is soccer, but the most popular spectator sport is cock-fighting (see page 209), also followed on the Spanish islands, but virtually unknown in the British Caribbean.

219

Baseball This is the national sport in Cuba, the Dominican Republic, and Puerto Rico, and has been played on the U.S. Virgin Islands since the Americans arrived. Just as many West Indian cricketers go to the U.K. to play, so the Dominicans and Puerto Ricans, as well as several Cuban defectors, play in American pro leagues. Sammy Sosa, star homerun-hitter for the Chicago Cubs, is Dominican. In the streets the children play a toned-down version of baseball, not unlike New York's stickball, in which they are not allowed to run.

The diamond at Charlotte Amalie, St. Thomas

GUN HILL SIGNAL STATION

Now restored, Gun Hill Signal Station stands in the center of the island with impressive views all around. It is one of a string of old military signal posts that could send messages (by mirror-flash or by colored lantern) across the island in minutes, warning the barracks of approaching ships, and the merchants of trading vessels. Set far away from the malarial swamps on the coast and bathed in fresh winds, the station was used as a hospital in the later colonial era.

The fishing village of Bathsheba on the wild and weather-beaten Atlantic coast

▶▶ Central Barbados

Inland from the capital, the land rises steadily through the Bridgetown suburbs (where Bajans grow their ground provisions of sweet potatoes and yams) into open country and cane fields, toward the cliffs that tower above the Atlantic coast. **Francia Plantation▶▶** gives a vivid idea of the privileged lifestyle of the old Barbados planters. Standing on high ground in attractive gardens, Francia is furnished with antique furniture and decorated with maps and prints of old Barbados. Another plantation house worth visiting is Sunbury, which has been restored following fire damage, with period furniture. In the gardens, there are cannon and a collection of old horse-drawn carriages. It is worth taking a quick look at **Codrington College▶**, an imposing religious seminary and school (buildings not open to visitors) that dates from the early 18th century and is approached along an avenue of splendid royal palm trees. **Harrison's Cave▶▶** is an extensive series of pale-gold limestone caverns off Hwy 2, complete with exquisitely formed stalactites amd stalagmites, subterranean streams, and a 40-foot waterfall.

The steep, somewhat remote east coast of Barbados is an unexpected find on an island usually associated with calm seas, gently sloping beaches, and palm trees. From the top of Hackleton's Cliff, the site of **St. John's Parish Church▶**, there is a marvelous view over small country villages and down to the east coast, where Atlantic waves roll in against huge sculpted rocks. The sea here is rough and unpredictable, and signs on the beaches warn of dangerous currents and advise people not to swim.

THE ATLANTIS HOTEL

In its dramatic setting atop the cliff in Bathsheba, the Atlantis Hotel has a fine view of the Atlantic waves. The hotel is past its best, but its Sunday brunch (a traditional West Indian buffet) has become legendary. The restaurant at the Round House is excellent.

Bajans tend to do so regardless, but visitors should not follow their example.

Andromeda Gardens▶▶, near Bathsheba, are set out on the hillside, with fiery blooms and flowering trees from the tropical world, including frangipani, orchids, and the Traveler's Tree (see panel, page 207). Bathsheba and Cattlewash are now fishing villages, but attractive seafront villas remain from when colonials would come here to escape the Bridgetown heat. The veranda of the Kingsley Club (tel: 433-9384. *Open* daily 9–5. *Admission charge*) at Cattlewash is an excellent spot for lunch or afternoon tea.

An old rhyme describes the rum punch drunk by planters in colonial days: "One of sour, two of sweet, three of strong and four of weak." The sour is lime, the sweet is cane juice, the strong is rum and the weak is water (more likely to be fruit juice nowadays). Mix these ingredients, sprinkle with grated nutmeg, and you have a genuine Caribbean rum punch.

Practically every Caribbean island distills its own rum, but the main producers are Cuba and Puerto Rico, where rums are traditionally light in color, and Barbados and Jamaica, where they are darker and fuller in flavor. On the French islands some of the finer rums are aged to be drunk like a brandy after dinner. Most islands also produce a white rum for local consumption. St. Croix produces both light and dark Cruzan rum.

Rum is a by-product of sugar, distilled from the fermented juice of sugar cane or a mix of cane-juice and molasses. Visits can often be arranged to rum distilleries, full of gurgling vats and stills, and the heady, sweet smell of fermentation. All distillations of rum result in a clear liquid; darker rums gain their color from the addition of caramel during the ageing process, and from the oak barrels in which the rum is stored. Barrels of rum were used as currency in colonial times, when rum first became an important export.

Perhaps the most famous rum manufacturer is Bacardi, which was based in Cuba before its revolution but now works mainly from Puerto Rico, where there is a huge factory outside San Juan. In Jamaica the biggest name is Appleton, producing gold rums of different ages and a strong white rum known as John Crow Batty (crow's backside). The Appleton factory can be reached from Montego Bay. From Barbados come Mountgay and Cockspur, as well as white rums such as Alleynes, and from Haiti the renowned Barbaucourt. The French islands have a long tradition of high-quality "rhum agricole" that includes Rhum St. James and Trois Rivières of Martinique (both of which can be visited). Caribbean rum is used as filling in expensive chocolates, and as the basis of a number of liqueurs such as Malibu.

RUM HISTORY
Rum first appeared in Barbados in about 1650, when it was known as "kill-devil" and "rumbul-lion." Pirates would drink an explosive mixture of rum and gunpowder. British sailors were entitled to a daily measure of rum from the 18th century until 1970.

221

Exotic liqueurs are produced all around the islands: Camerhogne is Grenada's mixture of rum, spices, and fruit

The Morgan Lewis Mill: one of the last of over 500 windmills that once turned on the island

SCOTTISH ORIGINS
As Barbados was once known as Little England, it is somehow fitting that there should be a hilly district to the north called Scotland. The parish is even named for St. Andrew. Many Scotsmen were banished to the east of the island, including Scotland, during an early episode of racial and religious segregation in the mid-17th century, and a few of their descendants still live there, in poor white communities. These settlers became known as Redlegs, supposedly because they did not tan under their kilts.

EUROPEAN INFLUENCES
St. Nicholas Abbey was built to European designs and included fireplaces; the settlers had not yet realized that even on winter nights they did not need a fire for warmth. Its curved gables help to date it to about 1650 (following the maxim "curly early, straighter later"). Competing in age with St. Nicholas Abbey is Drax Hall, a privately owned 1650s stone building off Highway 4, with a wood-paneled interior and mastic-wood staircase (open only once a year).

▶▶ Scotland

Scotland is a hilly district in northeast Barbados; a series of peaks, including Mount Hillaby, the island's highest, overlook the Atlantic coast. This remote district makes an interesting half-day drive, through isolated settlements where villagers collect water from standpipes.

The Flower Forest▶▶, just off Highway 2, has marked paths lined with trees such as mango and breadfruit, with their green cannonball-sized fruits, and a fine show of tropical blooms such as hibiscus and poinsettia. **Turner's Hall Woods▶** are the last remaining area of the natural woodland that covered Barbados until it was cleared for sugar plantations. Here you can see trees native to the island—fustic, West Indian locust, and sand-box trees—as well as birds and monkeys such as the Lesser Antillean bullfinch and the black Carib grackles.

In the days when it was carpeted with sugar cane, Barbados had about 500 windmills, whose sails turned constantly in the Trade Winds, driving the millstones that crushed the sugar cane to release its juice. The **Morgan Lewis Mill▶** is the last surviving example, and although it does not actually turn, the old crushing gear is on view. The **Grenade Hall Signal Station▶▶** is a recently restored link in the military communications chain (see panel, page 220). Close by, the **Barbados Wildlife Reserve▶▶** (Stateout Reserve: tel: 422-8826. *Open* daily) is a free-range reserve with paths laid out in a mahogany wood, where agouti (see page 24), spectacled cayman (which looks like an alligator), and iguana roam. A café in the grounds sells a range of snacks and Caribbean fruit juices flavored with mango or heavily sweetened tamarind.

St. Nicholas Abbey▶▶, in northern Scotland, is not actually an abbey, but a plantation house that is still working. An absorbing film shows shots of Barbados a century ago, with sugar workers, turning windmills, and "mauby ladies" serving the bitter mauby drink from vats which they carried on their heads.

▶ South Coast

The south coast of Barbados has a completely different feel from the better known, more sedate west coast. It attracts a younger, livelier crowd and lays a greater emphasis on activity outside the hotels, which are smaller and less expensive (package tourists often end up in this area, and there are also guesthouses here). Visitors tend to spend their days sunning themselves and windsurfing on the beaches; in the evenings they pour into the restaurants and bars, moving on to the clubs in St. Lawrence Gap and Bridgetown, where dancing and live music continue until the early hours. There are places to explore in the southeast, where isolated coves include Foul Bay, Harrismith Beach, and Bottom Bay, but most life centers around the "gaps," the small roads that lead down to the coast off Highway 7.

Highway 7 leads from Bridgetown past the Garrison Savannah and through the seemingly never-ending urbanized sprawl of Hastings, St. Lawrence and Worthing (hotels in this area are the Divi Southwinds Beach Resort, the Casuarina Beach Club and Southern Palms). Farther east, the Crane Beach Hotel sits on a hill-top overlooking the Atlantic. St. Lawrence Gap is a popular and busy area, with water sports facilities on the beaches around the small bay, and the main center for nightlife nearby with plenty of restaurants and bars where local bands play to packed crowds. There is usually a friendly atmosphere, but tourists have been robbed here, and you should be careful.

Beyond Maxwell, known for its windsurfing, is Barbados's fourth town, Oistins, a fishing community where the daily catch is sold on the waterfront. Recently, the fish market has gained a reputation as a lively place to eat out for simple dishes (especially fish), in the early evenings—worth a detour to join in.

At the rum factory and Heritage Park at Four Square, observe sugar and rum manufacturing, as well as contemporary Bajan artists at work in the foundry (tel: 426-2421. *Open* Mon–Thu 10–6. *Admission charge*).

LATE-NIGHT SNACKS
Baxter's Road was long a favorite with Bajans and tourists alike in search of late-night snacks of battered kingfish and a Banks beer. But allegiance seems to have switched to the fish market in Oistins, where 10 or 15 stalls sell simple fish and chicken meals in styrofoam boxes and on paper plates. In the early evening, you'll find music and a friendly crowd.

SAM LORD
Sam Lord's Castle (tel: 426-7350. *Open* daily. *Admission charge*), in Long Bay in the southeast, is now a large hotel, but it has a grim history. It was built in 1820 by Sam Lord, a scoundrel who imprisoned his wife (she eventually escaped), and made a fortune by defrauding and, some say, murdering rich victims. He is also said to have made a pretty penny by plundering ships that he lured onto the rocks by hanging lanterns in the trees at night to fool sailors into thinking they had spotted a harbor. He would then bring his haul along an underground passage to the castle. The tale may be fanciful—the underground passage is fictitious—but Sam Lord and his crooked ways were real enough.

Watching the world from a rum shop in Bridgetown

BIRD-WATCHING
With fruit-filled feeders just a few feet away, the veranda at the Asa Wright Nature Centre, one of the largest and finest in the whole Caribbean, provides people who are not normally bird-watchers with an excellent view of Trinidad's spectacular bird-life. It is said that you can see 25 species before breakfast: honey creepers, hummingbirds, *cro pendulas*, and toucans, among others (tel: 667-4655).

Trinidad and Tobago

This two-island nation offers a vivid contrast between bustling, cosmopolitan Trinidad and peaceful, rural Tobago. Trinidad is loud, lively, and full of ethnic and cultural diversity; Tobago tends to be less developed and much more traditionally Caribbean, with its delightful beaches and rolling countryside. Trinidad's Port of Spain attracts hundreds of thousands of spectators each year to its spectacular and exhilarating carnival, while Tobago is a better option for those looking for a quieter dose of sand and sun.

This southernmost nation of the Caribbean lies off the coast of South America. Trinidad was still joined to the continent 10,000 years ago and in some places its mountains (the Southern, Northern, and Central ranges), fertile plains, and mangrove swamps are separated from Venezuela by only 10 miles of water. Its spectacular flora and fauna are similar to the mainland's; there are hundreds of species of butterflies and

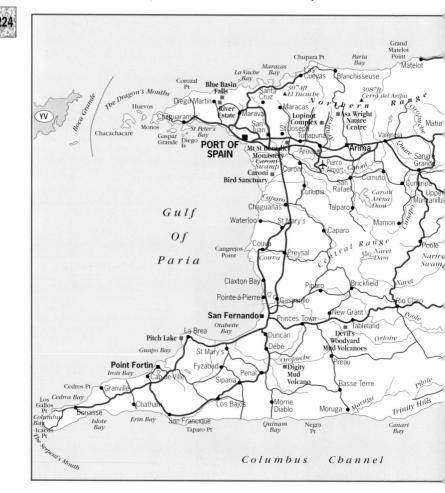

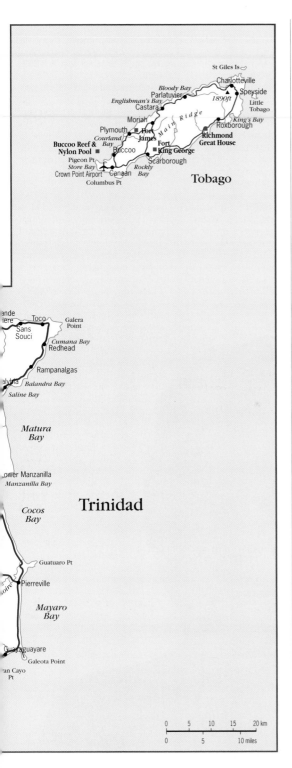

FESTIVALS
Divali is celebrated in Trinidad during October or November and honors Lakshmi, the Hindu goddess of light. During the festival, followers go from one open house to the next, drinking and feasting, and hundreds of coconut oil lamps are lit in small clay pots, illuminating whole valleys. Phagwa is celebrated in the streets in March with huge paper floats and bottles of red food dye, which is thrown over spectators, and the Muslim festival of Hosay (dates vary) commemorates the martyrdom of Hussein and features a parade of his tomb, accompanied by dancers and drummers. At the end of the year, you will hear traditional Christmas "parang" songs.

ANGOSTURA
aromatic bitters
Share
the
secret.

birds (more than can be found on any other Caribbean island), including 17 varieties of hummingbird and the scarlet ibis—the national bird—which can be seen flying in to roost in the Caroni Swamp (situated just south of Port of Spain) during the evening.

Tobago broke off from the continent in an earlier geological age and lies some 22 miles northeast of Trinidad. Its spine of volcanic mountains, the Main Ridge, is mantled with rainforest, which descends to a plain in the southwest. Much of the coastline is gouged with steep-sided bays and the underwater slopes are clad with corals, but in the gentler western end of the island there are some fine white sand beaches that are well worth seeking out.

HISTORY Christopher Columbus landed on Trinidad in 1498, during his third voyage to the Americas, and named it in honor of the Holy Trinity. During the 16th century, the island was used as a Spanish staging post in the search for El Dorado, the Golden One, whose kingdom was thought to be on the mainland near here. Tobago was probably not seen by Columbus, but after Europeans had settled there in the mid-17th century, there followed fierce battles for its possession, and the island changed hands more times than any other island in the Caribbean before it was eventually taken into British ownership in 1814.

Trinidad and Tobago were politically linked in 1888 and remained a British colony until 1962, so they retain similarities to other English-speaking islands in the area—but theirs is a far more complex heritage. Spanish place names can still be found everywhere, and there are strong traces of French Creole, a legacy of the Royalist settlers who fled from France in the wake of the 1789 Revolution.

The islanders joke that when the British took over, Trinidad became a Caribbean island with a French population, which was governed by the British according to laws laid down by Spain.

ISLAND LIFE The British added new strains to Trinidad's already potent mix of peoples, shipping in African slaves to work the sugar plantations and, later, after emancipation, turning to Asian "East" Indian, Chinese, and Middle Eastern immigrants, who worked as indentured laborers. The result is that Trinidad has a cosmopolitan population, of which nearly half is made up of descendents of Indian immigrants. Hindi, some French and French Creole are spoken as well as English; parish churches stand side by side with Islamic minarets; Indian and Chinese restaurants operate alongside tropical fruit stalls; and Hindu and Muslim festivals such as Divali and Hosay are celebrated as well as the Caribbean Carnival.

Tobago was also a plantation island and most of its population is of African descent, but for the traveler and the tourist, the two islands offer radically different experiences. Trinidad has a vibrant cultural life—theaters, a concert hall and festivals—while Tobago is altogether quieter (Trinidadians tend to go there for a rest), with secluded sandy coves. It has been developed somewhat in recent years, with new hotels and guesthouses springing up along the coast.

Trinidad is the place to experience hectic Caribbean bustle. Port of Spain is a lively and busy city, and music, heard everywhere, is an essential part of life. A visit to a calypso evening, or a "Tent" at Carnival time, is an essential Trinidadian experience (even though the language and repartee are hard to follow); the songs, which deal with island gossip and current affairs, are performed with great gusto by popular calypsonians, especially in the days leading up to the ultimate Trinidadian experience—**Carnival▶▶▶** (see pages 234–235). After a week of steel bands (which were invented here) and calypso shows, Carnival culminates on Mardi Gras with a two-day pageant around the streets of Port of Spain, with hundreds of thousands of costumed revelers and onlookers dancing in the streets.

The simple life in Buccoo, Tobago

BAMBOO CANNON
Loud explosions resounding through a Trinidadian valley (or elsewhere in the Caribbean) may indicate that someone has been given a bamboo cannon, a popular child's toy that is still used at Caribbean festivities. The cannon is made by hollowing out a length of bamboo, leaving only the bottom section untouched. A small hole is then cut about 6 in. from the end and kerosene is poured inside and warmed so that it turns into gas, which is lit with touch-paper, causing a heart-stopping bang.

Trinidad

Miguel Street is fictitious, created by Trinidadian writer V.S. Naipaul in his novel of the same name, but it has all the characters and life of a typical West Indian town. It could be almost anywhere in the Caribbean, but Naipaul, perhaps the Caribbean's best-known writer, was born in Trinidad and set his story in the island's capital.

Port of Spain is a large, active, modern city of about 300,000 people, lying on the Gulf of Paria in the northwest. In style it's a typical Caribbean mix, with modern high-rises and traditional Creole wooden houses overlooking the bustling streets, where vendors sell wares from their carefully arranged stalls.

The heart of the town is Independence Square, a wide avenue a couple of blocks in from the waterfront. At right angles to the square is one of the city's main shopping areas, Frederick Street. A walk up this street brings you to Woodford Square, named for Governor Woodford, who had the town rebuilt in 1813 after its destruction by fire five years earlier. On the square's western side is the **Red House**▶▶, Trinidad's parliament building, a massive Victorian pile whose two chambers can be visited, and diagonally opposite is the Anglican Cathedral of the Holy Trinity. The center of the square, tree-shaded and surrounded by iron railings, is a local gathering place. This was the spot where Dr. Eric Williams, the leader of Trinidad for many years before and after Independence, held his political rallies.

Farther along Frederick Street, beyond the Tourist Information Office (Nos. 134–138) is the **National Museum and Art Gallery**▶▶ (tel: 623-5941. *Open* Tue–Sun 10–6. *Admission free*), where displays of Trinidad historical and cultural life include the latest Carnival costumes. There is also an exhibition of the paintings of Trinidadian artist Michel Cazabon.

228

TRINIDADIAN DISHES
Trinidad's food is as varied as its racial heritage, and includes Indian, Chinese, and French as well as Caribbean cuisine. Probably the finest local fare can be bought at Veni Mange, at 67A Ariapita Avenue, where two sisters prepare meals for lunch only. The breakfast sheds on the waterfront in downtown Port of Spain sell rice and peas or callaloo at good prices, and street stalls sell snacks such as *rotis* (crêpe-like envelopes filled with chicken, beef, shrimp, or potato stew) or doubles (unleavened bread doubled over with a filling of split peas). Phulouri are batter balls served with a mango sauce.

King George III's cypher on a cannon that once protected Trinidad from rival European powers

Just north of Frederick Street, Port of Spain's vast central park, the 200-acre **Savannah**▶▶, officially called Queen's Park Savannah, is where Trinidadians go to walk, jog, play cricket, hockey and soccer, and buy their chilled coconuts and evening snacks. Look for the spectacularly extravagant houses known as the "Magnificent Seven" on the park's western side.

Among the plants displayed in the **Botanic Gardens**▶▶, north of the Savannah, are the red blossoms of the Trinidad national flower, the chaconia, a wild poinsettia that takes its name from the last Spanish governor, and an orchid collection. If you are lucky you might see some toucans flying home to roost here in the evening. Local animals such as the jaguar-like, buff-brown ocelot are kept in the **Emperor Valley Zoo**▶▶, next door to the grounds of the Presidential House.

OUTSIDE PORT OF SPAIN Beyond **Fort George**▶, an old defensive bastion with a line of cannons covering the approaches to Port of Spain, the Western Main Road passes through some of the city's most prosperous suburbs and continues to the northwestern Chaguaramas peninsula. At the head of the Diego Martin Valley is a museum with an original waterwheel devoted to the sugar era, at the **River Estate**▶▶.

During World War II the Chaguaramas peninsula was an American base and in the 1950s it was hoped that it would house the parliament building for the ill-fated Federation of the West Indies, in which the islands of the British Caribbean would come together in one political unit. A golf course is laid out near by, and the Anchorage is a popular swimming area, although the beach is not very attractive.

For the intrepid explorer, there are caves and colonial military ruins on Gaspard Grande Island, in the channel, and at the end of the peninsula is the Dragons' Mouths, the short channel that separates Trinidad from the Venezuelan coast.

Carib Beer, a Caribbean-wide Trinidadian export

VIEWS OF THE PAST
C.L.R. James and Eric Williams were two Trinidadian historians who between them overturned the conventional colonial view of British Caribbean history. James, who lived in London until his death in 1989, was a Marxist historian, best known for his account of the Haitian Revolution, *The Black Jacobins*. Williams, whose works include *From Columbus to Castro* and *A History of the Peoples of Trinidad and Tobago*, was Prime Minister of Trinidad for many years until his death in 1981.

When Europeans first arrived in the Caribbean, turtles provided a reliable source of food because they could be kept alive on their backs on board ship. Today, numbers have dwindled drastically, and some species of turtle are endangered. Their eggs (highly prized by some as an aphrodisiac) are often stolen and the turtles themselves are particularly vulnerable since they lay their eggs on the beach.

HELPING THE HATCHLINGS

Earthwatch (tel: 617/926 8200) sponsors a project to protect leatherback turtles in St. Croix (the largest population of leatherbacks in the U.S.). Volunteers can take part in nightly patrols to collect data on nesting females (measuring and tagging the turtles, counting eggs, and relocating nests in erosion zones). They also help hatchlings that are disoriented by the lights of Frederiksted, and keep predators away while they make their way to the sea.

HE OR SHE?

The sex of a turtle, like that of alligators and crocodiles, is determined by the temperature of the nest; the warmer the weather, the more females are hatched. The earlier hatchlings tend to be male (at the beginning of the year) and the later ones females, when the temperatures warm up.

Sea-turtles are seaborne reptiles with hard shells and flippers, which have remained basically unchanged for 250 million years. Five species of turtle live in the Caribbean: the loggerhead, the hawksbill, the ridley, the green turtle (once the most common, but now endangered), and, largest of all, the leatherback (also endangered), which can dive to 5,000 feet, weigh up to 1,550 lb. and live to 150 years old. Caribbean leatherbacks have been known to cross the Atlantic and swim as far north as Newfoundland.

The most fascinating part of a turtle's life-cycle is the way the young are hatched. The female leatherback nests

between April and June, arriving at night (often returning to the beach from which she originally came) and crawling laboriously up onto the beach to a point above the high water mark. For two hours she digs a hole with her hind flippers, to a depth of about 18 inches, and lays up to 200 eggs, each the size of a billiard ball. Then she covers them with sand and crawls back into the sea. The process is repeated perhaps 10 times during the season.

Over the next eight weeks the eggs incubate, and eventually the 4-inch hatchlings dig their way to the surface and set off for the sea, running the gauntlet of predators; apart from humans, herons and crabs lie in wait, and mongeese will actually dig them out of their nests. There is safety only in numbers. Several Caribbean hotels can arrange special trips to watch turtles nesting, and at the turtle farm on Grand Cayman, in the Cayman Islands, visitors can see turtles at different stages of development.

The beaches nearest to Port of Spain are on the north coast, over the mountains of the Northern Range, which tower above the city. The best route, and the most spectacular drive, is through the Maraval Valley. Maracas Bay, 1 mile wide, is flanked by massive headlands, thrown off by El Tucuche, Trinidad's highest peak. It's a traditional Trinidadian day out—part of the experience is to have a "shark and bake," a battered fish sandwich from one of the stalls. Here, the water is occasionally rough; it is calmer at Las Cuevas, a few miles beyond, where there are also beach facilities. From the north coast fishing village of Blanchisseuse, a road leads southward across the Northern Range, another long, twisting, and visually stunning drive.

The Eastern Main Road leads from just behind the waterfront in downtown Port of Spain toward St. Joseph, the original Spanish capital of the island. It then passes between the Northern Range and the northern edge of the **Caroni Swamp**▶▶▶ (tel: 645-1305. *Admission charge*), which harbors about half of the island's bird species, including the scarlet ibis, which flies in during the evening. It is said that up to 10,000 ibises can be roosting here at a time, and tours (with a guide) start at around 4:30 PM. Angostura Bitters is produced in a factory in St. Joseph which is open to visitors (see panel), and high above the town is the **Mount St. Benedict Monastery**▶, a peaceful spot with a fine view over the central plain.

A few miles up the Arouca river the **Lopinot Complex**▶▶ is an old cocoa estate cut into the huge valley early in the 19th century by the Comte de Lopinot, a refugee from turbulent Saint Domingue (Haiti). Part of the original estate house survives, set in pleasant gardens where Trinidadians picnic at the weekends. Early in the year the immortelle trees that were planted to shade the cocoa plants burst into a blaze of orange blooms. Several Native American descendants live in this area, where many locals speak French patois.

Whitehall, one of the "Magnificent Seven" houses that overlook the Savannah

ANGOSTURA BITTERS
Trinidad is the home of the world-famous aromatic Angostura Bitters, often added to cocktails. The business was started by the Venezuelan Siegert family in the 19th century, and the recipe is a secret, but involves a mixture of roots, barks, dried leaves, and spices with alcohol, boiled to give the dark bitters. The Angostura factory (tel: 623-1841), on the main road to St. Joseph, is open to visitors.

V.S. NAIPAUL

Vidiadhar Surajprasad Naipaul was born of a Brahmin family in Trinidad in 1932 and educated at Queen's Royal College, Port of Spain, and University College, Oxford. Many of his novels express pessimistic and critical views of his native culture. *A House for Mr Biswas* (1961), whose hero is based on Naipaul's father, describes the collapse of the Caribbean way of life, and his earliest books, *The Mystic Masseur* (1957), *The Suffrage of Elvira* (1958), and *Miguel Street* (1959) all satirize life and politics in Trinidad.

Maracas Bay, Trinidad

In the Arima Valley is another delightful retreat, the **Asa Wright Nature Centre**▶▶▶ (tel: 667-4655), a balconied estate house (with spartan yet elegant rooms for rent) looking out onto a vast, green valley. Here you can hear the strange "boing, boing" call of bell-birds and see the colorful flash of a toucan or an *oro pendula* in flight. Guided walks are offered in the grounds. Another excellent bird-watching spot is the Hollis Reservoir just north of Valencia (contact one of the bird-watching organizations listed in **Travel Facts**).

Beyond Valencia, southeast of the nature center, the strip of urban development gives way to forested and cultivated land. The road forks here and heads south toward the Atlantic coast at Manzanilla or north via Balandra to Toco, where there are good beaches.

To reach the south of the country from Port of Spain, turn right on the Uriah Butler Highway, just out of town, which skirts the Caroni Swamp and then heads out into the cane fields. The first major town is Chaguanas; V.S. Naipaul lived here and the house described in *A House for Mr Biswas* stands on Main Street. The road continues to San Fernando, Trinidad's second city; it passes the Pointe-à-Pierre oil refinery, a reminder that oil was once the island's chief export, funding its development during the boom years.

Trinidadians refer to the wilder country beyond San Fernando as the Deep South. At the town of La Brea, about 10 miles along the coast, is the **Pitch Lake**▶▶, a 100-acre cauldron of natural asphalt, fed by tar from beneath and forever turning; occasionally branches, ancient artifacts, and even bones are pushed up to the surface. It is worked as a mine and the pitch has been used in roads all over the world.

Tobago

With few large hotels and no crowds, this little island (only 20 miles by 6 miles) still has a tranquil charm. Tourism has gravitated around the southwestern tip of the island, where the best beaches are to be found, but elsewhere there are deserted coves set in the sinuous coastline, and quiet West Indian villages.

Most people arrive on Tobago at Crown Point Airport, on the far southwestern tip of the island. From here it is a short walk to most of the guesthouses and small hotels and to **Store Bay**▶▶, one of the island's liveliest beaches, where breakfast sheds have been set up selling such local dishes as "bakes" (like Johnny Cakes), served with salt fish buljol. Just north of Store Bay is the most popular beach, **Pigeon Point**▶▶, where there are palm-thatch bars and watersports. An entry charge can be avoided by walking in below the high-water mark (where the sand is not private). *Continued on page 236.*

A steel band performer making music on Tobago

SENSITIVE SOUVENIRS
Vendors at Caribbean beaches sell all sorts of trinkets and jewelry made from local materials. There is some good work made with calabash shells in Trinidad and Tobago, and from other local beads. Beware of buying jewelry made from turtle-shell or coral, because they may well have been obtained illegally.

Continued on page 236.

Trinidad's annual carnival is the Caribbean's largest, liveliest, and most flamboyant party. For two days before Lent, hundreds of thousands of revelers flood onto the streets of Port of Spain, clad in bright lycra, sequins, and feathered headdresses, and dance in "bands" of a thousand or more, all shuffling and strutting in rhythm. Mas, as it is familiarly known, has been adopted by other islands all over the Caribbean, but the Trinidadians still claim to do it better than anyone else.

234

Mas has its roots in Catholic pre-Lenten festivities of two centuries ago, in which the Trinidadian French Creoles would visit one another's houses for masked balls. After emancipation in the 1830s, ex-slaves adopted the masquerade, turning it into a drum-driven street-party. Suppressed by the authorities many times, it has grown since World War II into a massive, exuberant celebration.

Carnival begins to warm up soon after Christmas, when the calypsonians (see page 238) release their songs and the steel band preliminaries are held. "Mas Camps" are busily sewing the costumes to be worn by the carnival players—including the huge King and Queen costumes—which can be designed up to a year in advance, and depict themes as varied as birdlife and pirates.

The real action begins during the weekend before the beginning of Lent. On the Friday night, a competition is held to select the winning King and Queen of the Bands—magnificent centerpiece figures which can be up to 35 feet tall and are lavishly constructed.

These pirates—in carnival mood—sport sunglasses and wristwatches

On Saturday the children take their turn in Kiddies Carnival, and in the evening Panorama, the finals of the steel band competition (see pages 80–81), features the last eight steel bands, many 60 players strong, competing for the year's top title.

The Calypso Competition finals are held on Sunday night, with calypsonians vying for the year's most prestigious singing title, the Calypso Monarch. During the evening the winners of the King and Queen of the Band competitions put in an appearance.

On Monday the dancing begins and the revelers are out on the streets by 3 AM for jouvert (from the French Créole *jour ouvert*, but pronounced "jouvay"), with music provided exclusively by steel bands. Leading the parade are impish "djab-djabs" (from the French *diable*) and "moko-jumbies" who walk on stilts. Many dancers cover themselves in axle grease and mud (snazzily dressed onlookers are liable to be hugged). Jouvert comes to an end at about 9 AM, and is followed at midday by more formal music and dancing by the Carnival Bands.

Tuesday, Mardi Gras, is the day of the main procession, or road march, and judging day for the Carnival Bands. They assemble early in the morning and begin their strut around the streets, passing the four main judging areas—Independence Square, Adam Smith Square in Woodbrook, Park Street, and the Queen's Park Savannah. Each band, which may have as many as 2–3,000 players, is divided into sections, with players dressed in different costumes. At the rear of each band are the King and Queen. Music is provided by trucks interspersed among the sections, and the noise is deafening. In the full heat of the Trinidadian sun, dancing is exhausting work, and the players usually employ someone to wheel a portable bar around. By dusk the procession is finished, with dancing until the official finish at midnight.

Although most Caribbean carnivals are held on Mardi Gras and run along similar lines, some islands stage them in the summer, to celebrate the end of the cane-cutting season. In Barbados, Cropover is on the first Monday in August, and in Cuba, the Zafra celebrations are at the end of July. Perhaps the most enjoyable feature of Caribbean carnivals is that, unlike those of Rio or New Orleans, anyone can join in and dance.

CARNIVAL DANCES
Dances go in and out of vogue year by year, but the traditional step is the "chip," in which players drag their feet and swing their knees and hips, occasionally throwing their arms up in the air. Wining and grinding are dances in which players move their hips with their legs wide apart, sometimes alone, sometimes pushing up against another dancer (or in a conga). Groins and backsides feature prominently in the dance and partners perform in all imaginable combinations (back to back, back to front, etc).

CARNIVAL DESIGNERS
Carnival costume design is very big business in Trinidad. Peter Minshall is perhaps the best known of the carnival designers and his very elaborate creations, such as "Carnival is Colour" and "Jungle Fever," have won the Band of the Year prize several times. Other winning designers include Wayne Berkeley, an international stage-set designer who has been a leading competitor for over 20 years, and Raoul Garib.

235

PELICAN PERILS

Pelicans can often be seen throughout the Caribbean islands sitting on a rock or a convenient offshore post, diving for fish—hurtling arrow-like down at the water but barely entering it. In time, this battering damages their eyes, and many of them gradually go blind. Unable to fish well, eventually they die.

Continued from page 233.

Offshore are two Tobagonian landmarks: **Buccoo Reef▶▶**, although sadly overrun, still impresses with colorful coral and fish, which visitors can observe through a glass-bottomed boat, and the **Nylon Pool▶▶**, a waist-deep area of warm water with a silky, sandy bottom. On the other side of the bay is the village of **Buccoo▶▶**, where fishing boats with brightly painted diamond patterns lie on the sands. Hendrix bar in Buccoo is the scene of a weekly celebration that is known as **Sunday School▶▶**.

Past Mount Irvine Bay, the site of Tobago's 18-hole golf course, and Stonehaven Bay (both good beaches), is Courland Bay. The name Courland has a strange origin: it comes from a peninsula in what is now Latvia, from which a number of settlements of Tobago were attempted in the 17th century. There is a monument to their memory in **Plymouth▶**, Tobago's second town, where there are just a couple of streets, and Fort James, on the point overlooking the bay. **Back Bay▶▶**, on the other side of Plymouth, is an attractive stretch of sand.

Drinks-shack-cum-vegetable stall, Tobago

Beaching the boat in Tobago after fishing on the high seas

Beyond Plymouth, the road winds into Tobago's countryside, through hillside villages such as Les Coteaux and Moriah, before descending to the coast and a series of sandy, palm-backed bays: **Castara**▶▶, **Englishman's Bay**▶▶▶, and **Parlatuvier**▶▶. From Bloody Bay the main road leads up into the **Tobago Forest Reserve**▶▶, a rainforest with walking trails, reaching the island's south coast at Roxborough.

Scarborough▶ is the capital of Tobago, a quiet and undistinguished town set over the hills above Rockly Bay on the south coast. About 10,000 of the island's 55,000 inhabitants live here. At the top of the hill is the town's old defense, **Fort King George**▶, which is well preserved with its cannon covering the approaches to the town. Next door is the **Tobago Museum**▶▶, with displays of island history and Ameridian and colonial artifacts; and on the other side of town are the **Botanical Gardens**▶ (tel: 639-3970. *Open* Mon–Fri 9–5. *Admission charge).*

The road to the eastern end of the island winds its way along the palm-backed south coast, in and out of huge bays and through small Tobagonian settlements. **Richmond Great House**▶ is an old wooden estate house, now restored with a collection of African carvings and textiles. A 15-minute walk from Roxborough, near the junction of the inland and coastal roads, is the **Argyle Waterfall**▶▶, a three-stepped cascade where you can take a swim after the walk. There is another waterfall at **King's Bay**▶, to the east of Roxborough.

After climbing an impossibly steep hill the road reaches Speyside and then Charlotteville (lying at the island's eastern tip), two quiet Tobagonian towns with guesthouses, in the island's best scuba-diving area.

THE FRIGATEBIRD
The magnificent frigatebird, or Man-o'-War bird, nests on Tobago's northeastern cliffs. With its dark plumage, scissor-shaped tail, and a wingspan of over 3 ft., this is an impressive but aggressive bird which attacks other species for their food. It swoops from above or behind, shaking the victim until it disgorges its meal. Tours of Tobago's wildlife are arranged by David Rooks (tel: 639-4276).

Calypso is a flamboyant and witty singing tradition that originated in Trinidad. Styles range from rap to serenade, and lyrics touch on life, the universe, and everything. Some have a socially conscious edge; some are political; some are gossipy, and others are just plain "slack" (raunchy). But all calypsos entertain, and they jam the airwaves as Carnival approaches.

CALYPSO STARS

Most calypsonians adopt colorful singing names. The most popular prefixes are "The Mighty" and "Lord," and past winners include The Mighty Sniper and Lord Pretender. The two biggest names in the world of calypso are The Mighty Sparrow (alias Slinger Francisco), who first won the Calypso King title in 1956 and who, because of his saucy lyrics, has been crowned seven times since, and Lord Kitchener (Aldwyn Roberts), who is known for composing steel band songs and has won the Roadmarch title 11 times. Other names include Watchman (a policeman) and The Mighty Chalkdust (a schoolteacher). Calypsos are sung fast, in local dialect, so to get the best out of a calypso evening visitors should find out about the songs before hearing them performed.

Calypso is a legacy of Trinidad's dual African and French heritage. The first known calypsonian or "shantwell" was Gros Jean, who sang for a French planter 200 years ago. Since the beginning of this century calypsos have been sung in English, the language of Trinidad, and as their popularity has increased, other English-speaking Caribbean islands have adopted the tradition.

Calypsos are the major musical force behind Carnival, at the beginning of Lent each year (see pages 234–235). There are three main calypso competitions. The Roadmarch competition judges the year's best dancing tune in the parties (fêtes) and in the Carnival parade. The title is won by the calypsonian whose song is played most as the Carnival bands cross the judging stages.

In Ex-tempo, two calypsonians compete in quickfire singing, alternating verse by verse. A topic written on a piece of paper is handed to the singers, who are given 30 seconds to prepare a calypso. Teasing the opponent is more important than rhyme or meter, and the winner is usually the person who gets the biggest laugh. The most coveted and fiercely contested title is the Calypso Monarch (changed from Calypso King when women entered the field). Calypsonians release their songs in January, so that they become well known on the radio. Then they perform in calypso "tents," acting the songs out in an attempt to be selected for the next round. Calypso Monarch finals are held on the Sunday before

Lent—a cross between a variety show and a comedy evening. Calypsonians perform to huge audiences, making digs at the other singers and adding topical comments to their songs to provoke a response from the crowd.

238

Travel Facts

Arriving and departing

By air: The best way of getting to the Caribbean is to put yourself in the hands of an experienced tour operators, who usually command the best rates from airlines. U.S. Tour Operators include American Express Vacation (tel: 800/241-1700), GoGo Tours (tel: 201/934-3500, or 800/526-0405), and Travel Impressions (tel: 800/284-0044). Other specialized tour operators include Caribbean Concepts (tel: 800/423-4433) and Allen Tours (tel: 718/856-7711).

Airlines with regularly scheduled flights from the U.S. include Delta (tel: 800/221-1212), American (800/433-7300), B.W.I.A. (800/327-7401), Continental (800/231-0856), U.S. Air (800/622-1015), and Air Jamaica (800/358-3222). There are also numerous charter flights to the more popular destinations, mainly during the winter season (Dec–Apr).

It is possible to buy three types of Liat Air Pass to island-hop: the Liat Caribbean Explorer (valid for 21 days, max. three stopovers); the Liat Air Pass (max. 21 days, min. three stopovers, max. six); and the Liat Caribbean Super Explorer (linking the Caribbean with Guyana and Venezuela, max. stay 30 days, unlimited stopovers).

B.W.I.A. offers an Air Pass: unlimited travel for 30 days, although backtracking is not allowed. A.L.M. also has a number of hopper tickets, enabling you to link the Dutch Islands, usually with a link to a U.S. limb. There are some tiny inter-island airlinks (see individual listings), but their scheduling can be quixotic.

Departure tax is payable from most islands (usually about $20 U.S. a head and some exemptions for children).

By boat: Lines offering trips and cruises include: Carnival; Celebrity; Costa; Cunard; Dolphin; Fantasy; Holland America; Norwegian; Premier; Princess; Regency; Seabourn; Seawind; and Windstar.

Camping and student/youth travel

In general camping is discouraged in private and national park campsites on St. John in the U.S. Virgin islands.

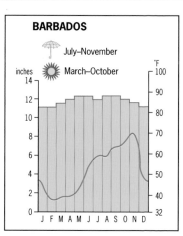

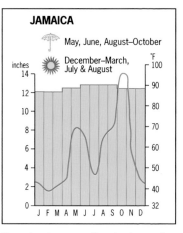

Some landowners allow tent-camping in the French Antilles. In Barbados, the Girl Guides (Girl Scouts), Boy Scouts, and Cadet Corps conduct organized camping for their worldwide counterparts.

The Caribbean is not known for budget accommodations, but there are inexpensive guesthouses and diving lodges on many islands, which usually do not appear in brochures. Write to tourist offices for a list.

Car rental

See individual island entries.

Climate

Temperatures generally average 78°F–85°F but are lower the greater the altitude. October and November are the wettest months (June in

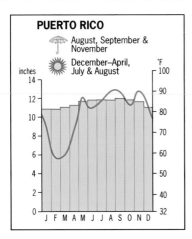

PUERTO RICO

August, September & November

December–April, July & August

Trinidad and Tobago); Dec–May is driest; the hurricane season is Jul–Oct.

Crime

Attacks and robberies are rare; the most hassle you are likely to encounter is from persistent souvenir salespersons, but be careful in large towns and cities. There is much poverty, which brings with it the temptation to petty theft. Keep doors locked, take care of your valuables and watch where you walk after dark. Don't take too much money out with you and don't display wealth. Most hotels have safes. Report lost property first to the hotel or apartment manager, and then to the police and/or the tourist board.

Dialing codes

Numbers given below should be prefaced with the international dialing code if you are calling from abroad or from an island with a different code. From the U.S.A., these numbers can be accessed by dialing 1, although the French and Dutch islands, and the other islands with a 599 area code, require an international prefix (011).
001-809 Dominican Republic
011-1473 Grenada
011-1876 Jamaica
011-1868 Trinidad and Tobago
011-1264 264-497 Anguilla
011-1268 Antigua and Barbuda
011-1246 Barbados
011-1345 Cayman Islands
011-1787 Puerto Rico
011-1664 Montserrat
011-1869 Nevis, St. Kitts

011-1758 St. Lucia
011-599 followed by: Bonaire (7), Curaçao (9), Sint Maarten (5), Saba (4), Sint Eustatius (3).
011-2978 Aruba
011-590 Guadeloupe, St. Barts, Saint-Martin
011-596 Martinique
011-767 Dominica
011-284 British Virgin Islands
011-784 St. Vincent and the Grenadines
011-40 U.S. Virgin Islands

Emergency telephone numbers

These telephone numbers are in the process of being standardized. Check the relevant numbers on arrival.
Anguilla Police and ambulance: 911
Antigua and Barbuda Police and ambulance 999 or 911
Aruba Police: 100; ambulance: 115
Barbados Police: 112; ambulance: 115
Bonaire Police and ambulance: 110
Curaçao Police: 114; ambulance: 112
Cayman Islands Police: 911; ambulance: 555 or 911
Dominica Police and ambulance: 999
Dominican Republic Police and ambulance: 911
Grenada Police: 911; ambulance: 434
Guadeloupe Police: 17; ambulance: 90-22-95
Jamaica Police: 119; ambulance: 110
Martinique Police: 17; ambulance: 70-36-48
Montserrat Police: 999; ambulance: 911
Puerto Rico Police and ambulance: 911
Saba Police: 63237; ambulance: 63288
St. Barts Police: 27-66-66; doctor 27-76-03
St. Eustatius Police: 82333; ambulance: 82211
St. Kitts and Nevis Police and ambulance: 911
St. Lucia Police and ambulance: 999
Saint-Martin Police: 87-50-04; ambulance: 87-74-14
Sint Maarten Police: 22222; ambulance: 22111
St. Vincent Police and ambulance: 999
Trinidad and Tobago Police: 999; ambulance: 990
Virgin Islands (British) Police and ambulance: 999
Virgin Islands (U.S.) Police and ambulance: 911

241

Health

Immunization against yellow fever may be required if arriving from an infected area. Otherwise immunization is not generally required, but typhoid, polio, and tetanus shots are often recommended, as well as hepatitis A for those staying outside tourist areas. Malaria is a problem in remote areas of Haiti and the Dominican Republic. The risks of H.I.V. are well known and apply in the Caribbean as anywhere else. Consult your doctor before leaving. Obtain health insurance prior to travel; those on regular medication should take supplies with them in case they are not sold on the islands. Tapwater is not always safe to drink. Check your destination on arrival.

Money

On islands where the official currency is the Eastern Caribbean dollar (EC$), the exchange rate is fixed to the U.S. dollar and U.S. currency is widely accepted: **Anguilla**; **Antigua**; **Dominica**; **Grenada**; **Montserrat**; **Nevis**; **St. Kitts**; **St. Lucia**; **St. Vincent**; **the Grenadines**
Other currencies
Aruba Aruban florin (AFl); **Barbados** Barbados dollar (BDS$); **Bonaire** Netherlands Antilles florin/guilder (NAf); **Cayman Islands** Caymanian dollar (C.I.$); **Curaçao** Netherlands Antilles florin/guilder (NAf); **Dominican Republic** Dominican peso (RD$); **Guadeloupe** French franc (FF); **Jamaica** Jamaican dollar (J$); **Martinique** French franc (FF); **Puerto Rico** U.S. dollar; Saba Netherlands Antilles florin/guilder (NAf); **St. Barts** French franc (FF); **St. Eustatius** Netherlands Antilles florin/guilder (NAf); **Saint-Martin** French franc (FF); **Sint Maarten** Netherlands Antilles guilder/florin (NAf); **Trinidad and Tobago** Trinidad and Tobago dollar (TT$); **Virgin Islands (British and U.S)** U.S. dollar. U.S. dollars are also accepted on all islands except the Dominican Republic and Trinidad and Tobago.

Public restrooms

There are not many of these. Some islands have basic beach facilities (not great), usually attached to a rustic bar. Stick to hotels and restaurants.

Travel insurance

This should cover accident, health, baggage and possessions, cancellation, etc. If you are taken ill or have an accident, you will nearly always be expected to pay, and health care is generally not cheap. Medicaments, if not already on the island, are usually flown in from the U.S., and there are plenty of pharmacies for over-the-counter medicines. Make sure your insurance policy covers you in the event of a watersports accident.

Travelers with disabilities

San Juan and Condado in Puerto Rico are well-equipped for wheelchair access; Luquillo Beach offers a ramp to allow disabled persons into the water. Puerto Rico and the U.S. Virgins are in compliance with the Americans with Disabilities Act. The Jamaica Tourist Board lists hotels with facilities, as does Trinidad and Tobago, but check before booking. Individual island tourist boards can give details about specific properties.

THE WINDWARD ISLANDS

Dominica (area code 767)

Car rental and driving

A local driver's license is required, obtainable from the airports or the Traffic Department, High Street, Roseau and at some of the rental companies (Mon–Fri). You must be 25–65 and have a valid driver's license and at least two years' driving experience. Rental companies include **Anselm's** (tel: 448-2730), **Budget** (tel: 449-2080), **SAG Motors** (tel: 449-1093), **Garaway Rent-a-Car** (tel: 448-3425), **C.I.C. Rental** (tel: 4485-5847), **Valley Rent-a-Car** (Roseau 448-3233; Portsmouth 447-2996), **Wide Range Car Rentals** (tel: 448-2198), good for four-wheel drive vehicles. Driving is on the left. The main roads are well maintained; others are full of potholes and hairpin bends and few road signs. The speed limit is 20 m.p.h (32 k.p.h.) in populated areas. Gas is paid for in cash. Seatbelts are not mandatory, but recommended. Drunk- driving laws are enforced. Get an Ordnance Survey map from the Tourism Office in the Old Market, Roseau.

Getting around

By air: Liat (tel: 448-2421 or 4458-2422) flies north and south from both airports (Canefield just outside Roseau, and Melville Hall, in the north) to all islands between Antigua and Trinidad. American Eagle (tel: 448-0628) links Dominica daily with San Juan. Cardinal Airlines (tel: 449-8922; fax: 449-8923) offers a charter service to other islands. Air Guadeloupe is represented by **Whitchurch Travel Agency** (tel: 448-2181): flights to Sint Maarten, Guadeloupe, Martinique.

By boat: Caribbean Express, a scheduled ferry service, offers connections between Roseau, Dominica, and Guadeloupe and Martinique. Dominica agent: **Whitchurch & Co.** (tel: 448-2181). **Atlantica** (tel: 448-6977) touches Dominica en route from Martinique to Guadeloupe.

By road: Taxis, minibuses and rental vehicles have license plates with H as the last letter. Taxi rates are fixed and quoted in EC$ and U.S.$: make sure you know which is being quoted. They are displayed at the airport and tourist office. In Roseau, try **Mally's Taxi Service** (tel: 448-3114), and **Izoe 24-hour Taxi/Tour Service Taxi** (tel: 449-8545). Few taxis work after 6 PM, except by prior arrangement.

Buses are cheaper; flag them down on the road by the airport.

Sightseeing and activities

Tours, including hiking and photo safaris, are offered by: **Antours Dominica** (tel: 448-6460), **Dominica Tours** (tel: 448-2638), **Ken's Hinterland Adventure Tours** (tel: 448-4850), **Mally's Tour & Taxi Service** (tel: 448-3114), **Nature Island Destinations** (tel: 449-6233), **Paradise Tours** (tel: 448-5999), **Rainbow Rover Tours** (tel: 448-8650), **Wide Range** (tel: 448-2198), **Whitchurch Travel Agency** (tel: 448-2181). You need an experienced guide for tours in the Morne Trois Pitons National Park. Dominica is excellent for scuba diving. Arrange trips to view corals and whale watching (Oct–May) through **Dive Dominica** (tel: 448-2188), the **Anchorage Dive Center** (tel: 448-2638), and **Dive Castaways** (tel: 449-6844). Book sailing in the dive shops.

Tourist information

Dominica Division of Tourism, P.O. Box 73, Roseau, Commonwealth of Dominica; Tourist Information Bureau, Old Market Plaza, Roseau (both tel: 448-2186); and offices at the airports. **Dominica Hotel Association** (tel: 448-6565), P.O .Box 384, Roseau, Commonwealth of Dominica, W.I.

Grenada (area code 473)

Car rental and driving

A local driving permit can be bought from most rental companies or the Fire Station on the Carenage; you need to show an international driver's license. Price EC$30. Car-rental companies include: **Avis** (tel: 446-2277); **David's Car Rentals** (tel: 444-3399); **Island Rent-A-Car** (tel: 443-5624); **Jerry's Auto Service** (tel: 440-1730); **Maitland's Motor Rentals** (tel: 444-4022); **M.C.R.** (tel: 440-5398); **C. Thomas** (tel: 444-4384); **Thrift Rent-a-Car** (tel: 444-4984); **Y&R Car Rentals** (tel: 444-4448); **Carriacou: Barba's Rentals** (tel: 443-7454). Driving is on the left. Seatbelts are recommended but not mandatory. Gas has to be paid for in cash.

Getting around

By air: Airlines linking Grenada with the rest of the Caribbean are: **Airlines of Carriacou** (tel: 444-3549), **Region Air** (tel: 444-1117) and **Liat** (tel: 440-2796, 440-2797). **American Eagle** (tel: 444-2222) fly from San Juan and BWIA (tel: 444-1221); from South America: **Aerotuy/Aeropostal** (tel: 444-4732).

By boat: Ferries operate daily from St. George's quayside to Carriacou and then to Petite Martinique on Mon, Wed, Fri. See list of local tour operators for yacht charter companies.

By road: Rental vehicles have a license plate with the letter H. Taxi rates are set by the government and quoted in U.S. dollars, but you can pay in either currency. Buses leave from Market Square, St. George's and can be flagged down elsewhere. Minibuses ply shorter routes. From Carriacou, buses link Hillsborough with Windwardside and Tyrrel Bay. Motorcycles and bicycles can often be rented from hotels or car-rental firms

Sightseeing and activities

Taxis can be rented as sightseeing guides. Contact local tour operators for excursions around Grenada, trips to Carriacou, Petite Martinique and the Grenadines, hiking tours, boat trips, car rental and taxi service. *St. George's*: **Arnold's Tours** (tel: 444-0531); **Fun Tours** (tel: 444-3167); **Grenada Hotels Taxi Drivers' Association** (tel: 444-4882); **National Taxi Association** (tel: 444-3640); **Sunsation Tours** (tel: 444-1656); **Henry Safari Tours** (tel: 444-5313); **Carib Tours/Carin Travel** (tel: 444-4363); **New Trends Tours** (tel: 444-1236); **Sunshine Tours** (tel: 444-4296). Sports and watersports operators include: **(scuba) Dive Grenada** (tel: 444-1092) and **Grand Anse Aquatics** (tel: 444-4129); horseback riding: **Ride Grenada** (tel: 444-1157) and **The Horseman** (tel: 440-5368); hiking: **Telfor Hiking Tours** (tel: 442-6200); deep sea fishing: **Captain Peters** (tel: 440-1349) and **Evans Chartering Service** (tel: 444-4422); Yacht charter companies include: **The Moorings** (tel: 444-4257); **Starwind Enterprises** (tel: 440-3678) and **Seabreeze** (tel: 444-4942) *Carriacou*: tours can be arranged through Bullen Tours (tel: 443-8590) and sports through Snagg (tel: 443-8293) and Tanki (tel: 443-8406).

Tourist information

Grenada Board of Tourism, The Cruise ship dock, St. George's (tel: 440-2001); on Carriacou (tel: 443-7948). **Grenada Hotel Association**, Ross Point Inn, Lagoon Road, St. George's (tel: 444-1353). In the U.S.: 820 2nd Ave. Suite 9000, N.Y., N.Y. 10017, U.S. (tel: 212/687-9554; 800/927-9554).

St. Lucia (area code 758)

Car rental and driving

A St. Lucia temporary driver's license must be purchased at the airport, the police station in Castries or the car-rental office. Take your current driver's license. Companies include **Avis** (tel: 452-2202), **Budget** (tel: 452-0233), **Courtesy Rent-a-Car** (tel: 452-8140), **A & E Auto Rentals** (tel: 451-3113), **Costless Rentacar** (tel: 450-3416), **St. Lucia Yacht Car Rental**

(tel: 452-5057). Some companies insist on a minimum number of years' driving experience. Motorcycles can be rented at **Wayne's Motorcyle Center** (tel: 452-2059). Driving is on the left. Speed limits are 48 k.p.h. (30 m.p.h.), and there are penalties for drunk driving and illegal parking. Gas must be paid for in cash.

Getting around

By air: Vigie airport is used for inter-island traffic, and is served by **Liat** (tel: 452-3056), **Air Martinique** (tel: 452-2463), **American Eagle** (tel: 454-6777), and **Helenair** (tel: 452-7196). A small plane charter service is available through **Eagle Air Services** (tel: 452-1900). Airlines operating from Europe and North America into Hewanorra include: **British Airways** (tel: 452-3951), **BWIA** (tel: 452-3777, 452-3789); **Air Canada** (tel: 451-6406); **American Airlines** (tel: 454-6777). Helicopter transfers are available from Hewanorra International Airport to Castries, and Windjammer Landing has a helipad. There are helipads at Pointe Seraphine and Rodney Bay. **Helicopters** (tel: 453-6950). **By boat:** A ferry service, **Caribbean Express** (tel: 452-2211), operates between St. Lucia and Martinique, Guadeloupe, and Dominica. A few hotels have their own boats: Jalousie, Windjammer, and Sandals (private yachts), and Anse Chastanet (motor boat). Other day sails include Endless Summer (tel: 450-8651) and Surf Queen (tel: 452-8351 ext 515). Yacht charter companies include: **The Moorings**, Marigot Bay (tel: 451-4357); **Vigie Motor Yacht** (tel: 452-9423); **Castries Yacht Center** (tel: 452-6234). **By road:** The north is well served by buses and private minibuses, until about 10 PM (later on Fri). The last bus from Soufrière to Castries leaves at noon. Taxis or minibuses are easily available and can organize tours: **Courtesy Taxi** (tel: 452-3555), **Vigie Taxi** (tel: 452-1599), **St. Lucia Taxi** (tel: 452-2492), **AA Taxi** (tel: 4451-6417), **AAA Taxi** (tel: 452-6077), **Boulevard Taxi** (tel: 452-1531).

Sightseeing and activities

Tours are usually organized through the hotel or tour company rep. Local tour operators include: **Barefoot Holidays** (tel: 450-0507), **Barnards Travel** (tel: 452-2214), **Carib Travel Agency** (tel: 452-3176), **Cox & Co.** (tel: 452-2211), **Fletcher's Touring Service** (tel: 452-2516), **Minvielle & Chastanet** (tel: 452-2811), **Pitons Travel Agency** (tel: 450-1486), **Spice Travel** (tel: 452-0865), **St. Lucia International Travel** (tel: 452-0865). For deep sea fishing contact: **Captain Mike's** (tel: 452-7044) and **Great White** (tel: 452-6112). Dive operators include: **Scuba St. Lucia** (tel: 459-7000) and **Dolphin Divers** (tel: 452-9485). Windsurfing: contact **Island Windsurf** (tel: 4454-7400, 454-3418) . For horseback riding: Trim's Riding Stables (tel: 452-8273) and Country Saddles (tel: 453-1231).

Tourist information
St. Lucia Tourist Board, Pointe Seraphine, P.O. Box 221, Castries, St. Lucia (tel: 452-4094, 451-6643). There are offices in Jeremie Street, Castries, and in both the airports. In the U.S.: 9th Floor, 820 2nd Avenue, N.Y., N.Y. 10017 (tel: 212/867-2950).

St Vincent and the Grenadines
(area code 784)

Car rental and driving
Take your normal or international license to the airport, the police station in Bay Street, or the Licensing Authority in Halifax Street to purchase a local license. The minimum age is 17, but some companies may insist on you being older. Rental companies on St. Vincent include: **David's Auto Clinic** (tel: 456-4026); **Kim's Rentals** (tel: 456-1884); **Lucky Car Rental** (tel: 457-1913); **Star Garage** (tel: 456-1743); **Sunshine Auto Rentals** (tel: 456-5380); **Unico** (tel: 456-5744). Drive on the left. Seatbelt laws do exist, and speed limits are 32 k.p.h. (20 m.p.h.), 24 k.p.h./15 m.p.h. for buses and trucks. Pay for gas in cash.

Getting around
By air: Connections for the U.S. are made in San Juan, from where **American Eagle** (tel: 456-5000) makes the link to E.J.Joshua Airport in St. Vincent. **Liat** (Kingstown tel: 457-1821; E.T. Joshua Airport tel: 458-4841; Union Island airport tel:

458-8230) links St. Vincent with Martinique, Barbados, St. Lucia and the other Grenadines; **Mustique Airways** (tel: 458-4380) and **S.V.G. Air** (tel: 457-5777; Mustique Airways waits for your international arrival. Also **Airlines of Carriacou** (tel: 444-2898), which flies through the Grenadines; **Air Martinique** (St. Vincent tel: 458-4528; Union Island tel: 458-8238) links St. Vincent with St. Lucia, Barbados, Mustique, Union Island, Canouan, and points north. **By boat:** Ferries leave St. Vincent every day to Bequia and three times a week to the Grenadines (Canouan, Mayreau, and Union): they depart from Grenadines dock in Kingstown harbor and arrive at Port Elizabeth in Bequia 70–90 minutes later. M.V. **Admiral I** and **II** (tel: 458-3348) and the **Sand Island** (tel: 458-3472) all serve Bequia. The **M.V. Barracuda** (tel: 456-5180) mail boat travels south on Mon and Thu at 10.30 AM, stopping at Bequia, Canouan, Mayreau, and Union Island, returning Tue and Fri. **Windward Lines** (tel: 457-2920) offers a weekly ferry service to St. Lucia, Barbados, Trinidad, and Venezuela. Yacht charter companies include, on St. Vincent: **Barefoot Yacht Charters**, Blue Lagoon (tel: 456-9526); **Lagoon Marina Yacht Charters** (tel: 458-4308). Bequia: **Frangipani Yacht Service** (tel: 458-3255); Union: **Anchorage Yacht Club** (tel: 458-8221). Day sails and boat trips to inaccessible beaches can be arranged by **Baleine Tours** (tel: 457-4089); **Fantasea Tours** (tel: 457-4477), and **Passion Day Charters** (tel: 458-3884). Based in Bequia, the traditional schooner **Friendship Rose** (tel: 458-3202) takes day trips to the southern Grenadines. Union Island, contact Captain Yannis (tel: 458-8513) or the **Anchorage Yacht Club** (tel: 458-8221). Scuba diving: **Dive St. Vincent** (tel: 457-4714); **Grand View Beach Hotel** (tel: 458-4811); **Dive Canouan** (tel: 458-8648); **Anchorage Dive Club** (Union tel: 458-8221); **Grenadines Dive** (Union tel: 458-8138). **By road:** The roads of St. Vincent and Bequia are rough and windy, but most areas are accessible by bus and taxi. Rates are fixed and a list is available at the Department of Tourism offices or at the airport. To

245

pre-arrange a taxi tour, ask in your hotel or contact the **Taxi Drivers' Association** (tel: 457-1807); or **Sam Taxi Tours and Yacht Agency** (456-4338; Bequia: 458-3686).

Minibuses depart from Market Square in Kingstown. Hail them anywhere along the route (indicated on the windshield). Smaller islands have taxi-vans and pick-up trucks with benches in the back. Water taxis are available from docks.

Bicycles can be rented from **Lighthouse**, Bequia (tel: 458-3084), and from **Sailors Cycle Centre**, St. Vincent (tel: 457-1712).

Sightseeing

Tours and trips can be organized through **W.J. Abbott & Sons**, Upper Bay Street, Kingstown (tel: 456-1511): **Barefoot Yacht Charters**, Blue Lagoon (tel: 456-9334); **Caribbean International Travel Services**, Granby Street, Kingstown (tel: 457-1841); **Corea & Co.**, Halifax Street, Kingstown (tel: 456-1201); **Emerald Travel & Tours**, Halifax St (tel: 457-1996); **Global Travel Service**, White Chapel, Kingstown (tel: 456-1601); **Grenadine Travel Co.**, Arnos Vale (tel: 458-4818); **Travel World**, Bay Street, Kingstown (tel: 451-7443). On Bequia: **Grenadine Travel Co.**, Port Elizabeth (tel: 458-3795). On Union: **Travel & Tours** (tel: 456-2572).

Tourist information

St. Vincent and the Grenadines Department of Tourism, P.O. Box 834, St. Vincent (tel: 457-1502). A tourist information office is located in Bay Street, Kingstown; also at E.T. Joshua Airport. Bequia's **Tourism Bureau** is on the main dock, Port Elizabeth (tel: 458-3286); **Union Island Tourist Information** (tel: 458-8350). In the U.S.A.: 801 2nd Ave. 21st Floor, N.Y., N.Y. 10017 (tel: 212/687-4981, 800/729-1726).

THE LEEWARD ISLANDS

Anguilla (area code 264)

Car rental and driving

You need a valid driver's license for a temporary license, on sale at rental companies or at the police station in The Valley. The minimum age for car rental can be 18; 21 or 25. Rental companies: **Apex** (tel: 2642); **Avis** (tel: 6221); **Budget** (tel: 2217); **Connors** (tel: 6433); **Triple K. Car Rental** (tel: 2934); **Island Car Rentals** (2723). Drive on the left. The speed limit is 48 k.p.h. (30 m.p.h.). Seatbelts are recommended. Smaller gas stations prefer cash.

Getting around

By air: Local airlines linking Anguilla with the rest of the Caribbean include **Winair** (tel: 2748), **Air Anguilla** (tel: 2643), **Tyden Air** (tel: 2719), **Liat** (tel: 5002), **American Eagle** (tel: 3131).

By boat: Ferries between Blowing Point and Marigot Bay, Saint-Martin, leave every 30 minutes from 7:30; also day trips to St. Barts. Ferry information (tel: 2643, 3290). Book boat trips with Chocolat (tel: 3394), Hoo Haa (tel: 4040) or Arvencia (tel: 2936). For offshore islands, Prickly Pear, and Sandy Island, contact Sandy Island Enterprises (tel: 6395). Scuba-diving: **The Dive Shop** (tel: 2020) and **Anguillan Divers** (tel: 4750).

By road: Use taxis or rental cars. Taxi rates are set by the government (no meters). There are no buses or maxi taxis: for larger groups, rental and taxi companies do have minibuses. Cycles (not motorbikes) can be rented through travel agents (see below).

Sightseeing

Tours are organized through your hotel, villa manager, or travel agent. Taxi drivers will also arrange tours (fees are negotiable). Local tour operators include: **Bennie's Travel & Tours**, Box 254, The Valley (tel: 2788) and **Malliouhana Travel & Tours**, Box 237, The Quarter (tel: 2431 or 2348).

Tourist information

Anguilla Tourist Office, The Valley (tel: 2759). In the U.S.: **Medhurst and Associates Inc**. 1208 Washington Drive, Centerport, N.Y. 11721 (tel: 516/425-0900).

Antigua and Barbuda (area code 268)

Car rental and driving

You need to purchase a provisional license (U.S.$20), issued on presentation of a valid driver's license. You have to be 18 to drive, and some companies set a minimum age for renting a car (21 or 25), and include "extras" in their quotes. Companies include **Budget** (tel: 462-3009), **National** (tel: 462-2113), **Capital** (tel: 462-0863), **Matthew's Car Rental** (tel: 462-9532) and **Avis** (tel: 462-2840).

It is virtually impossible to rent a car during Carnival, so if you're going to need one then, book ahead. To rent a car in Barbuda, arrange it before leaving Antigua. Driving is on the left, the speed limit 64 k.p.h. (40 m.p.h.). Seatbelts are recommended; and there are no drunk-driving laws. Gas usually has to be paid for in cash.

Getting around
By air: Services from the U.S. (via San Juan and other cities) are operated by American Airlines (local tel: 462-0952) and BWIA (tel: 462-0876), as well as a number of charter companies. Antigua is a hub for local island transportation: **Liat** (tel: 480-5600) has the greatest number of services, although **Air Guadeloupe** and **Air St. Kitts-Nevis** do fly in. Small charter planes are available through **Carib Aviation** (tel: 462-3147) and **Norman Aviation** (tel: 462-2445). **Liat** has several flights a day to Barbuda.
By boat: There are no ferries between Antigua and Barbuda, but there are catamarans for a day trip with swimming and snorkeling, etc., to Barbuda and Bird Island. Try **Shorty's** (tel: 464-6903), a glass-bottom boat, **Kokomo Cat** (tel: 462-7245), **Treasure Island Cruises** (tel: 461-8675), or *The Jolly Roger* "pirate" ship (tel: 462-2064). Watersports operators include: **Kelly's Watersports Antigua** (tel: 462-8693) and **Sea Sports** (tel: 462-3355); for windsurfing, **Windsurfing Antigua** (tel: 462-9463) and scuba diving, **Dive Antigua** (tel: 462-3483), **Deep Bay Divers** (tel: 463-8000) and, in English Harbour, **Dockyard Divers** (tel: 460-1178). To charter a yacht, contact: **Nicholson Yacht Charters** (tel: 4460-1530), **Sunsail** (tel: 463-6224) or **Sun Yacht Charters** (tel: 460-2615).
By road: Taxi rates are displayed at the airport and drivers should have a rate card with them. Check whether they are quoting the fare in U.S. or E.C. dollars. All taxi drivers double as guides, and hotels may have a team who take turns doing the tours. Alternatively contact **Capital Car Rental** (tel: 462-0863). A private bus system operates in the south and east, with no timetables and few stops; this is the cheapest way around (ask in your hotel for the nearest stop. There are no buses in Dickenson Bay or Barbuda: it is best to rent a jeep.

Bicycles can be rented from **Sun Cycles** in Antigua (tel: 461-0324).

Sightseeing
Local tour operators will also fix island and inter-island excursions. Try **Antours** (tel: 462-4788), **Alexander Parrish** (tel: 462-0638), and **Kiskidee** (tel: 462-0582).

Tourist information
The Antigua and Barbuda Department of Tourism, Thames and Long Streets, St. John's (tel: 462-0480). Also at the airport. Try also **Antigua Hotels Association**, Long Street, St. John's (tel: 462-0374). In the U.S.: 25 SE 2nd Avenue, Suite 300, Miami, FL 33131 (tel: 305/381-6762).

Montserrat (area code 1664)
Because of the volcanic activity, most car rental companies, watersports operators, and travel agents have ceased trading for the time being.

Car rental and driving
There are no rental companies at the airport, but it is normally possible to arrange delivery to meet your flight. Present a valid driver's license to purchase a temporary Montserrat driving permit from the car-rental company or your hotel. Car-rental companies: **Pauline's Car Rental** (tel: 491-2345); **Neville Bradshaw Agencies** (tel: 491-5270); **Jefferson's Car Rental** (tel: 491-2126). Drive on the left; the speed limit is 48 k.p.h. (30 m.p.h.). Small gas stations like cash.

Getting around
By air: At the time of writing the airport is closed. However, in normal circumstances connections are best made in Antigua, from where Liat (tel: 491-2533) schedule about four

flights a day. Alternatively, it is possible to charter a small plane from **Carib Aviation** (Antigua tel: 462-3147).
By boat: Prior to recent volcanic activity, round-island catamaran cruises could be booked through a travel agent or your hotel, or with the catamaran **Volcania** (tel: 491-5949). A general watersports operator is **Danny's Watersports** (tel: 491-5645)
By road: There are just a few minibuses, so rental cars and private taxis are preferable. Taxi fares between principal destinations are set by the government; check whether the fare quoted is in U.S. or EC dollars.

Nevis (area code 869)

Car rental and driving
Driving is on the left.Watch out for potholes and livestock on the roads.
  A local temporary driving license (price EC$30) must be bought from the traffic department, at the police Station in Charlestown. Rental companies will pick you up and help with the arrangements. Most insist on a minimum age of 25. A government tax of 5 percent is added to all rates, which start at about $40 a day (with insurance). Companies include: **Avis Rent-a-Car** (tel: 469-1240); **Nevis Car Rental** (tel: 469-9837); **Nisbett Rentals** (tel: 469-9211); **Noel's Car Rental** (tel: 469-5199); **Stanley's Services** (tel: 469-2597); **Striker's Car Rental** (tel: 469-2654), and **T.D.C. Rentals** (tel: 465-2991).

Getting around
By air: Connect in Antigua, Sint Kitts, or Sint Maarten. For internal flights contact: Liat (tel: 465-2286), Winair (tel: 465-8010), Air St. Kitts-Nevis (tel: 465-8571), Carib Aviation (tel: 465-3055) and Nevis Express (tel: 469-9755). Many of these fly to Newcastle Airport in Nevis. There is a departure tax of EC$27 (US$10).
By boat: There is a 45-minute link to St. Kitts from the ferry pier in Basseterre, with two sailings each way daily except Thu and Sun; see the current edition of *The Traveller*. Out of season you can sometimes get a transfer between the islands on the Four Seasons Hotel launch in Nevis, or charter a sea taxi from Oualie Beach to

Turtle Beach; contact **Nevis Watersports** (tel: 469-9060). For a day's catamaran tour, with snorkeling, contact **Leeward Island Charters** (tel: 469-9494).
By road: Private minibuses operate a bus service in both directions from Charlestown, leaving from the main square. Taxis have set rates, usually in EC dollars. Payment can be made in either currency; add 25 percent between 11 PM and 6 AM. For rates see *The Traveller*. Taxi numbers include the **City Taxi** stand (tel: 469-5621).

Sightseeing and activities
Taxis provide 3-hour island tours, or contact: **All Seasons Streamline Tours** (tel: 469-1138) or **Nevisian Travel** (tel: 469-5423). For walking tours to the rainforest, contact **Top to Bottom** (tel: 469-9080), and for a walking tour of the plantations try **Eco-Tours** (tel: 469-2091). Horseback riding is available through **Hermitage Inn** (tel: 469-3477). The Four Seasons Resort has a golf course (tel: 469-1111). Watersports are available on Pinney's Beach, and at Oualie Beach. Contact **Nevis Watersports** (tel: 469-9060) and **Windsurfing Nevis** (tel: 469-9682). For scuba diving Contact **Scuba Safaris** (tel: 469-9518).

Tourist information
There are offices in Charlestown (tel: 469-1042), on the waterfront, and at the airport. In the U.S.: 414 East 75th Street, N.Y., N.Y. 10021 (tel: 212/535-1234, 800/582-6208).

St. Kitts (area code 869)

Car rental and driving
Purchase local driving licenses from the traffic department at the fire station in Basseterre (tel: 465-2241). Regulations and prices as for Nevis. Rental companies: **Avis** (tel: 465-6507), **Caines Rent-a-Car** (tel: 465-2336), **Delisle Walwyn** (tel: 465-8449), **Island Car Rental** (tel: 465-3000), **Sunshine Car Rentals** (tel: 465-2193), **T.D.C. Rentals Ltd.** (tel: 465-2991), **Tropical Car Rental** (tel: 465-4039).

Getting around
By air: Robert Llewelyn Bradshaw Airport in St. Kitts is accessible via

charter flights from Europe and the U.S. For scheduled airlines change in Antigua or Sint Maarten, or link with **American Eagle** (tel: 465-2273) from San Juan, Puerto Rico. Within the Caribbean, St. Kitts is well served (see Nevis above). There is a departure tax of EC$27 (US$10).

By boat: There are ferries most days between St. Kitts and Nevis (see *The Traveller*), and you can also charter a sea taxi from Turtle Beach on the south peninsula for the 10-minute crossing to Nevis; contact **Pro Divers** (tel: 465-9086), or **Blue Water Safaris** (tel: 465-3223). **Leeward Islands Charters** (tel: 465-7474) operates the catamaran *The Spirit of St. Kitts* for day sails to Nevis. *Celica III* can be booked through **Tropical Tours** (tel: 465-4167).

By road: On St. Kitts privately run minibuses make regular but un-scheduled trips along the main coastal roads, starting at the ferry terminal on the waterfront in Basseterre. Taxis have set rates listed in *The Traveller*. Add 25 percent to the rates between 11 PM and 6 AM. Try **St. Kitts Taxi Association** (tel: 465-4253) and the **Circus Taxi Stand** (tel: 465-3006).

Sightseeing and activities

Island tours can be arranged through taxi drivers and tour companies: **Kantours** (tel: 465-2098), **Evelyn's Travel** (tel: 469-5238), **Kisco Travel** (tel: 465-4039), **Travel World** (tel: 469-1460, Nevis; 465-4085, St. Kitts), **Tropical Tours** (tel: 465-4167). An island tour takes 3 to 4 hours. For half- or full-day walking tours to the rain forest, contact **Greg's Safaris** (tel: 465-4121); for walks into the crater of Mount Liamuiga, **Kriss Tours** (tel: 465-4042). Horseback riding is available through **Trinity Stables** in Frigate Bay (tel: 465-9603). There is a golf course in Frigate Bay (tel: 465-1290). For windsurfers, sunfish, jet skis and snorkeling, contact **Mr. X. Watersports** (tel: 465-4995), which you will find next to the Monkey Bar on Frigate Bay. Scuba operators include **Pro Divers** (tel: 465-3223) at Horizons and Turtle Beach. There is a tourist information office in Pelican Mall on Bay Street (tel: 465-2620).

THE VIRGIN ISLANDS

British Virgin Islands (area code 284)

Car rental and driving

A temporary B.V.I. license must be purchased, issued on presentation of a current foreign license (obtained from rental companies). The minimum age for renting a car is 25. Cars can be rented in Tortola, from: **Alphonso Car Rentals** (tel: 43137); **Avis** (tel: 42193); **Budget** (tel: 42639); Hertz (tel: 54405); **National** (tel: 43197). In Virgin Gorda, L **& S Jeep Rental** (tel: 55297). Driving is on the left and the speed limit is 40 m.p.h. but 20 m.p.h. in residential areas. Most cars are left-hand drive. Gas stations take credit cards. Seatbelts are compulsory. You can usually share someone else's taxi in Virgin Gorda for a small contribution.

Getting around

By air: The best connections from the U.S. are through San Juan, Puerto Rico, or through St. Thomas. **Gorda Aero Services** (tel: 52271) link Virgin Gorda with Tortola. Tortola is linked to the U.S.V.I. by **American Eagle** (tel: 52559), **Liat** (tel: 51187); **Liat** and **Winair** (tel: 42210) fly down to the Eastern Caribbean. You can charter a small plane through **Fly B.V.I.** (tel: 495-1747).

By boat: There are daily passenger launches between Tortola, Virgin Gorda, Jost Van Dyke, St. Thomas, and St. John. Ferries from Tortola to St. Thomas and St. John are operated by **Native Son** (tel: 54617), **Smith's Ferry Services** (tel: 54495), **Inter Island Boat Services** (tel: 54166); from Tortola to Peter Island: **Peter Island Boat** (tel: 52000); from Tortola to Virgin Gorda: **Speedy's Fantasy** (tel: 55240), **Smith's Ferry Services** (see above) and **North Sound Express** (tel: 52271). From Virgin Gorda to St. Thomas, **Speedy's Fantasy** (see above) and **Native Son** (see above). From Tortola to Jost Van Dyke: **Jost Van Dyke Ferry Service** (tel: 42997). Bareboats can be rented for cruises, local boats for special tours. Contact: **The Moorings**, P.O. Box 68, Road Town (tel: 42331), **Sunsail**, P.O. Box

609, West End (tel: 54740), **North Sound Yacht Vacation**, P.O. Box 2812, Road Town (tel: 40096). Day Sails can be arranged through **White Squall II** (tel: 42564), **Kuralu** (tel: 54381) and the **Catamaran Ppalu** (tel: 42771). In Virgin Gorda contact **Misty Isle Yacht Charters** (tel: 55643). **Travel Plan** (tel: 442872) organizes day sails either in bareboats or crewed yachts. You can also take the Bomba Charger hydrofoil between Tortola and Virgin Gorda or St. Thomas.

Sightseeing and activities
Guided tours are offered by the **B.V.I. Taxi Association** (tel: 42322) and **Travel Plan Tours** (tel: 42347). On Virgin Gorda: **Los Taxi Service** (tel: 55297); **Mahogany Taxi Service** (tel: 55469) does tours for a minimum of two people. Scuba diving companies include **Underwater Safaris** (tel: 43235) and **Baskin in the Sun** (tel: 42858), both in Tortola. In Virgin Gorda try **Dive B.V.I.** (tel: 55513). For windsurfing contact **Boardsailing B.V.I.** (tel: 40422).

Tourist information
B.V.I. Tourist Board, Social Security Building, Waterfront Street, P.O. Box 134, Road Town, Tortola (tel: 43134) and in Virgin Gorda in the yacht harbor (tel: 55182). In the U.S.: 370 Lexington Avenue, N.Y., N.Y. 10017 (tel: 212/696-0400, 800/835-8530).

U.S. Virgin Islands
(area code 340)

St. Croix

Car rental and driving
The minimum age is 18; 25 with some companies. A full driver's license will suffice. Companies include: **Avis** (tel: 778-9355), **Budget** (tel: 778-9636), **Charlie's** (tel: 773-1678), **Hertz** (tel: 778-1402), **Olympic** (tel: 773-2208), **Thrifty** (tel: 773-7200). Drive on the left. The speed limit is 88 k.p.h. (55 m.p.h.). Drunk-driving and seat-belt laws are strictly enforced. Gas is cheap; credit cards accepted.

Getting around
By air: International carriers serving the U.S.V.I. are **American**,

Continental, **Delta** and **U.S. Air. American** and **American Eagle** for local flights (800/474-4884 all three islands). **Delta** (tel: 800/221-1212), **Air Anguilla** (tel: 778-1880). There is now a seaplane service (tel: 777-4491) linking Christiansted with St. Thomas. **By boat:** There is a hydrofoil link between St. Croix and St. Thomas: **Katran** (tel: 776-7417). For yacht charter, short cruises, and day sails try **Mile-Mark Charters** in Christiansted (tel: 773-2628), **St. Croix Yacht Club** (tel: 773-9531), **St. Croix Marine** (tel: 773-0289). Contact **St. Croix Watersports** (tel: 773-2035) or **Big Beard's Adventure Tours** (tel: 773-4482) for catamaran trips and general watersports. For scuba diving try **VI Divers** (tel: 773-6045) and **Dive Experience** (tel: 773-3307) in Christiansted and **Cruzan Divers** (tel: 772-3701) in Frederiksted. **By road:** Taxi vans can be called from your hotel or found at the airport and, when cruise ships are in, at the pier in Frederiksted. The **St. Croix Taxi Association** (tel: 778-1088) runs taxi vans on the main roads from Christiansted to Frederiksted; try also: **Cruzan Taxi Association** (tel: 773-6388); **Combine Taxi and Tours** (tel: 772-2828).

Sightseeing and activities
Island bus tours are offered by **St. Croix Transit Tours** (tel: 772-3333) and **The Traveller's Tours** (tel: 778-1636). Horseback tours are run by **Paul and Jill's Equestrian Stable** (tel: 772-2880). For a walking tour of Christiansted or Frederiksted, contact **Take-a-Hike** (tel: 778-6997). For biking contact **St.Croix Bike and Tours** (tel: 772-2343) in Frederiksted. For turtles and whales, contact the Virgin Islands Conservation Society, P.O. Box 3839, St.Croix 00822 (tel: 773-7545).

Tourist information
The **U.S. Virgin Islands Division of Tourism** has an office at Box 4538, Christiansted, St. Croix (tel: 773-0495) and at Strand Street, Frederiksted (tel: 772-0357). **St. Croix Hotel and Tourism Association**, P.O. Box 24238 (tel: 800/524-2026). In the U.S.: 1270 Avenue of the Americas, Suite 2108, N.Y., N.Y. 10020 (tel: 800/372-USVI).

St. Thomas and St. John

Car rental and driving

You need a valid driver's license, and the minimum age for drivers is 18; in general rental companies prefer you to be at least 25. On St. Thomas: **A.B.C. Rentals** (tel: 776-1222); **E-Z Car** (tel: 775-6255); **Cowpet Auto Rental** (tel: 775-7376); **Dependable** (tel: 774-2253); **Discount** (tel: 776-4858); **Hertz** (tel: 774-1879); **Sun Island** (tel: 774-3333). On St. John: **Avis** (tel: 776-6374); **Spencer's Jeep** (tel: 693-8784); **St. John Car Rental** (tel: 776-6103). Driving is on the left. Wearing a seatbelt is compulsory, and the drunk-driving laws are strictly enforced. The speed limit is 56 k.p.h. (35 m.p.h.). Credit cards are accepted; pay before filling up with gas.

Getting around

By air: Services from the U.S. include **American** (tel: 1-800/474-4884), **Delta** (tel: 1-800/221-1212), **U.S. Air** (tel: 800/622-1015) and **USVI Prestige Airways** (tel: 1-800/299-8784), or you can go via San Juan, Puerto Rico, from where there are links on **American Eagle** (tel: 1-800/ 474-4884). Links to other Caribbean islands can be made on **Winair** (tel: 775-0183), **Liat** (tel: 774-2313), and **Air Anguilla** (tel: 776-5789). Some airlines make the link to St. Croix, otherwise you can take the seaplane (tel: 777-4491). Two companies offer helicopter travel: **Air Center Helicopters** (tel: 775-7335) and **Hill Aviation** (tel: 776-7880).
By boat: There are two ferry routes between the islands: Charlotte Amalie to Cruz Bay (six a day) and Red Hook to Cruz Bay (daily, every hour). For more details, contact **Transportation Services** (tel: 776-6282). Hydrofoils link St. Thomas and St. Croix daily.
Ferries link St. Thomas and the British Virgin Islands (Tortola, Virgin Gorda, and Jost Van Dyke); proof of citizenship is required to embark here. Ferries from Red Hook (St. Thomas) to Jost Van Dyke, stopping en route at Cruz Bay (St. John) take an hour; contact **Inter Island Boat Services** (tel: 776-6597). Ferries from Charlotte Amalie (St. Thomas) to Tortola take 45 minutes to the West End or an hour-and-a-half to Road Town; contact **Native Son** (tel: 774-8685) or **Smith's Ferry** (tel: 775-7292). There are ferries from Red Hook (St. Thomas) to West End (Tortola), 30 minutes (contact Native Son or Smith's Ferry) and from Cruz Bay (St. John) to West End (Tortola), 30 minutes (contact Inter Island Boat Services). Ferries also leave from Charlotte Amalie and Red Hook (St. Thomas) for Virgin Gorda. From Charlotte Amalie, two hours; contact Native Son, Smith's Ferry, or **Speedy's** (tel: 1495-5235); from Red Hook, stopping at Cruz Bay, St. John.

Yachts can be chartered with or without crew, usually through a broker. Check that the vessel is a member of the V.I. Charter-yacht League (tel: 775-5959), the local professional association of crewed charter boats. A full list of brokers is available from the tourist office.

Powerboats with or without captains can be rented from numerous companies. Contact **Nauti Nymph** (tel: 775-5066) or Chill Out (tel: 775-6265). You can also book day sails, submarine rides or short fishing excursions with **Coconut Cruises** (tel: 775-5959), **Sundance** (tel: 779-1722) or **Winifred** (tel: 775-7898). **Atlantis Submarine** (tel: 776-5650) is based in Havensight Mall. Scuba operators include Chris Sawyer (tel: 777-7804) and **Caribbean Divers** (tel: 775-6384). In St. John day sails on **Jolly Mon** (tel: 776-6239) or **Stampede** (tel: 693-8000). For scuba diving contact **Low Key** (tel: 693-8999) or **Cinnamon Bay Watersports** (tel: 776-6330).
By road: On St. Thomas, taxis are usually found at the ferry, airport, shopping and resort areas, opposite Emancipation Gardens (behind the post office) and along the waterfront in Charlotte Amalie. In St. John they tend to cluster around Cruz Bay Dock, but can be hailed anywhere. Taxi fares are fixed and prices are published at the airport and hotels. St. Thomas taxis are usually station wagons or minivans that take five or six passengers to drop off at their stops; on St. John open safari buses serve as taxis. Public buses on St. Thomas are irregular, although there are some new buses operating east and west into Charlotte Amalie. Bus

service begins at 5:35 AM from the bus depot and the last one leaves around 10 PM. Open-air safari buses operated by the V.I. Taxi Commission run Charlotte Amalie–Red Hook, Charlotte Amalie–Havensight Mall: Mon–Fri 12:15–5:15 PM (every 15 min).

Sightseeing

St. Thomas: tours are mainly conducted in minivans or safari buses. The **Virgin Islands Taxi Association City-Island Tour** (tel: 774-4550) and **Worldwide Travel** (tel: 776-2424) offer a variety of island tours; **Tropic Tours** (tel: 774-1855) does half-day tours, including shopping and sightseeing, by bus.

St. John: the **St. John National Park Visitor Center**, Cruz Bay (tel: 776-6201) does guided tours on and offshore; a **St. John Taxi Association** (tel: 776-6060) island tour covers Cruz Bay, Annaberg Plantation and the north coast beaches.

Tourist information

The **U.S.V.I. Division of Tourism** can be contacted at P.O. Box 6400, Charlotte Amalie (tel: 774-8784, and at P.O. Box 200, Cruz Bay, St. John (tel: 776-6450). There are two Visitor Centers in Charlotte Amalie, one opposite Emancipation Square and the other at Havensight Mall. The National Park Service has visitor centers at the ferry areas on St. Thomas (Red Hook) and St. John (Cruz Bay). In the U.S.: 1270 Avenue of the Americas, Suite 2108, N.Y., N.Y. 10020 (tel: 212/332-2222, 800/372-USVI).

FRENCH ANTILLES

Guadeloupe (area code 590)

Car rental and driving

Normal driver's licenses are valid for up to 20 days, after which an international one is needed. The minimum driving age is usually 18. Cars can be rented at the airport from: **Avis** (tel: 21-13-54); **Budget** (tel: 21-13-48); **Hertz** (tel: 21-13-46); **Thrifty** (tel: 21-13-50), **Europcar** (tel: 21-13-52), **Karukéra Car** (tel: 83-78-79), **Citer** (tel: 21-13-58), **Pop's Car** (tel: 21-13-56), **Solincar** (tel: 21-13-60), **Soltour** (tel: 21-13-77). Car-rental companies also have desks at

hotels and in Pointe-à-Pitre and Basse-Terre. Drive on the right. Seatbelt and drink-driving laws are enforced. Most gas stations take credit cards.

Getting around

By air: Airlines serving Guadeloupe from the rest of the Caribbean include **Liat** (tel: 21-13-93, between Pointe-à-Pitre and Antigua, Barbados, Grenada, Montserrat, St. Kitts, St. Lucia, St. Vincent, and Trinidad); **Air Guadeloupe** (tel: 21-12-90, to Marie Galante, Désirade, Les Saintes, Saint-Martin, St. Barts, Dominica, St. Lucia, St. Thomas, Puerto Rico); **Air St. Barts** (tel: 21-12-87, to St. Barts), **Air Saint-Martin** (tel: 21-12-87, to Saint-Martin); **Air Martinique** (tel: 21-13-42) to Martinique, **Air France** (tel: 82-61-61) and **AOM** (tel: 21-14-84, to Martinique, Saint-Martin, Puerto Rico, Dominican Republic); and **Air Caraibes** (charter 21-13-34). Helicopter tours are offered by **Heli Inter** (tel: 91-45-00) and **Safari Tours** (tel: 84 -06-74).

By boat: Ferries to and from Marie-Galante, Les Saintes, and La Désirade are operated by **Trans Antilles Express** (A.T.E.) (tel: 83-12-45) and **Transport Maritime Brudey Frères** (tel: 90-04-48).

To Marie-Galante: Ferries leave three times a day from the pier at Pointe-à-Pitre, 35-min. journey; and from St-François on Tue and Thu, 45 min. To Les Saintes: daily ferries from Pointe-à-Pitre at 8AM, returning from Terre-de-Haut at 4 PM, 45 min.; twice a week from St-François, via Marie-Galante, one hour 20 min.; and daily from Trois Rivières (one-and-a-half hours from Pointe-à-Pitre), 30 min. To La Désirade: daily ferry from St-François (times vary).

Caribbean Express (tel: 83-12-45) services link Pointe-à-Pitre with Martinique, Dominica, and St. Lucia (in conjunction with A.T.E.). All times and prices are subject to change, so check before traveling. There are no ferries to St. Barts or Saint-Martin. Safe anchorages and marinas, for ferries and yachts, are at Marina du Bas-du-Fort, Gosier; Marina de St-François (in the heart of town); Marina de Rivière Sens, Basse-Terre. Numerous companies around the

Bas-du-Fort marina rent out bareboat or crewed yachts and motorboats, including: **A.T.M. Yacht** (tel: 90-71-03) **Cap Sud** (tel: 90-76-70), **Star Voyage Antilles** (tel: 90-86-26).
By road: Taxi fares are set by the government and prices are posted at the airport, taxi stands, and major hotels. Taxi stands in Pointe-à-Pitre are on Blvd. Faidherbe et Chanzy, rue Achille René Boisneuf, rue Alexandre Isaac, in front of the tourist office. In Basse-Terre: Cours Nolivos. For Radio cabs (French-speaking) tel: 20-74-74 (airport), 81-79-70 (Basse-Terre) or ring Taxigua (tel: 83-90-00) or C.T.P. (tel: 82-21-21). Taxi tours have set fares to various points, and the tourist office or your hotel can arrange for an English-speaking driver. A public bus service operates around the island, 5 AM–6 PM, stopping at *arrêtbus* signs, or wherever you hail it. The fare is paid when getting off. There are three bus stations in Pointe-à-Pitre, serving different parts of the island: La Darse, Mortenol, and Bergevin stations; fares are posted in the stations.

Vespas can be rented through: **Dingo Location** (tel: 88-76-08); **Easy Rent** (tel: 88-76-27); **Association Velo-Vert** (tel: 88-51-00). Bicycles: **Velo-Vert**, Pointe-à-Pitre (tel: 83-15-74); **Cyclo-Tours**, Gosier (tel: 84-11-34); **Rent-a-Bike**, Meridien Hotel (tel: 88-51-00); **Equateur Moto/Rent a Bike** (tel: 84-59-94).

Sightseeing and activities
Ask the tourist office for English-speaking guides. Pick-ups at the hotel, lunch, and guide services are usually included in the price. Sea excursions, particularly to the mangrove reserve, can be organized by companies around Bas-du-Fort Marina. **Organization des Guides de Montagne de la Caraïbe** (tel: 92-06-10) provide guides for hiking tours in the mountains. It is also possible to arrange trips to neighboring islands. Local operators in Basse-Terre include: **Agence Gerville Reache**, rue du Dr Pitat (tel: 81-10-00); **Agence Penchard**, 1 bis rue de la République (tel: 81-27-12). In Pointe-à-Pitre: **Agence Havas** (tel: 90-27-27); **Agence Marie-Gabrielle**, 21 rue Alexandre

CONVERSION CHARTS

FROM	TO	MULTIPLY BY
Inches	Centimetres	2.54
Centimetres	Inches	0.3937
Feet	Metres	0.3048
Metres	Feet	3.2810
Yards	Metres	0.9144
Metres	Yards	1.0940
Miles	Kilometres	1.6090
Kilometres	Miles	0.6214
Acres	Hectares	0.4047
Hectares	Acres	2.4710
Gallons	Litres	4.5460
Litres	Gallons	0.2200
Ounces	Grams	28.35
Grams	Ounces	0.0353
Pounds	Grams	453.6
Grams	Pounds	0.0022
Pounds	Kilograms	0.4536
Kilograms	Pounds	2.205
Tons	Tonnes	1.0160
Tonnes	Tons	0.9842

MEN'S SUITS

UK	36	38	40	42	44	46	48
Rest of Europe	46	48	50	52	54	56	58
US	36	38	40	42	44	46	48

DRESS SIZES

UK	8	10	12	14	16	18
France	36	38	40	42	44	46
Italy	38	40	42	44	46	48
Rest of Europe	34	36	38	40	42	44
US	6	8	10	12	14	16

MEN'S SHIRTS

UK	14	14.5	15	15.5	16	16.5 17
Rest of Europe	36	37	38 39/40 41	42	43	
US	14	14.5	15	15.5	16	16.5 17

MEN'S SHOES

UK	7	7.5	8.5	9.5	10.5	11
Rest of Europe	41	42	43	44	45	46
US	8	8.5	9.5	10.5	11.5	12

WOMEN'S SHOES

UK	4.5	5	5.5	6	6.5	7
Rest of Europe	38	38	39	39	40	41
US	6	6.5	7	7.5	8	8.5

253

Isaac (tel: 90-04-82); **Agence Petrelluzzi**, 2 rue Jean-Jaurès (tel: 82-26-40); **Agence R Poirier et Fils**, 16 rue François Arago (tel: 82-00-46); **Navitour**, 10 rue de Nozières (tel: 83-49-50); **Nouvelles Frontières**, 28 rue Delgres (tel: 90-36-36); **Riverainx Tours**, 18 rue Frebault (tel: 91-72-10). At Pôle Caraïbes airport: **CaribJet** (tel: 82-26-44). Scuba diving operators include: **Les Henres Saines** (tel: 98-86-63) and **Aux Aquanantes Antillais** (tel: 98-87-30). Charter sailboats are available through **The Moorings** (tel: 90-81-81) and **Star Voyage Antilles** (tel: 90-86-26).

Tourist information

Office Départemental du Tourisme de la Guadeloupe, 5 Square de la Banque, 97110 Pointe-à-Pitre Cédex (Guadeloupe) (tel: 82-09-30). **Office du Tourisme de Basse-Terre**, Maison du Port, 97100 Basse-Terre (tel: 81-24-83); **Office du Tourisme de St-François**, Avenue de l'Europe, 97118 St-François (tel: 88-48-74) and in Trios Rivièra (tel: 92-77-01). There is also a tourist information booth at the airport. In the U.S.: contact 610 5th Avenue, N.Y., N.Y. 10020 (tel: 212/315-0726).

Martinique (area code 596)

Car rental and driving

Drivers must be at least 21 and hold a driver's license; after 20 days you'll need an International Driver's Permit. Companies include **Antilles Location** (tel: 63-33-05); **Avis** (tel: 51-12-70), **Budget** (airport 63-69- 00, Fort-de-France 70-22-75); **Europcar** (tel: 51-33-33); **Euro Rent** (tel: 60-00-77 or 60-10-93); **Hertz** (airport 51-01-01; **Pop's Car** (tel: 51-50-50); **Thrifty** (tel: 66-09-59), **Croquet** (airport 42-17-08, Fort-de-France 60-54-54) and **Eura Dom** (airport 42-17-07). The speed limits are 100 k.p.h. (62 m.p.h.) on the highway and 50 k.p.h. (31 m.p.h.) in town. Seatbelts are mandatory; drunk-driving is strictly penalized.

Getting around

By air: Fly from Miami on **Air France** (tel: 55-33-33) and via American's hub in San Juan, Puerto Rico on **American Eagle** (tel: 42-19-19). Inter-island ser-

vices, to Guadaloupe are available on **Air Martinique** (tel: 51-08-09) and **Air Guadaloupe** (tel: 42-16-71), and on **Liat** (tel: 42-16-03). You can also take a sightseeing flight with **Envol** (tel: 68-45-49) or with **Helicaraibes** (tel: 73-30-03) by helicopter.

By boat: Caribbean Express is a power-catamaran linking Martinique with Guadeloupe, Dominica and occasionally St. Lucia. Information and reservations at all travel agents or tel: 63-12-11. **Malikera** (tel: 91-60-87) also offers ferry services to Guadaloupe via Dominica. A ferry service between Fort-de-France and Pointe du Bout leaves regularly from Quai Desnambuc on the sea front in Fort-de-France until 11 PM, returning from the Marina at Pointe du Bout (late returns on Sun and Mon) takes 20 minutes. There is also a service from Fort-de-France to Anse Mitan and Anse à l'Ane, several times a day. For information call **Somatour** (tel: 73-05-53) or **Madinina** (tel: 63-06-46).

By road: Taxis can be found mainly at the airport, in Fort-de-France, and at major hotels; radio taxis may be contacted on 63-63-62 and **Audio Communication** on 63-10-10 and **Taxi Parking** on 73-32-21. Fares are regulated by the government (list from the airport), and are expensive, especially if you arrive at night, when a 40 per cent surcharge is added. Private taxis: at the Savane, along Blvd. General de Gaulle and Place Clemenceau in Fort-de-France. You can also travel by bus or shared taxi: the main terminal is at Pointe-Simon, on the sea front in Fort-de- France, otherwise try around Boulevard General de Gaulle. Buses are run privately, from 5 AM to 8 PM, and leave when they're full. Shout *arrêt* to stop one. There is also an inter-urban bus network. Shared taxis (*taxi collectif* or *Taxicos*) start early and run until 6 PM with regular fixed routes. Most start at Pointe Simon and serve all the *communes*.

Motorscooters and bicycles can be rented from **Discount** of Trois-Ilets (tel: 66-05-58); **Funny** (Fort-de-France 63-33-05 and **St. Luce Location** (tel: 62-49-66). **V.T.T. Tilt** (tel: 66-01-01) offers Velo Tout Terrain 18-speed mountain bikes, as do **Diamant V.T.T.** (tel: 76-18-80) and **Location Vert** (tel:

254

72-41-75). The **Parc Naturel Regional de la Martinique** (tel: 73-19-30) has designated biking routes off the beaten track, and organizes bike and walking tours in beauty spots.

Sightseeing and activities

The following local agents will find you guided tours by car or bus, trips on sailing boats and cruise ships, excursions in glass-bottomed boats, trips to Dominica, St. Lucia, and the Grenadines: **Richard Flechon Voyages** (tel: 73-35-35), **S.M.C.R.** (tel: 63-44-54), **Jet Tours** (tel: 51-90-00), **Roger Albert Voyages** (tel: 71-71-71); **Caribtours** (tel: 50-93-52), **Madinina Tours** (tel: 70 65-25). **Azimut** (tel: 70-07-00) offers an excellent guided tour of Fort-de-France.

Scuba operators include: **Planète Bleue** (tel: 66-06-79) and **Histoires d'Eau** (tel: 76-92-98). Windsurfers can be rented from the east coast centers of **Club Nautique du Vauchin** (tel: 74-50-83) and the **Club Nautique du Marin** (tel: 74-62-02). General watersports operators include **Fun Alizé** in St. Anne (tel: 74-71-58). Charter sailing boats can be hired through **The Moorings** (tel: 74-75-39) and **Star Voyage** (tel: 66-00-72).

Tourist information

Office Départemental du Tourisme de la Martinique, rue Ernest Deproge, Bord de Mer, B.P. 520-97200 Fort-de-France Cédex (tel: 63-79-60). There are information offices on the waterfront in the town (same tel), at the airport (tel: 42-18-06), and in the towns of Le Marin (tel: 74-63-21) and St. Luce (tel: 62-57-85). In the U.S. contact: Maison de la France, 645 North Michigan Avenue, Chicago, IL 60611 (tel: 312/751-7800).

St. Barthélemy
(area code 590)

Car rental and driving

Cars can be rented at the airport, although in peak season there may be a three-day minimum. You need a driver's license. Some hotels have their own car fleets, and many offer 24-hour emergency road service. **Avis** (tel: 27-71-43); **Budget** (tel: 27-66-30); **Europcar** (tel: 27-73-33); **Mathieu**

Aubin (tel: 27-73-03); and **Island** (tel: 27-70-01). There are two gas stations, one near the airport (credit card-operated self-service pumps, open 24 hours, but closed Sun), the other in Lorient (closed Thu, Sat PM and Sun).

Getting around

By air: Air St. Barts (tel: 27-71-90) links with Guadeloupe, Puerto Rico, Sint Maarten/Juliana and Saint-Martin/L'Espérance, Antigua, and St. Kitts; **Air Guadeloupe** (tel: 27-61-90) links with Puerto Rico, Guadeloupe, Saint-Martin, and Antigua; **Winair** (tel: 27-61-01) links with Saint-Martin. Helicopter tours can be arranged with **Heli St-Barts** (tel: 27-81-11) and Trans Hélico-Caraibes (tel: 27-60-68).

By boat: Gustavia Express (tel: 27-77-24), an engine-driven, 12-seat power catamaran, links St. Barts with Sint Maarten (Philipsburg) and Saint Martin. **Marine Service** (tel: 27-70-34) does day trips around St. Barts and cruises to Saint-Martin, Anguilla, Saba, and the Virgin Islands on its four-cabin catamaran; also rents out powerboats; **Océan Must** (tel: 27-62-25) operate day sails around St. Barts and to neighboring islands. **La Maison de la Mer** (tel: 27-81-00) offers day charters and week cruises around St. Barts and Saint-Martin, and tours from Gustavia to Colombier beach.

By road: There are taxi stands at the airport (tel: 27-75-81) and in Gustavia on rue de la République (tel: 27-66-31). Cabs are unmetered, so you may be charged more if you stop on the way. Minibuses and taxis do island tours. Radio cabs can be called on tel: 27-66-31 or 27-63-12. Fares are 50 percent higher after 8 PM. Motorcycles can be rented near the airport and in Gustavia (helmet compulsory). Try **St. Barth. Moto Bike** (tel: 27-67-89) and **S'évader Rental** (tel: 27-52-81).

Sightseeing and activities

Tours can be arranged through your hotel, the tourist office or any of the taxi operators including **Hugo Cagan** (tel: 27-70 79), **Florian La Place** (tel: 27-63-58). Local operators include **St. Barth Voyages**, Gustavia (tel: 27-79-79). Scuba diving: **West Indies Dive** (tel: 27-91-79) and **Odyssée**

255

Caraïbe (tel: 27-55-94). Windsurfers can be rented at the **St. John's Beach** (tel: 27-52-77).

Tourist information
The **Office du Tourisme** is in the Mairie de St. Barthélemy (town hall), Quai du Général de Gaulle, Gustavia (tel: 27-87-27).

Saint-Martin/Sint Maarten
**(area code 599-5 Dutch;
590 French)**

Car rental and driving
Your own driver's license is sufficient to rent a car on both sides: you must be at least 25. Cars can be rented at Juliana Airport. Companies include: **Avis** (tel: 87-50-60 or 52847); **Budget** (tel: 87-38-22 or 54030); **Cannegie Car Rental** (tel: 54329); **Continental** (tel: 87-77-64); **Esperance** (tel: 87-51-09); **Express** (tel: 87-87-59); **Fantastic** (tel: 87-71-09); **Hertz** (tel: 54314 or 87-73-01); **Hibiscus** (tel: 87-74-53); **Island Trans** (tel: 87-91-32); **National** (tel: 42168); **Risdon's** (tel: 54239); **Safari** (tel: 53186); **Sandy G Car Rental** (tel: 87-88-25, 53186). Motorbikes and scooters are available through Moto Caraibes (tel: 87-25-91) and Eugène Moto (tel: 87-13-97).

Driving is on the right, and road signs are international. Speed limits are 80 k.p.h. (50 m.p.h.) outside the towns, 30 k.p.h. (19 m.p.h.) in towns; drunk-driving carries fines, as do illegal parking, speeding, and running traffic lights; seatbelts should be worn and gas is paid for in cash.

Getting around
By air: Saint-Martin/Sint Maarten is linked to many other Caribbean islands on regional and international carriers (lighter aircraft use L'Esperance Airport on the French side). From the U.S. **American Airlines** and **American Eagle** (tel: 52040) which fly via their hub in Puerto Rico, **Continental Airlines** (tel: 53444) and **B.W.I.A.** (tel: 54646). The island is well served from the rest of the Caribbean by **Air Guadeloupe** (tel: 54212) to other French islands and on **Air Martinique** (tel: 54212). **Liat** serves many of the former British islands between Trinidad and Puerto Rico

(tel: 54203). **ALM** (tel: 54240) flies to Curaçao. Nearby islands can be reached on **Air St. Barts** (tel: 877346) and on **Winair** (tel: 54230). **Trans Hélico-Caraibes** (tel: 29-05-41 in Grand Case) and **Heli-Inter Caraibes** (French side tel: 87-35-88) run sightseeing excursions and act as taxis or as emergency services.

By boat: There are anchorages around the island, and you can get to any of the neighboring islands of Anguilla, Saba, St. Eustatius, and St. Barts by boat. The St. Barts Express (tel: 87-99-03) leaves St. Barts Mon–Sat AM, stopping at Philipsburg and the deep-water harbor at Marigot (French side), returning later in the day. Ferries between Marigot and Anguilla leave from both every half hour between 8 AM and 5:30 PM, and there are two late-evening crossings. (about 20 min.). You will need a form of identification with a photograph, and there is a departure tax.

A catamaran service (tel: 42640, 24096) links Philipsburg (Pelican Marina) with Saba four times a week. Companies chartering boats, with or without skipper, include: **The Moorings** (tel: 87-35-26), in Oyster Pond and **Sunsail** (tel: 87-83-41).

Day trips by sail or motorboat and picnics to nearby islands or coves, including Anguilla, are organized from the Dutch side aboard **Bluebeard** (tel: 52898), **Sualiga** (tel: 22167) and, to Anguilla, **Sea Hawk** (tel: 87-59-49). From the French side, sailing excursions are organized through **Saint Martin Evasion** (tel: 87-13-60), **Rising Sun Tours** (tel: 87-14-22), **C.S.B.** (tel: 87-89-38) and through the marinas at Port La Royale (tel: 87-20 43) and Port Lonvilliers (tel: 87-31-94). General watersports operators offering equipment rentals include **Blue Ocean International** in Baie Nettlé (tel: 87-89-73), **Kakao Watersports** in Baie Orientale (tel: 27-49-94), and nearby **Kontiki Watersports** (tel: 87-46-89). Scuba diving : **Ocean Explorers** (tel: 45252) and **Scuba Fun** in Anse Marcel (tel: 87-36-13).

By road: Taxi rates across the island are fixed and standardized—you can get a list from the tourist offices, and rates are posted at the airport. Taxis can be called at tel: 87-56-54 (Marigot) or 54317 (Juliana Airport); also at 22359 (Dutch side). Authorized taxis display stickers of the Sint Maarten Taxi Association. Buses run between 7 AM and 7 PM from Philipsburg through Cole Bay to Marigot.

Sightseeing
For sightseeing, contact **Island Reps Tours** (tel: 52392), **Rising Sun Tours** (tel: 42855, 87-14-22), **St. Maarten Sightseeing** (tel: 52646) and **Dutch Tours** (tel: 23316).

Tourist information
Dutch side: **Sint Maarten Tourist Bureau**, Walter Nisbeth Road #23, Philipsburg, Sint Maarten (tel: 22337). There is a tourist information bureau on Cyrus Wathey Square, Philipsburg, at the cruise ship pier. French side: **Office du Tourisme de Saint-Martin**, Port de Marigot, 97150 Saint-Martin (tel: 87-53-21), on the waterfront in Marigot. In the U.S.: 10 East 21st Street, Suite 600, N.Y., N.Y. 10010 (tel: 900/990 0040).

NETHERLANDS ANTILLES

Aruba (area code 297-8)

Car rental and driving
You need a valid national or international license; age range policies may vary with different companies . All companies include unlimited mileage, but not insurance. Try **Airways** (tel: 21845); **Avis** (tel: 28787; airport 25496); **Budget** (tel: 28600; airport 25423); **Dollar** (tel: 22783; airport 25651); **Five Star** (tel: 27600); **Hertz**, **De Palm** (tel: 24545; airport 24886); **National** (tel: 21967; airport 25451); **Safari** (tel: 39670); **Thrifty** (tel: 35335); **Toyota Rent-a-Car** (tel: 34832; airport 34902). Main roads are in good condition, but most attractions are down dirt roads: four-wheel drive vehicles are recommended. Driving is on the right. Road signs are international. The speed limit in towns is 40 k.p.h. (25 m.p.h.), 60 k.p.h. (37 m.p.h.) out of town.

Getting around
By air Call the airport (tel: 24800) for information on **K.L.M.** (tel: 23546),

A.L.M. (tel: 38080) flights. A.L.M. links Aruba to Bonaire, Curaçao, Sint Maarten and other islands. Ask about its Visit Caribbean Pass. **American Airlines** (tel: 22700) links with Puerto Rico and the mainland U.S. **Air Aruba** (tel: 36600) links with the Dominican Republic (Santo Domingo), Sint Maarten, Bonaire, and Curaçao.
By boat: There is a ferry linking Aruba with Curaçao and Venezuela (cars carried), but it is not recommended for tourists—more of a cargo boat. There is also a fruit boat running between Oranjestad and Punto Fijo, Venezuela; contact **Agencia Maritima Seamar** (tel: 24790).

   Atlantis Submarine (tel: 36090) visits Barcadera Reef, 50 minutes. Sailing cruises around the island, or moonlight, catamaran or dinner cruises, with stops for swimming and snorkelling, can be arranged through **De Palm Tours** (tel: 24400), **Mi Dushi** (tel: 23513), **Red Sail Sports** (tel: 64500), **Pelican Watersports** (tel: 31228), **Wave Dancers** (tel: 25520), **Wonder Watersports** (tel: 78365), for a day's proper sailing contact **Windfeather Charters** (tel: 65842).
   The tourist office has a list of boats available for day or half-day charter for deep-sea fishing.
By road: Taxi rates are fixed—make sure you agree on the price before setting off; prices go up in the evening and overnight. Taxis can be flagged down, or tel: 22116 (main dispatch office, Oranjestad). Taxi drivers should all have Tourism Guide Certificates and speak English.
   Buses run between Oranjestad and the southeast of the island, and to the beach hotels, and between Oranjestad and the airport. Oranjestad bus station is on Zoutmanstraat. A free, colorful shopping tour bus, the Let's Go Town bus, departs every hour from 9:15 AM to 3:15 PM from the Holiday Inn, stopping at all major hotels (you have to make your own way back). There are also jitney cars that operate like shared taxis. A jitney or bus from Oranjestad to San Nicolas will drop you off at the airport. Buses stick to their timetables—which are available from the tourist offices—and run one or two an hour.

To rent motorcycles, scooters, and mopeds, contact **Donata Cycle Rental** (tel: 34343); **Ron's Motorcycle Rental** (tel: 62090); **George's** (tel: 25975); **Semver Cycle Rental** (tel: 66851).

Sightseeing and activities

The major local operator, **De Palm Tours** (tel: 24400 or 24545), has offices in most hotels offering a three-hour tour of Aruba's highlights, and a day-tour to Curaçao and to Caracas, Venezuela. **Corvalou Tours** (tel: 21149) organize archeological/geological tours, plus architectural, bird-watching, and botanical tours.

Other operators include.: **Pelican Tours** (tel: 31228); **E.C.O. Destination Management** (tel: 25353); **Aruba Taxi Transfer & Tours** (tel: 22116); **General Travel Bureau** (tel: 26609); **Friendly Tours** (tel: 23230); **Pacer Survival Tour** (tel: 36791; morning tour by 18-speed bikes); **Marlin Booster Tracking Inc** (tel: 45086 or 41513, six-hour historical and wildlife tour with archeologists); **Private Safaris Educational Tours** (tel: 34869, land cruisers into the interior).

Hiking: 3-hour guided trip to spots only accessible on foot, minimum four people, through **De Palm Tours** (tel: 24545). Scuba diving operators: **Aruba Pro–Dive** (tel: 22520) and **Mermiad Sport Divers** (tel: 835546).

Tourist information

Aruba Tourism Authority, L.G. Smith Blvd. 172, Box 1019, Oranjestad (tel: 23777) for brochures and guides. There are also tourist information centers at the harbor in Oranjestad and at the airport. In the U.S., contact 1000 Harbor Blvd., Weehawken, N.J. 07087 (tel: 201/330-0800, toll-free 1-800/TO-ARUBA).

Bonaire (area code 599-7)

Car rental and driving

A national or international license is required, and most of the 10 or so companies stipulate a minimum age. Try **A.B.C.** (tel: 8980); **Avanti Car Rental** (tel: 5661); **Avis** (tel: 5795); **Budget** (tel: 8300); **Dollar** (tel: 8888); **Everts Car Rental** (tel: 8099); **Total** (tel: 8313); **Island Car Rental** (tel: 5111); **Sunray Car Rental** (tel: 5230); **Trupial Car Rental** (tel: 8487).

Driving is on the right. The speed limit in built-up areas is 33 k.p.h. (20 m.p.h.), and outside towns 60 k.p.h. (37 m.p.h.) unless otherwise specified. There are no traffic lights, and the main roads are good, but there are 20 miles of unpaved roads that get very muddy during the rainy season. Roads are apt to become one-way halfway along. Beware of potholes, lizards, and herds of goats. There are very few watering holes: on island trips take food and drink supplies.

There are gas stations in Kralendijk, Antrejol, and Rincon, open Monday to Saturday 7 AM–9 PM; Kralendijk also open Sunday 9 AM– 3:30 PM.

Getting around

By air: Bonaire is connected directly with the U.S. by **American Airlines** (tel: 800/433-7300). **A.L.M.** (tel: 8300) and **Air Aruba** (tel: 7880). From Caracas, try **Avensa** (tel: 8361). Ask A.L.M. about their "Visit Caribbean Pass" for inter-island travel.

By boat: More people come to Bonaire to dive than to sail or putter around in boats (ask hotels about their diving packages). Klein Bonaire is reached by diving boats: hitch a lift if you do not plan to dive, and don't miss the return. Snorkeling, picnick-ing, and sunset cruises are offered by the Siamese junk *Samur* (tel: 5592), the *Woodwind* (tel: 8285) and the *Sea Witch* (tel: 5433).

By road: Taxis are not metered, but prices are fixed, and should be agreed with the driver beforehand. Taxis can be ordered through hotels or from a central dispatch office (tel: 8100); they do not drive around looking for fares. Any taxi will take you on an island tour. Motorbikes and scooters can be rented from **Caribbean Touring Scooters** (tel: 6877); **Avanti Scooters** (tel: 5661) and **Hotshot Rentals** (tel: 7166).

Sightseeing and activities

Ask in the tourist office about visits to the two flamingo nesting sites. **Bonaire Tours** (tel: 8778) and **BarankaTours** (tel: 2200) offer bus tours of the island. For a more active cycling or snorkeling tour, contact **Discover Bonaire** (tel: 7558, 5433). Scuba diving operators are in the hotels: **Captain Don Habitat** (tel: 8290), **Sand Dollar Dive and Photo** (tel: 5433), and the **Dive Inn** (tel: 8761). For windsurfing and kayaking: **Windsurfing Bonaire** (tel: 5363).

Tourist information
Bonaire Tourist Board, Kaya Simon Bolivar 12, Kralendijk (tel: 8322 or 8649) can provide a small amount of tourist information and leaflets but no maps. **Bonhata**, the Bonaire Hotel and Tourist Association, can be contacted at 5134. In the U.S: **Adams Unlimited**, 10 Rockefeller Plaza, Suite 900, N.Y., N.Y. 10020 (tel: 212/956-5911).

Curaçao (area code 599-9)

Car rental and driving
Your own driver's license must be presented. Many of the car-rental companies have airport offices, allowing you to compare prices. **Avis** (tel: 868-1163); **Budget** (tel: 8683466); **Caribe Rentals** (tel: 613089); **Dollar** (tel: 861-3144); **Love Car Rental** (tel: 869-0444); **National Inter-rent** (tel: 868-3489); **Pro Rent a Car** (tel: 8691489); **Romart Car Rental** (tel: 862-7688); **Ruiz Rent a Car** (tel: 373184); **24 Hours Car Rental** (tel: 868-9410). The north coast is worth seeing by car but much of it is down dusty lanes.

Driving is on the right, and international signs are used. The speed limit in built-up areas is 40 k.p.h. (25 m.p.h.), and out of town 60 k.p.h. (37 m.p.h.) unless specified. Traffic from the right has right of way.

Getting around
By air: Curaçao is well connected from the U.S. on **American Airlines** (tel: 800/433-7300, 8695707), **A.L.M.** (tel: 695533, 800/327-7230), which uses Curaçao as its hub, provides links with Miami, Trinidad, Aruba, Bonaire, Sint Maarten, Puerto Rico, Jamaica, Dominican Republic, and South America. **Air Aruba** (tel: 8683777, 800/882-7822) operates between Curaçao and Miami, Aruba, Bonaire, and Sint Maarten. **American Airlines** flies to Puerto Rico. Flights from Curaçao to Aruba or Bonaire take 15–20 minutes. **K.L.M.** information: 8652747; **B.W.I.A.** 8687835. Helicopter flights can be booked with

Pelican Air (tel: 862-8155).
By boat: A cargo/ferryboat runs between Aruba, Curaçao, and Venezuela (see Aruba). Contact **Sail Curaçao** (tel: 767-6003) for boat trips, sailing school, or yacht charter.
By road: Taxis have T.X. on their licenses. Fares are fixed, and should be agreed upon first. Meters are soon to be installed. There are taxi stands at the airport and hotels and Plaza Jojo Correa, downtown Willemstad. Fares go up by 25 percent after 11 PM, and there may be a charge for excess baggage. Central taxi office: 869-0752 or 862-8686. Tipping is not obligatory. Some hotels provide free transportation to and from the city center.

Yellow public buses (known locally as convoys) or private vans or cars with B.U.S. on their license plates, take 6–14 passengers and are an inexpensive way of getting around. There are regular bus routes between major sights, leaving from Punda Bus Terminal (market place) or Otrabanda Bus Terminal, Rif Fort. For information contact **A.B.C.** (tel: 767-5105).

259

Sightseeing and activities
For tours beyond Willemstad, try **Casper Tours** (tel: 737-6713, 465-3010); **Taber Tours** (tel: 376637); **Daltino Tours** (tel: 461-4888); **ABC Tours** (tel: 767-5105). Hourly tours of the Hato Caves are given by local guides, reservations and information 868-0379. Christoffel Park (864-0363) offers bird-watching and guided jeep trips—take the Westpunt bus from Otrobanda bus terminal, every two hours from 7 AM. The big hotels have scuba-diving operators, or you can try **Master Dive Inc** (tel: 465-4312).

Tourist information
There are three offices of the **Curaçao Tourism Development Board**: a booth at the airport (tel: 686789), the main office on Pietermaai 19, P.O. Box 3266, Willemstad (tel: 861-6000). There are also various visitor information kiosks, one at the Cruise Terminal in Otrabanda, another at Wilhelminaplein in Punda. **Curaçao Hotel and Tourism Association**, International Trade Center, Piscadera Bay (tel: 863-6260). In the U.S.: 474 Park Avenue South, Suite 2000, N.Y.,

N.Y. 10016 (tel: 212/683-7660, 800/270-3350).

Saba (area code 599-4)

Car rental and driving
Cars can be rented (produce your own driver's license), including a full tank of gas and unlimited mileage, from **Scout's Place** (tel: 62205); **Mikie's Car Rental** (tel: 63259) or **Juliana's** (tel: 62269).

Driving is on the right, along the island's only road, The Road. In the event of a breakdown, call the only gas station (Fort Bay) on 63272.

Getting around
By air: Winair (local: 62255; Sint Maarten 554210) flies several times a day between Saba and Sint Maarten and also to St. Eustatius. Reconfirm flights in advance.

By boat: An open-air, 50-passenger ferry, *Voyager* (Sint Maarten 24096), plies between Saba (Fort Bay) and Sint Maarten (Great Bay Marina, Philipsburg), taking 60 minutes.

The three dive operators on Saba, **Saba Deep** (tel: 63347), **Sea Saba** (tel: 62246), and **Saba Reef** at Fort Bay Pier have boats which are available for round-island trips, deep-sea fishing, trips to nearby islands or other parts of Saba; the latter is presently for sale and not currently operating.

By road: There are about 10 taxi drivers on Saba (tel: 62281); all do guided tours. They can also arrange diving or nature walks; some have guesthouses. It is also safe to hitch-hike: wait for a lift by the wall opposite the Anglican Church in The Bottom, or the wall opposite Saba Deep in Fort Bay. There are no buses.

Hiking: Saba has 18 nature trails through the rain forest and up Mount Scenery. For a botanical tour, try **James Johnson** (tel: 63307).

Tourist information
Saba Tourist Office, Windwardside (tel: 62231).

St. Eustatius (area code 599-3)

Car rental and driving
You will need a valid driver's license from your own country, or an inter-national driver's license. There is an **Avis** desk at the airport (tel: 82421); or you can try **Lady Ama's Services** (tel: 82451) or **Rainbow Car Rental** (tel: 82811). Cars are reliable, but the roads are not: watch out for potholes. Driving is on the right, but some roads are very narrow and liable to be frequented by cows, goats, and sheep. Road signs are in Dutch and English.

Getting around
By air: Windward Island Airways (tel: 82362 or 82381) flies to and from Sint Maarten several times a day, Saba (10 minutes), and occasionally to St. Kitts.

By road: Taxi drivers will give a tour of the island, which takes about an hour. More information from the Historical Foundation in Doncker/de Graaff House, 12 Van Tonningenweg (tel: 82288). Most places are within walking distance: the Historical Foundation has a brochure detailing a 90-minute walking tour of the Upper and Lower Towns. Taxi drivers include Hugh Richardson (tel: 82378) and Angelica Pole (tel: 82659).

Hiking: There are 12 nature trails (leaflet available from the tourist office). Or take a two-hour guided trek into tropical rainforest on the Quill volcano, organized through the tourist office. Scuba diving can be arranged through **Dive Statia** (tel: 82435) and **Blue Nature Watersports** (tel: 82725).

Tourist information
There are two tourist offices: at the airport (tel: 82433), and the main **St. Eustatius Tourist Bureau**, at the entrance to Fort Oranje, 3 Fort Oranjestraat, Oranjestad, St. Eustatius, Netherlands Antilles (tel: 82433).

OTHER CARIBBEAN STATES

Jamaica (area code 876)

Car rental and driving
Most major international companies are represented and there are many local ones; a list of the Jamica U-Drive Association members is obtainable from Jamaica Tourist Board, address below. A valid driver's license is required, and you must usually be at least 24. A sales tax of 15 percent is

added on top; accident and health insurance and collision damage waiver optional. Some gas stations are closed on Sundays, and gas must be paid for in cash. The speed limit is 48 k.p.h. (30 m.p.h.) in towns and 80 k.p.h. (50 m.p.h.) on the highway. Drive on the left.

In Montego Bay: **Anna Car Rentals** (tel: 953-2349), **Central Rent-a-Car** (tel: 952-3347) , **Chen's Rent-a-Car** (tel: 952-2398), **Jamaica Car Rentals** (tel: 952-5586). Negril: **Vernon's Car Rentals** (tel: 957-4354). Ocho Rios: **Campbell's Rent-a-Car** (tel: 974-2941), **Caribbean Rent-a-Car** (tel: 974-2123) Port Antonio: **Eastern Rent-a-Car** (tel: 993-3624). Kingston: **Island Car Rentals** (tel: 926-8012), **Galaxy Car Rentals** (tel: 925-4176).

Car rental firms can be contacted on the following U.S. toll free numbers: **Avis** (tel: 800/228-0668); **Bargain Rent-a-Car** (tel: 888/991-2111); **Island Car Rentals** (tel: 888/991-4255); **Sunbird** (tel: 800/306-5053).

Getting around

By air: Jamaica is well linked to the U.S. on scheduled and charter airlines: **Air Jamaica** (tel: 952-4300), **American Airlines** (tel: 952-5950), **Continental Airlines** (tel: 952-4495) and **Northwest** (tel: 952-4033). Montego Bay and Kingston are linked several times a day on **Air Jamaica Express** (tel: 922-4661). You can charter a small plane through **Tim Air** (tel: 952-2516). **Helitours** (tel: 974-1525) runs sightseeing trips, with pick-ups at most local airports. Helicopters can also be chartered.

By boat: Ask at your hotel or nearest tourist information center about private charters for deep-sea fishing, scuba diving, and sailing.

By road: Buses are by far the cheapest way of getting around. They run all over the island and can be flagged down at bus stops and in between. Bicycles and motorbikes can be rented at most resorts or through: **Montego Bike Rentals** (tel: 952-4984); in Negril: **Dependable Bike Rental** (tel: 957-4764); **CJ's Bike Rental** (tel: 957-4207). In Ocho Rios: **Abe's** (tel: 974-1008). Taxis are in all resort areas but are not often metered; prices between destinations are usually

fixed, so ask the price for the journey before starting, or be prepared to bargain with the driver. Look out for red P.P.V. plates (Public Passenger Vehicle).

Sightseeing and activities

Get the Tourist Board leaflet *Things to know before you go*, which lists main excursions and attractions. These might include: Boonoonoonoos Beach Party (reggae, dinner, floor show); guided half-day tour of Croydon in the Mountains (working plantation in Catadupa); Evening on the Great River (canoe trip, dinner); full-day guided tour of Hilton High plantation; one-hour rafting trip on The Great River with hayride and plantation tour, etc. Your hotel will be able to organize any tour, which may be in a taxi with driver-guide or minibus and include any admission price in the cost.

Local tour operators will organize your own island tour and inter-island travel: In Montego Bay: **Blue Danube** (tel: 952-2002); **Forsythe Tours** (tel: 952-0394); **Glamour Tours** (tel: 979-8207); **Greenlight Tours** (tel: 952-2636); **Jamaica Tours** (tel: 953-3700); **J.U.T.A. Jamaica** (tel: 962-0813); **Sun Holiday Tours** (tel: 952-5629); **Travel International Tours** (tel: 952-9362); **Tropical Tours** (tel: 953-9100). In Negril: **Caribic Vacations** (tel: 957-3881). In Port Antonio: **Valley Hikes** (tel: 993-2543) for walks and eco-tours. In Ocho Rios: **Touring Society of Jamaica** (tel: 975-7158), **Tourwise** (tel: 974-2323), **Holiday Services** (tel: 974-2948). In Kingston, contact **S.E.N.S.E.** (tel: 927-2097) and **Tourmarks** (tel: 926-8540). Scuba operators are based in all the main towns. In Montego Bay, try **Poseidon Divers** (tel: 952-3624), in Negril, **Dolphin Divers** (tel: 957-5069) and **Sundivers** (tel: 957-4069), in Ocho Rios **Sea and Dive Jamaica** (tel: 974-5762), in Port Antonio, **Lady G'diver** (tel: 993-9624).

Tourist information

Jamaica Tourist Board, 2 High Street, Black River (tel: 965-2074); Tourism Centre, 2 St. Lucia Avenue (tel: 929-9200); Cornwall Beach, Montego Bay (tel: 952-4425); Shop #9, Jackson

Plaza, Negril (tel: 957-4243); Ocean Village Shopping Centre, Ocho Rios (tel: 974-2570); City Centre Plaza, Port Antonio (tel: 993-3051); 801 Second Avenue, 20th Floor, N.Y., N.Y. 10017 (tel: 212/856-9727 U.S. toll free 800/233-4852).

Cayman Islands
(area code 345)

Car rental and driving

A valid driver's license mustshown and a Cayman driving permit produced. Different companies specify different minimum ages for renting cars. The main companies are: **Ace Hertz** (tel: 949-2280); **Andy's Rent-a-Car** (tel: 949-8111); **Budget** (tel: 949-5605); **C.I.C.O.-Avis** (tel: 949-2468); **Coconut Car Rentals** (tel: 945-4377); **Economy Car Rental** (tel: 949-9550); **Just Jeeps** (tel: 949-7263). Gas is sold in imperial (160-ounce) gallons. Rental firms can be contacted on their U.S. toll-free numbers: **Ace Hertz** (tel: 800/654-3131), **Budget** (tel: 800/527-0700), **Coconut** (tel: 800/949-4377), **Cico Avis** (tel: 800/228-0668).

Driving is on the left, and some rental vehicles have left-hand drive; drunk-driving laws are strictly observed; seatbelts are recommended.

Getting around

By air: Flights to the Cayman Islands are available on: **Cayman Airways** (tel: 949-8200), **American Airlines** (tel: 949-8799) and **U.S. Air** (tel: 949-7488).

Between the three islands of Grand Cayman, Cayman Brac, and Little Cayman, **Cayman Airways** (tel: 949-8200) and **Island Air** (tel: 949-0241) fly regular services.
By boat: Boat excursions can be arranged through **Red Sail Sports** (tel: 949-8745) and **Cockatoo Sailing** (tel: 949-7884). Diving can be organized through: **Quabbin Dives** (tel: 949-5597); **Fisheye** (tel: 945-4209); **Aquanauts** (tel: 945-1953) and **Sunset Divers** (tel: 949-7111), **Calico Jacks** (tel: 949-4373), **Divers Down** (tel: 945-1611, **Ocean Frontiers** (tel: 947-7500).
By road: There is a limited public bus system on Grand Cayman but there are plenty of cars, motorscooters and bicycles to rent and taxis to hire. Taxi

rates are determined by the government and published in C.I.$, so always ask the driver how much the trip will cost before you start.

Motorcycles and bicycles can be rented from: **Cayman Cycle Rentals** (tel: 945-4021) and **Soto Scooters** (tel: 945-4642). Private bus services run between West Bay and George Town at irregular intervals. Buses can be flagged down along the route.

Sightseeing and activities

There are numerous local travel agents (see those listed below) which offer land and water-based excursions and tours; all such activities can be booked on your arrival in Grand Cayman. Local tour operators are mostly in Grand Cayman: **Evco Tours** (tel: 949-2118); **Majestic Tours** (tel: 949-7773); **Reid's Premier Tours** (tel: 949-6531); **Rudy's Travellers Transport** (tel: 949-3208); **Tropicana Tours** (tel: 949-0944). In the smaller islands, go through the hotels.

Tourist information

Department of Tourism The Pavilion, Cricket Square, George Town (tel: 949-0623). In the U.S.: 420 Lexington Avenue, Suite 2733, N.Y., N.Y. 10170 (tel: 212/682-5582).

Cuba (area code 537)

Getting there

Contrary to popular opinion, Americans can legally visit Cuba—they just can't spend American dollars there, which is meant to make traveling impossible. Exceptions are made for former Cubans with relatives in need, government officials, journalists, and professional researchers, all of whom must obtain an official license to go. The licenses are issued by the Treasury Department (tel: 202/622-2480). A second option for U.S. citizens is to sidestep the embargo by going through a third country: Canada, Mexico, and Jamaica offer regular flights in and out of Havana, Varadero, and Santiago de Cuba. Many of the other Caribbean and Latin American nations offer flights as well. The Cubans know the drill—they issue Americans a tourist card instead of stamping passports, so it is rather easy to "get away with it." The tourist cards are generally provided by travel agencies in these "third countries" which specialize in arranging American tours of Cuba. Law-abiding American citizens, be forewarned: under the terms of the current embargo, these trips are not legal.

For non-American citizens: from Mexico, try Tijuana-based **Cubatravel** (tel: 310/842-4148, cubatravel.com.mx). Up north, Canada's major airline, **Air Canada**, offers package tours (tel: 514/422-5788). The Toronto-based **Hola Sun Holidays** offers package tours as well (tel: 905/882-5184, 800/098-HOLA, 800/668-8178). From Jamaica, **Caribic Vacations** in Montego Bay offers Cuba packages (tel: 876/95-9895/ 9896, fax: 876/95-9897, caribic@cwjamaica.com). **Cubana Airlines** flies into Cuba from major European and Latin American cities (in Cuba tel: 55-550/04, fax: 55-5507). Arrivals fly in to Jose Marti International Airport, just outside Havana. An airy new international terminal (Terminal 3) makes your time at the airport quite pleasant.

Package tours of the island, arranged by any of the companies listed above, provide an organized, hassle-free if somewhat constrained way to see a lot of the island in a little time. If you are planning to travel on your own, by train or rental car, you'll probably need to make reservations in advance through one of the Cuban tour specialists listed above, since calling directly to Cuba from the United States can be quite problematic.

Getting around

Getting around within the country is relatively easy by plane or train, although trains are crowded and seats should be reserved well in advance. Contact your tour company for further information.

By air: Air Cubana (tel: 55-5503/04) flies from Havana to most of Cuba's major cities and resorts. Tickets are relatively inexpensive.

By road: Roads connecting all the country's major regions and towns are in decent condition. Car rentals from **Havanautos** or **Cubacar** (tel: 537-335546) are best arranged

through tour companies such as **Caribic** or Hola Sun (see above), **Havanatur** (in Cuba tel: 537-24-2121/ 2161/2248/227, fax: 537-24-2199/ 2681), or **Travelcoast** at the Havana Libre Hotel (tel: 537-66624). Rental prices range from around $25 to $45 a day plus $8–12 in mandatory insurance. Cuba is subject to intermittent gas shortages, so if you see an open station, fill your tank. In Havana almost everyone with a car, whether an official designated taxi or not, will pick up tourists and taxi them where they want to go for dollars.

Tourist information

Health Cuba has a large number of well-trained doctors, part of the most advanced health-care system in Latin America, but the U.S. embargo has caused serious shortages of medical equipment and all medicines. Visitors should not expect to refill prescriptions or even to obtain basics such as aspirin or ibuprofen. Bring your own basic medicines and prescriptions. Never drink the tap water. Aside from potential *turista* symptoms, some travelers have been known to pick up type A hepatitis.

263

Money Driven by the tourist sector, the dollar seems to be taking over the Cuban economy, making it easier for tourists but more expensive for tourists and locals alike. Prices were rising fast in 1999, and it was becoming more difficult for visitors to avoid the tourist economy, which runs on dollars only. Credit cards from American banks are acceptable. But the currency of choice on the ground in Cuba is without a doubt the American dollar, so take as much cash as you need, and/or are comfortable carrying.

Crime Police are ubiquitous in Havana, but increasing tourism and economic desperation has led to a rise in street crime—robbery and muggings, primarily—in Havana, Varadero, and other touristed areas. Prostitution is technically illegal, but there are many women, some, sadly, very young, patroling around the lobbies of the tourist hotels, nightclubs, and streets.

Dominican Republic
(area code 809)

Car rental and driving
Your own driver's license, or an international license, allows you to drive in the Dominican Republic for 90 days. The minimum age for renting a car is 25.

The following companies all have offices in Santo Domingo: **Avis** (tel: 533-3530); **Budget** (tel: 567-0173); **Dollar** (tel: 546-6801); **Nelly** (tel: 535-8800); **Hertz** (tel: 221-5333); **Honda Rent-a-Car** (tel: 567-1015); **National** (tel: 562-1444); **Patsy** (tel: 686-4333); **Thrifty** (tel: 687-9369). Rental is expensive because of high tariffs on vehicles; credit cards are accepted and a large deposit taken, usually twice the weekly rental fee.

Driving is on the right, but local drivers can be erratic; watch out also for motorcyclists in towns. Tolls of a few cents are levied on all principal roads out of the capital. Speed limits are 80 k.p.h. (50 m.p.h.) on highways, 60 k.p.h. (37 m.p.h.) in suburban areas; 40 k.p.h. (25 m.p.h.) in cities unless otherwise specified. Gas stations are few and far between in country areas and generally close at about 6 PM. Avoid night driving as narrow mountain roads are dark and treacherous. Cars driven by tourists are often stopped by police at the entrance to and exit from towns—this is nothing to worry about.

Getting around
By air: Several regional carriers serve neighboring islands, including **A.L.M.** (tel: 687-4569, to Sint Maarten and Curaçao); **American Eagle** (tel: 682-0077, to Puerto Rico from La Romana airport); **Air France** (tel: 686- 8419, to Martinique, Guadeloupe and Haiti); **Aeropostal** (tel: 566-2334, to Curaçao); **Dominicana** (tel: 532-8511, to Puerto Rico). **Columbus Air** (tel: 571-2711) organizes tours by plane to Haiti or the Turks and Caicos Islands, and domestic flights between Santo Domingo, Puerto Plata, and Samana. **Agencia Portillo** (tel: 565-0832) offers air taxi services from Santo Domingo (Herrera airport) to Puerto Plata and Punta Cana. Other domestic flights (linking Santo Domingo, Puerto Plata,

Santiago, Samana, Barahona, Portillo, and La Romana) are operated by **Servicio Aereo Dominicano** (tel: 541-2667) and **Aeronaves Dominicanas** (tel: 567-7195).
By boat: Leisure craft take you on trips to offshore islands, such as Cayo Levantado, from the dock at Samana and from Los Cacaos.
By road: Taxis are unmetered. Although fares are government-regulated, they are negotiable assuming you and the driver speak the same language. Fares to destinations outside the city are posted in major hotels and at the airport.

Telephone-dispatched taxi services are another option: this is a 24-hour service with rates agreed over the telephone, roughly depending on distances covered (but you usually need to speak Spanish). Taxi firms include **Taxi Anacaona** (tel: 530-4800); **Emely Tours** (tel: 687-7114) and **Taxi Raffi** (tel: 689-5468).

Publicos, blue-and-white or blue-and-red cars that run regular routes stopping to let passengers on and off, are much cheaper; rates are fixed between cities. The cars are often crowded and uncomfortable.

Private buses—*conchos* or *colectivos*—are the colorful way to get around. Most leave from around Parque Independencia in Santo Domingo; exact change required.

Private air-conditioned buses make regular trips from Santo Domingo to Santiago, Puerto Plata, etc. To reserve a seat call **Metro Buses** (tel: 544-4580 in Santo Domingo, 563-7929 in Puerto Plata or **Caribe Tours** (tel: 538-2229), whose prices tend to be cheaper. Also **Apolo** (tel: 586-2751); **Linea Sur** (tel: 682-7682).

Motoconchos—motorbike taxis—are found on the streets of Puerto Plata, Sosua, and Jarabacoa: flag them down on the road and in town and negotiate the fare.

Motorcycles can be rented out around Puerto Plata and Playa Dorada; you must ensure that you always use the lock, as there is no insurance on motorcycle theft.

Bicycles can be rented from many of the hotels on the north coast. Ask at reception.

Sightseeing and activities

Prieto Tours (tel: 685-0102) offers half-day bus tours of Santo Domingo, beach tours, tours to Cibao Valley and the Amber Coast, and others. **Turinter** (tel: 685-4020) does a full-day tour of Samana, and specialty tours (museums, shopping, fishing, casino). **Apolo Tours** (tel: 586-6610) offers a full-day tour covering Playa Grande, Santiago, and Sosua. **Ecoturisa** (tel: 221-4104) does wildlife tours of the western end of the country. **Museo de Historia y Geografia** (tel: 689-0106) does archeological and historical bus tours of the east of the country. **Go Caribic** (tel: 586-4075) for a variety of land and sea excursions and jeep safaris. Diving is best arranged through the hotels.

Tourist information

There is a Secretary of Tourism on the Avenida Mexico (at the corner of Avenida 30 de Marzo) (tel: 221-4660) and in Puerto Plata, at Malecon 20 (tel: 586-3676). Tourist information can be obtained in most local town halls, and there are offices at Las Americas International Airport, La Union Airport, in Ayuntamiento, Santiago (tel: 582-5885), in Jimani, Samana, and Boca Chica. In the U.S., contact 2355 Salzedo Street, Suite 307, Coral Gables, Miami, FL 33134, toll-free (tel: 800/752-1151).

Puerto Rico (area code 787)

Car rental and driving

Your bational driver's license is preferred by companies to an international license. There are about 13 rental agencies including **Avis** (tel: 800/800/374-3556), **Hertz** (tel: 791-0840), **National** (tel: 791-1805), and **Budget** (tel: 791-3685).

Driving is on the right, with maximum speed on the expressway 88 k.p.h. (55 m.p.h.). Take a phrasebook if you are heading off the beaten track.

Getting around

By air: San Juan is a Caribbean hub and has excellent connections to the continental U.S. on **American Airlines** (tel: 749-1747), **Continental** (tel: 800/525-0280), **Delta** (tel: 800/221-1212) and **Northwest** (tel: 800/225-2525). **American Eagle** run domestic flights every hour between San Juan and Ponce. Several local airlines operate services within Puerto Rico and between Puerto Rico and the rest of the Caribbean, including **American Eagle** (tel: 749-1747), **Liat** (tel: 791-3838), **Towers Air** (tel: 800/221-2500), and **Dominicana Airline**. All have offices at the Luís Muñoz Marín International Airport (tel: 462-3147). **Vieques Air Link** (tel: 722-3736) flies from Isla Grande Airport and from Fajardo on the east coast to Vieques, about $28 one-way, and **Flamenco Airways** (tel: 725-7707) to Culebra.

By boat: Passenger ferries run by the Fajardo Port Authority (tel: 863-0852) only between Fajardo Beach and Vieques twice daily, taking 80 min. From Fajardo to Culebra there are daily ferries; from Vieques to Culebra, ferries go three times a week.

265

By road: All taxis are metered but can be hired unmetered for sightseeing, etc. Shared taxis (*publicos*) have yellow license plates with P. or P.D. at the end and operate all over the island, stopping in each town's main plaza. They take up to 17 passengers, and their routes and fares are fixed by the Public Service Commission. Main terminals are at the airport and Plaza Colon in Old San Juan. Information **Metropolitan Bus Authority** (tel: 250-6064). **Airport Limousine Service** (tel: 791-4745) provides a minibus or shared-taxi service from the airport to hotels in Isla Verde, Condado, and Old San Juan. **Dorado Transport Co-operative** (tel: 796-1214) serves hotels and villas in the Dorado area.

The city buses in San Juan (*guaguas*) travel on a special route against the traffic flow. Bus stops, which are yellow posts, are marked *Parada de Guaguas*. City buses are not frequent: 30–45 minutes apart, and not after 10 PM. The main terminals are Intermodal Terminal on Calles Marina and Harding in Old San Juan and Capetille terminal in Rio Piedras, next to the Central Business District.

Elsewhere on the island, **Puerto Rico Motor Coach Co.** (tel: 725-2460) has daily scheduled service between San Juan, Arecibo, and Mayaguez through Caguas and Cayey or

Salinas. Bus T1 goes between the airport and Plaza Colon in San Juan; people take precedence over luggage if the bus is full. Open-air trolleys also rattle around Old San Juan, leaving from La Puntilla and the marina; you can board anywhere and there is no charge. Bicycles can be rented at Boqueron Balnearios (beaches), and from Hyatt hotels (tel: 796-1234).

Sightseeing and activities

For scuba diving contact **Caribbean School of Aquatics** (tel: 728-6606) and **Caribe Aquatic Adventurer** (tel: 724-1882). In the southwest, contact **Parguera Divers Training Centre** (tel: 899-4015). Tours of San Juan, the Bacardi Rum plant, the beaches, and the rain forest, etc., can be arranged through: **Rico Suntours** (tel: 722-2080); **United Tour Guides** (tel: 723-5528); **Cordero Caribbean Tours** (tel: 786-9114). Some eco-based tours include **Tropix Wellness Tours** (tel: 268-2173) and **Encantos Ecotours** (tel: 272-0005).

Tourist information

Puerto Rico Tourist Bureau, P.O. Box 4435, San Juan 00905. There are tourist information offices at the international airport (tel: 791-1014 or 2551), at Convention Center Condado (tel: 721-2400 ext 2280), at La Casita, near Pier 1, Old San Juan (tel: 722-1709), and also in Ponce at Casa Armstrong-Poventud, Plaza, Las Delicias (tel: 840-5695). Town halls throughout the country will have information desks. The government-sponsored **Puerto Rico Tourism Company** (tel: 721-2400) is good for maps, brochures, etc., and *Que Pasa*, the official visitors guide. In the U.S.: 575 Fifth Avenue, 23rd Floor, N.Y., N.Y. 10017 (tel: 212/599-6262).

Barbados (area code 246)

Car rental and driving

A visitor's driver's license must be purchased price B.D.S.$10.00 from car-rental companies, the airport, or Oistins, Hastings, Worthing, Holetown, District E, or Bridgetown Police Stations; drivers must have held a full license for at least two years and be over 24. There are car-rental companies in every district (the tourist board has the complete list), including: **Corbin's Car Rentals** (tel: 427-9531); **Courtesy Rent-a-Car** (tel: 431-4160); **Regency** (tel: 427-5663), **National** (tel: 426-0603), **Sunny Isle Car** (tel: 435-7979), **Sunset Crest Rentals** (tel: 432-2222), **P&S Car Rentals** (tel: 424-2052).

Motor scooters and bicycles also available from **Fun Seekers Inc.** (tel: 435-6852). Driving is on the left, and speed limits are 34 k.p.h. (21 m.p.h.) in towns and 80 k.p.h. (55 m.p.h.) on the highway. Seatbelts are not mandatory, and there are no drunk-driving laws as such, although police could stop you for bad driving. Gas generaly has to be bought in cash.

Getting around

By air: Barbados has good international services from North America on: **American Airlines** and **B.W.I.A.**. It also has excellent connections with the Caribbean islands nearby: to Antigua, St. Lucia, Grenada, Trinidad, and Tobago on **Liat** (tel: 434-5428) and to the Grenadines: **Mustique Airways** (tel: 435-7009) and T.I.A. (tel: 418650). Helicopter tours, a stomach-lurching way of seeing the island, are offered by **Bajan Helicopters** (tel: 431-0069). **By boat: Windward Lines** (tel: 431-0449) has a weekly scheduled ferry touching St. Lucia, St. Vincent, Trinidad, and Venezuela. The *Bajan Queen* makes sunset trips (both tel: 436-6424). For a lower-key sail with snorkeling and lunch stops, try *Tiami* (tel: 427-7245), *Secret Love* (tel: 432-1972), or *Heat Wave* (tel: 423-7871). For deep-sea fishing contact **Blue Jay** (tel: 422-2098).

By road: Bright yellow minibuses with blue stripes, run by the Barbados Transport Board, provide a regular service around the island, with destinations usually displayed at the bottom left-hand corner of the windshield. There are two terminals in Bridgetown, plus Speightstown Terminal in the north providing a service to Bridgetown along the west coast, to eastern areas, and a bypass service from Speightstown to the south coast. For information on routes call the Transport Board

Headquarters (tel: 436-6820). A number of privately owned maxi-taxis (minibuses) and route taxis also operate (not color-coded). These can be picked up at normal bus stops.Taxi fares between principal destinations are set in Bds. dollars—check first.

Sightseeing and activities

Tours can be organized through hotels or through companies such as: **L.E. Williams Tour Co.** (tel: 427-1043); **Sunflower Tours** (tel: 429-8941); **Gem Tours** (tel: 436-1640). For a four-wheel-drive tour to remote areas, contact **Island Safari** (tel: 432-5337). **V.I.P. Tour Services** (tel: 429-4617), which runs private air-conditioned cars with driver/guides.

The Barbados National Trust (tel: 436-9033) organizes interesting guided Sunday walks. For visits to the Grenadines, St. Lucia, Grenada, Tobago, and Angel Falls by sea and air: **St. James Travel & Tours** (tel: 432-0774); **Chantours** (tel: 432-5591); **Grenadine Tours** (tel: 435-8451).

Scuba diving operators include: **Explore Sub Barbados** (tel: 435-6542) on the south coast. **Blue Reef Watersports** (tel: 422-3133), **Scuba Barbdoes** (tel: 435-6565), and/or **Dive Boat Safari** (tel:427-4350). For wind-surfing contact **Mistral** (tel: 428-7277) on the south coast.

Tourist information

Barbados Tourism Authority, P.O. Box 242, Harbour Road, Bridgetown, Barbados (tel: 427-2623 or 4). **Barbados Hotel Association** (tel: 426-5041). In the U.S.: 800 Second Avenue, N.Y., N.Y. 10017 (tel: 212/986-6516, toll-free 800/221-9831).

Trinidad and Tobago
(area code 1868)

Car rental and driving

To rent a car you must have a valid driver's license and be at least 21. For a comprehensive list of car-rental companies in Port of Spain, Piarco Airport, San Fernando, and the south of Trinidad, and Tobago, ask for the *Discover Trinidad and Tobago* booklet from the tourist office. Beware: in Trinidad it can sometimes take an entire morning for a satisfactory

rental car to be delivered. **Singh's Auto Rentals** (tel: 625-442, **Thrifty** (tel: 669-0602); **Econo Car Rentals Ltd** (tel: 622-8074, airport 669-2342); **Johnny's** (tel: 674-0463). On Tobago it is more economical to rent a jeep than take a taxi, although there are some great taxi driver/guides. Tobago Car Rental: **Auto Rentals** (tel: 639-5330); **Rattan's Car Rental** (tel: 639-8271); **Sunflower Tours** (tel: 429-8941); **Tobago Travel** (tel: 639-8778).

Driving is on the left, and the roads are good in cities and towns, but check with the locals before venturing elsewhere, particularly in Tobago; you might be halfway down one side of the island only to find the road you are on is impassable.

There is a front-seatbelt law, and drunk-driving laws are strictly enforced (fining or detention). Speed limits are 80 k.p.h. (50 m.p.h.) on the highways, 40–60 k.p.h. (25–37 m.p.h.) on minor roads and 30 k.p.h. (18 m.p.h.) in residential areas.

Getting around

By air: Both islands are well served from the U.S. on **B.W.I.A.** (tel: 627-2942) and **American Airlines** (tel: 669-4661). Regular 15-minute flights on **Air Caribbean** Trinidad (tel: 623-2500), Tobago (tel: 639-2500) and **Liat** (Trinidad tel: 627-2942, Tobago tel: 639-8541) link Trinidad and Tobago (up to 10 a day) so you can hop from one to the other for a day. **Liat** also links Trinidad and Tobago with the rest of the Caribbean. Charter aircraft in Trinidad from **Sun Island** Aviation (tel: 669-3101); **Diamond Air** (tel: 623-3300); **Nealco Travel Services** (tel: 664-5416); or through **Trinidad & Tobago Sightseeing Tours** (tel: 628-1051). **By boat:** A car ferry/passenger service from Port of Spain to Tobago (Scarborough) leaves daily, taking between five and six hours, with food and drink on board; you can return by plane . You can rent a cabin if you take the evening sail. Reservations can be made through the tourist board (see below); buy tickets at ferry offices in Port of Spain (tel: 625-3055) and Scarborough (tel: 639-2416).

For scuba diving and snorkeling, try **Tobago Dive Experience**

267

(tel: 639-7034), **Aquamarine Dive Ltd,** Speyside (tel: 660-4341); **Man Friday Diving**, Charlotteville (tel: 660-4676). For trips to Buccoo Reef, day sails, and general watersports, contact the hotels or **Kalina Catz** (tel: 639-6304) and **Ron's** (tel: 660-4941).

By road: There are two types of taxis: rental and route, identifiable by their H license plates. Rental taxis are private, carrying you where you want. They do not have meters and although their rates are theoretically fixed, they tend to be negotiable (especially during Carnival) if you have the energy to haggle. An official list of rates for some routes, quoted in TT dollars (although some taxi drivers will accept U.S. dollars), is posted at the airport or obtainable from the Tourist Board. Drivers do tours also: prices depend on how many passengers there are, how far you wish to travel, and how long you want the driver to wait for you: take the official rate as the basis for all your negotiations.

Less expensive are route taxis, which operate like buses on prescribed routes, picking up as many passengers as can fit in their vehicles. They tend to start and finish their journey around Independence Square, Port of Spain, and come in two forms: cars taking four or five passengers (some with small signs on their dashboards denoting the route—otherwise you have to spot the H. license plate, flag one down and ask where it is going), and maxi-taxis. These are color-coded, 11- or 25-seat minibuses that ply particular routes according to their color (you can hail them anywhere also).

Yellow taxis operate around Port of Spain, red in eastern Trinidad, green for south Trinidad, black for Princes Town, brown for San Fernando, and blue in Tobago. Both kinds of taxi will sound their horns as they go, to let you know if they still have some room on board. Public buses run by the Public Transport Service Corporation (P.T.S.C.) are either very old (the blue ones) or spanking new and air-conditioned (the red, white, and black ones). They follow special bus lanes from Port of Spain to San Fernando, to Arima, and to

Chaguanas. Check with your hotel or the tourist board for rates and pick-up points for all modes of transportation.

Sightseeing and activities

On Trinidad two of the most popular excursions are to the Caroni Swamp during the flight of the scarlet ibis, and to the Asa Wright Centre in the rainforest. Tours of the Caroni Bird Sanctuary are run by naturalists **Winston Nanan** (tel: 645-1305, 658-0308) and **David Ramsahai** (tel: 663-4767). Other tour companies in Port of Spain include: **Bacchus Taxi and Car Rentals** (tel: 622-5588); **Hub Travel**, Hilton Hotel Lobby (tel: 624-3111); **Legacy Tours** (tel: 623-0150); **St. Christopher Taxi Service**, Hilton Hotel (tel: 624-3560); **The Travel Centre** (tel: 623-5096, 623-8785); **Trinidad & Tobago Sightseeing Tours** (tel: 628-1051).

For operators outside Port of Spain, look in the *Discover Trinidad & Tobago* booklet from tourist office. David Rooks of **Nature Tours** offers guided walks and trips to offshore bird colonies (tel: 639-4276). Other companies in the sightseeing business include **Ansyl Tours** (tel: 639-4125); **Southeast Eco-Tours** (tel: 644-1012); **Pax Nature Tours** (tel: 662-4084); **Naipaul's Tours & Travel** (tel: 623-5516); **Bibi's Tours & Travel** (tel: 679-4584); **Tobago Travel** (tel: 639-8778); **Trinidad & Tobago Sightseeing Tours** (tel: 628-1051).

Tourist information

Tourism and Industrial Development Co. (T.I.D.C.O.), 10 14 Phillip St Port of Spain (tel: 623-1932). **Tobago N.I.B. Mall**, Scarborough (tel: 639-2125). T.I.D.C.O. is also at Piarco Airport (tel: 669-5196) and Crown Point Airport (tel: 639-0509). **Trinidad and Tobago Hotel and Tourism Association**, Unit B, 36 Scott Bushe Rd, Port of Spain (tel: 624-3928). **Trinidad and Tobago Bed and Breakfast Co-operative Society**, P.O. Box 3231, Diego Martin (tel: 637-9329); **Tobago Bed and Breakfast Association** (tel: 627-2337).

In the U.S.: 7000 Blvd East, Guttenburg, N.J. 07093 (tel: 201/662-3403), National Carnival Commission (tel: 627-1530).

Accommodations & Restaurants

ACCOMMODATIONS

Styles and standards of Caribbean accommodations vary enormously, as shown by the differences in price. There are very sophisticated beach clubs where individual cottages have ocean views, but most hotel rooms are in large resort complexes. In every recommendation except the very cheapest, rooms have their own bathrooms. A number of villas and short-term apartments are mentioned below. For independent travelers there are a few guesthouses and local business hotels on each island. Most hotels are set on the beach; if not, this is indicated. Most also have swimming pools.

There is no standardized system of classification in the Caribbean, but all hotels booked through tour operators and travel agents will be registered with the tourist board on the island and checked by the operators.

Prices, highest from January to April, are reduced by 20–25 percent during the rest of the year. Each island has a different system, with supplementary room taxes. A service charge of 10–15 percent is often levied.

Hotels are divided into four price categories, based on the rate for a double room in high season:

($) = budget (a double room for less than U.S.$75)
($$) = moderate (a double room for between U.S.$75 and $200)
($$$) = expensive (expect to pay between U.S.$200 and $400)
($$$$) = very expensive (expect to pay more than U.S.$400)

Dialing codes From the U.S., dial 1 and the area code only (although the French and Dutch islands and other islands with the 599 area code require 011).

THE WINDWARD ISLANDS

Dominica (011-767)
Hotels on Dominica levy a 15 percent government tax on all bills.

Evergreen Hotel ($$)
tel: 448-3288
South of Roseau, with a pool and pleasant waterfront setting. Small and welcoming.
The Garraway Hotel ($$)
tel: 449-8800
Modern high-rise building well positioned on the waterfront in town. Very comfortable rooms with a good restaurant, and good service.
Papillote Wilderness Retreat ($)
tel: 448-2287
Ten rooms set in a grand tropical garden fed by the Trafalgar Falls. Good walking.
Picard Beach Cottage Resort ($$)
Roseau tel: 445-5131
Eight beach cabins, comfortable Caribbean style, to the south of Portsmouth.

Grenada (011-1473)
Hotels on Grenada and Carriacou levy an 8 percent government tax on all bills.

The Caribbee Inn ($$)
Carriacou tel: 443-7380
Charming old colonial-style inn set on a hillside a short walk from the extremely fine cove, Anse la Roche. Intimate and friendly; home-cooked Caribbean cuisine.
Coyaba ($$)
tel: 444-4129
Friendly beach resort in Grand Anse. Comfortable rooms in large buildings in a neat tropical garden. Entertainment in the bar and thatch-roof restaurant; good sports facilities on the beach.
Petit Bacaye ($$$)
tel: 443-2902
Set in its own cove, Petit Bacaye has just a few palm-thatched cottages and a central bar. Very friendly, fresh fish from local fishermen.
Spice Island Inn ($$$)
tel: 444-4258
High luxury on Grand Anse beach. The 56 rooms are large and air-conditioned, and some stand directly behind the palms and sand. Entertain-ment in the beachfront restaurant and bar.

The Grenadines (011-784)
Hotels charge 7 percent government tax.

Cotton House Hotel ($$$$)
Mustique tel: 456-4777
Set in the ancient stone estate building of a former cotton plantation; sumptuous beds and furnishings. Pool and fantastic views to go with superb food.
Dennis's Hideaway ($–$$)
Mayreau tel: 458-8594
Six rooms with a restaurant and bar near by; modern but made special by Dennis himself, who plays the guitar and sings.
Frangipani ($$)
Bequia tel: 458-3255
Set in an old family vacation villa on the Port Elizabeth waterfront. Antique gentility and personable West Indian style.
Friendship Bay Hotel ($$$)
Friendship Bay tel: 458-3222
Brightly colored complex on the south side of the island. Passable beach; excellent beach bar; some watersports.

St. Lucia (011-758)
All hotels on St. Lucia levy an 8 percent government room charge.

Anse Chastanet ($$–$$$)
Soufrière tel: 459-7000
Forty-eight rooms and villas scattered on the hillside and on the gray sands of secluded Chastanet bay; good diving and seclusion.
Candyo Inn ($–$$)
tel: 452-0712
Small, friendly inn a short walk of Reduit Beach and Rodney Bay. Self-contained apartments.

Ladera Resort ($$–$$$)
tel: 459-7323
A magnificent setting on the shoulder of one
of the Pitons. Antique furniture rooms open to
the view and the noise of tree-frogs.
Marigot Bay Resort ($$)
tel: 451-4974
In the wonderful setting of Marigot Bay, a nar-
row, steep-sided inlet festooned with palms.
Villas and cottages; charming and laid-back.
Royal St. Lucian ($$$)
Reduit Beach tel: 452-9999
A grand and luxurious hotel, with central
atrium and wings, commanding the beach.
Every modern convenience in the huge rooms.

St. Vincent (011-784)

All hotels on St. Vincent levy a 7 percent
government room tax.

Petit Byahaut ($$)
tel: 457 7008
Tents above the secluded beach of Petit
Byahaut bay, which can be reached only by
boat. Stylishly rustic, but has hot running
water.
Umbrella Beach Hotel ($)
tel: 458-4651
Set in lively strip of restaurants and bars at
Villa. Small and simple.
Young Island ($$$$)
tel: 458-4826
A Caribbean gem—cottages scattered around
the tropical garden of Young Island, 200 yds.
off St. Vincent's southern coast. Pool, bar,
restaurant, and sports.

THE LEEWARD ISLANDS

Anguilla (011-264)

Hotels on Anguilla add a government tax of
8 percent.

Cap Juluca ($$$$)
tel: 497-6666
A mile-long line of bright, white Moorish domes
rising out of the Anguillian scrub along the
stretch of Maunday's Bay in the southeast.
High luxury with sunken baths and richly col-
ored Oriental rugs.
Harbour Villas ($$)
tel: 497-4393
Self-catering apartments in the fishing village
of Island Harbour, in the northeast of the
island. Plenty to do near by, but you may want
to rent a car.
Malliouhana ($$$–$$$$)
tel: 497-6111
On a cliff overlooking the superb Mead's Bay,
Mailliouhana has a mix of styles; terra-cotta
tiles, slender columns and arches, touched
with colorful Haitian prints. Smoothly run
hotel, with every luxury and a very elegant
dining room.
La Sirena ($$)
tel: 497-6827
A small and friendly hotel perched above
Mead's Bay, at an affordable price on an
island of heavyweights. Some entertainment.

Antigua (011-268)

Hotels on Antigua add a government tax of 8.5
percent; the tax is 7 percent for restaurants.

Admiral's Inn ($$)
tel: 460-1027
Within the historic walls of English Harbour;
rooms quite simple. A lively crowd of sailors
collects at the bar.
Catamaran Hotel ($–$$)
tel: 460-1036
Well-priced accommodations with kitchenettes
not far from the activity of English Harbour in
the south.
Copper and Lumber Store ($$–$$$)
tel: 460-1058
A small hotel set in the grounds of English
Harbour; functional brick walls beautified with
tropical plants and urgent naval air
transformed into a retreat of historic laziness.
Curtain Bluff ($$$$)
tel: 462-8400
Once again the height of Antiguan elegance
since its renovation. Main house on the bluff,
between two excellent beaches. Lavish in the
dining room and wine cellar.
Hawksbill Beach Resort ($$$–$$$$)
St. Johns tel: 462-0301
Very comfortable beach-front resort. Cottages
ranged above a series of bays; plenty of water-
sports.

Montserrat (011-1664)

Hotels on Montserrat add a government tax of
7 percent.

**Providence Estate House
Bed and Breakfast** ($)
tel: 491-6476
Set in lovely gardens in the north of the island
far away from the volcano. Two charming
rooms.
Vue Point Hotel ($$)
tel: 491-5210
Friendly hotel with cabins ranged on the hillside above Old Road Bay. Beach bar down
below; a crowd gathers some evenings.

Nevis (011-1869)

Hotels on Nevis add a government tax of
7 percent.

Four Seasons ($$$$)
tel: 469-1111
A reliable beach vacation spot. Elegantly deco-
rated and luxurious rooms. "Olde Worlde"
decor and tropical profusion in the garden.
Hermitage ($$$)
Charlestown tel: 469-3477
A gem of the Caribbean, set in one of its most
ancient wooden houses. Rooms modern, in
cottages embellished with gingerbread point-
ing, each with a hammock with a view.
around a lawned garden with palms.
Oualie Beach Club ($$)
tel: 469-9735
Twelve comfortable rooms on the calm Oualie
Beach in the north of the island, overlooking
St. Kitts. Low-key but fun.

271

Accommodations and Restaurants

St. Kitts (011-869)

Hotels on St. Kitts add a government tax of 7 percent.

Rawlins Plantation ($$$)

Mount Pleasant tel: 465-6221

The closest you can come to the lavish grandeur of plantation life. Ten luxurious rooms scattered around the estate grounds; fine, home-cooked West Indian cuisine and rum punch with a view from the impressive 18th-century great house.

Timothy Beach Resort ($$)

tel: 465-8597

Good value suites on the fine strip of sand in Frigate Bay. Beach hotel, but pretty quiet.

THE VIRGIN ISLANDS

British Virgin Islands (011-284)

Hotels in the B.V.I. add a government tax of 7 percent to all bills.

Anegada, Jost van Dyke and Necker Island

Cooper Island Beach Club ($$)

tel: 494-3721

Comfortable rooms in pretty cottages on the friendly, active Cooper Island.

Necker Island ($$$)

tel: U.S. 1-800-557-4255

You and a crowd of friends (up to 20) can rent the island. Huge Indonesian-style villa with split-level pools and all the trimmings of Caribbean luxury.

Tortola

Cane Garden Bay Beach Hotel ($–$$)

tel: 495-4639

A lively hangout on Tortola's busiest beach. Rooms air-conditioned and simple, but plenty of activity all around.

Long Bay Beach Resort ($$$)

tel: 495-4252

Delightful rooms and villas in Long Bay in Tortola's northwest. Some on stilts above the beach, others nestled in the profusion of the tropical gardens. Quiet but classy.

Virgin Gorda

Bitter End Yacht Club ($$$–$$$$)

tel: 494-2746

Lively resort for watersports fans—sailing school, windsurfing, short hops to nearby beach bars. Some entertainment, but also hideaway hillside cabins of high luxury.

Little Dix Bay ($$$$)

tel: 495-5555

Low-key high luxury. Cottages in spacious and neatly tended grounds, looking onto an excellent strip of sand. Very quiet, but activity if you want it.

Olde Yard Inn ($$)

The Valley tel: 495-5544

Quiet retreat with the beach a short drive/ride away. Attractive open-terrace restaurant.

U.S. Virgin Islands (011-340)

St. Croix

Hotels in the U.S.V.I. add a government tax of 8 percent.

Club Comanche ($$)

tel: 773-0210

Old colonial town house in Christiansted that has sprouted terraces, wings, and verandas, all connected by walkways. Cozy and hip, piano entertainment in the bar in the evenings.

Cormorant Beach Club ($$$)

tel: 778-8920

Low-key beach hotel—very attractive rooms with terraces or balconies overlooking the palms and sea. Quiet and refined with an excellent restaurant.

Villa Madeleine ($$$–$$$$)

tel: 778-7377

Set on a hillside in the east of St. Croix, each of the suites of the Villa Madeleine has its own pool and is charmingly decorated. Very plush.

St. John

Caneel Bay Resort ($$$–$$$$)

tel: 776-6111

A very elegant resort on St. John's north shore, where rooms are set in beautifully tended gardens around a great house. Watersports on the resort's seven beaches, otherwise reliable relaxation.

Gallows Point Suites ($$)

tel: 776-6434

Elegant suites with all modern comforts. Just a short walk from downtown Cruz Bay.

Raintree Inn ($–$$)

tel: 776-7449

In the heart of Cruz Bay, a small and friendly hotel with 11 rooms set in an oddly alpine timber house. Seafood restaurant attached.

St. Thomas

Bolongo Bay Beach Club ($$$)

tel: 775 1800

Lively sporting resort—watersports, scuba, tennis—on a charming sandy bay on the south of the island. Sport activities by day, entertainment by night.

Hotel 1829 ($$–$$$)

tel: 776-1829

A lovely townhouse hotel with a quiet, sophisticated air. Dinner is usually served to a piano accompaniment.

Ritz Carlton ($$$–$$$$)

tel: 775-3333

The most luxurious in St. Thomas: a large suite-hotel set around a bay on the east coast. Watersports (excellent windsurfing) and gourmet dining.

Sapphire Beach Resort ($$$)

tel: 775-6100

Large resort hotel right on Sapphire Beach where there are good snorkeling and watersports. All the Caribbean comforts are available in the rooms; there is a lively beach party each Sunday.

THE FRENCH ANTILLES

Guadeloupe (011-590)
Some hotels on Guadeloupe add a room tax of a few dollars.

Auberge de la Vieille Tour ($$$)
Montauban tel: 84-23-23
Large but genteel resort, rooms ranged in dwellings on the hillside around an old windmill tower. Dining room above the private hotel beach.

Auberge des Petits Saints aux Anacardiers ($$)
Terre de Haut, Les Saintes tel: 99-50-99
A charming bungalow in the main town of Terre de Haut. Fine French cuisine.

Les Flamboyants ($–$$)
Gosier tel: 84-14-11
On a hilltop just outside town, an old family villa with neat and simple rooms. A walk from the beach; pool and kitchen .Breakfast only.

Le Hamak ($$$–$$$$)
St.-François tel: 88-59-99
Rarified relaxation in private bungalows, tucked away in a beautiful profuse Guadeloupean garden on the seafront. As the name suggests, each bungalow has its own hammock.

Martinique (011-596)
Some hotels on Martinique add a room tax of a few dollars.

Auberge de l'Anse Mitan ($–$$)
tel: 66-01-02
A friendly hotel, still with some old West Indian charm; tucked away at the end of Anse Mitan beach, but not far from the action of the town.

La Bonne Auberge ($)
Trois-Ilets tel: 66-01-55
Small and friendly hotel, with simple rooms set in modern buildings in the heart of the tourist town of Trois-Ilets. Nice tropical dining room.

Habitation Lagrange
tel: 536060
Set in a superb restored plantation house in the banana groves in the northeast of the island near Le Marigot. No beach but elegant relaxation and fine cuisine.

Hotel Diamant les Bains ($$)
Diamant tel: 76-40-14
Quiet and very friendly hotel; 24 rooms overlooking a pretty garden; views of Diamond Rock. An ideal retreat.

Saint-Barthélemy (011-590)
Some hotels on St. Barts add a room tax of a few dollars.

Club la Banane ($$$)
Lorient tel: 27-68-25
Amusing crowd in the bar; rooms decorated with traditional Caribbean flourishes, lost in a tropical garden that overhangs a pool.

Hotel Manapany ($$$$)
Anse des Cayes tel: 27-66-55
The finest luxury; 52 rooms in sumptuous suites and cottages, near a good beach.

Isle de France ($$$$)
tel: 27-61-81
On the sand of the Baie des Flamands, a variety of rooms decorated with antique furniture. Sophisticated beach resort; sports room and fine dining.

Saint-Martin (011-590)
Some hotels on Saint-Martin add a room tax to your bill.

Captain Oliver's ($$$)
tel: 87-43-706
Small hotel on Oyster Pond lagoon, from where many of the guests take to the seas to sail. Short water-taxi ride to the beach.

Esmeralda Resort ($$$–$$$$)
Baie Orientale tel: 87-36-36
A new resort that has taken traditional gingerbread style and added to its luxurious cottages, each of which has its own pool. Sports and restaurants.

Hévéa Hotel ($$)
tel: 875685
In the center of the Grand Case, it has an easy charm.

La Samanna ($$$$)
Terres Basses tel: 87-51-22
Very chic and stylish, standing above the excellent sand of Long Beach. Built in a curious mix of styles, with vast rooms, fine views, extreme luxury, and extreme prices.

273

THE NETHERLANDS ANTILLES

Aruba (011-2978)
Hotels on Aruba add a government tax of 5 percent to all bills.

Americana Aruba Hotel ($$$)
tel: 64500
High-rise, large, plush, and brightly painted, on excellent Palm Beach. Watersports. Casino and floor shows in the evenings.

Divi Aruba Beach Resort ($$$–$$$$)
tel: 23300
Low-rise hotel in the land of high-rises; excellent beachfront setting. Attractive gardens.

Bonaire (011-5997)
Hotels on Bonaire add a government tax of 5 percent to all bills.

Captain Don's Habitat ($$–$$$)
Kralendijk tel: 8290
Has grown from a small diving resort to a very comfortable and laid-back hotel, now with cottages and villas as well as rooms.

Carib Inn ($–$$)
Kralendijk tel: 8819
Excellent choice for relative comfort and price. Nine simple rooms, good diving. No restaurant, but kitchenettes.

Harbour Village Hotel ($$$)
Playa Lechi tel: 7500
The most comfortable hotel on Bonaire, with plush and brightly painted suites in villas dotted around a sandy garden and pool.

Accommodations and Restaurants

Curaçao (011-5999)

Hotels on Curaçao add a government tax of 7 percent to all bills.

Avila Beach Hotel ($$–$$$)
Willemstad tel: 461-4377
The most elegant and traditional of Curaçao's hotels, now modernized. On edge of town with a small beach and a dining room open to the breezes.
Princess Beach Hotel ($$)
Willemstad tel: 736-7888
A large resort spread out along the seafront. Sports and gambling.

Saba (011-5994)

Hotels on Saba add a government tax of 5 percent to all bills.

Captain's Quarters ($$)
tel: 62201
A lovely old Saban house at the foot of the hill in Windwardside; antique furniture and ambience but with a lively bar.
Cranston's Antique Inn ($)
tel: 63203
Set in a classic wooden Saban house in the Bottom. Creaking floorboards and some four-poster beds, local island charm.
Scout's Place ($–$$)
tel: 62295
Intriguing spot on the hillside in Windwardside. Comfortable rooms and a lively bar.

St. Eustatius (011-5993)

Hotels on St. Eustatius add a government tax of 7 percent to all bills.

The Kingswell Inn ($)
tel: 82538
Upper Town. Just a few apartments and a small, lively restaurant.
La Maison sur la Plage ($$)
Zeelandia Bay tel: 82256
Isolated and a little past its best but comfortable and a certain charm.

Sint Maarten (011-5995)

Hotels on Sint Maarten add a government tax of 5 percent to all bills.

The Horny Toad ($$)
tel: 54323
Excellent setting on Simpson Bay, attentive service and friendly, fully equipped rooms.
Passangrahan ($$)
Philipsburg tel: 23588
Old colonial air in the louvered lobby and some rooms; a welcome oasis of peace and quiet in the shopping turmoil of Front Street. Thirty rooms, restaurant, and bar.

OTHER CARIBBEAN STATES

Jamaica (011-1876)

Hotels in Jamaica add a general consumption tax of 10 percent to all bills.

Black River, Blue Mountains

Ivor Guest House ($–$$)
Jack's Hill tel: 977-0033
Beautifully restored colonial home perched on the mountains above Kingston. Just three bedrooms, dining room, and terrace with a magnificent view of the capital.
Natania's ($–$$)
tel: 963-5342
Outside Whitehouse, set in a charming modern wooden house on the waterfront, small beach and very friendly.

Kingston

Terra Nova Hotel ($$)
New Kingston tel: 926-9334
Elegant grand old uptown house in lawned gardens; 33 attractive rooms, pool, and a good dining room.
Morgan's Harbour Hotel ($$–$$$)
tel: 967-8030
A pleasant, shady two-storey motel with an open-air restaurant, pool, beach and yacht marina, five minutes' walk from Port Royal and a breezy ferry ride to downtown Kingston.

Mandeville

Astra Hotel ($–$$)
tel: 962-3265
Set in a modern building just outside the town, 40 rooms. Family-run and friendly. Tours can be arranged to the surrounding countryside.

Montego Bay

Coral Cliff Hotel ($)
tel: 952-4130
Graceful old villa near town center. Some rooms in the modern buildings behind. Pool, beach within walking distance.
Half Moon Club ($$$–$$$$)
tel: 953-2211
Simply the classiest in Jamaican high luxury, on a fine beach. Elegant rooms decorated in black and white; 19 pools, tennis, golf, riding, health club, and very fine dining.
Richmond Hill Hotel ($$)
tel: 952-3859
On the hilltop above the Montego Bay, an elegant town house, now with rooms added.

Negril

Catcha Falling Star ($$)
tel: 957-0390
On the cliffs in the south of the town, simple cabins set in a charming garden.
Charela Inn ($$)
tel: 957-4648
Beach hotel, with an intimate feel; 49 rooms, watersports, and a fine French restaurant.
Grand Lido ($$$$)
tel: 957-5010
On the fine sand of Bloody Bay, a top-grade all-inclusive hotel—champagne on command.

Ocho Rios

Boscobel Beach ($$–$$$)
tel: 975-7330
All-inclusive resort on a fine beach, designed especially for families with children. Finger-painting instruction through to kiddies' disco lessons to occupy them while you indulge in watersports and sunning.
Hibiscus Lodge Hotel ($–$$)
tel: 1974-2676
Simple rooms on the clifftops, near the action of town. Garden, good restaurants, watersports, short walk to the beach.

Port Antonio

De Montevin Lodge ($–$$)
tel: 993-2604
A throwback to a century ago: a classic town-house of gingerbread and brick. Rooms simple, some with balconies.
Trident Villas ($$$–$$$$)
tel: 993-2602
An enclave of supreme elegance, stunningly presented main house and rooms in manicured gardens. On a ledge of coral reef, small beach, but a fine pool. Overpriced dining.

The Cayman Islands (011-1345)

Hotels on the Cayman Islands add 6 percent government tax to all bills.

Beach Club Resort ($$$)
tel: 949-8100
Low rise with pleasant setting right on Seven Mile Beach with all watersports right there. Rooms comfortable to luxurious.
Divi Tiara Beach Hotel ($$)
Cayman Brac tel: 948-1553
In the southwest, right on the seashore. Diving is the primary activity, but the rooms are extremely comfortable.
Hyatt Regency ($$–$$$$)
tel: 949-1234
The most luxurious accommodations in Cayman, just across the road from Seven-Mile Beach. Modern building, but with attractive old-colonial flourishes. Three restaurants, golf course, dip-and-sip pool bar, watersports on the beach.

Cuba (011-537)

Havana

Havana Libre ($$$)
tel: 24-40-11
Tall building at the head of La Rampa, built as the Havana Hilton in the 1950s and renamed the Havana Libre by the young revolutionaries.
Hotel Valencia ($)
tel: 57-10-37, fax: 33-56-28
A small, elegantly remodeled house in the heart of Old Havana, the 12-room Valencia features a sunny, cozy courtyard café and a fine cigar store on the premises.

Inglaterra ($$–$$$)
tel: 33-85-39
On the Parque Central at the edge of the colonial city. Pleasant bar in the elaborate foyer. Rooms comfortable, short walk to the sights.
Plaza ($$$)
tel: 240-575
A fine, colonnaded building on the Parque Central, grand breezy interior with palms and pillars. Newly decorated, comfortable rooms.

Outside Havana

Club Gran Hotel ($$)
Varadero tel: 535/668-2431
With 331 room sand 300 yards of beach, two pools (one with a children's section), air-conditioning, all-inclusive meals and watersports, and all the American amenities, this is a prudent option for families or budget watchers visiting Varadero.
Horizontes Villa Playa Giron Bay of Pigs ($$)
tel: 53-594-118
History buffs will appreciate the pool, air-conditioning, and other comforts of this 292-room beachfront bungalow complex after visiting the nearby Bay of Pigs museum.
Hotel Casa Granda Santiago ($$–$$$)
tel: 53-226-86600
Built in 1914 and recently renovated, the elegant Casa Granda has 58 fully equipped rooms right in the heart of atmospheric Santiago.
Pelican ($$–$$$)
Cayo Largo tel535-48-333
The island of Key Largo off the south coast offers great beaches and the best diving in all of Cuba. The 230 beachfront rooms of Pelicano come with an all-inclusive package. Amenities include a pool, half a dozen restaurants, multiple bars, and plentiful watersports.
Hotel Herradura ($$)
tel: 63703
On the Avenida de la Playa on the beach. Midsize with two-star facilities.
Motel Los Jazmines ($)
Viñales tel: 93265
Not a motel at all, but an old villa standing high above the Viñales valley, fine views.
Paradiso ($$)
Varadero tel: 63917
One of Cuba's new resorts. Luxury rooms in beach villas; good Caribbean beach vacation with watersports, bars and clubs.

Haiti (011-509)
Some hotels in Haiti add an energy tax of a few dollars.

El Rancho ($–$$)
Pétionville tel: 257-2080
Grandest of the hotels built before Haiti's present troubles. Spanish revival decor, lavish rooms, antique furniture. Pool.
Mont Joli Hotel ($$)
Cap-Haïtien tel: 262-0300
A small, elegant hotel on the hill above town, very comfortable rooms, good restaurant. Driving distance to the beach and sights.

275

Accommodations and Restaurants

Oloffson Hotel ($)
Port-au-Prince tel: 223-4000
Set in a wonderful gingerbread building, former presidential palace. Amusing and lively bar full of travelers and passing journalists. A bit run down these days.
Villa Créole ($–$$)
Pétionville tel: 257-1570
Charming and elegant hotel in a quiet street. Attractive rooms, tennis, pool with a view.

The Dominican Republic (011-809)

Hotels in the Dominican Republic add a government tax of 6 percent.

Altos de Chavon and the Southeast, Cordillera Central

Bavaro Beach Hotel ($$)
Punto Cana Higuey tel: 686-5797
Behind the superb palm-fringed beach are four hotels, with a strong resort feel. Comfortable air-conditioned rooms, plenty of restaurants and bars, every watersport, golf, and tennis.
Casa de Campo ($$$–$$$$)
La Romana tel: 523-3333, 800/877-3643
A top resort complex with some of the Caribbean's most chic villas and hotel rooms— polo, golf, beach sports, nine restaurants in beautifully landscaped grounds.

Puerto Plata and the Amber Coast

Auberge du Roi Tropicale ($–$$)
Cabarete tel: 571-0770
A hotel dedicated to windsurfing, right on the beach. Rooms simple, pool under palms, restaurant on the sand.
Tropix Hotel ($)
Sosua tel: 571-2291
A charming, guest house, beloved of travelers. Friendly atmosphere, honor bar, home cooking. A short walk from the beaches and the downtown restaurants.

Samana

Hotel Gran Bahia ($$–$$$)
tel: 538-3111
Supremely elegant gingerbread mansion east of Semana, opposite fine beaches of Cajo Levantado. Old Caribbean air and comfort and high standards of service.
Hotel Tropic Banana ($)
Las Terrenas tel: 240-6110
One of the best travelers' haunts in the Caribbean. A lively crowd gathers for music at the poolside; 30 rooms in a spacious palm garden near the beach.

Santo Domingo

Boca Chica Resort ($$)
tel: 523-4621
The closest beach resort to the capital (about 30 minutes). All-inclusive plan, but sophisticated ambience. Elegant rooms.

Hostal Nicolas de Ovando ($–$$)
Calle de las Damas tel: 687-3101
The historic grandeur of the colonial city continues into the hotel, in the flagstones, courtyards, and corridors. Ideal for exploration of sights, but some rooms noisy at night.
Jaragua ($$–$$$)
Avenida Independencia tel: 221-2222
Luxury in a large and glitzy hotel on the Malecon. Four restaurants, club with entertainers, casino. Tours arranged.

Puerto Rico (011-1787)

Hotels in Puerto Rico add a government tax of 7 percent (9 percent in hotels with a casino).

Cordillera Central

Hacienda Gripinas ($–$$)
Jayuya tel: 828-1717
A charming timber-framed coffee estate house. Not elaborate, but wonderful old-time Caribbean feel.
Horned Dorset Primavera ($$$)
tel: 823-4030
Luxurious rooms that overlook the hotel garden or the sunset out to sea. Elegant central area with a library for afternoon tea and cocktails. Very fine cuisine.

Ponce

Hotel Melia ($)
tel: 842-0260
Just off the central square in Ponce. The rooms are modern and air-conditioned.

San German and the South West

Parador Boquemar ($)
Boqueron tel: 851-2158
A modern building near beach. Comfortable rooms; pool and restaurant.
Villa Parguera ($–$$)
Parguera tel: 899-3975
Welcoming resort hotel on the waterfront, set in a tropical garden. Pool and good local restaurant on the bay.

San Juan: New City

Casa Mathieson ($–$$)
Calle Uno 14 tel: 762-8662
Simple rooms near Isla Verde beach. Air-conditioning, restaurant.
Hotel Condado Beach ($$)
Condado tel: 721-6090
The Vanderbilt family home, built in 1919, now converted but still with many of its original features—antique furniture and marble floors. Large resort hotel.
El Prado Inn ($–$$)
1350 Calle Luchetti tel: 728-5925
Set in a neat family villa, between Condado and Isla Verde; walls festooned with tropical blooms. El Prado has 10 simple rooms and a swimming pool.

San Juan: Old City

Gallery Inn ($$)
tel: 722-1808
Restored town house with circular staircases, courtyards and terraces: bohemian feel; art gallery.
Gran Hotel El Convento ($$–$$$)
tel: 723-9020
A magnificent old building in the colonial city—checkerboard tiles, stained paneling, and tapestries hung on the walls. Once a convent, retains a calm and cloistered air.

Vieques

La Casa del Francés ($$)
tel: 741-3751
A charming old estate house, with checkerboard tiles and a cool courtyard. It is owned by a Hemingway-like character who is always amusing. Pool, home-cooked food.

Barbados (011-1246)

Hotels on Barbados add a 5 percent government tax to all bills.

South Coast

Crane Beach Hotel ($$–$$$)
St. Philip tel: 423-6220
In a superb setting on the cliffs, where the pool and restaurant, above the pretty cove 100 feet below, have magificent views. Eighteen rooms in a small apartment building and in a coral stone castle.
Windsurfing Club Hotel ($)
Maxwell tel: 428-9095
On the Maxwell shoreline, a simple but comfortable hotel with windsurfers and a lively bar. 15 rooms.

West Coast

Cobbler's Cove ($$$$)
tel: 422-2291
South of Speightstown, Cobbler's Cove has 39 beautifully decorated suites set above a fine strip of sand.
Sandy Lane Hotel ($$$$)
St. James tel: 432-1311, 800/223-6800
A legend in Caribbean elegance and hospitality. Sandy Lane has recently undergone a complete remodel.

Trinidad and Tobago (011-1868)

All hotels in Trinidad and Tobago add V.A.T. of 15 percent to published prices.

Trinidad

Asa Wright Nature Centre ($$)
Arima tel: 667-4655
Grand colonial estate house with an enormous screened veranda, which is lost in the forests of the northern range. This nature center makes an ideal base for birdwatching and general relaxation.

Hilton ($$)
on the edge of Port of Spain tel: 624-3211
Busy center for those passing through capital, also quite well organized for tourists. Superb views over the Savannah.
Hotel Normandie ($–$$)
St. Ann's tel: 624-1181
Quiet hotel tucked away in a valley that has now been swallowed up by the town. Fine French fare.

Tobago

Arnos Vale ($$)
tel: 639-2881
In its own steep-sided valley festooned with tropical blooms, the Arnos Vale has 30 rooms in a complex and in a central estate house. Beach bar, pool, boutique.
Old Donkey Cart House ($$)
tel: 639-3551
On a hillside just outside Scarborough, with very comfortable rooms clustering around a pool. Private and secluded, attached to an excellent restaurant.
Plantation Beach Villas ($$–$$$)
tel: 639-0455
Very attractive, old colonial style villas situated above the beach at Stonehaven Bay. Self-catering; swimming pool and bar down below; cooking can be arranged.

277

RESTAURANTS

Many of the hotels listed above have good restaurants but those listed below are also worth a visit. They are divided into the following categories:

($) = budget
($$) = moderate
($$$) = expensive

THE WINDWARD ISLANDS

Dominica

Castaways ($)
Mero Beach tel: 449-6244
A good lunchtime stop on the black-sand beach at Mero; popular on Sundays.
Garraway Hotel ($$$)
tel: 449-8800
Excellent fare overlooking the waterfront in Roseau itself.
Guiyave ($$)
Roseau tel: 448-2930
Pretty balcony setting above the street for a hearty local lunch (no dinner).

Grenada

La Belle Créole ($$$)
Grande Anse tel: 444 4316
The terrace dining room of the Blue Horizons hotel, *nouvelle cuisine* with a West Indian lilt.

Accommodations and Restaurants

The Boatyard ($$)
L'Anse aux Epines tel: 444-4662
Bar and restaurant in marina, simple fare, bar
livens up at the weekend, some entertainment.
Canboulay ($$$)
Grand Anse tel: 444-4401
Charming dining room set above the bay, with
innovative West Indian fare.
Coconuts ($$$)
Grand Anse tel: 444-4644
Classic Caribbean beach setting, tables inside
the pretty house or just above the sand. Also
known as the French restaurant; fine French
creole cuisine.
Mamma's ($$)
Lagoon Road St. Georges tel: 440-1459
A legendary haunt for its local fare. Set menu
with a striking variety of dishes that never
seem to stop coming.

The Grenadines
On the small Grenadine islands you will be
dependent on your hotel.

Basil's Bar ($$)
Mustique tel: 458-4621
In a charmed setting on stilts on a magnificent
bay; the favorite haunt of island visitors and
passing yachtsmen. Entertainment.
Dennis' Hideaway ($$)
Mayreau tel: 458-8594
Bar and dining room on a terrace on the hillside, good local fare. Dennis himself sings
occasionally.
Mac's Pizzeria ($$)
Bequia tel: 458-3474
Wooden deck above a tropical garden, excel-
lent pizzas.

St. Lucia

Bang Between the Pitons ($)
tel: 459-7864
Courtyard surrounded by old wooden creole
houses between the comical pitons. Local and
international fare with flair.
Dasheene($$$)
tel: 459-7323
Dasheene's Ladera Resort location between
the Pitons and high above the sea will take
your breath away—as will the top-notch international nouvelle Creole cuisine and the fine wine
list. A must for gourmets.
Jimmie's ($$)
Vigie Bay tel: 452-5142
Veranda with colored lights, tucked away in
Vigie Harbour. A variety of seafood and fish.
The Snooty Agouti ($$)
tel: 452-0321
Whole food, great coffee, jazz, internet connection, all upstairs in the Rodney Bay area.

St. Vincent

Aggie's ($$)
Grenville Street tel: 456-2110
Upstairs dining room and bar popular with the
locals, good local fare.

Basil's Bar ($$)
Kingston tel: 457-2713
Downstairs from the Cobblestone Inn. In the
old stone setting of a trading warehouse;
international and local fare.
Lime N' Pub ($$)
Villa tel: 458-4227
Video bar and terrace for meals overlooking
Young Island on the Villa strip. Has been
known to get lively.

THE LEEWARD ISLANDS

Anguilla

Blanchard's ($$$)
tel: 497-6100
Top-notch international fare offered in a charm-
ing and elegant house in Mead's Bay.
Lucy's Harbour View ($$)
above Sandy Ground tel: 497-6253
Tables on a large veranda with a view. Classic
West Indian chicken or fish dishes.
Mango's ($$$)
Barnes Bay tel: 6479
Above the beach on a breezy veranda, well pre-
pared new American cuisine. Reserve.

Antigua

Admiral's Inn ($$–$$$)
tel: 460-1027
Housed in a lovely Georgian building dating
from 1788, the Inn offers fresh seafood, home-
made soups, and other fare in a lively nautical
atmosphere. The secluded dining terrace overlooks the harbor.
Lemon Tree ($$)
Long Street, St. John's tel: 462-1969
Lively dining room in town with entertainment.
Local and international food.
Shirley Heights Lookout ($$)
tel: 460-1785
High above English Harbour, a veranda with a
view. Burgers and salads or West Indian
dishes, best known for riotous Sunday afternoon assembly.

Montserrat
In the present situation, you have to eat in the
hotels that are open, but you might try Ziggy's
in the Belham River Valley (tel: 491-8282),
which serves sandwiches, steaks, and local
fish—if it is open.

Nevis

Hermitage Plantation ($$$)
tel: 469-3477
Elegant, candle-lit veranda in the main house
of the hotel, adventurous and delightful West
Indian cuisine. Reserve.
Nisbet Plantation ($$$)
tel: 469-9325
In the charming old colonial setting of the main
house, often dinner with piano
accompaniment. Continental and Caribbean
dishes. Reserve.

Prinderella's ($$)
tel: 469-8291
Views across the Channel to St. Kitts from a pretty tropical garden veranda, local and international food.
Unella's ($$)
Charlestown tel: 469-5574
An upstairs terrace above the waterfront, good local fare as well as continental dishes.

St. Kitts

Ballahoo ($$)
Basseterre tel: 465-4197
On a balcony right above the Circus in town center. Salads, snacks and bigger meals.
The Georgian House ($$$)
tel: 465-4049
Elegant dining in Basseterre in the setting of an old colonial townhouse.
Golden Lemon ($$$)
Dieppe Bay tel: 465-7260
Exquisite local and Continental fare in the delightfully restored historic surroundings. Fine lunchtime stop, but even better at dinner.
Rawlins Plantation ($$$)
Mount Pleasant tel: 465-6221
Some of the best West Indian food in the islands, served in the charming setting of an 18th-century plantation house. Good lunchtime stop, dinner also available.

THE VIRGIN ISLANDS

The British Virgin Islands

Cooper Island Beach Club ($$)
tel: 494-3721
(V.H.F. Channel 16). The only bar on Cooper Island, a bright patio right above the sand where you can enjoy a grill and a salad with a passing sailing crowd.
Peter Island ($$$)
tel: 494-2561
Worth the short ride from Roadtown to Peter Island for top Caribbean and international cuisine after a day out on the island.

Tortola

Brandywine Bay ($$$)
tel: 495-2301
With a magnificent view of the Channel from the breezy terrace, fine Italian cuisine. Reserve a table.
Mrs. Scatliffe ($$)
Cane Garden Bay tel: 495-4556
Delectable local fare, pumpkin soup and curry goat followed by tropical fruit ice-creams.
Pusser's Store and Pub
Road Town tel: 494-2467
Lively haunt, located near the ferry terminal; warmly decorated with burnished brass and paneled walls.
Sugar Mill Restaurant ($$$)
Apple Bay tel: 495-4355
In a candle-lit stone building from old colonial times; extremely fine West Indian cuisine. Make a reservation.

Virgin Gorda

Chez Bamboo ($$)
Spanish Town tel: 495-5752
Brightly painted dining room in town serving French and international fare.
Pirate's Pub
Saba Rock, North Sound tel: 495-9537
Riotous bar on a tiny blip of rock. Popular with passing sailors. Instruments at hand for those who want to play them.

The U.S. Virgin Islands

St. Croix

Blue Moon ($$$)
Frederiksted tel: 772-2222
Deep and dark setting under the arches in an old Front Street trading building. Jazz and cajun fare, gets busy.
Duggan's Reef ($$)
Teaque Bay tel: 773-9800
A breezy deck overlooking the beach and Buck Island offshore. Sandwiches and salads, international fare at dinner.
Top Hat ($$$)
Company Street, Christiansted tel: 773-2346
Very pleasant restaurant in an old town house, menu international, particularly notable for its Danish dishes.

St. John

Morgan's Mango
tel: 693-8141
Great veranda setting with new Caribbean and some Argentinian fare. Live music sometimes, right in Cruz Bay.
Paradiso Restaurant ($$$)
Cruz Bay tel: 693-8899
Decor worthy of a Manhattan nightclub, cocktail bar and quiet music, Italian dishes.

St. Thomas

Café Wahoo ($$)
tel: 775-6350
Seafood and fish on a deck above the lagoon at Red Hook; lively and fun.
Craig and Sally's ($$$)
tel: 777-9949
Set in Frenchtown, a varied and interesting menu with an excellent wine list.
Eunice's ($$$)
Smith Bay tel: 775-3975
With a charming setting on a veranda with wicker chairs. Serves excellent West Indian cuisine.

THE FRENCH ANTILLES

Guadeloupe

Château de Feuilles ($$$)
Grande-Terre tel: 223030
Worth a trip to the far northeast of Grande-Terre, where you dine on a terrace in a profuse garden. Excellent French and local fare.

Accommodations and Restaurants

Chez deux Gros ($$$)
Grande-Terre tel: 84-16-20
Hidden in overgrown garden beyond Gosier.
Easygoing dining room and good international
fare.
Côté Jardin ($$$)
tel: 90-91-28
Elegant, air-conditioned dining with a good wine
list in the lively marina at Bas du Fort.
Les Oiseaux ($$)
Saint François tel: 88-56-92
Pleasant, veranda setting for an eclectic combi-
nation of French and creole food.
Le Rocher de Malendure ($$)
overlooking Pigeon Island tel: 98-70-84
Covered terraces on the hillside. Fish and
seafood on the menu, with the best of
Caribbean vegetables. Good stop for lunch.
Le Vieux Port ($$)
tel: 88-56-24
On the St. François waterfront, this lively and
rustic setting has fresh fish and lobster.

Martinique

Aux Délices de la Mer ($$)
tel: 76-97-36
Waterfront setting for traditional Créole cuisine
in the far south of the island. A good retreat
from the island's best beach, the Grand Anse
des Salines.
Le Colibri ($$)
Morne des Esses tel: 69-91-95
A veranda with a fantastic view and some of
the most adventurous French Creole food in
the island, all prepared by Clothilde Palladino.
La Fontane ($$$)
route de Balata, Fort-de-France tel: 64-28-70
In the charming setting of a gingerbread house.
Top French cuisine. Reserve, jacket and tie
required.
La Savane ($)
A series of snackwagons with loud music
where you can sit out in the crowd and eat
sandwiches and simple dishes.

Saint-Barthélemy

Chez Maya ($$$)
Public tel: 27-75-73
Popular waterfront restaurant under the palms
in public. Fish and Créole specialties.
Eden Rock ($$)
Saint-Jean tel: 27-72-94
Beachfront deck for a lunchtime break, light
and international fare.
Le Sapotillier ($$$)
Gustavia tel: 27-60-28
Charming and elegant Gustavia setting.
Excellent classical french cuisine.

Saint-Martin

Bar de la Mer tel: 87-81-79
Cocktail bar just off the waterfront in Marigot,
open all day for snacks and drinks.
Bistrot Nu ($$)
on an alley in Marigot tel: 87-77-39
Some of the best Creole food in the island.

The Fishpot ($$$)
tel: 87-50-88
Elegant French cuisine on a balcony above the
bay in Grand Case.
Les Lolos ($)
Grand Case
Very cheap barbecued food and beer from the
roadside in the middle of town. Worth a
lunchtime stop.
Le Tastevin ($$$)
Grand Case tel: 87-55-45
On a tropical terrace, above the waves. Classic
French cuisine and service.

THE NETHERLANDS ANTILLES

Aruba

Charlie's Bar ($)
tel: 45086
Bar and restaurant at the east end of the
island, hung with memorabiliia,famous for
jumbo shrimp.
Gasparito ($$)
Gasparito 3 tel: 67044
The best in Dutch Antillean food in a traditional
old Aruban country house, behind Palm Beach.
Papiamento ($$$)
Washington 61 tel: 64544
The best Aruban cuisine in the best setting, a
country house where tables are inside or by the
pool. A delightful experience. Reserve.

Bonaire

Mi Poron ($$)
Kralendijk
Home-cooked Bonaire cuisine in the courtyard
of a traditional house, in the middle of town.
Rendez-vous ($$$)
Kralendijk tel: 8454
Charming restaurant set in a modern
townhouse. You dine on the veranda or inside.
Continental dishes, with some local cuisine.
Richard's ($$$)
Kralendijk tel: 5263
Easy-going spot on a seafront terrace in the
south of the town. Locals stop over at the bar
after work. Excellent local cuisine and seafood.

Curaçao

De Taveerne ($$$)
Salinja tel: 737-0669
Intimate atmosphere in the low-lit cellar of an
old estate house. Menu continental, using the
best of local fish and vegetables.
Fort Waakzamheid ($$)
off highway, Otrobanda tel: 623633
Open-air setting in an old fortress high on a hill
in the west of Willemstad.
Golden Star ($$)
Dr. Maalweg tel: 654795
Cold and over-decorated dining room, but the
finest West Indian food in town.
Plaza Biejo
next to the market building in Willemstad
Vats of *sopi, toetoe, funchi*. Simply point at
something that looks good. Lunchtime only.

Rum Runners ($$)
tel: 623038
St. Annabaai waterfront, Otrabanda side. Hip, lively cocktail bar and restaurant.

Saba

Chinese Restaurant ($$)
Windwardside tel: 62268
Modern house high on the hill with a long list of Chinese dishes to eat in or take out.

In Two Deep ($)
Fort Bay
Café for sandwiches and salads and a drink after scuba-diving.

Scout's Place ($$)
Windwardside tel: 62295
Drinks with a view, wholesome and hearty portions of Caribbean food, and some entertainment.

St. Eustatius

La Maison sur la Plage ($$)
Zeelandia Bay tel: 82256
Fine French fare, using the best local ingredients, set in a bamboo-covered courtyard on the eastern side of the island.

Stone Oven ($)
Oranjested tel: 82247
Good Caribbean food—curry goat and fried fish—in a small town house set with neat wooden tables.

Sint Maarten

Da Livio ($$$)
Front St. tel: 22690
Delectable Italian fare on a waterfront terrace in Philipsburg. Very popular.

Kangaroo Court Café ($–$$)
tel: 24278
Great baked goods and fine coffee make this pleasant courtyard café the best breakfast spot in Philipsburg. On a side street not far from the cruis ship dock.

Le Perroquet ($$$)
Simpson Bay tel: 44339
In a pretty house overlooking a tropical garden, menu French with some very exotic extras like lion and ostrich.

OTHER CARIBBEAN STATES

Jamaica

Restaurants add a General Consumption tax of 10 percent to all bills.

Black River, Blue Mountains

Blue Mountain Inn ($$$)
Gordon Town tel: 927-1900
Old plantation house setting, very fine fare of Creole dishes as well as international classics.

The Gap Café ($)
tel: 923-7078
Stupendous view over Kingston, good stop for lunch or tea.

Ivor Lodge ($$)
Jack's Hill tel: 977-0033
Wonderful view over Kingston and West Indian cuisine in a restored country house. Intimate; make a reservation.

Kingston

Chelsea Jerk Centre ($)
Chelsea Avenue tel: 926-6322
Very local; pork and chicken jerked meat; watch the hot pepper sauce.

Guilt Trip ($$)
tel: 977-5130
Hip gathering point, with cakes by day and international and new Jamaican cuisine by night, on Barbican Road.

Indies Pub ($$)
Holborn Road
Popular pub with garden in New Kingston with a crowd of locals and visitors.

Montego Bay

Marguerite's ($$)
Gloucester Avenue tel: 952-4777
Terrace on the sea and under the stars, for cocktails and light meals. Margueritaville, next door, offers international fare in a rowdy, sport-bar atmosphere.

Norma's ($$$)
Reading tel: 979-2745
Stunning waterfront setting opposite the town, very fine Caribbean cuisine. Reserve.

Pork Pit ($)
Gloucester Avenue tel: 952-1046
Take-out or sit at the garden benches, pork, chicken, fish, and spare ribs with coconut milk or beer.

Negril

Hungry Lion ($$)
On the cliffs. Great garden setting for natural foods and juices. Hip, popular spot; get there early or be prepared to wait.

Paradise Yard ($)
tel: 957-4006
Inland from the rotary.Classic rustic setting on a terrace under palms, local Jamaican fare.

Ocho Rios

Almond Tree ($$$)
Hibiscus Lodge Hotel tel: 974-2676
Fine setting on the cliffs with floodlit greenery around; local cuisine.

Double V Jerk Centre ($)
tel: 974-0174
Main Street heading east. A wooden cabin in a tropical garden, good stopover for jerk.

The Mug ($$)
Runaway Bay tel: 972-1018
Waterfront bar popular with locals. Light meals.

Parkway ($$)
tel: 974-2667
Tasty local fare on a modern West Indian veranda setting.

Accommodations and Restaurants

Port Antonio

Daddy D's ($)
West St tel: 993-2116
Best local fare in a typical West Indian setting.
Huntress Marina ($$)
tel: 993-3053
On the waterfront in the harbor, rustic and local fare.
Trident Villas ($$$)
tel: 993-2602
Very elegant setting of a colonial-style veranda, top local cuisine. Living on past gourmet glories. Reserve.

The Cayman Islands

Apollo 11 North Sound. Very cool waterfront bar in an old shed. Live music.
Cracked Conch ($$)
West Bay tel: 945-5217
Very lively bar and restaurant, where conch is served cracked (beaten to tenderness) along with other fish.
Grand Old House ($$$)
Church Street tel: 949-9333
In a charming old colonial house; excellent Continental dishes as well as few local ones. Make a reservation.
Ristorante Pappagallo ($$$)
Spanish Cove tel: 949-1119
Huge palm-thatched, air-conditoned cabana set on an isolated lagoon. Northern Italian menu. Reserve a table.

Cuba

Havana

La Cecilia ($$$)
5th Avenue, Miramar tel: 33-15-62
Top Cuban cuisine in an attractive town house.
Don Giovanni ($$)
Calle Tacon, colonial city tel: 62-35-60
Italian dishes in an old colonial house.
Floridita ($$$)
Calle Montserrate tel: 63-10-60
A favorite of Hemingway's, famed for its daiquiris (worth going just for them). Elegant if ritzy dining room, fine cuisine.
Hemingway Marina
west of the city tel: 24-11-50
Restaurant and marina complex, popular with foreigners, particularly for the lively disco.
El Patio ($$)
Cathedral Square, colonial city tel: 61-85-04
Charming setting under the arches. Café downstairs on the cobbles, meals upstairs.

Outside Havana

Las Americas ($$$)
Varadero
Once a private home on the waterfront, now serving international dishes; fine views.
Los Jazmines ($)
Viñales
Magnificent setting. Local Cuban cuisine.

El Meson de Quijote ($$)
Varadero. Set in open grounds far down the peninsula; Spanish menu.
1900 ($$)
Calle San Basilio, Santiago de Cuba tel: 23507
Charming old town house; local Cuban food.

Haiti

La Belle Epoque ($$)
rue Grégoire, Pétionville tel: 257-0984
Covered veranda and courtyard setting, menu French and kreyol.
Champs de Mars ($)
Port-au-Prince
Stalls selling barbecued chicken and beer.

The Dominican Republic

Altos de Chavon

Café del Sol ($$)
tel: 523-3333
Pizzas, pasta, and salads on an open-air terrace lost in tropical greenery.
Casa de Rio ($$$)
tel: 523-3333
Fantastic setting above floodlit river with a mix of Caribbean and international dishes.

Puerto Plata and the Amber Coast

De Armando ($$$)
Calle Separacion, Puerto Plata tel: 586-3418
Very neat, air-conditioned townhouse dressed up in pink for an intimate meal. Fine international and Dominican cuisine. Reserve.
Leandros ($)
Cabarete
Local dishes in a lively palm-thatch dining room.
La Louisianne ($$)
tel: 884434
French cuisine right on the beach in Cabarete.
Valther's ($$)
Calle Hermanas Mirabal tel: 586-2329
Dinner on the veranda of a charming wooden Caribbean house; international menu with Caribbean ingredients.

Samana

L'Hacienda
tel: 538-2383
Grilled food on a breezy veranda to Latin music and hot salsa.
La Salsa ($$)
tel: 240-6049
Great bar with wooden floors and thatched roof above the waves. French menu.

Santo Domingo

El Conuco ($$)
Calle Casimiro de Moya tel: 686-0129
Riotous restaurant with decorations from the *conuco* (country). Waiters sing to you.

Independencia ($)
just off Parque Independencia
Some of the best local food around, slightly chaotic service but a good Dominican experience all in all.
Vesuvio ($$$)
on the Malecon tel: 221-3333
Big, very popular restaurant. Top Italian and Dominican fare.

Puerto Rico

San German and the Southwest

I Bohio ($$)
Playa Joyuda tel: 851-2755
On a breezy deck above the waves. Unpretentious but the best of local fish.
Vista Bahia ($$)
Cabo Rojo
Right on Playa Joyuda; fresh fish and seafood.

Ponce

El Ancla ($$$)
Playa de Ponce tel: 840-2450
Out of the city center, an air-conditioned lounge, menu mainly seafood with copious local vegetables.

San Juan

Amadeus ($$)
Calle San Sebastian tel: 721-6720
Stylish restaurant serving Italian food, near the lively bars of Plaza San Jose.
Bistro Gambaro ($–$$)
Old San Juan on Calle Fortaleza
Bistro with adventurous international fare.
La Casita Blanca ($$)
eastern outskirts of the city
Small but very lively restaurant specializing in Puerto Rican food, and lots of it. Charming setting, amusing waiters.
La Mallorquina ($$$)
Calle San Justo tel: 722-3261
Set in a century-old house, still with its antique furnishings. Good local food.

Barbados

Atlantis ($$)
Bathsheba tel: 433-9445
The hotel itself is clearly past its prime, but the setting on the clifftops and the food, a West Indian buffet, is still superb.
Carambola ($$$)
tel: 432-0832
Superb setting on the cliff of the west coast, delectable Caribbean and Continental cuisine.
The Cliff ($$$)
tel: 432-1922
Topnotch international cuisine in an extremely elegant setting.
David's Place ($$)
Main Road, Worthing tel: 435-9755
Breezy setting above pretty St. Lawrence Bay; excellent Bajan food, delicious desserts.

Fathoms ($$)
Payne's Bay tel: 432-2568
Fine position on the cliffs for candle-lit dinner, good seafood and fish.
Josef's ($$$)
tel: 435-6541
Private home turned into elegant restaurant in St. Lawrence Gap. The cuisine is international and excellent.
Pisces ($$)
tel: 435-6564
Charming setting on a trellis-lined veranda above St. Lawrence Bay. Mainly seafood and fish, some other dishes.

Trinidad and Tobago

Trinidad

The Breakfast Shed ($)
(24-3404)
Waterfront, Port of Spain
Refectory-style dining room with vast pots and pans bubbling away, fine local fare.
Le Chateau de Poisson ($$)
Ariapita Avenue Port of Spain tel: 622-6087
Charming gingerbread townhouse hung with greenery; seafood and fish is served in a variety of spices.
Moon Over Bourbon Street ($$)
West Mall tel: 637-3448
A delightful cocktail bar and rooftop restaurant out of town, decked out like a transatlantic liner. Some entertainment.
Pelican Pub
St. Ann's tel: 624-7486
Usually busy with ex-pats on Thursday and Sunday evenings.
Rafters ($$)
Warner Street Port of Spain tel: 628 9258
Hip video bar and restaurant located in an old warehouse.
Tiki Village ($$)
Kapok Hotel (622-6441
Busy restaurant on top floor; Polynesian and Chinese menu.
Veni Mange ($$)
Ariapita Avenue, St. James tel: 624-4597
Popular lunchtime (only) haunt. Delicious West Indian cuisine. Highly recommended.

Tobago

Black Rock Café ($$$)
Black Rock tel: 639-7625
Veranda painted pink with white louvers. Creole dishes with salads and steaks.
Old Donkey Cart House ($$$)
just out of Scarborough tel: 639-3551
Charming floodlit garden and pretty house, good local and international fare.
Rouselle's ($$)
Scarborough tel: 639-4738
Upstairs lounge bar with tables where you get good local food.
Store Bay ($)
Local take-out meals, curry goat, crab and dumpling, and delicious local fruit juices.

Index

Index

Index/Acknowledgments

Picture credits

The Automobile Association would like to thank the following for their assistance in the preparation of this book:
ALLSPORT UK LTD: 219a Cricket. **BRIDGEMAN ART LIBRARY:** 178–9 *Voodoo Dance* by Jean Pierre; 178 *Voodoo ceremony around a tree* by Valcin. **S CAMPBELL:** 162 Sunrise at Brac Reef; 163 Totem pole; 164 Swimming with stingrays; 165 Straw-weaver. **MARY EVANS PICTURE LIBRARY:** 25a Raiding cattle ranches; 28–9a Columbus's fleet 1492; 28 Columbus lands San Salvador; 29 Columbus; 30–1 Drake attacks Spanish; 30 Pirates; 31 Buccaneer; 32–3a Slaves working; 32 Slaves dancing; 33 Slave in chains; 34–5 Treadmill; 35 Sugar mill; 36–7 Emancipation parade; 36 Emancipation; 37 Burke in House of Commons; 43b Spaniards and Caribs; 100b Blackbeard; 101 Spaniards loading ship. **J HENDERSON:** 9a Barbados; 10a St. Vincent; 12–13 Children; 15b Oranjestad, Aruba; 16–17a Church, Trinidad; 18–9a Poster; 27 Arawak carvings; 40 Calabas Hotel; 49 St. Georges; 50a Market, St. Georges; 52 Maurice Bishop, St. Georges; 53 Admiralty Harbour; 68 Man; 70 Boat; 76 Barbuda; 83 Nevis; 83 Old windmill; 91b Bombas, Tortola; 96 Jost van Dyke; 98 Frederiksted, St. Croix; 103 Legislature, Charlotte Amalie; 112a Guadaloupe cemetery; 113a Boats; 113b Deshaires; 120 Islands; 121a Airport, St. Barts; 121b Club La Banane; 124a Aruba; 124b Bolatabla, Curaçao; 125–6 Sailing ship; 125 Saba; 126 Craft stall; 128–9 Oranjestad, Aruba; 129a Windmill; 129b Jet ski; 130, 131 Salt stacks, Bonaire; 134–5 Handelsgade, Willemstad; 134a b Floating market; 135 Fisherman; 136 House; 137a Windwardside, Saba; 137b Flags; 137c sign; 138 Sint Eustatius; 139a Sign; 139b Children; 140 Car; 141a St. Georges; 143c Breadfruit; 166 Car; 167 Main Square, Trinidad, Cuba; 168 Poster; 169a Santa Clara; 169b House, Cuba; 170a Old Havana; 170b Cathedral, Old Havana; 173 Cien Fuegos; 176 Taptap; 177 Fishermen; 180–1 Dessalines barracks; 181a Sans-Souci Palace; 181b Man; 183 Carvings; 186 Windsurfers; 187 Hotel Sousa; 189 Palm fronds; 190 Boats; 191 Sugar mill; 192 Children; 193a Columbus lighthouse; 193b Columbus Palace; 197b Festival of the Innocents; 198 Hacienda Gripinas; 210 Fire station, Ponce; 203 Sunset, Puerto Rico; 206 Croton; 210 Casa del Frances, Vieques; 211 Limers Bar, Esperanza; 215a Bridgetown Harbour; 215b Sombaero; 219b Baseball; 228 Canon, Trinidad; 234b Carnival, St. Lucia; 236 Shack; 238b Calypso singer. **IMAGES COLOUR LIBRARY:** 179 Mask. **IMAGES DES ANTILLES:** 109 Course de Yoles; 155 Images des Antilles. **INTERNATIONAL PHOTOBANK:** 20a Ocho Rios market; 24 drinks; 45b Dunn's River Falls; 47, 50b St. George's Saturday Market; 58b Woman and bananas; 80–1 Steel band; 155 Straw market, Montego Bay; 159 Beach, Ocho Rios; 160 Port Antonio; 206–7 Royal Poinciana tree; 233 Tobago steel band. **NATURE PHOTOGRAPHERS LTD:** 74–5 Orange clown fish, Queen Angel fish (S C Bisserot); 116a Scarlet Ibis (P R Sterry); 117 Iguana (E A Janes); 230a Green turtle (D A Smith); 230b Loggerhead turtle (J Sutherland). **PARIA PUBLISHING CO LTD:** 61a The Soucouyant; 61b Mama Dio; 61c Pappa Bois. **PICTURES COLOUR LIBRARY LTD:** Cover Carnival, Port of Spain, Trinidad. **REX FEATURES LTD:** 152a,c Shabba Ranks; 152b Shaggy; 156a,b Bob Marley. **ROYAL GEOGRAPHICAL SOCIETY:** 25 Map **SPECTRUM COLOUR LIBRARY:** 6 Bequia; 22–3a Buffet; 38 Nightlife; 81 Musician; 95a Faune Sous Marine; 111 Rainforest; 131 Kralendick Town, Bonaire; 133 Curaçao; 162 Drinks; 171 Tropicana cabaret, Havana; 184 Mexican night; 185 market; 188 Restaurant, Puerto Plata; 189 Palm-fringed beach; 200 Shell; 234–5 Carnival; 238a Nightlife. **THE MANSELL COLLECTION LTD:** 26 Indians sowing maize. **ZEFA PICTURE LIBRARY (UK) LTD:** 200a Coral.
All remaining pictures are held in the Association's own library (**AA PHOTO LIBRARY**) with contributions from: **P BAKER:** Spine; 2; 4; 7; 9b; 11; 13b; 14–5; 16b; 19; 20b; 21; 25b; 39; 41; 42; 43a; 44; 48a,b; 51; 54a,b; 55; 56; 57; 58a; 59; 62–3a; 62b; 63; 64; 65; 66; 67a; 68–9; 71; 72; 73; 77; 78a; 79; 80; 84; 85a,b; 86; 87a,b; 90; 91a; 92a,b; 93; 94a,b; 96–7; 99; 102; 105a,b; 106a,b; 107; 108; 109a,b; 110a,b; 111b,c; 112b; 114; 115a,b; 118; 119a,b; 122; 123a,b,c; 140; 141a,b; 142a,b; 143a,b; 144–5; 161a,b; 191a; 194; 194–5; 196; 197a; 199a,b; 202; 204a,b; 207; 208; 209b; 210b; 213; 214; 216; 217; 218; 220; 221a; 222; 23; 226a,b; 227; 229; 231; 232; 269a. **R HOLMES:** 100–1. **D LYONS:** 8; 60. **S & O MATHEWS:** 77. **C SAWYER:** 174, 175. **A SOUTER:** 209a. **R VICTOR:** 5a,b; 10b; 12; 23b; 45a; 88; 89; 95b; 116b; 146; 149a,b; 150; 151a,b; 153; 154; 157; 158; 161c; 239a. **J WYAND:** 3; 67b; 78b; 125; 239b; 269b.

Acknowledgments

The Automobile Association would also like to thank the Sandridge Beach Hotel, Barbados, and the Ocean View Hotel, Barbados for their assistance in the making of this book

Contributors

Revision copy editor: Grapevine Publishing Services

Original copy editor: Nia Williams Revision verifier: Justin Henderson